The World In Their Web

Frederick Clairmonte and
John Cavanagh

. . . When these prodigies
Do so conjointly meet, let not men
 say,
'These are their reasons: they are
 natural'
For I believe, they are portentous
 things . . .

 Julius Caesar
 Act I, Scene iii

Last season's fruit is eaten
And the fullfed beast shall kick the empty pail.
For last year's words belong to last year's language
And next year's words await another voice.

 T.S. Eliot
 Little Gidding

The World In Their Web

Dynamics of Textile Multinationals

Frederick Clairmonte and John Cavanagh

Zed Press, 57 Caledonian Rd., London N1 9DN

The World in their Web was first published by Zed Press, 57 Caledonian Road, London N1 9DN in November 1981.

Copyright © Frederick Clairmonte and John Cavanagh, 1981.

ISBN 0 905762 95 9

338.8
C585w

Copyedited by: Mandy MacDonald
Typeset by: Margaret Cole
Proofread by: Penelope Fryxell
Designed by: Mayblin/Shaw
Cover design by: Jaque Solomon
Printed and bound in Great Britain by
Redwood Burn Ltd., Trowbridge, Wiltshire.

British Library Cataloguing in Publication Data

Clairmonte, Frederick and John Cavanagh
The World in their Web: Dynamics of Textile Multinationals.
Fibre and Allied Textile Ologopolies.
1. Textile industry
2. Oligopolies
I. Title   II. Cavanagh, John
338.8'2677   HD9854

U.S. Distributor   83 - 8561
Lawrence Hill and Co., 520 Riverside Avenue, Westport, Conn. 06880, U.S.A.

Acknowledgements

A number of individuals played a crucial role in assisting our research and in critically evaluating every phase of the book. Of these many friends and well-wishers, special thanks are offered to: Reginald Green, Andrew Cornford, Hans Singer, Stuart Ozer, Robin Broad, Roy Rothwell, Samir Amin, Robert Molteno, and the textile group at the Max Planck Institute in Starnberg. The countless hours Judy Mann and Kathie Clark spent typing and commenting on the manuscript will never be forgotten. The work, however, would never have assumed its present format (despite its obvious and apparent short-comings) were it not for Gertrude Clairmonte who in all ways could be considered a co-author. Her expertise as a statistician, editor and critic — not to mention her persistence — were priceless.

The authors also wish to thank the following libraries for their sustained support during the months that were required for the preparation of this work: the United Nations Library in Geneva; the Library of Congress; the British Museum and a large number of specialized libraries too numerous to mention. In addition, there were several friends and officials at the Anti-Trust Division of the U.S. Department of Justice, the Security and Exchange Commission and the U.S. Federal Trade Commission who gave invaluable advice bearing on specialized chapters, notably those embracing the activities of the giant traders and the operations of the futures markets, but who would prefer to remain anonymous.

We also acknowledge the assistance and at times active stimulus from certain persons within the corporate world but who, for understandable reasons, have selected anonymity. Apart from proffering their trivialized balance sheets, most corporations either adamantly refused to answer our queries, or did so with the greatest reluctance on the simple grounds that their records, policies and pursuits were not open to public scrutiny: a tragic comment itself on the non-accountability of the modern corporation.

The final perspective of the work remains that of the authors and in no reflects that of the UNCTAD Secretariat.

Contents

Tables

Abbreviations

CMEA	Council for Mutual Economic Assistance		Trade and Industry (Japan)
CPE	centrally planned economy	NEDC	National Economic Development Council
CFTC	Commodity Futures Trading Commission	NEDO	National Economic Development Office
DCE	developed capitalist economy	ILO	International Labour Office
EEC	European Economic Community	OECD	Organization for Economic Co-operation and Development
FAO	Food and Agriculture Organization	OPEC	Organization of Petroleum Exporting Countries
GATT	General Agreement on Tariffs and Trade	TNC	transnational corporation
ICAC	International Cotton Advisory Committee	UCE	underdeveloped capitalist economy
ICAITI	Instituto Centroamericano de Investigacion y Tecnologia Industrial	UNCTAD	United Nations Conference on Trade and Development
IFCATI	International Federation of Cotton and Allied Textile Industries	UNIDO	United Nations Industrial Development Organization
MFA	Multi-fibre Arrangement	USDA	United States Department of Agriculture
MITI	Ministry of International		

Preface

Frederick Clairmonte and John Cavanagh's work on the way the contemporary economic system operates in the textile fibres sectors hardly needs an introduction. With their usual attention to detail, the authors have built up a collection of documents which, in this field, is without comparison. Not content with this immense task, they have conducted a particularly acute political analysis of the policies and strategies which enable a handful of monopolies to dominate the sector so completely. Through this analysis, they enable us to see the mechanisms by which monopoly capital exploits not only the workers in the specific industries concerned, but also all the workers in the various sub-sectors directly connected with textile fibres, notably the millions of peasants who produce natural fibres in the Third World.

The monopolies in question are, of course, American, European and Japanese. In the three post-war decades we have come to think of the organization of these monopolies in terms of how they fit into a world system based on 'free enterprise' and 'free competition' under the aegis of a 'pax americana' which has many parallels with the British hegemony of 100 years ago. The fact that productive processes, especially in the textile fibre sector, are now interlinked on a world scale obviously does not exclude competition between monopolies. But it does mean that this competition is organized within a global political framework in which United States hegemony plays a key role.

It is on this aspect of the question, bordering as it does on Clairmonte and Cavanagh's work, that I propose a few reflections. By integrating issues of world policy into a more directly economic analysis, I hope to indicate the possible forms of equilibrium between the imperialist powers in the given context.

1) American hegemony presupposed the maintenance of a specific set of conditions, namely: (a) that national liberation in the peripheries would 'stabilize' at the bourgeois stage; American military power was supposed to prevent the process developing any further. The United States was thus led to intervene in Korea and Vietnam, and to attempt a reconquest of China throughout the 1950s and 1960s; the Zionists were assigned the task of policing the Middle East and preventing any 'radicalization' there.

(b) that Europe would remain both dependent on American military protection and economically fragile. (c) that the Soviet Union would remain confined to its own territory.

2) These conditions have, on the whole, not been met.

a) Bourgeois power in the peripheries cannot be stabilized: In the Far East, American intervention proved incapable of halting the liberation movements. The US was eventually forced to recognize China in 1971 and to evacuate Indochina in 1975. Elsewhere, the bourgeois powers allied to imperialism are less directly threatened by revolutionary forces. In the Middle East, the US has managed to force Arab nationalism to retreat. But the US had only just succeeded in reasserting its hold over Egypt when the prospect of a populist explosion, starting in Iran in 1979, began to loom on the horizon. In Central America, although Cuba was effectively isolated, the US could not prevent popular revolution in Nicaragua. In Southern and Eastern Africa it failed to prevent the popular movements calling in Soviet aid. Finally, in Afghanistan, the US was, at least for the moment, forced to accept a *fait accompli*.

The defeat of the United States in the Far East is one of the major events of our era, exposing the fact that this great power can no longer impose 'free enterprise' by force. As a result the sovereignty of the Third World countries has been reinforced and their manoeuvring space increased. Without that defeat, it is unlikely that OPEC would have dared assert itself, or that the Third World countries could have launched their struggle for a New Economic Order. That those same countries are still too weak to impose a new and more favourable international division of labour is mainly due to the 'extroverted' development of Third World growth throughout the previous period. This is as much a characteristic of the newly industrializing countries – the NIC – as of the less developed countries. Precisely because it is extroverted, development remains fragile and the bourgeoisie which underpins it is still very vulnerable. As a result, the 'South' as a whole continues to be the weak link in the world system and seems increasingly likely to become, once again, the world's 'stormy weather area', as the crisis and the populist explosions it will provoke proceed apace.

b) Europe and Japan are no longer economically 'inferior' to the United States: The reconstruction of Europe and Japan always carried within it the germ of reversal. Japan, and to a lesser extent Germany and Europe, are now as competitive as the United States in the world market, in some cases more so. Their efforts have already brought about a reversal of the structural tendencies of the balance of payments. After the War the US had a chronic and increasing trade surplus. Now it is the trade surplus of the new economic powers which is growing day by day. Hence the contemporary crisis, which first manifested itself in the field of international monetary relations. The collapse of the Bretton Woods system in 1971 marked the end of the American era. But, as we shall see later, analysis of the relative competitiveness of the US, Japan and Europe is not quite so simple and straightforward. On the military level, Europe and Japan on their own still could not face the nuclear and conventional forces of the Soviet Union.

   c) The strategic aims and means of the USSR must be reassessed.
The USSR appears to have entered a new phase of its development, to
become a world military power which can now rival the United States.

   3) For a long time the European 'economic miracle' seemed to be merely
a by-product of world growth within the 'free enterprise' system set up under
American hegemony. This was indeed the case up to 1973. Rapid growth
(5 per cent a year on average), (nearly) full employment and very limited
inflation (3 per cent a year on average) made it possible for the structures
of final demand and production to be brought into close alignment, not just
in the six EEC countries but also in adjoining areas (notably Spain and
Greece). Only Britain proved incapable of reversing its decline.

   Admittedly, the resulting unequal development is not unconnected with
the implantation abroad of American multinationals. The fact remains
though that the threat of nationalist reactions restricted the US in the
Gaullist period and that by the mid 1960s the balance of foreign trade
had been reversed. It therefore seems quite legitimate to interpret the United
States' benevolent neutrality towards OPEC in 1973 as an 'American counter-
offensive' designed to remind Japan and Europe of the fragility of their growth.

   Yet the American counter-offensive failed. True, the Europeans and Japan
were not all equally able to cope with the new challenge. Only Japan and
Germany managed to reorient their industrial exports (especially towards
the semi-industrialized countries and the Eastern Bloc), by sacrificing employment to relative monetary stability and by concentrating on the new technology sectors. The other European countries found themselves reduced to a
level where they have to cope with competition not only from Germany and
Japan, but also from the semi-industrialized countries and the Eastern Bloc.
Under these conditions, the expansion of the EEC to include a chronically
ailing Great Britain and, soon, the still fragile Spanish, Greek and Portuguese
economies is by no means a guarantee of future success. The class alliances
which characterize each of the European formations have different historical
roots, which limits the possibilities for a common economic policy. The
EEC's 'two faced' attitude to agriculture is a case in point. The northern
farmers benefit from common price support policies for cereals, meat and
milk products, while those in the south, who are excluded from the hegemonic alliance within Europe, get little or no support for their produce
(wine, fruit and vegetables) under the unconvincing 'technical' pretext that
these goods are very difficult to stockpile. Will the reinforcement of the
southern European presence in the EEC force Germany, for political reasons,
to 'finance' a common agricultural policy which will help Europe as a whole
(and not just Germany) to become more competitive internationally? And
will the European Monetary System and the various EEC Funds provide
for a generally acceptable solution? It remains to be seen.

   4) There are thus two main possibilities facing Europe. According to the
first thesis, Europe will effectively 'fragment' under the pressures separating
Germany from the other European countries. The latter will be increasingly

exposed to competition from the semi-industrialized and Eastern Bloc
countries, while the three 'majors', the US, Germany and Japan, engage in
ever more acute competition for the new expanding markets. There are
already many examples of this competition, for example the growth of
German investments in Brazil, contrary to American interests (in the nuclear
industry there was open conflict) or the US counter to Japanese competition
in electronics by shifting their own production to Taiwan and Korea, an
attempt which was foiled when the Japanese also moved their plants to those
countries. From this viewpoint, Germany's chances of pulling through on its
own are much slimmer than is generally believed. German superiority in the
'spearhead' industries is still both recent and fragile. Indeed from 1958 to
1973 German industry's share in world production fell (by 1.3 per cent)
as did that of the US (by 6.9 per cent), Great Britain (by 2.5 per cent) and
France (by 0.7 per cent). In contrast the share of the socialist countries
increased (by 6.3 per cent), and so did Japan's (by 5 per cent). Furthermore,
Germany's push forward only really showed itself after 1973, while Japan's
is more firmly rooted. On the other hand, while the outcome of the struggle
between the US, Germany and Japan is not yet settled, there is no reason to
believe that the old industrial countries of Europe will be reduced to the level
of the semi-industrialized states of the periphery. There is still a qualitative
difference between centres and peripheries.

Given these considerations, Europe may opt for a second strategy: to
reinforce its unity and use the German 'push forwards' to benefit the
Community as a whole. The advantages, including political and military
advantages, of such a development are obvious. Unity of this kind would
not, of course, exclude unequal development within a broader and fuller
EEC, nor would it preclude the emergence of an eventual leader.

5) Could Europe then become a real rival to the United States? Europe's
advantages (perhaps even more than Japan's) should not be underestimated.
In strictly economic terms, the US will probably find it difficult to 'climb
back up' and cancel out the factors which favour Europe. Of course, in the
abstract, if the American firms 'wanted' to concentrate their research and
development efforts to counterbalance the recently won advantages of
certain European and Japanese industries, they would most likely succeed.
But what this abstract line of argument glosses over is the range of intangible
but real structural effects of the 'laziness' inherent in any hegemonic position.
Furthermore, as Wallerstein has demonstrated, the 'decline' of a form of
hegemony is not a feature of the hegemonic power itself but simply to the
more rapid growth of its competitors.

The United States is now handicapped by the gigantism which was once
its main historical advantage: American monopolies are less flexible than
many European and Japanese firms, and they cope badly with the administrative parasitism which often afflicts them. As a result the US companies lose
many battles in the struggle for markets now made much more competitive
by the crisis. Girded up to fight and win a favourable conjuncture by
launching new products, they find this oligopolistic approach ill-suited to

the need for rapid reductions in costs provoked by the crisis, but these are adjustments which Japan, even more than Germany, have successfully implemented.

Secondly, America's very wealth has itself become an impediment to the country's ability to maximize profits by integrating as fully as possible into an increasingly world-wide economy. The American subsoil contains an important portion of the natural resources the US consumes, and its agriculture and industry produce a complete range of goods. In Europe, the less interesting sectors can be dropped more or less at will, but in the US they are defended by powerful interest groups. For instance, in the days when Europe and Japan were getting their energy at ridiculously low prices, the US was enfiefed to its own oil monopolies. Obviously, there are strategic and political advantages to having an abundant supply of raw materials within one's own territory, but it may involve shouldering a fairly heavy economic burden.

Thirdly, on the political level, Europe's division into separate states is also an advantage. It enables European capital to present a united front against disparate 'national' political forces, and thus the European Left has suffered successive defeats throughout the 1970s. Under such conditions Europe can only be the Europe of European capital. The idea of a 'workers' Europe' is clearly an illusion. The fact that so many political forces, of both Left and Right, have rallied round the idea of Europe testifies to the advantage the old but self-rejuvenating continent enjoys in its efforts to hoist itself into a hegemonic position, in economic terms at least. The phenomenon is reminiscent of events within the Second International in 1914, when the working classes of each country fell into line behind 'their' national monopolies. It signals the partial elimination of the local or national contradictions which in the 1950s had cast the Southern European countries in the role of a series of weak links in the central imperialist chain. One should add that even the strength of the European working classes is not a major inconvenience, since it operates in the context of a political polarization which divides the European societies into two more or less equal forces, a liberal Right and a social-democratic Left. The latter not only accepts the rules of the political game but also shares in forms of solidarity which supposedly cut across class, the so-called 'national interests' engendered by access to the Third World's raw materials and the super-exploitation of its labour force. In fact the Left-Right polarization in Europe fulfills certain salutary political functions. It imposes coherent and generally right-wing policies (notably in periods of restructuration), with occasional tilts to the Left to provide an effective safety valve. By contrast, because it lacks any autonomous worker's party, even a social-democratic one, American political life is backward, retarded and fragmented by the inflection of minor contradictions, petty local quarrels, interest lobbies, etc. It is consequently extremely difficult for the country to put a coherent political plan into effect. The 'irrationality' of US policy and the mediocrity of the Presidential competition are clear symptoms of this handicap.

On the ideological level, ever since 1968, capitalist growth has lost much

of the moral legitimacy it had until then possessed in both Europe and
America, but the problem is more acute in the United States. In Europe,
this legitimacy has been partially replaced by the effects of a 'social-
democratic' alliance of much greater lucidity, for example German Social
Democracy. Such alliances clearly make it easier for the working class to
accept a measure of unemployment and for the petty bourgeoisie to tolerate
constant inflation, both of which are essential to the restructuration of the
economy.

Our analyses of Japan and Europe's great strides and of the resulting
American decline do not, as the reader can see, rest entirely on a comparison
between the respective countries' breakthrough's in developing new technology, for here, it is still too early to talk of an American decline. True, Japan
has acquired a definite lead over its competitors in terms of microprocessors
and robotization, a lead which is qualitative as well as quantitative. The
Japanese have concentrated on assembly line production and the installation
of simple and reliable robots which permit a sharp reduction in costs. The
romanticism which prevails in the literature on the subject (the factory with
no workers) is not borne out by the Japanese experience, which has shown
that only partial robotization, notably of handling operations, is profitable.
However, there are no great secrets in the robot field, and the American
companies could soon catch up, especially as the US scientific effort is
already being oriented in this direction. In other domains, such as atomic
science, space and undersea exploration, American technical and scientific
superiority is still considerable.

There is thus little point in analysing economic advances and decline
purely in terms of technological breakthroughs. The progress or decline of an
economy does not result from technology itself but from the social capacity
to put that technology into operation. The case of robotization in Japan
illustrates that the new technology, like Taylorism before it, has as its
essential function the increased subordination of the labour force to the
logic of capital. It therefore requires favourable social conditions which may
not be so easy to establish elsewhere. It is no accident that Japan and
Germany are the two countries whose development most threatens the
United States. Both were defeated in the last war. This meant that their
destroyed industrial infrastructure could be rebuilt on ultra-modern lines,
while their defeated working classes were unable to resist the projected
restructuration of capital. In contrast, Britain's decline and France's difficulties stem from effective working class resistance. The American Right, now in
power, talks a great deal about the 'reindustrialization' of the country. An
inflow of European and Japanese capital is facilitating this renovation and
strengthening the south and west of the US against the old north-east and
its AFL-CIO trade unions. But it is still open to question whether this restructuration will be both rapid and efficacious.

The economic decline of the United States is relative; Europe's and Japan's
lead has only just been opened up and is still fragile. The American multinationals continue to enjoy an overwhelming predominance. But there is

good reason to believe that, far from demonstrating the vitality of North American capitalism, the growth of these firms' foreign investments is a reaction to decline. The American monopolies fight shy of the effort involved in an internal restructuring of their national base and prefer to look for easy profits abroad. The same choice was made by Britain towards the end of the last century and is the main cause of its present accelerated decline. Clearly, it is on the military level that the United States can react most efficaciously. The US retrenchment following the defeat in Vietnam is almost certainly temporary. But although a military reassertion will obviously reopen the question of relations with the USSR, it can have no direct effect on economic competition with Europe. In any case Europe has chosen to concentrate on its economic aims and has thus adopted a much less antagonistic position towards the Soviet Union, to the extent of tolerating the *fait accompli* in Afghanistan. The Soviets have successfully counterposed a Moscow-Bonn-Paris detente axis to the Washington-Tokyo-Peking axis, thereby reducing the scope for American 'nuclear umbrella' blackmail. This choice illustrates after the fact that European reconstruction is by no means a neatly fitting component in a strategy for American hegemony (as those analysts who speak of a German-American Europe suppose). On the contrary, European reconstruction is based on economic competition with the United States. Of course, in the last analysis, the future will be decided on another level, in terms of the relations between the US and the USSR, but that is a separate matter altogether.

6) Finally, there is no real symmetry between Japan in the East and Europe in the West. In terms of economic competition, Japan is even better placed than Europe. But geography cannot be ignored. Japan is forced to tie its fate to the Sino-American alliance, and thus to link itself with its own economic rival and with a socialist country which has no intention of giving up its own autonomy. Analyses which stress the 'brilliant capitalist future' of the 'Confucian Zone' (China, Japan, Korea and Vietnam) and see it taking over where the West leaves off are thus not only based on a rather unrealistic view of the Chinese system; they also cheerfully ignore the problems and contradictions of the coming decades.

Samir Amin
February 1981

1. Introduction

The central concern of this book is to analyse the dynamics of oligopolistic structures in the production of cotton, chemical fibres, and allied textiles, dominated by the transnational conglomerate corporation. We examine the impact of international oligopolies on some of the major actors within contemporary capitalism: the millions of peasants, both small-scale and landless, the industrial proletariat and capitalist classes in the developed and underdeveloped capitalist economies, and the finance and trading capitalists. No less crucial for our analytic perspective is the dialectical interaction of these class forces and the intensifying crises generated by oligopolistic capitalism.

Up to the present, studies on monopoly and oligopolistic capitalism have remained almost exclusively at a highly theoretical level: they have illuminated such conceptual categories as accumulation and appropriation of the economic surplus. In practice this has meant that few studies were centred on either specific primary commodities or specific industrial sectors within the global framework of capitalist relations. Our researches have been motivated by the conviction that an understanding of the mechanisms of 20th Century capitalism requires an enquiry into the interlocking corporate structures of major primary commodities and industries. Cotton and allied textiles are not only one of the major primary commodity exports of the underdeveloped capitalist economies (UCEs), but also involve vital industrial sectors of both developed and underdeveloped countries. Thus the contours and trajectories of contemporary capitalism must be analysed through a specific study of commodities which have been closely interrelated.

The Rise of Oligopoly

This book is concerned with three products which are normally understood as separate commodities: namely, textiles, chemicals and petrochemicals. We have broken these up into eight sectors in order to examine the determinants and impact of oligopoly within the global context of oligopoly's growth from 1895 to the present. These sectors are cotton, cotton trade, petrochemicals, chemical fibres, textiles, clothing, wholesaling/retailing, and textile machinery. Although it has several variants, oligopoly is operationally defined as an irreversible phase in the process of capital accumulation at which a sector is dominated by a few giant corporate enterprises who, by the use of economic and political power, determine prices and output, thereby maximizing profits. Three major phases of oligopolistic capitalism are discernible in the following approximate periodization: 1895—1945, depicted by the emergence and consolidation of oligopoly in key sectors within North America, Western Europe, Japan, and Russia up to 1917; 1946 to the mid 1960s, which witnessed the full-blown emergence of the transnational corporation as the paramount force in the world economy in many sectors; and the mid 1960s to the present day, a period which has experienced the dramatic entrenchment of transnational conglomerate oligopoly that largely provides the time-frame for this study.

Phase 1: 1895—1945

This fifty-year span embodies the most convulsive stage in capitalism's long and tempestuous history. It brings to the fore its inherently degenerative features, such as wars, economic stagnation and the thrust of economic annexationism. In economic terms this stage can be defined as the move from relatively competitive conditions to monopolistic and oligopolistic structures whose culmination was the pool, the trust, the modern corporation, the finance holding company, and the complex scaffolding of a massive and supportive legal framework.

Enhanced economic concentration from 1897 to 1914 was related to the expansionism of industrial and finance capital, improved technology, economies of scale, and the growth of the world market. In the United States, the advent of the corporate revolution (1895—1907) saw the annual average absorption of 266 firms; in 60 per cent of these consolidations a single giant corporation acquired control of at least 62.5 per cent of its industry's market as measured by capitalization. By 1904, 318 corporations owned 40 per cent of all the country's manufacturing assets.[1] Economic annexationism was now ceasing to be confined to a single country, as can be glimpsed in the merger of the American Tobacco Company with the Imperial Tobacco Company, producing the British American Tobacco Company. James Buchanan Duke (1857—1925), the architect of ATC, BAT's first chairman of the board, and master of successive waves of consolidation, grasped the lineaments of the merger movement as pioneered by Standard Oil: 'If John D. Rockfeller can do what he is doing in oil, why should I not do it in tobacco?'[2]

The drive towards consolidation, while reaching its pinnacle in the United States, straddled all developed capitalist economies — the United Kingdom, Germany, France, Japan, Sweden, Switzerland and Russia — albeit in varying degrees and intensities. One of the motives behind this drive was revealed in the exhaustive testimony presented to the United States Federal Industrial Commission at the turn of the century: 'It is clearly the opinion of most of those associated with industrial combinations that the chief cause of their formation has been excessive competition. Naturally all businessmen desire to make profits, and they find their profits falling off first through the pressure of lowering prices of their competitors. The desire to lessen too rigorous competition naturally brings them together. A second way of increasing profits is through the various economies which they think will come by consolidation.'[3] Control of pricing policy and market dominance, control over patents, 'horizontal' and 'vertical' mergers, integration of the marketing and distribution network, were the immediate goals to be obtained through large-scale production. Horizontal mergers were those among companies producing identical or very closely interchangeable products – for instance, two manufacturers of textile products. Vertical mergers were those between companies in an integrated buyer-seller relationship – for example, a textile manufacturer and an apparel retailer. Vertical integration, as envisaged by Andrew Carnegie, stemmed from the implacable logic of economic expansionism: 'Yes, we have been erecting several new departments, including what I believe will be the largest axle factory in the world. Why, it may be asked, should steel makers make plates for other firms to work up into boilers, when they can manufacture the boilers themselves, or beams and girders for boilers, when they can turn out and build up the completed article, or plates for pipes when they can make pipes? I think the next step to be taken by steel makers will be to furnish articles ready for use. In the future, the most successful firms will be those that go farthest in that direction.'[4]

Interpenetration of technologies, the opening up of mass markets, and capital resources contributed to path-breaking innovations in power-generating equipment, new processes in the iron and steel industry, chemistry and engineering, and revolutions in communications, related primarily to railroads, telephone, telegraph, as well as efficient postal services. Taken singly and as a complex whole, these innovations exercised cumulative spread effects on a wider spectrum of industries.[5] 'In brief', wrote Professor Faulkner, 'mechanical improvements made big business not only possible but imperative.'[6] The invention of the modern corporation – and specifically the holding company[7] – provided the ideal instrument for mobilizing capital commensurate with the demands of large-scale industry and beyond the ambit of partnerships and individuals.

The techniques of the 'new competition' included such tested practices as 'cutting prices in one locality to meet local competition while recouping in another, the operation of bogus "independent" concerns to maintain the fiction of competition, the insistence upon "tying clauses" or exclusive arrangements, the securing of rebates and preferential agreements, and use of blacklists, boycotts, espionage, coercion and intimidation.'[8] The sheer expansion of corporate capital led J.B. and J.M. Clark to write that 'the mere size of the consolidations which have recently appeared is enough to startle those who saw them in the making. If the carboniferous age had returned and the earth had repeopled itself with dinosaurs, the change made in animal life would have scarcely seemed greater than that which has been made in the business world . . .'[9]

Imperial Germany perhaps best exemplified the relationship of investment banking, industrial expansion and imperialism. 'Our banks', noted one of the chief executives of the Dresdner Bank in 1908, 'are largely responsible for the development of the empire, having fostered and built up its industries. It is from 1871 that our real development dates and it is since that year that our great banks have been organized. To them more than any other agency may be credited the splendid results thus far achieved.'[10]

Although more rigidly traditionalist in its adherence to economic liberalism, the United Kingdom was not exempt from restrictive business practices. In the 1870s, shipping cartels and nitrate cartels were incubated by British concerns. By 1919, the British Royal Commissioners were writing: 'We find that there is, at present, in every important branch of industry in the United Kingdom an increasing tendency to the formation of Trade Associations and combinations having for their purpose the restriction of competition and the control of prices.'[11] In the United Kingdom, the greatest surge toward oligopoly occurred from 1919 to 1930, fuelled largely by a spate of mergers. It was precisely in this period that 'rationalization', a movement dedicated to the liquidation of millions of working men and women (and less potent capitalists), was to be defined sanctimoniously by its creator, Lord Mond of ICI, 'as the application of scientific organization to industry by the unification of the processes of production and distribution with the object of approximating supply and demand'.[12] The growth of the market shares of the top ten corporations in five major British industries (as measured by market valuation of a company's capital) indicates this trend (see Table 1.1). Textiles was the only industry where mergers were relatively less important, due primarily to massive internal growth by such textile giants as Courtaulds, whose market value rose from £16 million to £52 million over this period.[13] It should be added that many of the industrial giants of today, such as ICI, Unilever and BAT, owe their origin to mergers in this period.

While certain corporations in North America and Europe were extending their sales and production overseas, none approached the transnational power exerted by the Japanese *zaibatsu* (or 'financial clique'), which operated in alliance with the State. 'The usual means of welding the numerous companies in a *zaibatsu* organization into a cohesive group', noted an official US report, 'has been the wide use of interlocking directorates, accompanied by the use of one individual as officer in several companies.'[14] The widespread diffusion of *zaibatsu* directors in key government posts ensured government subsidies and monopolistic grants in the *zaibatsu*'s formative years and after. *Zaibatsu* control of banks, other financial institutions, and raw material supplies armed these giant corporations with ample power to prevent new entry into their industrial and trading domains. In the total absence of anti-trust law, the largest *zaibatsu* dominated trade as well as most industrial sectors. Mitsubishi, the second largest *zaibatsu*, accounted for over 10 per cent of

Japan's 1940s production in many sectors, including flour milling (50 per cent), aircraft engines (45 per cent), sugar (35 per cent) electrical equipment (35 per cent), and shipbuilding, shipping and iron ore (25 per cent).[15] Despite efforts during the US occupation to dismantle the *zaibatsu* in 1945, a new species of *zaibatsu* was created, and continues to operate in close conjunction with the Ministry of International Trade and Industry (MITI).

Table 1.1
Market Share of Ten Largest Corporations in British Industry (%)

Industrial Sector	Share in 1919 (a)	Change due to Merger (b)	Change due to Internal Growth (c)	Share in 1930 (a + b + c)
Food	52.9	+ 30.7	+ 1.5	85.1
Tobacco	98.2	+ 1.8	+ 0	100.0
Chemicals	76.7	+ 14.2	+ 2.3	93.2
Textiles	60.7	+ 9.2	+ 8.3	78.2
Paper and Publishing	56.0	+ 25.5	+ 7.3	88.8

Source: L. Hannah and J.A. Kay, *Concentration in Modern Industry* (London, 1977), pp. 69–70.

Phase 2: 1948 to the mid-1960s
Rising out of the technological explosion after the Second World War, the Japanese transnational corporate prototype became generalized, despite the formal endorsement of anti-trust legislation in all countries – including Japan. The growth, nature, and composition of world trade and investment were revolutionized in this period. The epicentre of this transformation has been the transnational corporation, now enveloping roughly 70–80 per cent of world trade outside the centrally planned economies (CPEs). Significantly, transnational corporation intra-firm transfers grew during this period to a point where they account for around 30 per cent of international trade.

The emergence of international oligopoly was predicated upon the internationalization of output, finance, and commerce. Technological innovation in four crucial areas fuelled the internationalization process: dispersed production facilities became profitable only after revolutionary advances in containerized shipping; unprecedented breakthroughs in satellite engineering provided the complex communications network crucial to international capitalism that depended on speed of operations; the rise of the computer provided for the instantaneous data-processing so vital for the maximization of global profits; and relatively cheap and dense international air networks facilitated the transnationalization of business through personal contacts. These innovations were especially crucial to the stupendous growth of the giant multi-commodity trading corporations, whose cotton-trading activities are dissected in Chapter 3.

Other factors that furthered capital concentration[16] included the banks, advertising media — which were swiftly brought under the control of transnational power, and the increasing interpenetration of the state and corporate capital. Congressman Wright Patman, Chairman of the US House Subcommittee on Banking and Currency, elucidated the role of US banks, a role which was to be universally valid for the entire transnational banking structure: 'One of the favourite pastimes of concentrated financial power is promoting concentration in non-financial industries. There is substantial evidence that the major commercial banks have been actively fuelling the corporate merger movement.'[17]

Despite laws that limit US banking control of industry, throughout the 1950s and 1960s the big banks invested billions of dollars in industrial stocks. By the early 1970s, the top 49 banks had a 5 per cent share or more in 147 of the top 500 US industrial corporations.[18] In other leading developed capitalist economies (DCEs) such as Germany and Japan,[19] banks, unimpeded by legal constraints, grew to control major industries at home and abroad. In this symbiotic relationship banks grew rapidly, due to the high cash-flow requirements of industry, and many of the major global banks appropriated the bulk of their profits from overseas operations, while major industrial enterprises were becoming predominantly transnational. The birth of the Eurodollar market in the 1960s also played a pivotal role in financing the international operations of large-scale industry. Credit borrowed from this market scaled $100 billion by the 1970s.[20]

Transnationalization of advertising emerged as a decisive instrument of the global corporation in carving out new market shares. While the top United States advertising firms derived only a little over 5 per cent of their 1954 revenues overseas, by the mid 1970s the world's ten largest agencies accounted for 35 per cent of world advertising billings ($7.2 billion), with 43 per cent of their activities in foreign countries.[21] But the final major component of concentration indirectly contributing to the internationalization of capital, has been the state. Using techniques described in subsequent chapters, state organs such as the Industrial Reorganization Corporation in the United Kingdom, the state planning agency in France, and MITI in Japan, have spurred industrial concentration.

The 1960s thus saw a quantitatively new dimension of the scale of operations of the transnational oligopolistic corporation. Whereas there were only two or three giant (product-specialized) corporations with assets reaching $500 million in 1906, in the ensuing decades, size and diversification grew apace, as was trenchantly pointed out by Willard Mueller in his testimony on corporate growth and secrecy:

> In contrast, by the first quarter of 1971, there were 111 industrial corporations with assets of $1 billion or more and nearly 200,000 partnerships and proprietorships engaged in manufacturing. These 111

corporations held at least 51 per cent of the assets and 56 per cent of the profits of all corporations engaged primarily in manufacturing; the 333 corporations with assets of $500 million or more accounted for fully 70 per cent of all industrial assets, excluding their unconsolidated holdings. Indeed, by 1970, the two largest industrial corporations alone had sales of nearly $40 billion, which is about as great (in constant dollars) as those of the over 200,000 manufacturing establishments operating in 1899.[22]

The picture in the United Kingdom is no less revealing. The largest 100 manufacturing firms in terms of net output, which had accounted for a relatively stable share of manufacturing (22–24 per cent) between the early 1920s and the late 1940s, a share which had moved up to 27 per cent by 1953, saw their share spurt sharply to slightly over 40 per cent by 1970. In fact the United Kingdom's industrial structure is already more concentrated than that of the United States.[23] Indeed, two analysts concluded 'that the period from 1955–73 must be considered as the most sustained period of merger activity in the history of the U.K. economy, certainly since 1880 and probably since the emergence of British capitalism. There is at least a *prima facie* case for arguing that it has contributed largely to the most sustained and rapid change so far experienced in the centralization of manufacturing, and distribution and finance, since the First World War.'[24]

Phase 3: the mid-1960s to the Present
The current phase of transnational conglomerate oligopoly, which grew in most industrial sectors over the 1960s, was consolidated by an unprecedented spate of worldwide mergers from 1967 to 1969. This periodization does not imply that conglomerates are a product of the 1960s. In the United States, for example, during the 1948–65 period, there were 711 mergers of large firms, 454 of which were conglomerate.[25] As the Chairman of the US Federal Trade Commission, Michael Pertschuk, explained, there was a qualitative difference between the mergers of the earlier period and those of today. Referring to the 1950s and 1960s, he testified: 'You had product-extension and territorial extension mergers, more horizontal and more vertical during that time.'[26] Conglomerate mergers are those between any two companies that are neither direct competitors nor in a buyer-seller relationship with one another. Within this general category, the product-extension mergers mentioned above include mergers between companies that are functionally related in production and/or distribution but sell products that are not in direct competition with each other (e.g. a yarn spinning company merging with a textile weaving company). Territorial extension mergers include mergers between companies producing identical products but selling in separate geographical markets.

These mergers contrast with the largely 'pure' conglomerate mergers of the 1970s, which Mr. Pertschuk described as: 'firms with piles of cash that are buying up solid firms'.[27] These involve firms acquiring functionally un-

related enterprises, a process epitomized by ITT, which, according to one of
its annual reports, 'is constantly at work around the clock, in 67 nations on
6 continents, in activities extending from the Arctic to the Antarctic and
quite literally from the bottom of the sea to the moon'.[28] Moreover, the
percentage of mergers which were conglomerate rose in the USA from 64 per
cent in the 1948–65 period to 88 per cent in 1975.[29] Any hope of stemming
this tide via anti-trust legislation appears naive, as was recognized even by
such spokesmen of the system as Congressman Neil Smith of Iowa: 'Enforcement of this nation's existing anti-trust laws rests with whoever may be in
power at the Justice Department; and, if and when those laws are enforced,
the process is so time consuming that the injured firms may be long out of
business before a decision is reached.'[30] Also underlining the limitations of
the legislative approach, Mr. Ralph Nader has observed: 'The posture of two
agencies (the Anti-Trust Division of the US Justice Department and the
Federal Trade Commission) with a combined budget of $20 million and
550 lawyers and economists trying to deal with anticompetitive abuses in a
trillion-dollar economy, not to mention an economy where the 200 largest
corporations control two-thirds of all manufacturing assets, is truly a
charade.'[31]

No less dramatic is the virtual powerlessness of Canada's Anti-Combines
Branch of the Department of Consumer and Corporate Affairs. 'We have a
great concern over the size of these mergers,' commented Mr. Paul Mitchell
of the Combines Branch, 'but the law is toothless. Mergers are impossible
to stop. We must prove an "undue" loss of competition to the public's detriment before that happens'.[32] Mr. Robert Bertrand, Director of the Anti-
Combines Branch, comments: 'What we will have if this march of increased
concentration continues is a national oligarchy in which a few dozen people
will interact to bargain about the economic future of millions.'[33]

Another testimony to the brisk pace of conglomeration is that the total
value of conglomerate mergers and acquisitions was less than $1.5 billion
in 1972. By 1977, after what one corporate mergers' expert termed 'an orgy
of cannibalism which has reached unprecedented levels',[34] it had jumped
to nearly $6 billion.[35] For Europe, the extent of transnational conglomera-
tion is depicted by the growing number of firms in the *Fortune 500* list of
industrial corporations outside the US that span several industrial categories.
This pace of concentration and conglomeration is evidenced not only in the
DCEs, but also in certain select UCEs, of which South Korea is a glaring
example. The Hyundai Group alone accounts for about 10 per cent and
Samsung 4 per cent of that country's GDP.

Dr Walter Adams recently testified to the overwhelming impact of conglomerates, even in sectors which have not been significantly penetrated by
oligopoly: 'A conglomerate giant is powerful, therefore, not because it has
monopoly or oligopoly control over a particular market, but because its
resources are diversified over many different markets. Its power, as Corwin
Edwards says, derives from the fact that it can outbid, outspend, and out-
lose a smaller firm. It occupies a position much like the millionaire poker

player who, in a game of unlimited stakes, can easily bankrupt his less opulent opponents, regardless of his comparative mastery over the dizzy virtues of probability theory.'[36]

In fact, conglomerates derive benefits from oligopolistic market structures and the two, working in concert, present an economic unit of almost unparalleled power. While different markets expand and contract, the conglomerate that belongs to several industrial oligopolies can ride the ebbs and flows by shifting its resources into whatever happens to be most profitable at the moment. This technique is known as 'cross-subsidization', since the conglomerate can use profits earned in its prospering sectors to subsidize losses in some of its temporarily depressed lines of business. With the same facility it is able to engage in a swift and constant process of shifting its large cash reserves between currencies to protect itself against devaluation, inflation and other monetary turbulence. It can thereby earn maximum interest payments and reap windfall profits on changes in relative currency values.

In addition to cross-subsidization, another mechanism of conglomerate power is business reciprocity, which is the practice of making sales to and purchases from corporations that are already customers of the conglomerate. Not only does this practice raise barriers to new entrants but also reciprocal arrangements of this kind drastically reshape the competitive market mechanism. As such arrangements proliferate, 'trade relations between the giant conglomerates tend to close a business circle. Left out are the firms with narrow product lines; as patterns of trade and trading partners emerge between particular groups of companies, entry by newcomers becomes more difficult.'[37] The further consequence, as *Fortune* notes, is that the United States economy 'might end up completely dominated by conglomerates happily trading with each other in a new kind of cartel system'; and, as will be seen below, the phenomenon is not confined to the United States.

It is in this general overall framework that the specific evolution of oligopoly in the majority of our eight sectors can be understood.

The Mechanisms of Oligopoly

In the most general economic sense, oligopoly is characterized by large corporations acting as 'price makers'. This differs from competitive capitalism where the individual enterprise is a 'price taker'. The oligopoly sets a price, then produces and sells at that price whatever quantity the market will take. It is for this reason that price in an oligopolistic industry is sometimes referred to as an 'administered' price, or a political price. The basic principle is that price is seller-determined and aimed at maximization of profits of the oligopoly's member firms.[38] While varying according to different historical and legal contexts, oligopolistic pricing has traditionally assumed one basic mode of operation: price leadership. Arthur Burns defined the concept as follows: 'Price leadership exists when the price at which most of the units in an industry offer to sell is determined by adopting the price announced by one of their number.'[39] Price leadership implies not only that pricing policies must be coordinated, but also that the price, once agreed upon, must be sustained by its members until a further change is required by the oligopolists collectively.[40] Such leadership is most pronounced when one firm stands far above the others in the industry in terms of assets, revenues, and general market power — a firm such as US Steel and General Motors in the United States, or Courtaulds and Unilever in Britain. Other firms in the oligopoly accept price changes by the leaders since those prices are generally profitable, and because they are aware of the self-destructive nature of price warfare in which the less powerful inevitably lose out.

When no single firm clearly dominates the field, price leadership takes on varying guises. In the cigarette and chemical industries, for example, the giants share the responsibilities of initiating price changes. In petroleum, before the 1973 OPEC embargo, different firms took the lead in different regional markets. In other industries, no such regularity is noticeable, and the following situation emerges: 'The initiating firm may simply be announcing to the rest of the industry, "We think the time has come to raise (or lower) the price in the interest of all of us". If the others agree, they will follow. If they do not, they will stand pat, and the firm that made the first move will rescind its initial price change.'[41] Other characteristic techniques within oligopolies include product differentiation where, through advertising, brand names and other forms of non-price competition, rival corporations try to carve out separate market spheres where they can command consumer loyalty.

Certain oligopolies do make the decision to move from tacit collusion to open cartels, where oligopolistic firms agree on prices and occasionally on market shares and areas of operation. As an OECD committee of experts recently noted, firms sometimes 'consolidate their economic power and draw advantages from it not only individually but also by means of agreements or concerted actions with other enterprises, particularly in oligopolies where most multinationals are to be found. Such agreements are facilitated by the possibility in many countries of legalizing certain types of cartels: for example, rebate, rationalization, import and specialization cartels in which the subsidiaries of multinational firms may participate and which may, and in fact sometimes do, serve as the nucleus for an international system of restrictive agreements.'[42]

Although the data are not sufficiently exhaustive to assess precisely the role of export cartels on an industry by industry basis or to quantify exactly their economic significance, it can be concluded from the Federal Cartel Office that transnationals participate in around 70 per cent of all the export cartels of West Germany. In the United Kingdom an analysis of 41 international export cartels (32 per cent of all export cartels) showed that 20 out of 29 with transnational participation had both British and foreign transnational members.[43] Also noteworthy is the fact that the oligopoly in an international export cartel can induce other corporations engaged in domestic and foreign trade not to undermine the cartel's export prices.

A central mechanism deployed by capitalism, especially in its oligopolistic phase, has been the appropriation of science, glimpsed in the chemical industry's emulation and transcendence of natural products (cotton, rubber, wool, soya, and so on), in the search for an increased market. 'The scientific technical revolution', as Harry Braverman incisively puts it, 'cannot be understood in terms of specific innovations . . .' rather, it 'must be understood in its totality as a mode of production into which science and exhaustive engineering have been integrated as part of ordinary functioning. The key innovation is not to be found in chemistry, electronics, automatic machinery . . . or any of the products of these science-technologies, but rather in the transformation of science itself into capital.'[44] No less vital is the transformation of capital into science, through the billions of dollars which the chemical fibre oligopoly pumps into research and development mobilizing tens of thousands of scientists. Knowledge is power, profit and survival, an equation well understood by the executors of Big Capital: 'We must move towards company structures', noted Mr John Davies, former Director General of the Confederation of British Industries, 'capable of competing in research and development, in scale of production, in market coverage and financial strength . . . not even on a national plane — but on an international plane.' This is a theme which permeates the present work, and is no less relevant to the export-oriented UCE oligarchy.[45]

One important caveat to the understanding of oligopolistic mechanisms is that the general traits described here apply in particular to industrial oligopolies. In primary commodity trade there are certain marked variations in oligopolistic practices: the mechanisms of price leadership, advertising, and brand names, as described in their deployment by industrial oligopolies in Chapters 6 to 9, either do not exist or operate differently for trading corporations. Pricing for the primary commodity trading giants is more like a highly complex game, where secrecy and sophisticated hedging, speculating and arbitrage produce profits. However, a close similarity between oligopoly in primary commodity trade and industry remains: both entail a minuscule number of giant firms exercising economic and political power to determine prices geared to profit maximization. Likewise, certain techniques, such as cross-subsidization, characterize both variants of oligopoly.

Methodological Departures

Our approach deviates radically from both neo-classical microeconomic theory and traditional oligopoly theory. At the most fundamental level of microeconomic theory, we reject the notion that marketing proceeds as if price structures were reproduced in an idyllically competitive milieu between buyers and sellers of equal bargaining strength. The transparent inequality of corporate forces provides evidence that this is not the case. As regards the behaviour of large firms with oligopolistic power, formal economic theory has largely bypassed this issue. Rather, it continues to centre on the role of the profit-maximizing entrepreneur who has occupied the pivotal position in traditional theories since well before the onset of the industrial revolution of the 18th Century. This body of traditional doctrine, therefore, likens the functioning of the corporation to that of an individual entrepreneur. Instead of this ahistorical equation of individual and firm behaviour we propose a systematic enquiry into the forces producing the accelerating shift from small to larger corporate units, whether this is sealed by literal agglomeration of smaller business units or through their dependent integration (e.g. through supplier contracts) into a larger corporation's marketing realm. In contrast to the apologetics of traditional theory, our approach both pinpoints the historical interactions of the corporate structures pioneering chemical fibres and allied textiles, and describes the engines of economic power they have been able to deploy (not least in research).

Turning now to traditional oligopoly theory, we start from Willard Mueller's assertion that

> Theories of oligopoly . . . that were framed to explain market conduct and performance in terms of the market structure of an industry, are no longer adequate tools of analysis in an age in which conglomerate firms are enjoying greater and greater dominance. For the power that such firms can bring to bear within a particular industry — and, hence, the influence they can exert over prices, output, new entry, and innovation — depends on their market position not just in that one industry but also in all their many lines of business at home and abroad.[46]

In this spirit, our study delves into the new mechanisms of corporate power as they are evolving under transnational conglomerate oligopoly.

Not surprisingly, our conclusions likewise differ substantially from those of our neo-classical critics. International organizations have responded to the fluctuations and crises of the cotton and allied textile industries with price stabilization schemes and reducing trade barriers to UCE manufacturers (although their practice frequently deviates from this). We do not aim to disparage such gestures of international benevolence. But we do wish to throw light on the protean forces of national and international class power within the developed and underdeveloped capitalist economies. We thereby focus attention on — among other related elements — the appropriation of the economic surplus, an appropriation which international commodity agreements are largely incapable of altering. Indeed, these commodity agreements could not have even a marginal effect on the redistribution of global economic power unless they were framed on the basis of a clear understanding of production, marketing and reproduction relations. Our conclusions flow from this theoretical framework.

Our approach departs from traditional methodological constructs in two major respects. First, we examine commodities in their totality, relating to their shifting global output and export structures, and in their interconnections with other commodities. Secondly, we study commodities by unveiling the configuration of corporate power at each specific stage of commodity output. The first approach, that of viewing commodities in their totality, is based upon two novel concepts: processing and marketing chains, and a new conceptualization of the international division of labour. This approach stems from the conviction that any attempt to confine analysis to a single commodity is erroneous, as the generalized process of global accumulation has led to an interlacing of inter-commodity flows through the political, economic and marketing mechanisms of corporate expansion.

Processing and Marketing Chains

This part of the analytic framework, which also provides the rationale for later chapters, consists of examining the two basic integrated and overlapping marketing chains that comprise the industry: the cotton/yarn/textile/clothing and other end-use chain, which also embraces textile machinery; and the petroleum and natural gas/petrochemicals/chemical fibres chain. Our analysis delineates the underlying corporate structures and the technological imperatives of successive production phases, leading ultimately to a retail breakdown of clothing items into the proportions annexed by actors at various links in the chains.

The first chain begins with the primary commodity — cotton. Cotton output, which is our first link in this chain, is largely dominated by the USSR USSR, China, and the United States; the remainder is produced in over sixty underdeveloped countries. By any benchmark of concentrated economic power, this is the most fragmented stage of operations. In sharp contrast to such fragmentation, the second link — the multi-commodity traders (who market cotton to spinners) — is the embodiment of transnational conglomerate oligopoly. The giant traders who transport the bulk of globally traded cotton have their headquarters mainly in the United States, Switzerland, and Japan.

Yarn preparation, the first stage of processing, is increasingly carried on outside the DCEs, with UCEs lifting their world share of cotton yarn production from 19 per cent in 1950 to almost 40 per cent in 1978.[47] Textile weaving and knitting, the second phase of processing, is by far the most capital-intensive segment. With high levels of economic concentration and automation, this sector continues to be primarily the domain of DCEs. In contrast, the clothing industry, the major textile end-use, has so far proved less amenable to comprehensive mechanization and is implanted mainly in lower-cost capitalist countries (Hong Kong, South Korea, Taiwan, and India) where the industry is still overwhelmingly distinguished by fairly competitive small-scale economic units.[48] The same is true of most DCEs where clothing sweatshops are still conspicuously prevalent. The inroads of automated processes into the clothing industry, however, will gather speed in the 1980s, with concomitant economic concentration. Inexorably, this will place considerable pressures on UCEs to automate (and hence to slash the industrial workforce massively and swiftly — and this in the context of a rapidly swelling labour force) if they are to maintain their still tenuous world market shares.

After clothing, the chain's next link is the wholesaling/retailing of textile and apparel items. This sector operates within all national markets, and its market structure varies from medium levels of concentration in many DCEs to much more fragmented markets in most UCEs. The final link of this first chain consists of the textile machinery industry. This branch is one of the highest expressions of contemporary engineering design and research and is directly germane to the erosion of cotton's market share compared with chemical fibres. Geographically, the industry is highly concentrated, with UCEs holding less than 5 per cent of the world export market, and having only bleak prospects of enhancing that share.

Chemical fibres' pivotal linkage with the world cotton economy necessitates a study of a second marketing chain, which begins at the oil-fields and meanders through refineries and petrochemical complexes to the fibre plants. The geographic configuration of the first link — petroleum and natural gas — stems, as with almost any primary commodity (notably non-agricultural commodities), from unequal natural endowments. The leaders are the United States and the Soviet Union, trailed by a limited number of UCEs, mostly in the Middle East, to a lesser extent in Latin America, and including China.

The processing of natural gas and petroleum into petrochemicals — the prime feedstock of chemical fibres — has historically been dominated by the DCEs. Over the last decade, however, a number of socialist industrialized economies, several of the thirteen OPEC nations, and Mexico have leapt headlong into this sector. Their intrusion presages further extensive rever-berations on the world market in the 1980s through overcapacity pressures on the traditional petroleum and chemical oligopolies. A similar but rather less convulsive intrusion is being made by the chemical fibre industry into UCEs and socialist countries.[49] However, in both petrochemicals and chemical fibres it is important to distinguish between the physical setting up of plants in UCEs, and the highly complex basic and applied research pushed through at astronomical capital costs in DCE corporate laboratories. The central importance of this second chain is that it intersects the first at the stage of textile manufacturing, and it is here that the corporate structures promoting chemical fibres are systematically and irreversibly eroding cotton's share in fibre end-uses.

The International Division of Labour

We have seen how viewing commodities in their totality involves examining the industry's two marketing chains. But it is necessary to supplement this with a new conceptualization of the international division of labour. The aftermath of the Second World War saw a colossal and unprecedented burgeoning of the world's productive resources, partnered by major shifts in their geographical distribution via the transnational corporations. To describe the global network — where and why goods and services are generated geographically — we turn to the concept of the international division of labour. Theoretically rationalized by the classical Ricardian paradigm, based on the fixed notion of comparative advantage operating through unimpeded 'market forces', a two-fold vision and division of the world economy separated colonial and semi-colonial raw-material-producing countries from metropolitan manufacturing ones. This simplistic schema has been outdated as certain UCEs emerged as industrial sites for investing corporate capital from the DCEs, a process clearly visible in the giant dwarfs: South Korea, Hong Kong, Taiwan, Singapore, India, Brazil and Mexico.

This shift in manufacturing locations is being fed essentially by three currents: DCE corporations, UCE private and public sector enterprises, and permutations of these through joint ventures. This drive springs from the quest for lower-cost raw materials and labour inputs and for more lucrative investment outlets; the striving to penetrate and expand potential industrial markets; the allurements proffered by several UCEs (including free trade zones and tax write-offs), enhancing the profitability of overseas investments; and flight from increasingly costly environmental regulations in the DCEs.

A seminal distinction must be drawn here between the dominant and expansionist industrial bourgeoisie within the leading six underdeveloped capitalist economies, and the remainder of the UCEs, who themselves are objects of predatory action, not least by this group of six. These six account for four-fifths of aggregate UCE exports of textiles, clothing and chemical fibres. To date, a significant share of output is still generated by subsidiaries of transnational corporations (TNCs), but the pattern is changing toward one of dependent partnership by domestic state and private capital. Indeed, it is precisely the state and industrial oligarchies of this limited list of UCEs that are now aggressively cutting wider salients into the world market.

Given this social perspective, the designation 'farmers' or 'peasants' with respect to UCE agriculture is generally misleading. Rather we explicitly recognize several levels of class differentiation within the agrarian structure: landless labourers, tenants, sub-tenants, landlords, independent farmers, etc. Each social class and its sub-categories are affected in specific ways by price, volume and technology changes in the specific commodities involving their production relations.

The Configuration of Corporate Oligopoly

Our second major methodological point of departure is to identify the specific corporate forces engaged in production, processing and marketing, which leads to the demystification of the traditional concept of 'inter-fibre competition' and, for that matter, competition between all natural and synthetic commodities. While the designation 'inter-fibre competition' is used occasionally in this work as a convenient piece of shorthand (as is the notion of the 'Third World'), it should not be taken as a denial of the pedestrian truth that commodities in themselves do not 'compete'. Rather, commodities are the objects of corporate forces within the global economy, and hence are not independent of the political economy of oligopoly, This section merely provides an overview of the conglomerate and oligopolistic forces in the individual segments of the cotton and allied textile industries.

If at one end of the chemical fibre chain we find the strategic deployment of corporate chemical and petrochemical output with their marketing and research power, at the other end are millions of small peasant farmers, sub-tenants and landless labourers within the UCEs. For the bulk of this prole-tarianized mass, subsistence wages (often sub-subsistence wages) are the established norm. In Central America, this plantation wage income averages around US$1.25 per day, and in Africa it is often lower for tenants and landless labourers. This is a major factor in cotton's still competitive stance in the international market. However, this extreme fragmentation at the producer level perceptibly alters at the highly sophisticated plantation level, notably in certain Central American UCEs, such as Nicaragua, Guatemala, and El Salvador.

The situation can be compared to a river. As the multiple production tributaries of the natural fibre river approach the delta of the world market, massive build-ups of economic power, enshrined in fifteen giant traders controlling 85–90 per cent of globally traded cotton, make their appearance. Concentration of capital at the trading level now becomes synonymous with the ascent of the multi-commodity conglomerate corporations whose global hegemony has become more discernible over the last two decades. Their sheer operational scale requires them to extend their trading supremacy beyond a single commodity (in the case of the Japanese *Sogo Shosha* to a large range of manufactured commodities as well). Nowhere is this embodiment of power so blatant as in futures markets, where multi-commodity traders often manipulate prices. But, what has been invariably obscured in analyses of the futures market is that they abet economic concentration, specifically in industries dominated by vertically-integrated firms that trade in futures.

In contrast to the fragmented state of the world cotton economy and its paltry annual research funds of around US$55–65 million, billions of dollars are being injected into widening the applications of current chemical fibres and the creation of new ones. Here the bulk of chemical and petrochemical giants have extended their economic realm to other energy sectors, with serious implications for the marketing of cotton and natural fibres. Indicative of this is Dow Chemical Corporation's new and inexpensive catalyst to turn coal into oil (low in sulphur and free of solid contaminants) by a liquefaction process expected to be on stream by 1990. This is by no means an isolated one-shot research plunge but involves, to a greater or lesser extent, all the petrochemical majors. In fact, the manipulation of chemical and physical properties so that fibre products can be varied according to desired qualities has been the basic rationale of fibre chemistry for some decades.

World petrochemical production is dominated by about five oil giants and ten chemical corporations, often working in concert through joint ventures. Likewise, the chemical fibre oligopoly has traditionally been highly concentrated. By 1979 around thirteen giant firms (now twelve) produced about three-fifths of the world's chemical fibres, encompassing about 80–90 per cent of world trade (see Table 1.2).

Table 1.2
World Ranking of Major Synthetic Fibre Producers (based on mid-1979 nominal capacity)

	Nylon		Polyester		Acrylic		Total	
	Rank-	%	Rank-	%	Rank-	%	Rank-	%
Producer Group	ing	Share	ing	Share	ing	Share	ing	Share
Du Pont	1	17	1	14	2	8	1	14
Celanese USA[1]	11	1	2	12	11	–	2	6
Monsanto	2	8	9	3	1	9	3	6
Akzo	3	8	5	6	8	2	4	6
Toray	6	5	6	6	9	2	5	4
Teijin	8	2	3	7	–	–	6	4
Hoechst	13	–	4	7	6	3	7	4
Rhone Poulenc	5	5	7	4	10	2	8	3
ICI[1]	4	6	8	3	–	–	9	3
Courtaulds	12	1	12	–	3	6	10	2
Montedison[2]	10	1	10	1	5	5	11	2
Bayer	9	1	13	–	4	6	12	2
Snia Viscosa[2]	7	3	11	–	7	3	13	2
Others	–	42	–	37	–	54	–	42
Total		100		100		100		100

1. ICI and Celanese have a joint subsidiary whose sales are included in Celanese.
2. Merged fibre divisions in 1978.

Source: Trade sources.

In general, chemical fibres represent only one-fifth of the chemical corporations' sales, because of their highly diversified product lines. This has enabled them to withstand the battering of financial losses in the chemical fibre sector in excess of $4.5 billion between 1974 and 1979.

The textile processing stage has a less cohesive oligopolistic structure than that of cotton trading and chemical fibres. Approximately thirty-five to forty giant textile corporations (several of whom will undoubtedly be bought out by others in the next decade – the liquidation of the powerful Boussac Group in France is a recent example) envelop a wide spectrum of textile and non-textile activities.

These thirty-five to forty textile transnationals (several of whom are chemical corporations) largely dominate world textiles in both DCEs and UCEs. Their power (as with chemical, petrochemical, oil and textile engineering) is rooted in six countries: the USA, Japan, France, the United Kingdom, West Germany and Italy. While all major fibre manufacturing sectors have been caught in the avalanche of concentration, there are marked sectoral and geographical variations. DCE textile industries are increasingly characterized by vertically and horizontally integrated corporations. Such leading world textile firms as Courtaulds, Burlington, ICI and the Agache Willot Group in France exemplify the peaks of concentration within specific national markets. These have, of course, overspilled onto the international economy.

Yet, for a complex concatenation of reasons, such levels of concentrated power do not occur at all phases of the global textile production chain. The clothing industry is still highly fragmented but technological innovations have recently opened the gateways for future concentration. In certain DCEs, the textile and clothing industries have fused, an example is the textile giant Courtaulds, whose estimated share of the British apparel market is 15–20 per cent. The clothing industry in the United States, notoriously fragmented, in fact includes giant conglomerates such as Gulf and Western, the largest US apparel manufacturer (aside from the denim giants Levi and Blue Bell), whose clothing sales ($725 million in 1978) are a trifling 17 per cent of its aggregate sales.

Apart from the clothing sector, oligopolistic power structures have become much tighter at the wholesaling and retailing level. Gross margins now represent as much as half the retail price of textile products. The rapid growth of these colossal aggregations of purchasing power over the last three decades, (promoted by the creation of new fashion trends), has generated tempestuous marketing stratagems within the world fibre and textile economy. The giant wholesaler/retailers are strategically placed in the marketing chain, able to dictate supplier discounts by playing off national and non-national producers against each other.

Finally, any enquiry into the economic power structures of cotton and allied textiles would remain incomplete without a review of the corporate entities that control textile machinery, since they directly impinge on fibre choice. Almost every advance in textile engineering technology since the end of the Second World War has been at the cost of natural fibres, and parallelled by closer corporate links between the chemical fibre oligopoly and the textile machinery producers. As with the petrochemical, chemical fibre and textile industries, the entire world market for textile machinery is controlled by a handful of transnational machinery producers originating in the developed economies: West Germany, the United States, Britain, Switzerland, France,

Belgium, and Italy. Not only does it affect fibre choice, the textile machinery oligopoly also unloads increasingly sophisticated engineering technology on the global market. Its high capital intensity of course spells reductions in the workforce.

The Overall Impact of Oligopoly

We are concerned with the impact of oligopoly, in its current transnational conglomerate stage, on the major regions of the world economy (UCEs, DCEs, and CPEs) as well as on the trajectory of the world capitalist economy itself. Beginning first with the underdeveloped capitalist economies, the growth of oligopoly in the sectors outlined above has redirected the entire course of both primary commodity and industrial development. For the millions engaged in cotton production, the grossly unequal configuration of corporate power in petrochemicals/chemical fibres versus cotton production continues to erode cotton's share in fibre end-use markets, allocating meagre financial returns to this powerless mass of peasantry. Moreover, the relationship of the cotton trading oligopoly to the peasantry can only be exploitative. Nor has the plight of cotton been aided by the traders, who, as multi-commodity corporations, do not suffer excessively when cotton exports decline.

Conglomerate oligopoly has contributed to two forces in UCE industry. First, with the movement of subsidiaries and industrial capital principally to six or seven leading UCEs, existing divisions within the so-called 'Third World' have been heightened. The 'industrialization of the Third World' in reality amounts to a proliferation of manufacturing only within this coterie of countries. Secondly, it is the corporate members of the oligopolies who continue to appropriate the gains of this industrialization which are only partially shared with a growing but still subordinate UCE industrial bourgeoisie.

In the developed capitalist economies, the most direct effect of the growth of conglomerate oligopoly has been the winnowing out of smaller firms in most industrial sectors, with harmful consequences for employment. In literally hundreds of pages of testimony from United States Congressional hearings (relevant to all DCEs) the evidence is overwhelming:[50] the internationalization of capital has generated massive job displacement and will continue to do so. Moreover, the unrelenting growth in the capital intensity of most industries contributes both to overcapacity production and unacceptably high levels of unemployment. Such labour and industrial strategies have given oligopolistic capitalism a greater flexibility on the national and global market, but one which simultaneously exacerbates the conflicts within the system as a whole. In his testimony Mueller underlined that 'as corporations operate across a growing spectrum of industries and own plants in many nations, they achieve great flexibility and discretion at the bargaining table . . . Industrial conglomeration may dissipate the bargaining power of an individual trade union if its members are in an industry that represents a small part of the total business of a huge conglomerate.'[51]

Although the CPEs are of peripheral concern to our study, we should note that the early 1970s boom and subsequent overcapacity in DCEs (notably in the petrochemical and chemical oligopolies) provided them with certain economic benefits. In their quest for profitable investment outlets, many DCE petrochemical and chemical corporations turned to the CPEs in the 1970s and arranged buy-back contracts whereby plants were set up in CPEs with payment in kind. As one after another of these firms came on-stream in the late 1970s, they also contributed to the growing global crisis of overcapacity.

At the level of the world capitalist crisis, a detailed study of five post-war United States recessions found conglomerates exercising a direct and harmful impact on unemployment and inflation. In highly concentrated industries, conglomerates managed to induce price mark-ups as high as 14 per cent during recessions, whereas firms in the less concentrated sectors reduced price mark-ups, as one would expect in a more competitive economy.[52] Such increased mark-up practices will multiply as conglomeration invades increasing numbers of industries. Inflation is not only a systemic emanation of oligopolistic capitalism but also reinforces oligopolistic structures by driving out smaller firms. To the extent that large corporations tend to have lower labour, utility, and raw materials costs as a percentage of aggregate sales than smaller firms, they are less adversely affected by the batterings of inflation.

In the face of mounting recessionary forces, we can anticipate an even closer relationship between the state apparatus and corporate capital in both DCEs and UCEs. MITI of Japan offers perhaps the most vivid illustration of a superbly honed state instrument which, in conjunction with corporate leadership, periodically rationalizes Japan's chemical and textile industries. State intervention has proliferated over the last decade and is now openly incorporated into the national and international economic policies of the leading underdeveloped capitalist countries. With the deepening synchronization of the world economic crises, interventionist measures become a major policy weapon in the armoury of all UCE ruling political and economic castes. It is deemed, and in fact has become, a precondition of breaking into the world market and even of beating back import onslaughts on the national market.

Whether state interventionism can stem the crisis, slash global unemployment, open markets for the unused productive capacity, and rehabilitate world capitalism, remains dubious at best. For the fundamental conflict within oligopolistic capitalism — generating an ever greater surplus without providing adequate mechanisms of surplus absorption — has never been addressed by the spokesmen of big capital, nor can it be, given the nature of the system. The mechanisms at work within conglomerate oligopoly, as revealed in this work, can only aggravate the crisis in the forthcoming decade.

References

1. Alfred S. Eichner, *The Emergence of Oligopoly: Sugar Refining as a Case Study* (Baltimore, 1969), p.1.
2. *The New York Times,* 11 October 1925.
3. *Review of Evidence, Report of the Industrial Commission on Trusts and Industrial Combinations,* Vol XIII (Washington, DC, 1901), p. v.
4. *Iron and Coal Trades Review,* London, 12 May 1899. Quoted in J.M. Blair, *Economic Concentration: Structure, Behaviour and Public Policy* (New York, 1972).
5. J.D. Bernal, *Science in History,* (London, 1969).
6. H.U. Faulkner, *The Decline of Laissez-Faire, 1897–1917* (New York, 1951), p. 171.
7. The holding company has been defined as 'any company, incorporated or unincorporated, which is in a position to control, or materially to influence, the management of one or more other companies by virtue, in part at least, of its ownership of securities in the other company or companies'. Cf. T.C. Bonbright and G.C. Means, *The Holding Company: Its Public Significance and Its Regulation* (Reprint; New York, 1969), p. 10. The holding company is fundamentally an American institution which began its career in the last decade of the 19th Century through new corporate laws. Before then, corporations were generally prohibited by common law from owning shares in other corporations, a prohibition which largely precluded the possibility of using the holding company as a means of industrial consolidation.
8. Faulkner, p. 171.
9. J.B. Clark and J.M. Clark, *The Control of Trusts* (New York, 1912), pp. 14–15. The two were academic theorists and leading Federal investigators.
10. Quoted in J.H. Clapham, *The Economic Development of France and Germany, 1815–1914* (Cambridge, 1963), p. 393. For a description of the organization of the Deutsche Bank and how its structure facilitated the interpenetration of finance and industrial capital, cf. F.E. Lavington, *The English Capital Market* (London, 1921), p. 210; also F. Stern, *Gold and Iron: Bismarck, Bleichroder and the Building of the German Empire* (London, 1977).
11. *Report of the Committee on Trusts* (Cmd. 9236, London, 1919). The Chairman was Sydney Webb. See also *Findings and Decisions of the Tobacco Sub-Committee Appointed by the Standing Committee on Trusts* (Cmd. 558; London, 1919); *Report on the Committee on Finance and Industry* (MacMillan Report; London, 1931); P.F. Fitzgerald, *Industrial Combination in England* (London, 1927).
12. Quoted in W.J. Reader, *Imperial Chemical Industries: A History,* Vol. I (Oxford, 1970), p. 456. See Chapter 6 of the present work for a discussion of Lord Mond's role in the creation of ICI. Lord Mond's ruminations were little more than a rehash of the ideas of the American, Frederick Winslow Taylor, 'father' of modern management and an implacable enemy of the trade union movement. Its revolutionary significance of 'rationalization' however, was that its theory and practice, as preached by Lord Mond and his associates in ICI, now received the

supreme plaudits of the big boardrooms of global corporate capital.
It was destined to become one of the ideological pillars of oligopolistic
capitalism.

13. L. Hannah and J.A. Kay, *Concentration in Modern Industry* (London,
1977), p. 68.

14. *Report of the Mission on Japanese Combines, A Report to the Department of State and the War Department* (Washington, D.C., March 1946),
p. 4.

15. *Ibid.*, p. 133.

16. In certain specific national settings, as in the Netherlands, the loss of its
sizeable Asian empire stimulated the post-war merger movements in
textiles. See, H.W. de Jong, *Ondernemingsconcentratie* (Leiden, 1971).

17. 'Other People's Money', *The New Republic*, 17 February 1973. He
went on to note: 'A 1971 congressional report, for example, found that
the major banks financed acquisitions, furnished key financial personnel
to conglomerates, and were even willing to clean out stock from their
trust departments to aid in takeover bids. Thus Gulf and Western, one of
the most aggressive conglomerates of the 1950s and 1960s (92
acquisitions involving almost a billion dollars in eleven years), expanded
hand in glove with Chase Manhattan. Friendly representatives of Chase
made funds available and provided advice and services that assisted Gulf
and Western in its acquisitions. In return, in addition to the customary
business charges for Gulf and Western's account and loans, Chase secured
banking business generated by the newly developing conglomerate that
formerly had gone to other banks, and was recipient of advance inside
information on proposed future acquisition.'

18. Quoted in Richard Barnet and Ronald Muller, *Global Reach*, (New York,
1974), p. 234.

19. Fear of capital liberalization, that is, intensified penetration of foreign
capital, boosted the number of cartels in Japan from 150 to 1,973
between the mid-1950s and mid-1960s. See the perceptive comment of
Mr. K. Yamamura in United States, Senate, *Hearings Before the Subcommittee on Antitrust and Monopoly* (Washington, DC, 1964, 1965
and 1967). The push to cartelization was partnered by significant strides
towards conglomeration, which, as in the inter-war years, was bankrolled
by finance capital in conjunction with MITI.

20. *Ibid.*, p. 28.

21. UNCTAD, *The Marketing and Distribution of Tobacco* (TD/B/C.1/205)
(Geneva, United Nations, 1978), p. 82.

22. United States Senate, *The Role of Giant Corporations in the American
and World Economies, Corporate Secrecy: Overview, Hearings before the
Subcommittee on Monopoly of the Select Committee on Small Business*,
92nd Congress, 1st session, (Washington, DC, 9 and 12 November 1971),
pt. 2: 1111. See also Federal Trade Commission, *Economic Report:
Conglomerate Merger Performance. An Empirical Analysis of Nine
Corporations* (Washington, DC, 1972). By the mid-fifties in the US,
four firms controlled over two-thirds of the market in the following
industries: automobiles, aluminium, copper, rubber, cigarettes, soap and
detergents, whisky, heavy electrical gear, computers, sugar, iron. Cf.
John K. Galbraith, *The New Industrial State* (Toronto, 1968), p. 190.

23. S.J. Prais, *The Evolution of Giant Firms in Britain: A Study of the Growth of Concentration in Manufacturing Industry in Britain, 1909–1970* (Cambridge, 1976). As Hannah and Kay (pp. 89–91) point out, the top 10 UK firms' market share (as measured in market valuation of a company's capital) from 1957 to 1969 rose as follows: in food, 62 to 81 per cent; tobacco, 100 per cent throughout; chemicals, 81 to 86 per cent; textiles, 60 to 74 per cent; and paper and publishing, 64 to 78 per cent. The extent of market concentration in continental Europe can be seen in Germany and France. In certain key industries in Germany, the market share of the ten largest enterprises in 1960 was as follows: oil, 92 per cent; tobacco, 85 per cent; transport, 67 per cent; rubber, 60 per cent; and iron and steel, 58 per cent. In 1963, the percentage of workers employed in the eight largest enterprises in major industries in France exhibited similar traits: oil, 91 per cent; non-ferrous metals, 66 per cent; iron and steel, 63 per cent; transport, 53 per cent; and rubber, 51 per cent; Cf. Lawrence G. Franks, *The European Multinationals* (London, 1975), p. 18.
24. S. Aaronovitch and M. Sawyer, *Big Business, Theoretical and Empirical Aspects of Concentration and Mergers in the United Kingdom* (London, 1975), p. 145.
25. United States Senate, *Mergers and Industrial Concentration; Hearings before the Subcommittee on Antitrust and Monopoly of the Senate Judiciary Committee*, (Washington, DC, 12 May, 27 and 28 July, and 21 September 1978), p. 151. 'Large firms' refers to acquired firms with assets of $10 million or more.
26. *Ibid.*, p. 152.
27. *Ibid.*, p. 152.
28. *Ibid.*, p. 172.
29. *Ibid.*, p. 151.
30. House of Representatives Transcript Record of 'Excerpts from the Testimony of Neil Smith before the Subcommittee on Livestock and Grains', 30 October 1979, Washington, DC, p. 7.
31. Quoted in M. J. Green, B.C. Moore and B. Wasserstein, *The Closed Enterprise System* (New York, 1972), p. xii. See also M.S. Lewis-Beck, 'Maintaining economic competition: the causes and consequences of antitrust', *Journal of Politics*, vol. 41, 1979. By 1980, twenty US corporations employed over 100 in-house lawyers apiece, led by AT&T with 902 and Exxon with 384. DuPont allocated 39 corporate lawyers exclusively for antitrust work. See *Business Week*, 1 September 1980.
32. Quoted in *The New York Times*, 'Canada's industry plays Monopoly for real', 25 March 1980. Indeed, Canada recorded only one monopoly conviction since 1945, and that presumably on the basis that the defendant pleaded guilty.
33. *Ibid.*
34. United States, Senate, *Mergers ...*, p. 252.
35. *Ibid.*, p. 143.
36. *Ibid.*, p. 172.
37. *Fortune*, June 1965, and Willard Mueller, 'The social control of economic power', University of Wisconsin, Working Paper Series, June 1977.

38. For a discussion of this issue, see Paul Baran and Paul Sweezy, *Monopoly Capital* (New York, 1966), pp. 69–71.

39. Arthur Burns, *The Decline of Competition: A Study of the Evolution of American Industry* (London, 1936), p. 76.

40. See A.S. Eichner, *The Megacorp and Oligopoly: Micro-Foundations and Macro-Dynamics* (Cambridge, 1976).

41. Baran and Sweezy, pp. 70–1.

42. OECD, *Restrictive Business Practices of Multinational Enterprises: Report of the Committee of Experts on Restrictive Business Practices* (Paris, 1977), para. 57.

43. *Ibid.,* para. 59.

44. Harry Braverman, *Labor and Monopoly Capital* (New York, 1974), p. 166.

45. *Financial Times,* 9 February 1966.

46. United States, Senate, *Mergers . . .* , p. 463.

47. *Le Monde,* 7 October 1977, and data supplied by IFCATI.

48. The structural differences between the textile and apparel industries bear comparison with the cigarette and cigar industries. The cigar industry did not lend itself to mechanization until the early 1920s. By the late 1920s, the ranks of the fragmented small-scale cigar producers had been winnowed, ultimately to give way to comprehensive mechanization and concentration in the 1930s. The thrust of automation in the clothing industry should exercise the same cumulative effect over the next decade in view of rising costs and the lure of an $18 billion global apparel market.

49. The further complexity of the technical phases of setting up chemical fibre industries in UCEs was noted by Enka Glanzstoff's deputy chairman: 'Anybody can make nylon fibres and that's what developing countries usually produce first. Polyester fibres require more know-how. Carpet yarns are more difficult to make than those for apparel. And technical fibres require the most sophisticated technology and it will be years before developing countries can make them.' See *Chemical Week,* 4 June 1975.

50. See United States, Senate, *Mergers . . . ;* and United States House Committee on the Judiciary, *The Celler-Kefauver Act: The First 27 Years,* a study prepared by Willard F. Mueller for the Subcommittee on Monopolies and Commercial Law (Washington, DC, 1978).

51. United States, Senate, *Mergers . . .,* p. 471.

52. *Ibid.,* p. 126. These were the findings of Howard Wachtel.

2. The Structure of the World Cotton Economy

Despite its fragmentation, the world cotton economy has not evaded economic concentration in either developed or underdeveloped countries To understand the morphology of these changes, we present an overview of the evolution of cotton and its allied industries, notably in the UCEs, followed by a dissection of the shifting class alignments and the exploitative class practices extending from the plantations of Central America to the parcellized holdings of the Sahel. Thus the subject of this chapter is not oligopolistic capitalism but concentration and its corollaries. However, oligopolistic capitalism inflects and overwhelmingly determines prices, output and the nature of class formations within agriculture as examined in this and subsequent chapters.

This brings us to a contrast between the relatively weak power configurations within the cotton economy and the serried ranks of the petrochemical and chemical fibre oligopoly. Clearly, these forces confront each other not only in cotton but in a number of other primary commodities, such as soya, rubber, jute, and sugar.

No less germane to our perspective on cotton's future are rapid population growth and the exigencies of growing more food in a limited arable area. This is combined with the demands of the UCE industrial bourgeoisie and foreign capital for domestic processing of cotton. We assess the impact of this shift on the international division of labour and the diminishing UCE (and Chinese) supplies of raw cotton entering the global market. The chapter closes with a glimpse of cotton's minuscule retail share in several textile and clothing items.

Historical Foundations

'King Cotton' and the textile industry laid the foundations of the first industrial revolution and became one of the generators of an integrated world market, notably between 1814 and 1914.[1] It is ironic to recall that though cotton is now being embattled, and its defences breached in traditional end-use markets, the incipient cotton textile industry, with its attendant technological imperatives, fathered the modern chemical[2] and dyestuff industry.[3]

The chemical industry was in its turn to acquire autonomy precisely as it incubated cotton's antithesis – chemical fibres – at the turn of the century. Thereafter the destinies of cotton and chemical fibres were to become inextricably enmeshed in their processing and marketing trajectories. Moreover, as with a myriad of other industrial lines, the direction of the cotton textile industry was to be conditioned by the advent of several specialized textile machinery producers that have influenced inter-fibre competition through new blending techniques and machines.

19th Century technical breakthroughs were matched by shifts in the international division of labour. Symptomatic of this relationship was the clear demarcation between raw cotton producers in the colonial and semi-colonial regions, and industrial processors in the imperialist centres. This is, of course, a highly schematized portrayal. A full-blown textile industry already existed in India but it was deliberately annihilated by a series of neo-mercantilist decrees that left the industry vulnerable to British textiles.[4] Nor was India unique; most of Asia, North Africa, and Ireland had created textile industries sophisticated in both quality and scale, that were undermined in the age of colonialism. Even the resurgence of the UCE textile industry has been on the basis of a new international division of labour involving technological and marketing subordination to DCE transnational corporations.

The division between UCE raw material producers and DCE industrial processors, however, was neither absolute nor immutable. The United States remained the largest single cotton producer and exporter long after it had become a central industrial economy with a major textile/clothing industry. Tangible shifts in the international division of labour began to surface prior to 1914, and deepened in the inter-war years as expansion of the textile and clothing industry became conspicuous in several now underdeveloped countries, notably India, China, Brazil, Argentina, Chile, Mexico, Egypt, and the Sudan.

Since the Second World War, more specifically since 1955, the world textile economy has witnessed the upsurge of other UCEs in dramatic new roles, stemming in part from the expansionary momentum of foreign capital. With textiles, this often involved complex relationships between foreign and domestic capital and firms. Certain of these UCEs, bereft of raw cotton, succeeded in building up and retaining a sizeable segment of world textile and apparel output, especially the 'giant dwarfs' of the world textile industry – South Korea, Taiwan and Hong Kong, the leading trinity of UCE producers. Over the last two decades, several UCEs have embarked on processing cotton and other fibres.

In conjunction with the shifting international division of labour, and in turn impacting on it, have been the differential growth rates among major fibre groups. Synthetic fibres' encroachment on fibre markets since their inception in 1940 has been unrelenting (see Table 2.1). There are significant variations within this global picture on a national and regional level indicative of the thrust of corporate chemical power most clearly manifest in the DCEs.

There are likewise marked national variations due to unequal distribution of oil resources and corporate penetration. In Pakistan and Egypt, cotton's share of total fibre production remains above 90 per cent; in Brazil it is now less than 60 per cent.[5]

Table 2.1
World Output of Cotton, Wool, Cellulosic and Synthetic Fibres, 1955–79 (%)

Year	Cotton	Wool	Cellulosics	Synthetics	Total
1955	69.9	9.8	18.2	2.1	100.0
1960	68.3	9.9	17.2	4.6	100.0
1965	62.2	8.1	18.4	11.3	100.0
1970	55.5	7.2	15.8	21.5	100.0
1971	54.0	6.7	15.0	24.3	100.0
1972	53.0	6.3	14.6	26.1	100.0
1973	51.3	5.4	14.0	29.3	100.0
1974	52.2	4.9	13.8	29.1	100.0
1975	52.7	5.6	12.0	29.8	100.0
1976	50.5	5.6	11.9	32.0	100.0
1977	50.1	5.2	11.8	32.9	100.0
1978	46.7	5.3	11.9	35.9	100.0
1979	47.8	5.1	11.3	35.6	100.0

Source: Computed from data in: World Bank Staff Commodity Paper No. 2, *International Cotton Market Prospects,* New York, 1978; and *Textile Organon,* June 1980.

Cotton's Contribution

Output and trade of natural and man-made fibres is of seminal importance to the developed and underdeveloped economies. Cotton embraces almost one-half of the world fibre supply, with output jumping from 30 to 65 million bales between the mid-1950s and the late 1970s. Roughly one-third of its output, with an estimated value of $6.1 billion, entered the global market in 1979. As with all agricultural commodities, its relative value in the composition of world trade has steadily shrivelled. Yet raw cotton continues to be one of the basic inputs of the textile and clothing industry which, in most countries, is still a major propellant of industrialization. Table 2.2 shows the pace and trajectory of change.

Natural fibres' production and manufacturing contribution to GDP is highly significant for underdeveloped countries: 5.3 per cent, as against a trifling 1.2 per cent for developed countries. These numbers are lower than the previous decade, reflecting the widespread inroads of man-made fibres. In both major segments of the world economy, processing accounts for larger value increases than raw fibre production (see Table 2.3): in underdeveloped countries about twice as large; in developed countries almost six times.[6]

Table 2.2
Composition of World Trade by Sector, 1913, 1953 and 1973 (%)

Commodity	1913	1953	1973
Agricultural Produce[1]	45	36	21
Minerals[2]	8	13	14
Manufactures:	44	49	63
Machinery and transport equipment	7	18	33
Textiles and clothing	14	6	6

1. Does not include animal and vegetable fats and oils (SITC 4).
2. Includes fuel.

Source: GATT, *International Trade,* various issues; P.L. Yates, *Forty Years of Foreign Trade* (London, 1958).

Table 2.3
Annual Contribution to GDP of Natural Fibres ($ billions)

| | 1961–65 | | 1972 74 | |
	DCEs	UCEs	DCEs	UCEs
Output of natural fibres	2.4	3.5	3.2	6.9
Textile manufactures in natural fibres	8.9	5.1	11.9	11.9
Clothing manufactures in natural fibres	4.3	1.2	5.9	3.2
Total	*15.6*	*9.8*	*21.0*	*22.0*
All productive activities	655	149	1,820	400
% from natural fibres	2.4	6.6	1.2	5.3

Source: R. Robson, 'Importance of natural fibres . . .', Shirley Institute, December 1977.

Employment distribution is disproportionate to output value, particularly in UCEs, where natural fibres are as important as fibre processing in job creation: 38.5 million jobs depend on fibre production out of 74.7 million that depend on natural fibre output and manufacture.[7]

Over the last three decades the world cotton economy has undergone vast structural mutations. As one of the world's leading agricultural commodities, cotton is produced in over 80 countries, overwhelmingly underdeveloped, including 17 of the 29 least developed economies.

In addition to fibre, the cotton plant also produces cotton seed, which after crushing provides edible oil and cotton seed meal (cake). Cotton seed is also one of the world's principal oil seeds (second to soya), of which one-fifth is crude protein; it comprises 5–6 per cent of aggregate world protein supply. Among other cotton end-uses, the hulls or empty seed shells are processed as fertilizers, and the linters (short, non-spinnable fibre) serve as an industrial cellulosic fibre input. Cotton stalks can be processed into multi-purpose building materials, or pressed into fuel briquettes.[8]

In its fibre form, cotton is a foreign exchange earner in more than 60 countries. For nine of them – Chad, Sudan, Yemen Arab Republic, Egypt, Mali, Central African Republic, Benin, Nicaragua, and Upper Volta – its earnings exceed 25 per cent of total exports: over 45 per cent for the Sudan, and as much as 70 per cent for Chad. For certain countries, the overall population dependent on cotton for their livelihood is marked: Chad (71 per cent), the Nicaragua (35 per cent), Guatemala (20 per cent), Syria (16 per cent) and the Sudan (13 per cent).

As against any natural comparative advantage, Mali's colonial history provides clues to modern UCE single-commodity economies. In the largely subsistence agricultural economy of 1929, the French imposed a tax on every adult over fifteen, payable by growing 5–10 kilos of cotton. Taxes had increased by 1960 to the equivalent of 40 kilos. Post-colonial policy continued the escalation so that at the time of the 1970 drought, the government was levying a tax of 48 kilos or their equivalent in cash.[9]

Mali's historical predicament was symptomatic of the majority of British, French, Portuguese, Belgian and Dutch colonies. To ensure a supply of raw materials to their domestic capitalists and food to the world market, colonial officers often expropriated the most fertile areas, evicted the indigenous population (or physically liquidated them), and reincorporated them as quasi-slave labour on tracts of land given over to one or two commodity crops. In most cases the mono- and duo-economic structures became crystallized between the 1890s and 1914. In the inter-war period, world capital accumulation through the rapid expansion of industry, finance and trade, consolidated this process. The transition from colonialism to neo-colonialism in most African and Asian nations did not appreciably shift the pattern of exploitation, since both local oligarchies (political and economic) and international capital were part of a profitable and integrated production and trading circuit. At present, the World Bank, the International Monetary Fund (IMF), and most segments of international capital are pursuing inter-related strategies designed to preserve this economic format, while at the same time tailoring UCE industrialization to ensure continued subordination.

More specifically, IMF and Lome Convention compensatory finance schemes offer inducements to continued dependence on single-crop economies. Likewise, the World Bank[10] and USAID via their project approaches generate and reinforce a kulak class mobilized to adopt 'green revolution' technology, which is beyond the budgets of poorer UCE peasants. Continued emphasis on the single crop, accompanied by the destruction of subsistence agriculture and the reorientation of marketed output towards the world market, has exacerbated malnutrition (which often borders on famine conditions) in most UCEs. In both Africa and Asia, many small-scale cotton producers gain some protection against malnutrition by supplementing cotton cultivation with basic food crops, cattle, or other livestock. This pattern of cultivation is often a hedge against food shortages and, to a lesser extent, against price fluctuations. Such integrated practices, however, are inoperative for large, irrigated blocks farmed by smallholders involved in mono-cropping (e.g. Office du Niger in Mali at some phases of its history) or fixed rotation patterns (eg. Gezira in the Sudan).[11]

One of the reasons for the conspicuous absence of TNCs in cotton plantations as opposed to their no less conspicuous presence in banana-growing (eg. R.J. Reynolds through its Del Monte subsidiary, United Brands, and Castle and Cooke), in rubber (eg. Goodyear, Firestone, and Dunlop), and sugar (eg. Tate and Lyle, Gulf and Western) is that, at the height of TNC plantation agriculture in the early 20th Century, there were no textile corporations with the marketing power to manage and sustain UCE plantations. Furthermore, few corporations felt the need to ensure supplies in this manner, since the close co-operation between trading companies and colonial governments ensured adequate, cheap cotton supplies.

Thus, revolutionary movements in many cotton-producing countries have directed their historical analyses of oppression not only against TNCs, but also against the domestic landed oligarchies which reap the greatest gains from agricultural output. In October 1979, when the Guatemalan Guerilla Army of the Poor (EGP) targeted important national figures to highlight the terror exercised by the regime, they abducted the son of one of Guatemala's wealthiest cotton growers, a relative of the President, General Romeo Lucas García (who is himself one of the biggest *latifundistas* in the country). Not surprisingly, the family was able to raise overnight the hundreds of thousands of dollars required to finance the many international newspaper statements demanded by the EGP.[12]

While the world's majors (the USSR, China and the United States) in 1978 staked out close to 56 per cent of global output, their relative shares have altered drastically (see Table 2.4). The ascent of the two socialist nations at the expense of the United States means that today almost two-fifths of the world's cotton is grown on socialist production units (the Sovkhoz, Kholkoz and Commune). The Soviet Union led the world in cotton output in five of the eight years between 1971 and 1978.[13] In addition to increasing cotton acreage steadily since the Second World War, the USSR has maintained its lead through rapid jumps in yields and irrigation of almost 100 per cent of its land. China's production peaked in 1974; recent declines may be attributed to farmers shifting into more lucrative and less risky grain production. The Chinese claim to have improved the situation by pushing up internal cotton prices by 25 per cent in 1979, providing more raw materials for a booming textile industry.[14]

Table 2.4
Growth of Cotton Output in Selected Countries, 1950–78 (000 bales)

	1950 bales/(%)	1960 bales/(%)	1970 bales/(%)	1978 bales/(%)
USSR	4,800 (15.9)	6,850 (14.6)	10,800 (19.9)	12,400 (20.6)
USA	9,878 (32.8)	14,453 (30.8)	10,269 (18.9)	10,885 (18.1)
China	3,000 (10.0)	6,500 (13.9)	9,200 (16.9)	10,000 (16.6)
India	2,775 (9.2)	4,650 (9.9)	4,400 (8.1)	6,220 (10.3)
Brazil	1,650 (5.5)	1,950 (4.2)	2,740 (5.0)	2,650 (4.4)
Turkey	545 (1.8)	780 (1.7)	1,845 (3.4)	2,200 (3.7)
Pakistan	1,244 (4.1)	1,405 (3.0)	2,502 (4.5)	2,090 (3.5)
Egypt	1,762 (5.9)	2,205 (4.7)	2,346 (4.3)	2,022 (3.4)
Mexico	1,145 (3.8)	2,100 (4.5)	1,440 (2.7)	1,570 (7.6)
Argentina	566 (1.9)	559 (1.2)	390 (0.7)	815 (1.3)
Guatemala	4 (–)	95 (0.2)	265 (0.5)	760 (1.3)
Greece	118 (0.4)	290 (0.6)	508 (0.9)	705 (1.2)
Sudan	440 (1.5)	525 (1.1)	1,130 (2.1)	635 (1.1)
Nicaragua	23 (0.1)	150 (0.3)	360 (0.7)	515 (0.9)
Peru	404 (1.3)	557 (1.2)	410 (0.8)	400 (0.7)
Colombia	38 (0.1)	308 (0.7)	540 (1.0)	375 (0.6)
El Salvador	29 (0.1)	185 (0.4)	252 (0.5)	325 (0.5)
Others	17,221 (5.7)	5,374 (7.2)	4,994 (9.2)	5,551 (9.2)
World	*30,145 (100.0)*	*46,936 (100.0)*	*54,391 (100.0)*	*60,118 (100.0)*

Source: Computed from data in ICAC, *Cotton World Statistics,* April 1980.

United States supremacy in global cotton production was maintained through the 1950s and 1960s by lavish subsidies and support prices. Since the early 1970s, as is detailed in Chapter 4, the United States government has cut back supports and, as a recent visitor to the South observed, 'King Cotton' has been 'battered by erratic prices and high production costs, and usurped in the marketplace by a pretender named polyester. The synthetics, cotton farmers like to say, are the boll-weevils of the 1970s.'[15]

In contrast, cotton output in the UCEs doubled from 1950 to 1978; and almost tripled in the socialist economies.[16] Cotton's importance cannot be gauged simply by export earnings, but also by its income – and employment-generating effects. Iran serves as an illustration. Though dwarfed by petroleum and natural gas, which provide well over nine-tenths of its export earnings, raw cotton embraces almost half of Iran's foreign exchange earnings from the agricultural sector, despite the fact that between 35 and 45 per cent of the crop is retained for domestic textile manufacturing. Almost 4 per cent of the nation's population, roughly 1.4 million people, are supported by cotton cultivation.[17]

Land allocated to cotton cultivation globally has remained relatively constant in recent years, but is now lower than in the 1950s. The UCEs, CPEs and DCEs produce roughly 42, 40 and 19 per cent respectively of the world's cotton on 61, 24 and 15 per cent of the world's cotton acreage.[18] Despite the general productivity drawbacks of the UCEs, cotton yields per acre in ten of them are higher than in the USA (see Table 2.5). The tremendous diversity in yields in fact transcends the categories 'developed', 'underdeveloped' amd 'centrally planned' economies. China and the United States rank considerably below UCEs such as Madagascar, Syria, and Mexico. Apart from the extended use of irrigated land, the productivity boost in recent years stemmed from enhanced crop rotation, larger inputs of farm chemicals, and wilt-resistant varieties. In both China and the USSR, new varieties are being adapted to very short growing seasons.

Traditionally, yields are considered almost exclusively a function of inputs. While this functional relationship is valid, some variations between producing countries may be ascribed to different climatic conditions and land management techniques. Iran and Mexico demonstrate these divergences: the former spends over two dollars per kilogram of output as against the latter's one dollar. Thus boosting financial and physical inputs by itself is not a sufficient condition for raising yields.

Trade Flows

Initially, the accelerated growth in world cotton trade in the underdeveloped countries was in response to industrialization in the centres of world capital accumulation between 1846 and 1914. To cite one major case Egypt's rapid integration into the world cotton economy pinpoints how colonial countries were sucked into the vortex of the international division of labour.[19] Egypt's cotton exports rose four-fold from 1858 to 1865 (stimulated by the cotton famine arising from the Union blockade of Confederate ports), and six-fold from 1866 to 1914.[20]

In aggregate terms, while a third of world cotton was traded globally in the mid-1970s, there were marked variations from one country to another (see Table 2.6).

For the world's two leading exporters, the USA and the USSR,[21] cotton represents roughly 1.5 and 2.9 per cent of their aggregate exports. Both the import and export pattern and the relative national shares of the world market have been appreciably modified since the twenties, for instance in the USSR, the USA, Egypt, Hong Kong, India and the United Kingdom (see Tables 2.7 and 2.8). In the early 1970s, cotton represented 2.6 per cent of all UCE exports, and was fifth in rank among primary commodities after petroleum, coffee, sugar, and copper. However, if cotton and its allied textile products are considered as one sector, it ranked second to petroleum, encompassing more than 8 per cent of UCE global export earnings.[22] As against the rapid export growth of man-made fibres, world cotton trade exhibited a faltering and fluctuating growth of less than one per cent yearly from the sixties to the mid-seventies. Fluctuating growth has been the result of the speculative and manipulative practices of multi-commodity traders on the futures exchange as well as the vagaries of nature to which all farm commodities are victims. Such fluctuations stand in stark contrast with the controlled and sustained growth and pricing patterns of the chemical fibre oligopoly.

Table 2.5
Cotton Yields in Selected Countries, 1975−76

	Area (000 hectares)	Output (000 metric tons)	Yields (kg per ha)	Proportional Yield (Israel = 100)
Israel	38.0	49	1,289	100.0
Guatemala	83.2	100	1,201	93.2
USSR	2,890.0	2,526	874	67.8
Australia	29.2	25	856	65.4
Mexico	232.4	197	848	65.8
Syria	205.6	158	768	59.6
Nicaragua	142.4	109	765	59.3
Madagascar	16.0	12	750	58.2
Turkey	662.4	480	724	56.2
Egypt	558.8	382	684	53.1
Peru	95.6	63	659	51.1
Bolivia	30.0	17	567	44.0
USA	3,518.4	1,808	514	39.9
China	4,800.0	2,385	497	38.6
Colombia	248.8	121	486	37.7
Iran	286.8	139	485	37.6
Mali	86.4	39	451	35.0
Thailand	60.0	22	367	28.5
Argentina	408.8	133	325	25.2
Sudan	405.2	98	242	18.8
Iraq	52.0	12	231	17.9
Brazil	1,880.0	396	211	16.4
Chad	3,332.4	65	196	15.2
CPEs	7,596.0	5,053	665	51.6
DCEs, UCEs	24,519.2	6,974	284	22.0
World	32,115.2	12,027	374	29.0

Source: Computed from data in ICAC, *Cotton World Statistics*, 1977.

Table 2.6
Share of Nationally Grown Cotton Marketed Internationally, mid-1970s (%)

Nicaragua	95	Turkey	32
Guatemala	86	USSR	30
Tanzania	84	Pakistan	21
Egypt	49	Brazil	18
USA	40	China	1

Tables 2.7 and 2.8 reveal the shifting cotton trade flows over the last fifty years. Whereas in 1925 the Indian and Egyptian colonies dominated global exports along with the USA, by the mid-1970s the first two had been ousted by the new powerhouses of Turkey and the USSR. On the import side, the hegemony of Japan and the United Kingdom was partially supplanted by the ascendancy of several of the giant dwarfs: Hong Kong, Taiwan and South Korea.

One facet of the international division of labour is revealed by the main destinations of major exporters. For the United States, the Japanese market remains paramount, trailed by South Korea and other Asian countries. The USSR's major trading partners include Eastern Europe, Japan and the EEC. For Egypt and Syria, Eastern Europe accounted for about half their exports, and a comparable share of Mexican cotton is destined for Japan.[23]

A scrutiny of world imports since the 1960s indicates a relatively stable condition for all major importing regions, with the exception of EEC imports, which have plummeted, owing mainly to man-made fibre encroachment.

Class Forces

Obviously what the trade flows cannot tell us is the exploitative mechanisms of surplus generation related to its specific class configuration. Just as it is mandatory to look beyond commoditized relations to the corporate structures which create them, it is likewise imperative to look beyond aggregate export earnings of UCEs to their relative impact on different socio-economic classes. Throughout the capitalist cotton world the direct cotton producers are by no means homogeneous in class: they may be landlords, tenants and sub-tenants, landless labourers, or independent small-scale producers. As might be expected, the gains from exports do not redound in the same proportion to these highly differentiated class groupings. The real earnings of tenants and landless wage-earners are not generally affected by a rise in cotton prices on the international market. In many cases a tenant's output is marketed through the landlord at prices well below international or marketing board levels. On landless labourers, Guatemalan data are revealing. Although 370,000 people inhabit Guatemala's cotton-growing lowlands in the picking season, as many as 600,000 Indians migrate for 30–90 days to earn

Table 2.7
Major Cotton Exporters, 1925-78 (000 bales)

	1925 bales/%	1950 bales/%	1960 bales/%	1970 bales/%	1978 bales/%
USA	8,052 (57.2)	4,108 (34.0)	6,632 (39.4)	3,740 (21.2)	6,206 (31.3)
USSR	—	1,100 (9.1)	1,750 (10.4)	2,550 (14.5)	4,000 (20.2)
Turkey	74 (0.5)	349 (2.9)	271 (1.6)	1,128 (6.4)	966 (4.9)
Mexico	110 (0.8)	742 (6.1)	1,602 (9.5)	756 (4.3)	920 (4.6)
Sudan	103 (0.7)	373 (3.1)	439 (2.6)	1,053 (6.0)	817 (4.1)
Egypt	1,459 (10.4)	1,538 (12.7)	1,589 (9.4)	1,403 (8.0)	750 (3.8)
Guatemala		–	75 (0.4)	248 (1.4)	707 (3.6)
Syrian Arab Rep.	6 (–)	110 (0.9)	447 (2.6)	617 (3.5)	553 (2.8)
Nicaragua	1 (–)	24 (0.2)	139 (0.8)	382 (2.2)	520 (2.6)
Argentina	97 (0.7)	275 (2.3)	76 (0.5)	210 (1.2)	321 (1.6)
Iran	84 (0.6)	106 (0.9)	240 (1.4)	495 (2.8)	319 (1.6)
El Salvador	10 (–)	23 (0.2)	139 (0.8)	224 (1.3)	260 (1.3)
Pakistan		1,043 (8.6)	245 (1.5)	471 (2.7)	256 (1.3)
India	3,159 (22.4)	147 (1.2)	277 (1.6)	138 (0.8)	250 (1.3)
Brazil	116 (0.8)	698 (5.8)	698 (4.1)	1,015 (5.8)	143 (0.7)
Colombia	—	–	119 (0.7)	205 (1.2)	70 (0.3)
World	*14,083 (100.0)*	*12,104 (100.0)*	*16,828 (100.0)*	*17,594 (100.0)*	*19,809 (100.0)*

Source: ICAC, *Cotton World Statistics*, April 1959, October 1966, April 1980.

Table 2.8
Major Cotton Importers, 1925-78 (000' bales)

	1925 bales/%	1950 bales/%	1960 bales/%	1970 bales/%	1978 bales/%
Japan[1]	3,288 (21.7)	1,961 (15.7)	3,550 (20.5)	3,684 (19.5)	3,396 (16.8)
China[1]	504 (3.3)	275 (2.2)	300 (1.7)	500 (2.6)	2,400 (11.9)
Rep. of Korea[2]	7 (—)	35 (0.3)	232 (1.3)	539 (2.8)	1,360 (6.7)
Italy	1,093 (7.2)	1,022 (8.2)	999 (5.8)	819 (4.3)	1,024 (5.1)
Hong Kong	—	140 (1.1)	503 (2.9)	876 (4.6)	878 (4.3)
Taiwan	—	—	217 (1.2)	738 (3.9)	858 (4.2)
Germany[3]	1,555 (10.3)	337 (7.5)	1,432 (8.3)	1,889 (5.8)	818 (4.1)
France	1,469 (9.7)	1,066 (8.5)	1,414 (8.2)	1,065 (5.6)	808 (4.0)
Poland	235 (1.6)	400 (3.2)	661 (3.8)	775 (4.1)	738 (3.6)
Czechoslovakia	597 (3.9)	280 (2.2)	550 (3.2)	530 (2.8)	530 (2.6)
Yugoslavia	—	138 (1.1)	235 (1.4)	426 (2.3)	485 (2.4)
Portugal	67 (0.4)	144 (1.2)	311 (1.8)	394 (2.1)	476 (2.4)
Hungary	19 (0.1)	175 (1.4)	289 (1.7)	360 (1.9)	440 (2.2)
United Kingdom	3,676 (24.3)	1,971 (15.8)	1,146 (6.6)	746 (4.0)	432 (2.1)
USSR	494 (3.3)	20 (0.2)	650 (3.8)	1,100 (5.8)	250 (1.2)
World	*15,147 (100.0)*	*12,504 (100.0)*	*17,311 (100.0)*	*18,863 (100.0)*	*20,168 (100.0)*

1. Figures for 1925 include Taiwan.
2. Figures for 1925 and 1950 include all of Korea.
3. As from 1950, refers to Federal Republic of Germany (West Germany).

Source: ICAC, *Cotton World Statistics*, April 1959, October 1966, April 1980.

$1.25 for a twelve-hour shift.[24] Such wage levels have helped to sustain cotton's globally competitive stance. In northern Costa Rica, the bulk of the crop has historically been picked by low-cost Nicaraguan migrants who enter the country illegally.[25]

The size and yield of cotton holdings illuminate the class forces at work. Through the interaction of technology, size and profitability, the large mechanized farm unit has become paramount in the United States, where 3,400 cotton growers accounted for a third of 1965 sales, and where their numbers have since dwindled further.[26]

These numbers must be evaluated within the larger context of land and capital concentration within American agriculture. Between 1929 and 1979, farm employment dropped by 69 per cent, involving the exodus of millions of farmers and hired farm workers and a parallel march to concentration.[27] As 1979 data indicate (see Table 2.9), a mere 6 per cent of farms accounted for over half the nation's farm sales, whereas 70 per cent sold a precarious 10 per cent. Hence, the scope for further concentration is considerable.

Table 2.9
Distribution of US Cotton Farms, 1979

Gross Farm Sales ($000s)	Number of Farms (000s)	% Farms	Sales
Over 100	162	6.0	52.0
40 – 100	348	12.9	25.6
20 – 40	321	11.9	11.1
Under 20	1,875	69.2	10.7

Source: United States Department of Agriculture, *The Structure of American Agriculture,* Issue Briefing Paper No. 16, 6 July 1979.

This points to the inescapable conclusion that the smaller farmer faces extinction in the 1980s. His predicament is exacerbated by oligopolistically determined price overcharges on his basic inputs: fertilizers,[28] fuel,[29] pesticides,[30] seeds,[31] and machinery.[32] In addition, he faces soaring land values, which have tripled between 1967 and 1979, and the onset of two-figure inflation in the late 1970s.[33] The combined onslaught of these forces (similar to those beating down upon the small-scale textile and apparel producers and retailers) proves the contention of a leading mid-western banker that 'the control of agriculture is moving to those who control capital.'[34]

Enlargement of the farm unit is not confined to the DCEs but is also moving apace in certain UCEs, such as Iran, where state-aided measures were pushed through to enlarge the size of farm units through farm corporations (1968–79). Likewise in Chad, the country *par excellence* of small-scale producers, with one of the lowest average cotton holdings and yields in the world (averaging less than one hectare),[35] hesitant attempts are being pushed to consolidate land. In Nicaragua, the average cotton plantation area sky-rocketed from 21,000 hectares in 1948–52 to 132,000 in 1968.[36] Perhaps unequalled in contemporary history, the Somoza clan alone controlled 30 per cent of all cultivable land, embracing the entire gamut of Nicaragua's cash crops, from cotton to bananas.[37]

Despite official myths, land reforms of the type advocated by the World Bank have not realigned class relations within agriculture. The Pahlavi dynasty's highly-touted 'White Revolution' (which did not touch the plantations and mechanized farms where most cotton was grown) is an odious reminder of this truth. Likewise, the 1979 colonization of Guatemala's central jungles was passed off officially as 'land reform' to alleviate the plight of the 'impoverished Indian'. However, much of 'the best land has fallen into the hands of wealthy farmers and army officers', reported the *International Herald Tribune*.[38] About 1.4 million acres of a 2.2-million-acre tract were annexed by these two groups, who promptly expelled the Indian squatters who had been selected as 'new settlers' and engaged them 'as peons on the large farms'. Infra-structural costs borne by the state under-pinned the giant farms — evidence of the collusion between state apparatus and the oligarchy.

This is taking place in a country where 2 per cent of the rich farmers own 53 per cent of the cultivable land. It is not surprising in this context that Guatemala's president, General Romeo Lucas Garcia, who in 1977 was in charge of resettling the landless Indians, 'is reported to own three estates totalling 130,000 acres. Several other army officers, including defence minister Otto Spiegler, also have been given land to 'colonize'. One district near Sebol is known as 'the area of the generals'. As is often the case, the Guatemalan state and its oligarchy (military and civilian) is not alone in its blatant theft of public lands. It is abetted in this effort by a $5.6 million handout from the US Agency for International Development (AID), but, as a foreign analyst in Guatemala pointed out, 'by the time the [AID's] experiment is completed, there'll be no land left to distribute.'[39]

The size of a cotton farm varies significantly not only between but within most countries, revealing the enormous class cleavages manifest in UCE agriculture. Whilst 85 acres is the average for El Salvador, 60 per cent of its total acreage is in farms of around 200 acres, with 27 giant farms (exceeding 1,000 acres) producing a quarter of total output. In Nicaragua, there are 600 farms of less than nine acres and at the other end of the spectrum, 15 farms of nearly 2,000 acres. This situation is expected to be changed with the extensive land reform programme for the 1980s.

Marked disparities in farm concentration are matched by very different cost structures. While labour costs represent 38 per cent of total production costs in Turkey, for South Africa they are a mere 5 per cent. In general, countries with high labour components enjoy relatively lower costs for petroleum related inputs. In Colombia, petrochemical inputs (pesticides, fertilizers and pre-emergents) comprise as much as 40 per cent of total costs.[40] In most cases they are massively subsidized: in Tanzania, insecticides and fungicides to the tune of 75 per cent; fertilizers by 50 per cent. On a global scale, mechanization is playing an even greater role in reshaping cost structures. In the United States, the cost per hectare of power and equipment – indicative of a global movement – jumped from $89 at the beginning of the 1970s to over $200 in 1976.

The concentration of land into large farm units over the last two decades has also been matched by higher levels of concentration at the stage of processing. In 1973, about 3,300 gins processed the United States cotton crop compared with 7,400 in 1952 and 13,000 in 1932. Although the smallest gins turn out only 1,000–1,500 bales annually, today's minimum economic size is considered 5,000 bales, and the largest produce up to 50,000.[41] The drop in number of gins and their increased productivity have been accompanied by a sharp rise in construction costs of modern ginning complexes, often exceeding one million dollars.

The techniques employed in raising productivity also illuminate the interplay of class forces. In the Guatemalan coastal lowlands, cotton yields are the highest in the western hemisphere and pesticide spraying is the highest in the world. As cotton pests multiply the large cotton *latifundistas* are boosting insecticide inputs. However, as a result of more resistant strains of pest, more toxic sprays are being used, with cataclysmic consequences for workers. 'At this time of the year, we treat 30–40 people a day for pesticide poisoning,' said a Guatemalan nurse to a *New York Times* reporter. 'The farmers often tell the peasants to give another reason for their sickness, but you can smell the pesticide in their clothes.'[42] In a graphic description of such cultivation practices, *The New York Times* continues:

> According to the government, there were no fatalities among the 1,039 cases of pesticide poisoning recorded last year in Guatemala. But doctors, priests and peasant leaders believe that there are numerous unreported deaths each year and that many more people are poisoned than the government admits. In the absence of government controls over most insecticide spraying, researchers report dangerous levels of pesticide residue in mother's milk, cow's milk, beef, fish, chickens, ducks and pigs in the area. Rivers carry the poison to the sea, where it pollutes seafood. But the political strength of the cotton planters and the importance of cotton exports to Guatemala's economy have blocked attempts to curb the pesticides. Last year, a delegation from La Noria could not find a ministry willing to take responsibility for monitoring insecticides.[43]

The widespread misuse of pesticides in UCEs is by no means fortuitous: the chemical oligopoly has long employed coercive marketing techniques to dump on them surplus pesticides and certain brands of pesticides banned in DCEs. Further danger results from the application of pesticides under unstable weather conditions. In Guatemala, it was estimated that about 75 per cent of the amount sprayed falls outside the cotton fields under conditions of temperature inversion and moderate winds. A large amount of the $70 million spent yearly on pesticides in Central America's cotton lands is lost because of drift. From a health perspective, according to the Central American Nutrition Institute, the amounts of DDT in mother's milk in Guatemala are the highest in the Western hemisphere. One sample from La Gomera contain 9.26 parts per million of DDT. This, the study concluded, 'is 185 times higher than the limit'.[44] And while formally the law stipulates that pickers should not enter fields within 72 hours of spraying and that cotton should not be grown within 100 metres of roads, houses, rivers, cattle grazing areas, or grain crops, no measures exist for enforcing the law. The political implications are serious, as *The New York Times* further notes: 'Because the victims of the spraying have little voice in Guatemalan politics, the use of pesticides is rarely discussed in the capital and so far the issue has not been raised . . . But its political potential has at least been recognized by Guatemala's leftist guerillas. Last year, the Guatemalan Army of the Poor destroyed 22 crop-dusting planes at La Flora . . . Within days, the cotton planters had replaced them and spraying was resumed.'[45] In the wake of the 1979 Sandinista victory in Nicaragua, we are witnessing an intensified armed opposition to the traditional oligarchies in several Central American countries. Given the symbiotic relationship between corporate capital and the oligarchies, the onset of revolutionary governments must lead to a funda-mental re-evaluation of relations with the chemical corporations and the multi-commodity traders that dominate their agricultural exports.

The Political Economy of the Food/Cotton Playoff

Cotton producers, large and small, have almost no control over the prices they receive. In no national market do they exercise monopolistic or oligo-polistic power. In the 1970s, cotton prices swung wildly compared to the oligopolistically controlled prices of most manufactured goods. For many countries, such as Mexico, these fluctuations have been devastating:

> The serious repercussions which the violent price changes had on the earnings of Mexican farmers and the unpromising outlook (including ecological problems affecting certain regions) were the determining factor in their decision to reduce the areas given over to cotton-growing, and in spite of their efforts to increase productivity per unit of land, production fell considerably . . . The peasants and smallholders under the *ejido* system who grow cotton are part of the [agricultural] sector where economic and social conditions are the worst in the whole of Mexico, and they are the least well endowed to protect themselves from changing international conditions which affect demand for their produce.[46]

Global demands to grow more food and raise nutritional levels are placing increasing pressure on cotton producers. Further, in the substitution war between man-made fibres and cotton, what looms ominously large is rising demand for textile fabrics. Mexico, a significant world cotton producer, exhibits the forces at work: a sharply rising demographic curve, grossly in-adequate nutritional levels, rising internal use of cotton in textiles – and this despite the well-orchestrated technocratic ballyhoo of the country that pioneered the 'green revolution' with its 'wonder wheat strains'.

'While malnutrition has long been a chronic problem in Mexico,' reports *The New York Times,* 'the recession of the last four years has brought even more serious under-nourishment to millions of families, both in city slums and villages. Reliable statistics on nutrition levels do not exist, although the 1970 census concluded that 30 per cent of the population (then more than 60 million) were under-nourished, 30 per cent suffered malnutri-tion, and at least 20 per cent were obese because of poorly balanced diets.'[47]

Data for the period 1960–75 for nine major cotton countries record marked population growth, except in Chad (see Table 2.10). Increasingly, this has placed pressure on available land as seen in all nine, strikingly so in Nicaragua where per capita arable land is less than half its 1960 level. Not-withstanding these demographic pressures, per capita cotton exports jumped as much as eight-fold for six of the countries, which suggests that cotton exports have been encouraged by the UCE oligarchies and trading oligopoly to the detriment of domestic food requirements. In all cases there has been an upsurge in per capita food imports over the period, such as the staggering ten-fold jump in Iran. Output indices further dramatize this point: in Chad *per capita* food production declined by 20 per cent between 1961 and 1978, in contrast to a 150-per-cent jump in *per capita* cotton production; and in Turkey, *per capita* food production increased by only 14 per cent over those seven years, as opposed to a 67-per-cent leap in *per capita* cotton output.[48] Needless to say, food imports, now absorbing massive foreign exchange earnings, are not even meeting minimal nutritional needs in these nine countries.[49]

The food crisis becomes more poignant against the backdrop of rising nutritional expectations. Yet there is no implication that the relationship between cotton and nutrition is exclusively related to land availability. Given the present highly inegalitarian income distribution in all UCEs, a reallocation of cotton lands would not necessarily lead to higher nutritional levels. The wretchedly low income of the masses precludes a rise in food consumption *regardless* of food availability. In the bulk of UCEs, with the exception of certain emerging CPEs (eg. Cuba), food imports supply almost exclusively the upper income groups in urban areas. Nevertheless, it is to be expected that revolutionary political pressures in certain countries (eg. Iran and Nicaragua) will increasingly call for a shift from cotton into food production to end endemic malnutrition. One indication of such a trend came from Abba Sidick, Secretary General of the National Liberation Front of Chad, a peasant-based movement that now controls extensive areas of Chad. He emphasized that the growing of food crops, as distinct from cash crops, was one of the Front's major goals.[50]

Table 2.10
Population, Land and Agricultural Indicators in Selected Countries, 1960–75

	Population Growth Rate (%) (1960–75)	Per Capita Arable Land and Land Under Permanent Crops (1960 = 100)	Per Capita Value of Food Imports ($US)[4] 1960	1975	Per Capita Value of Cotton Exports ($US)[4] 1960	1975
Brazil	2.9	93.68	2.86	7.23	0.65	0.91
Chad	1.8	77.16[1]	1.03	4.47	2.65	5.53
Egypt	2.5	78.47[1]	5.25	26.96	14.98	13.79
Guatemala	3.9	74.87[1]	3.67	6.81	1.50	12.05[2]
India	2.2	74.00	0.85	2.66	0.04	0.04
Iran	3.3	86.93	4.21[3]	47.10	1.41	3.78
Mexico	3.7	68.28	1.02	12.62	3.41	2.10
Nicaragua	2.9	46.62	4.04	17.84	10.41	44.25
Turkey	2.3	78.99	1.09	5.47	1.66	5.75
World	*1.9*	*81.90[1]*	*6.71*	*n.a*	*0.81*	*1.11*

1. 1961–5 = 100
2. 1974
3. Including beverages and tobacco
4. Current US dollars

Source: Computer from data in UN, *Demographic Yearbooks;* FAO *Production Yearbooks;* FAO *Trade Yearbooks;* and UN *Yearbook of International Trade Statistics.*

In addition to food demand pressures on cotton, the following model spells out cotton yields required to meet world demand in 1990 under two scenarios: the first postulating that the chemical fibre/cotton ratio remains at the 1976 level of 44:50; the second postulating that this ratio shifts to 65:30. The model is based on three assumptions for 1990:[51] (1) area under cotton remains around the 1960 and 1976 levels of 32 million hectares; (2) world average *per capita* fibre consumption continues to rise, attaining the *per capita* European and Japanese average 1976 levels of 13.5 kilograms; (3) world population grows at approximately 2 per cent yearly to 5.4 billion.

On these assumptions, in the first case, unchanging fibre ratios, the volume of cotton required to meet world demand would be 36.7 billion metric tons, or world average yields of 1,147 kilograms per hectare. This implies a three-fold jump from the 1976 world average to levels approaching those of the world's leaders, Israel and Guatemala. The ecological implications of the increased use of fertilizers and pesticides this would require have been spelt out in our findings on Guatemala. The vast capital outlays needed to attain such yields would depend on much larger farm units than the present atomistic structure of the world cotton economy.

In the second scenario, in which cotton would drop to 30 per cent of total fibre consumption, the cotton required to meet world demand would be 22 billion metric tons, or world average yields of 688 kilograms per hectare (about the yields of Egypt and Peru). The same effects on ecology, farm size and capital inputs would again result, but on a lesser scale.

State Interventionism

At a national level, the cotton/food playoff occurs within frameworks of differing state regulatory measures. State intervention, including cotton subsidies and acreage controls, is a familiar feature of American agriculture, now almost universally emulated. Most governments, with the assistance of state or private banks, provide special credit facilities to cotton farmers. These loans are usually available at the beginning of the growing season to cover fertilizers, insecticides and seeds. In a few countries, such as Pakistan, ginners advance credit to landlords on a selective basis, and the same is true of the giant multi-commodity traders within a large number of producing countries.

A factor bearing directly on cotton's position *vis-a-vis* other crops has been the outright subsidies offered in many countries. New varieties are often subsidized to stimulate production. Other subsidies of up to 100 per cent for certain inputs are offered for selected demonstration farms and special government projects. Smaller subsidies for machinery, fertilizers, and insecticides have been used in India, Iran, Kenya, Niger and Pakistan.

Attempts to ensure that farmers at least cover production costs in bad years are made in many countries through minimum price guarantees. A frequently used method of state intervention has been acreage control. In its minimal institutional form this means that governments prescribe specific zones where cotton may be grown; examples are Pakistan, Kenya and Mali. Other governments, such as those of Niger and Syria, enforce definite limits on cotton land. One should not be deceived, however, into thinking that governmental assistance is in any way neutral — as Guatemala's experience shows. In many countries, cotton plantation owners and *latifundistas* slide back and forth into and out of the state apparatus, often representing their governments *and* their own interests in international cotton conferences. In the United States, agricultural subsidies flow disproportionately to big-scale corporate holdings, and in many ways these subsidies have massively contributed to boost the level of farm concentration.[52]

Although state intervention has been significant in buttressing cotton in its war with man-made fibres, public sector promotional assistance has been far less significant. Global research and development expenditures on cotton are estimated at around $55—65 million, of which Cotton Incorporated (USA) accounts for approximately $20 million.[53] That organization is now under investigation by the United States government for corrupt financial practices.[54] By contrast, the self-reinforcing research and development budgets of the chemical giants already exceeds $1.8 billion, a total which includes research on cotton itself to enhance its ability to blend with synthetics. Other research on cotton comes from the big textile machine producers working in conjunction with technical specifications of chemical corporations.

Research by Cotton Incorporated is split into four major areas: agricultural research; processing/handling; services research; and product research. In the Soviet Union and China the bulk of research and development funds is allocated to the production phase, involving weed and insect control, yields and quality crop physiology, irrigation and basic inputs. Product research in both the DCEs and CPEs is basically oriented towards finding ways for finishing cotton fabrics to ensure durable press and fire-retardant properties.

UCE states have pushed cotton in other directions, most notably into increased domestic processing. Over the last five decades there has been a shift in cotton consumption (as measured in the geographical distribution of cotton spindleage) from the DCEs to the rest of the world, particularly the UCEs (see Table 2.11). This shift may in part to be imputed to national import-substitution policies, underpinned in many cases by foreign capital. At the epicentre of this historical change has been the literal dismantling of cotton spindleage in the United Kingdom, the pioneer of the textile-based industrial revolution.[55]

Table 2.11
Cotton Spindles in Selected Countries, 1928—78 (% of world total)

	1928	*1955*	*1973*	*1978*
DCEs	*82.8*	*66.1*	*37.9*	*33.8*
United Kingdom	34.9	19.4	1.9	1.5
USA[1]	22.2	17.1	13.2	11.6
UCEs	*7.4*	*17.4*	*32.8*	*36.2*
Brazil	1.6	2.6	2.8	3.0
India	5.3	9.2	12.9	13.3
CPEs	*9.8*	*16.5*	*29.3*	*30.0*
China	2.1	4.4	12.5	13.2
USSR[1]	4.4	7.8	11.0	10.6
World	*100.0*	*100.0*	*100.0*	*100.0*

1. These percentage shares are slightly inaccurate since the extensive rotor spinning capacities are excluded.
Source: Computed from data in *IFCATI* publications.

Another consumption trend is seen in the per capita end-use of cotton compared with other textile fibres. In the two decades 1955–75, world fibre consumption practically doubled from 12.5 to 26.1 million tons. Such overall consumption averages, however, conceal significant growth disparities: polyester fibre end-use expanded yearly by 28 per cent and that of cotton slipped from 70 per cent of fibre end-use in 1955 to under 50 per cent at present.

In its war against cotton, the chemical oligopoly has wielded innovational product lines, advertising, and an ability to ensure supplies at relatively stable prices. The oligopoly's capacity to respond swiftly with this concatenation of weapons has shifted the *per capita* fibre consumption pattern (see Table 2.12).

Table 2.12
Per Capita Fibre Consumption in Selected Countries 1965–74 (kilograms)

	Cotton		*Cellulosics*		*Non-Cellulosics*		*Total Fibres*	
	1965	*1974*	*1965*	*1974*	*1965*	*1974*	*1965*	*1974*
USA	10.8	7.5	3.6	2.4	4.0	12.0	19.2	22.2
East Germany	5.2	5.4	8.5	9.7	0.7	6.3	15.8	21.9
West Germany	5.8	5.7	4.0	2.8	2.7	8.6	15.1	18.4
Bulgaria	6.9	9.3	3.3	1.4	0.1	4.3	12.4	17.2
UK	6.5	4.8	3.7	3.1	2.4	7.2	14.8	16.6
Czechoslovakia	5.9	6.4	5.1	4.7	0.9	4.1	13.3	16.4
France	4.0	5.0	1.7	2.4	1.4	5.1	8.3	13.6

Source: FAO, *Per capita fibre consumption, 1965–1974* (Rome, 1976).

Retail Breakdown

Available data is inadequate to offer us a cost image of the different components of a global cotton retail breakdown.[56] National marketing data, however, have been obtained for the United States, Britain, West Germany, and Mexico, and suggest the main cost elements of certain selected manufactured cotton items.

The United States cotton farmer's share of the retail dollar reflects the subordinate role of the direct producer in the marketing chain, influenced by the chemical fibre industry (see Table 2.13). In essence, this means that the operating costs and pricing policies of fibre producers, textile manufacturers, and multi-commodity traders bear directly on farm retail margins. Thus, for example, the direct producer is reduced to about 8.8 per cent (which is susceptible to price swings) of the total retail value of a pair of cotton denim dungarees, equivalent to a return of about $1.14 per pair retailing for $12.95. As with most primary commodities, processing and final marketing account for the bulk of the cotton dollar. During processing and finishing, raw cotton is spun into yarn, dyed and woven into denim fabric. These manufacturing industries — which, as will be seen, are highly capital-intensive — account for one-fifth of the denim dollar. They are either large integrated firms performing all three operations at one location, or firms specializing only in spinning yarn or in spinning and finishing.

Clothing manufacturing, the next stage in the production-marketing chain, corrals about 30 per cent of retail value. The finished product is then sold by the manufacturer to clothing wholesalers or directly to retailers who annex the remaining 42 per cent. In other words, the three major segments of the production-marketing chain have staked out about 90 per cent of the cotton denim dollar.

For the United Kingdom, the breakdown for denim jeans over a short period in the first half of the 1970s depicts shifts in marketing composition and the fluctuating margins to which they have been subjected (see Table 2.14). As with United States denim, raw cotton costs are a minor component of the aggregate costs. Of great significance at the downstream end of the chain has been the systematic build-up of distributors' (wholesalers'/ retailers') gross margins, now accounting for over 43 per cent. Whilst denim jean prices escalated by 82 per cent in three years because of alleged rising costs, the increase in the British consumer price index was 64.2 per cent for the corresponding period, for a cost boost in real terms of 17.5 per cent.

Table 2.13
US Retail Breakdown of Denim Jeans, 1976

Economic Agent	Cost per pair of jeans ($)	% of Total Cost
Cotton farmer	1.14	8.8
Ginner	0.14	1.1
Transporter to textile mill	0.12	0.9
Textile manufacturer	2.38	18.4
Apparel manufacturer	3.73	28.8
Wholesaler/Retailer	5.44	42.0
Total	*12.95*	*100.0*

Source: USDA, *Cotton and Wool Situation,* February 1977.

Data for West Germany in 1976 suggest a higher level of wholesale/ retail control of the marketing chain than for the United Kingdom — and/ or higher distribution costs resulting from higher wages in these relatively labour-intensive retailing activities (see Table 2.15). Although it would appear that raw material costs in both commodities (the examples are a cotton towel

Table 2.14
UK Retail Breakdown of Denim Jeans and Baby's Napkins, 1976 (%)

	Sep. '72	Mar. '73	Sep. '73	Denim Jeans Mar. '74	Sep. '74	Mar. '75	Sep. '75
Manufacturer's cost							
Raw cotton	8.1	7.2	7.2	8.9	12.3	10.0	8.4
Direct labour costs	13.4	16.7	15.5	12.8	13.8	14.8	14.0
Other costs	21.6	22.2	21.6	21.2	22.6	25.9	20.2
Profits	16.0	13.3	14.4	15.4	9.0	5.4	14.4
Distributor's gross margin	40.9	40.6	41.3	41.7	42.3	43.9	43.0

	Sep. '72	Mar. '73	Sep. '73	Baby's Napkins Mar. '74	Sep. '74	Mar. '75	Sep. '75
Manufacturer's cost							
Raw cotton	14.9	14.0	13.0	10.7	13.7	13.5	11.5
Direct labour costs	18.5	18.3	18.7	14.7	13.1	17.0	18.5
Other costs	16.5	17.1	18.3	18.6	16.2	20.1	19.9
Profits	7.4	7.8	8.0	15.1	15.2	6.0	6.8
Distributor's gross margin	42.7	42.9	42.0	40.9	41.8	43.4	43.4

Source: Computed from data in Price Commission, *Raw Material Movements and Retail Prices* (London, 1976).

47

and a polyester/cotton shirt) are widely divergent (15 per cent and 3.5 per cent respectively), this stems from processing differences between the two articles. The cotton towel, like the baby's napkin, requires little making-up.

Turning to Mexico, a leading UCE, we perceive that there are wide differences in the cost breakdown of different clothing items (Table 2.16). It would appear here that the more restricted the distribution of the apparel item (as in the case of specialty apparel), the wider the margins the apparel and wholesale/retail industry are able to garner. This is due to wide income disparities, and the role clothing plays as an upper-class status symbol. The clothing and marketing sectors have skilfully capitalized on these attitudes in a restricted market.

Table 2.15
West Germany: Retail Breakdown of Cotton Towels and Polyester-Cotton Shirts, 1976

	Cotton Towels		*65–35 Polyester/Cotton Shirts*	
Cost Items	*% of Total Cost*	*Cost Items*		*% of Total Cost*
Cotton	15.0	Cotton-polyester		3.5
Spinning	4.0	Spinning and winding		3.5
Weaving	6.0	Weaving		4.2
Dyeing & finishing	3.0	Bleaching and dyeing		4.0
Making-up	5.0	Finishing		2.0
Overhead	6.0	Dispatching		5.0
Other costs	13.0	Making-up		29.8
Wholesale/Retail	48.0	Wholesale/Retail		48.0

Source: Computed from F. Egbers, 'La production textile europeenne', *Industrie Textile,* March 1977.

Table 2.16
Mexico: Retail Breakdowns of Cotton Items, 1977 (% of total cost)

Cost Item	*Speciality apparel*[1]	*Men's Shirt*[1]	*Cotton T-Shirt*
Cotton	1.7	3.0	18.0
Ginning	0.1	0.2	1.3
Transport[2]	0.1	0.1	0.5
Textile Manufacture	12.5	23.0	15.0[3]
Apparel Making-up	35.0	32.0	40.0
Wholesale/Retail	46.0	38.0	23.0
Other	4.6	3.7	2.2

1. 35 per cent cotton; 65 per cent synthetic fibre.
2. From production areas to factory site.
3. Includes textile processing through the yarn stage.
Source: Computed and designed from data of the Banco Nacional de Co Comercio Exterior, SA, Mexico.

In the more specialized items, the share of raw materials diminishes significantly. In items with longer production runs, such as underwear and T-shirts (where product homogeneity and a fragmented retail structure have made the market more competitive), wholesale/retail mark-ups are smaller. Hence raw material costs are relatively more important in the final retail price.

References

1. For an amplification see E.J. Hobsbawm, *The Age of Capital, 1848–1875* (London, 1975). For the earlier period see the classic work of Paul Mantoux, *The Industrial Revolution in the 18th Century* (London, 1925).
2. Cf. J.D. Bernal, *Science in History* (3 vols; London, 1969). This author earlier noted that the chemical industry, 'though born from a union between the physician's and miner's art, was all through the nineteenth century largely an ancillary to the rapidly expanding textile industry'; J.D. Bernal, *Science and Industry in the Nineteenth Century,* (London, 1953), p. 73.
3. One of the offshoots of the textile dyestuffs industry was the discovery of the explosive properties of nitrated cotton and glycerine that provided the main impetus for the nitric acid industry which, in turn, provided one of the sinews for the armament industry. Cf. Archibald and Nan Clow, *The Chemical Revolution* (London, 1952), and J.D. Bernal, *Science in History.*
4. See F.F. Clairmonte, *Economic Liberalism and Underdevelopment: Studies in the Disintegration of an Idea* (London, 1960).
5. USDA, *Foreign Agriculture,* 7 March 1977.
6. R. Robson, 'Importance of natural fibres . . .'. Shirley Institute, 1977.
7. For developed countries, clothing manufacture is an important employment source, 3.4 million (or about 40 per cent) of 9 million persons being dependent on natural fibre output and processing. If man-made fibres are included, employment dependence climbs to around 23 million and in underdeveloped countries to about 84 million. The total for all productive activities for these countries does not include persons in the subsistence sector, nor are small self-employed tailors/garment makers included in 'clothing manufacture' figures.
8. International Institute for Cotton, *Cotton's Importance to the Developing World* (Brussels, 1976).
9. See *Le Monde Diplomatique,* May 1976, p. 11.
10. The World Bank's project selection criteria involve cost-benefit analysis, whereby all projects must ensure a high rate of return. Time and again this has led to projects geared to, and servicing the needs of, richer peasants and big landowners. See Joe Collins and Frances Moore Lappe, 'Whom Does the World Bank Serve?', *Economic and Political Weekly,* 12 May 1979.
11. *Le Monde Diplomatique,* May 1976, p. 11.
12. See the nine-thousand-word statement in *The New York Times,* 26

October 1979, which alone cost $24,187.

13. USDA, Foreign Agriculture Circular, *Recent Developments in Cotton in the USSR,* August 1978, pp. 1–3.
14. *Textile Asia,* August 1978, p. 84; *Financial Times,* 22 June 1979.
15. *The New York Times,* 12 November 1978. The United States is still at a higher level of cotton farm mechanization than the USSR and China, and roughly half of all Soviet cotton is still hand picked. The US crop is entirely machine picked, with most of the 70,000 cotton-picking machines produced by two highly diversified agricultural machinery giants: International Harvester Co. (1976 sales, $5.5 billion) and Deere & Co. (1976 sales, $3.1 billion). See USDA, *US Team Reports on USSR Cotton Production and Trade* FAS-M-277 (Washington, DC, June 1977).
16. Calculated from ICAC, *Cotton World Statistics,* April 1980.
17. 'Cotton in Iran', *Indian Cotton Mills Federation Journal,* 1977.
18. E. Thigpen, *Draft Paper on Cotton* (Washington, DC, World Bank, 1977), p. 13.
19. See E.R.J. Owen, *Cotton and the Egyptian Economy 1820–1914,* (Oxford, 1969), and A.E. Crouchley, *The Economic Development of Modern Egypt* (London, 1938).
20. UNCTAD, *The Maritime Transport of Cotton,* TD/B/C.4/157, 10 February 1977.
21. Cotton is the Soviet Union's most valuable agricultural export. The decision to grow cotton rather than grain on the irrigated land of Central Asia is motivated in part by the $1,400 return on one hectare of cotton land (plus $250/hectare for cottonseed), as against $675 for wheat. Cf. USDA, *US Team Reports on USSR Cotton Production and Trade,* p. 16.
22. UNCTAD, *Handbook of International Trade and Development Statistics* (New York, 1976).
23. United Nations, *Commodity Trade Statistics,* New York, 1974, Series D; *Vneshniaia torgovlia SSSR,* Moscow, 1975; FAO, *Trade Yearbook,* Rome, 1975.
24. *The New York Times,* 17 November 1977.
25. NACLA, 'Agribusiness targets Latin America, *NACLA Report on the Americas,* XII, 1, (January-February 1978), p. 31.
26. Nick Kotz, 'Agribusiness', in Richard Merril (ed.), *Radical Agriculture* (London, 1976), p. 42.
27. Calculated from data in *Economic Report of the President,* Washington, DC, January, 1979.
28. Towards the end of the 1970s the top ten fertilizer producers (including 'food' processors such as Esmark and Borden) accounted for 47 per cent of estimated sales; the top sixteen for almost two-thirds.
29. Oligopolistic price abuses by the 'seven petroleum sisters' have been extensively documented, their conglomerate structures are studied here in Chapter 6.
30. By 1979, only two firms accounted for four-fifths of all United States cotton pesticide sales. See USDA, Issue Briefing Paper No. 16, *The Structure of American Farming* (Washington, DC, 6 July 1979), p. 5.
31. Petroleum and chemical giants are spearheading the movement to oligopoly in this sector, which includes such corporate notables as Shell,

The Structure of the World Cotton Economy

ITT, Monsanto, Union Carbide, Ciba-Geigy, General Foods and Cargill. See P.R. Mooney, *Seeds of the Earth: A Private or Public Resource?* (Ottawa, 1979).

32. According to the findings of the Council on Wage and Price Stability, seven companies produce 90 per cent of all tractors and combines, three of them (International Harvester, John Deere, and Massey Ferguson) annexing three-quarters of farm machinery markets. See Council on Wage and Price Stability, *Report on Prices for Agricultural Machinery and Equipment*, Washington, DC, 1976.

33. *The Structure of American Farming*, p. 3.

34. L. Finch, 'Structural changes in the agricultural industry: their meaning for American business and world food production', in *Feeding the World's Hungry: The Challenge to Business* (Conference sponsored by Continental Bank, 20 May 1974), p. 108.

35. One hectare equals 2.47 acres.

36. J.M. May and D.L. McLellan, *The Ecology of Malnutrition in Mexico and Central America* (New York, 1972), pp. 254–5.

37. *Le Monde*, 18 July 1979.

38. *International Herald Tribune*, 7–8 April 1979. This is in line with the 14 giant landowning families that dominate agriculture in El Salvador. This oligarchy's interests also have historically been protected by the military and state apparatus, as seen in the ruling class's brutal liquidation of 30,000 threatening peasants in the uprising of 1932. This represented 3 per cent of the entire population. See Amnesty International, *Campagne Le Salvador* (in French), London, 1979, and *Neue Zurcher Zeitung*, 2 June 1979.

39. *International Herald Tribune*, 7–8 April 1979.

40. Calculated from USDA, FC 14-77, *Cotton*, August 1977.

41. *International Herald Tribune*, 7–8 April 1979.

42. *The New York Times*, 17 November 1977.

43. *Ibid.* 'With an integrated pest control programme, we think that 6 or 7 sprayings would be enough in a 90-day growing cycle', one agronomist noted, 'but here we have plantations sprayed 30, 40 and even 50 times in three months'.

44. Instituto Centro-americano de Investigacion y Tecnologia Industrial (ICAITI), *An Environmental and Economic Study of the Consequences of Pesticide Use in Central American Cotton Production, Final Report* (2nd edition; Guatemala City, 1977).

45. *Ibid.*

46. UNCTAD, *Impact of the Fluctuations of Cotton Prices on the Profitability of the Mexican Cotton Industry* (Geneva, 22 January 1979, TD/B/IPC/COTTON/L.3), pp. 4, 11.

47. *The New York Times*, March 9, 1978. Inadequate nutrition has induced high rates of infant mortality. 'The first indication is when we see infant mortality rising again', – Dr Adolfo Chavez of the National Nutrition Institute. 'In some really depressed rural communities, few children born since 1974 have survived. We have what we call generational holes. But infant mortality is also growing in slum areas of the cities . . . more than 100,000 children die here each year because of the relationship between malnutrition and transmittable diseases, and of the 2 million or so who

are born each year, at least 1.5 million will not adequately develop their mental, physical and social functions.' Nutritional deficiencies have also been stimulated by the advertising onslaught of the transnational corporations which bend consumer preferences, notably among the poor, towards non-nutritive food consumption patterns.

48. Computed from FAO data.
49. J.M. Bengoa and G. Donoso, 'Prevalence of protein-calorie malnutrition, 1963 to 1973', *PAG Bulletin* (World Health Organization), 1974.
50. Frances Moore Lappe and Joseph Collins, *Food First*, (Boston, 1977) p. 103.
51. Based on: World Bank Staff Commodity Paper No. 2 *International Cotton Market Prospects*, (New York, 1978); *IMF Staff Papers, xxiv,* 2, July 1977; United Nations, Department of Economic and Social Affairs, *World Population Prospects as Assessed in 1968,* (New York, 1973); *Wool Record,* October 1977.
52. *The New York Times,* 2 March 1979; also Kotz, p. 44.
53. This compares with $55 million spent by the International Wool Secretariat.
54. *Wall Street Journal,* 20 March 1979.
55. The rise and fall of the British cotton textile industry can be seen in the increase of cotton cloth from 40 million yards in 1785 to 6,500 million in 1887. By 1912, it had reached an all-time high of 8,000 million yards and then fell to 3,600 in 1937 and 2,100 in 1950. Cf. Bernal, *Science and Industry in the Nineteenth Century,* p. 20.
56. The distinction must be made between profit margins of individual firms (which measure revenues minus costs) and retail margins depicted in these breakdowns. The latter indicate the relative shares of a retail dollar redounding to the major economic actors at every phase of the production and marketing chain.

3. The Trading Conglomerates

Oligopoly, by the 1960s, became the subject of both Marxist and conventional academic enquiry. However, private trading conglomerate oligopolies have so far eluded any systematic probes into their operations and their devastating impact on commodity prices, UCE peasants, and global trading patterns. This chapter elucidates the critical connexions between commodity exchanges, national marketing institutions, and multi-commodity traders. The linchpin in this triad has always been the group of big traders, whose numbers over the last half-century have decreased steadily to the point at which fifteen companies now control 85–90 per cent of the world cotton trade.[1] This extent of control is paralleled on many other primary commodity markets, for instance leaf tobacco, where roughly 85–90 per cent entering international trade is under the direct control of six transnational leaf buyers,[2] bananas, where 70–75 per cent of the world market is dominated by three companies,[3] and cocoa, where five corporations hold over 75 per cent of world cocoa trade.[4]

In the history of capitalism, private family-owned enterprises were by far the dominant institutions until the American invention of the holding company in the 1870s. This marked the advent of the modern public corporation, created to expand their capital base (through the issue of publicly held stock) to exploit the openings in transportation, industry, and the Western American frontier. Since that time in all DCEs, the public corporation has become the major catalyst of imperialism and has usurped dominance in all industrial sectors. Perhaps the only international sector where family-owned companies still predominate is commodity trading. Their continued supremacy stems from their mode of operation, combining speedy decision-making and absolute secrecy together with non-accountability.

The sole exception to widespread family control of commodity trading has been the Japanese *sogo shoshas*. Their high degree of corporate autonomy within Japanese conglomerate structures permits them, in many ways, to operate with the flexibility of family concerns. In all ways possible, such private modes of operation have impeded and intimidated researchers from any systematic enquiry into their activities. We have attempted to remove a little of the secrecy that shrouds these operations by investigating the general mechanisms of market control, and the specifics of manipulative pricing practices. Further investigation of these concerns is vital for an analytical grasp of the specifics of contemporary oligopoly.

The Giant Traders

International cotton traders emerged out of the crystallization of the world cotton economy between 1846[5] and 1871, with the United States Civil War serving as a major catalyst. In the subsequent four decades the strength of the giant traders was vastly reinforced as the textile industry gathered universal momentum and capital concentration moved briskly ahead. By 1921, twenty-four firms with annual sales of over 100,000 bales handled over 60 per cent of the United States cotton crop. 'The fundamental changes in the marketing of the cotton crop', writes Alfred Chandler, 'came swiftly in the years immediately following the Civil War, as the impact of the railroad, telegraph, cable and steamship was fully felt.'[6] The winnowing out of smaller traders was speeded up in the inter-war years, reaching more or less their present numbers in the 1960s.[7]

Three distinct groupings dominate world cotton: two giant European corporations, five Japanese conglomerates (of the giant *sogo shosha* type), and eight US public and private corporations (see Table 3.1).

While their outer forms differ, their inner cores reveal certain striking similarities:

(1) Giant traders contend that they operate on very slim margins of 1–2 per cent of sales value. Such a claim can often be highly misleading, as it is at present impossible to disentangle the intertwined financial and marketing operations of the conglomerates, be they multi-commodity traders or otherwise.[8] In such organizational structures, characterized by interlocking directorates, vertical and horizontal integration and their several variations, there is ample room for sufficient financial chicanery to obscure the real value and volume of profit margins. Traders have been known to take advantage of price hikes in a manner similar to the oil transnationals. In Mexico, when domestic cotton prices jumped $19 per 100 lb from 1974 to 1976, traders increased their average margins from $9.50 to $16.50 (per 100 lb) on cotton traded to North European spinners.[9]

(2) The vast bulk are private corporations who are in no way publicly accountable. Even for the public corporations, who are obliged by law to disclose a formal balance sheet, the rudimentary data are presented in ways contrived to conceal rather than reveal their mode of operation. The balance sheet of Bowater (the parent holding company of Ralli), for example, gives an aggregate sales figure for international trading and transportation. There are no clues, however, as to the breakdown of cotton (or any other commodity) in that total.

(3) Most are in a position to shift margins from one financial account to another due to their extensive operations in several commodity markets, a manoeuvre similar to the now familiar transfer pricing techniques of the large

industrial transnationals.

(4) Most of the giants are dominant world marketeers in other commodities: Volkart in coffee, Cargill and Bunge in grains and soybeans, Ralli
Brothers in tropical hardwoods, grain, coffee, tea, rubber, metals, and hard
and soft fibres, and the *sogo shosha* in all commodities, manufactured and
non-manufactured.

(5) Due to their self-reinforcing backward and forward linkages (Ralli and
Volkart in ginning, Bunge in plantations, spinning and weaving, and massive
penetrations into warehousing by almost all), they are strategically positioned
through perfectly legal engineering to outfox national marketing institutions
with whom they deal:

(6) The payoff complex is another component in their marketing
operations. As with other corporate activities, certain members of the UCE
oligarchy have been the object of special financial solicitude. To cite but
one example of a widespread practice, a large trader bribed a high official
in an African marketing board to delay sales until prices dropped, to the gain
of the large trader.

(7) Very close links have developed over time between the giant traders
and the transnational banking structure, best exhibited in the case of one of
the trading giants, which has a permanent overdraft account of around
$100 million with one of the world's largest commercial banks.[10] Close
collaboration with the banks is aided by trading company executives on the
boards of transnational banks, such as Eikichi Itoh of C. Itoh & Co., who
serves with the Societe de Banque Suisse. The chairman of the board of
Volkart Brothers, Peter Reinhart, was elected to the Board of the giant
Union des Banques Suisses in 1939 and served as vice-chairman from 1961 to
1978. In its encomium to Reinhart, the 1978 *Annual Report* aptly acknowledged: 'For decades, he placed his wide experience and extensive knowledge
at the disposal of our Bank and assisted us through countless valuable suggestions and recommendations.'[11] In the USA banks finance a large segment
(slightly above 85 per cent in some cases) of the cotton traded by certain
US traders, *Sogo shoshas* in Japan include banks as part of their conglomerate
structures.

(8) In the field of economic and trading intelligence, the giants all possess
highly sophisticated networks which lend a staggering speed and flexibility
to their operations in a way unmatched by national marketing institutions.
Among members of the oligopoly, swapping of information for specific
marketing goals occurs, although competition based on concealing key
information alternates with it.

(9) The giants are major hedgers and speculators on the New York Cotton
Exchange and other exchanges either with their own seats or operating
through their own brokers.

(10) While considerable attention has been focused on their external
trading activities, many of the giants are dominant in domestic trade within
large producing countries. Brazil and the United States are prime examples.

(11) Almost universally, traders buy and sell on the basis of common

rules, contract terms, and arbitration embodied in the Liverpool Cotton
Association (LCA). The LCA provides traders and mills with a common set
of rules whereby the former can be held legally accountable for abrogating
contract terms. This accountability has been used by traders to draw mills
away from direct purchases from cotton growers (with whom legal arbitration is less certain). Traders actively engender loyal, long-standing relations
with mills by providing a constant flow of information on price movements
and availability of specific qualities. Pulling new mills into a trader's
sphere often involves offering low-priced cotton compared to world
averages; the price is raised later as loyal ties are forged.

(12) As with most commodities, brand names play an important marketing
function as a sales booster for the more prestigious traders, primarily because
mills seek a commercial guarantee whereby they can hold the marketeer
accountable for defective merchandise.

While it is true that greater competition amongst traders has given way to
oligopolistic competition, this is not at all incompatible with collusive trading
practices. It can be noted that in countries where some cotton is sold through
auction[12] large traders have on occasion colluded in their bids.[13] In the
demarcation of geographical spheres of influence the level of collusion
amongst members of the oligopoly is so high as to bring about a situation
almost of monopoly. Examination of individual national markets reveals that
in all cases (with the exception of the United States) three to five giant
traders dominate the export business.[14] At this juncture it should be added
that there are around ten additional large traders that are very significant in
certain national markets (eg. Esteve and Anderson Clayton in Brazil and
Mexico, and Bambax and Blanchard in the USSR), but which fall short of
the big fifteen in global market shares.

A counterpart to this economic concentration has been the ascendancy
of Switzerland (and in particular Geneva) as a world centre of actual (as
opposed to futures) cotton and textile marketing. This geographical pull
primarily away from Liverpool, the USA and Egypt reflects a new constellation of forces associated with the complex exigencies of world capitalism.
Paramount among them are: political stability related to the absence of any
attacks on their mode of operations; news and communications media hostile
to any investigative activities against the transnationals; a milieu highly
congenial to multi-commodity activities, since many key corporations trading
in almost all primary commodities are located in Switzerland; a vitally
important international hub for marketing contacts of all kinds; and, of
course, a highly streamlined transnational banking structure in which money
and secrecy move in easy consonance. Due to a special constellation of
historical forces in the nineteenth century (primarily due to US cotton
dominance) the cotton futures market was born in New York, and its
perpetuation there is related to the city's emergence as the world financial
centre after 1918.

The case histories of Cargill, Bunge & Born and the Japanese *sogo shoshas*
highlight the evolving oligopolistic power of the trading juggernauts.

Table 3.1
Major World Cotton Traders

Rank[1]	Trader[2]	Place of Origin	Remarks
1	Ralli Brothers	UK. (Liverpool)	Average annual turnover well over 1 million bales, at times going up to well over 2 million.
2	Volkart Brothers	Switzerland (Winterthur)	Operational offices include New York, Osaka, and Bremen.
3	McFadden/Valmac	USA (Memphis), and Brazil (Sao Paolo)	Ranks probably equal with Volkart, at times ahead and at times just behind.
4	W.B. Dunavant	USA (Memphis)	Trades nearly exclusively on the American continent, but otherwise (in turnover) equal to Ralli.
5	Bunge & Born	USA (New York) and Brazil (Sao Paolo)	Argentinian family firm with major operational headquarters in New York, Latin America, London, Antwerp, Osaka, etc.
6	Cargill	USA *(Minnesota)*	
7	Allenberg Cotton Co.	USA (Memphis)	
8	Weil Brothers	USA (Memphis)	
9	H. Molsen & Co.	USA (Dallas)	German/American owned operation.
10	Cotton Import/Export Co.	USA (Dallas)	
1	Toyo Menka Kaisha	Japan (Osaka)	Deals foremost in American cotton. Average annual turnover 1 million bales.
2	Sumitomo Shoji Kaisha (and Sumitomo Menka)	Japan (Osaka)	Deals foremost in USSR cotton — turnover 1 million bales.
3	C. Itoh & Co)		Average annual turnover over 500,000 bales.
4	Marubeni-Iida Co.)	Japan (Osaka)	
5	Nichimen Co.)		

1. Ranking is not absolute, as volumes traded by companies vary greatly from year to year.
2. Cook Industries has been omitted because of their precarious financial posture at the time of writing.

Source: Trade sources.

Cargill

With 1979 aggregate sales outstripping $12 billion (as compared to $9 billion
in 1975), this multi-commodity giant is now larger than such huge
corporations as Du Pont, Atlantic Richfield, Imperial Tobacco Company,
and Tenneco. If Cargill were placed on the *Fortune 500* list of the largest
industrial corporations, it would rank just below Standard Oil of Indiana.
Few corporations reveal so clearly the morphology of oligopolistic capitalism
as this 116-year-old family corporation, the largest privately owned US
corporation. Over four-fifths of its stock is owned by the Cargill and
MacMillan families and the tax-exempt Cargill Foundation. Headquarters
in Minneapolis serve as the nucleus of a transnational empire of 140
subsidiaries in 36 countries. 'Cargill's money', writes Dan Morgan, 'may be
made thousands of miles away; but the decisions are made in Minneapolis,
or rather, in the woods outside it.' There, it 'operates its own foreign office,
gathering information, keeping in touch with its emissaries in dozens of
countries . . . and assessing the impact of political, financial and economic
developments on Cargill's foreign relations. This is the seat of the
"government of Cargill".'[15]
   Cargill is the third largest food enterprise in the world, after Unilever and
Nestle. Until 1950, its exclusive concern was grain, and grain still occupies
a significant place in its total sales. In 1974, its shares of United States grain
exports were as follows: barley, 42 per cent; oats, 32 per cent; wheat, 29 per
cent; sorghum, 22 per cent; soybeans, 18 per cent; and maize, 16 per cent.
Since that date its takeover and build-up of the Hohenberg cotton interests
has made it one of the decisive agents in world cotton trading.
   Fully half of its projected profits, and about two-thirds of its projected
profits, will emanate from its non-trading activities, thus exhibiting the tendency
towards accumulation characteristic of all oligopolies, whose overriding goal is
infinite growth in a finite environment. Cargill's conglomerate expansion into
cotton and metals trading, flour processing, chemicals, steel manufacturing,
coal merchandizing, poultry processing, salt mining, sunflower and other
oilseed processing, meat, coal, sugar, molasses, barge construction and
commodity futures trading, are but part of a larger realm that will be
extended in the 1980s. Cargill's Investor Services serve commodity speculators; its Summit National Life Insurance offers individual and group life
programmes, and its expertise straddles bulk commodities, agriculture
marketing and speculation, handling and transportation logistics.[16]
   The sizes of its recent annexations indicate Cargill's direction. Amongst
others, they include the MBPXL Corporation, the number two US meat-
packer, with annual revenues of over one billion dollars. In addition to these
mergers, $150 million is now being invested annually to boost the company's
grain-handling capacity by 50 per cent by 1984, a drive that could well push
its US market share to around 35 per cent. But the annexationist thrust will
not and cannot be confined solely to the United States, 'for Cargill is also
strengthening its position in foreign markets, thus grabbing additional sources

of supply as a buffer against any·dips in the USA.[17] The anatomy of just one
of Cargill's subsidiaries. Tradax, expresses the conglomerate nature of the
'big fifteen'. In 1955, Tradax was embedded in Geneva and had become
one of the largest grain (and other commodities) corporations in its own
right. Supra-nationalism, be it in Geneva, the Bahamas or the EEC, is not an
aberration, as Tradax attests. In several ways, its links with the Swiss Credit
Bank (which has 30 per cent of its shares) have proved a bonanza. In 1974–5
Tradax sales were over $2 billion, but it paid a trifling $3.3 million in US
taxes. Tradax International, its Panamanian creation, deferred US taxes at
the rate of 97.6 per cent in 1973, 71.8 in 1974, and 86.1 in 1975. In a
luminous understatement, a senior executive stated: 'In order to operate
successfully in the Common Market you've got to be a world trader. If you're
just domestic, you don't have the same tools as Tradax. The things that
influence the market may not be known to a domestic economy.'[18]

But offshore operations for tax write-offs and big-scale marketing are
only one aspect of the problem. For Cargill, as for other giant trading corporations, the secrecy of its corporate behaviour would make the dissembl-
ing antics of both Standard Oil at the turn of the century and the seven
petroleum sisters of today look like a libertarian's dream. This high secrecy
is typical of the global operations of all transnationals who are publicly unaccountable. When in 1975, to take but one example, the staff of the Senate
Subcommittee on Multinational Corporations began investigating the grain
juggernauts, it routinely asked libraries for documentation. It was not fortuitous that one library after another informed the Subcommittee that no
such materials existed. In the scathing rebuke of Senator Frank Church:
'No one knows how they operate, what their profits are, what they pay in
taxes and what effect they have on our foreign policy – or much of any-
thing else about them.'[19]

The ambience of secrecy has not altered appreciably since then. Swiss
law provides an alibi which continually inhibits US Congressional investigators. In its categorical refusal to transmit information to the United States
government, Cargill's subsidiary could pontificate: 'Tradax and its employees
would be subject to criminal prosecution if they supplied this information to
a US government entity.'[20] This in itself is a tragic commentary. It takes no
great effort to imagine the response to an underdeveloped country which had
the temerity to raise such awkward questions.

Bunge & Born

Baptized 'The Octopus' by the Argentine Movimiento· Peromista Montonero,
Bunge & Born is the most vertically integrated of the non-Japanese giant
traders. The president of the company's United States division described
Bunge's principal difference from the other cotton oligopolists as 'the
company's thrust toward developing a domestic presence in the countries
where it operates, as distinct from relating investments solely to export

trade opportunities'.[21] The Bunge family business launched its first trading operations in 1818 in Amsterdam, importing spices and hides from the Dutch colonies. Later, its headquarters were shifted to Antwerp (in 1850, when cotton trading activities were launched); Buenos Aires (in 1884); and recently to Sao Paulo (in the wake of the highly publicized 1974 kidnapping and $60-million ransom of two Born brothers).

Bunge's estimated 50,000 employees fuel a conglomerate which is a world leader not only in the cotton trade, but also in grain trading, soybean processing, flour milling, and various agricultural processing industries.[22] In Latin America, Bunge moved from trading Brazilian and Argentine cotton into textile manufacturing and a wide range of industrial processing, including paints, tin cans, jute sacks, etc. It has formed joint ventures with European drug and chemical majors, such as Bayer and BASF, and has also moved into banking, mining and resort properties. As an agribusiness concern, Bunge has substantial land holdings in fruit, vegetables, soybeans and grains.

The Sogo Shoshas

The Japanese writer Yoshie Hotta, in one of his novels on Japan's corporate community, observed that the constellation of *sogo shoshas* 'is the nation'. Capitalists and capitalism have always sought to rationalize their existence by making this erroneous identity. Undoubtedly, however, within the perspective of Japanese capitalism over the last hundred years, the general trading companies have become the conspicuous actors of the Japanese economy at home and abroad. They were the crack divisions that mounted the economic offensive responsible for driving the nation's GNP from $24 billion in 1955 to over $562,940 million in the mid-1970s. The *shoshas* were the trading arms of the giant Japanese *zaibatsu* until their dissolution by the United States after World War II. Their existence was enhanced by this change as they became the even more powerful trading extensions of the modern Japanese corporations that continued the *zaibatsu* tradition. Their trading activities – which are but a sub-system of their global activities – have four major segments: imports, exports, domestic trading transactions and trading between third countries. Whereas Japan's foreign trade in 1979 was $212 billion, the total trading transactions of the nine majors surpassed $268 billion (see Table 3.2) or 27 per cent of the nation's national income. In general, each *sogo shosha* handles 20,000–25,000 products, demonstrating the penetrative power of these transnational conglomerates. A glimpse of their diverse trading power and shifting structures is seen in the sectoral breakdown of their global revenues. (See Table 3.3).

Although there are more than 5,000 'trading companies', that designation is, and has been for decades, singularly inept to describe the nine *sogo shoshas* (reduced from ten in 1978 when No. 4 – Itoh – annexed No. 9 – Ataka) that straddle the entire spectrum of Japanese economic, social and political life. Several of these corporations (in which family and kinship ties are still important) have roots and legends that hark back to the 19th century and earlier: Mitsubishi,[23] Mitsui, Marubeni, Itoh, Sumitomo, Nissho Iwai, Toyo Menka Kaisha, Kanematsu-Gosho, and Nichimen.

Table 3.2
The *Sogo Shoshas*: Global Sales ($ billion) 1974—79

Corporations	1974	1979	1974 = 100
Mitsubishi	32.5	52.6	161
Mitsui	27.1	48.8	180
C. Itoh	17.8	38.6	217
Marubeni	19.4	36.5	189
Sumitomo	17.8	33.1	186
Nissho-Iwai	13.7	25.1	184
Toyo Menka	8.3	12.1	146
Kanematsu-Gosho	7.9	12.0	152
Nichimen	7.1	10.0	141
Total Sales	*151.6*	*268.8*	*177*

Source: Company *Annual Reports* and trade sources.

While we are specifically concerned with the five Japanese 'cotton traders', the corporate pursuits of the cotton 'big five' are inseparable from the activities of the *sogo shoshas* as a whole. Others play a role in the purchase and sale of cotton although this may be a minute share of their total sales. In 1978, for example, around 17 per cent of the world's marketable cotton entered the Japanese market. Of this, the Mitsubishi Corporation (with overall sales topping $40 billion in that year) handled 8 per cent — not including its sales to other countries.

The formal rules for the operation of the *shoshas,* according to the United States Department of Commerce, are: strong ties to manufactures; product specialization; powerful and highly flexible foreign sales networks; the ability to tap enormous amounts of credit, both foreign and domestic; an extensive range of products and markets; and speed of operations.[24] It was not an advertising stunt when a Mitsubishi spokesman declared that 'first of all, our 13,000-man network of offices — 120 abroad and 60 in Japan — keeps us closely informed on market conditions everywhere, so that we know the actual demand for any product anywhere, anytime. Secondly, we deal in a great diversity of goods totalling over 20,000 lines. From raw materials to consumer products, Mitsubishi covers the entire spectrum of economic activities.'[25]

Because of the sheer volume of their business transactions (based on relatively low margins of 2—3 per cent recouped by high volume turnover), the 'big nine' are ideally placed to make economies of scale in transportation, warehousing and marketing. Further, the scale of primary commodity

The World in their Web

purchases often yields massive discounts that boost the competitive status of
Japanese industry. While rivalry among the giants, as John G. Roberts noted,
seems to have been as keen as ever, 'much' of it is illusory because in fundamental matters they work together much more than they compete'.[26] Indeed,
in conjunction with the phalanx of the state apparatus, the Economic
Planning Agency and the Ministry of International Trade and Industry, to
which could be added that tested battle wagon, the Bank of Japan, 'they have
quietly supplanted the pre-war *zaibatsu* as masters of the Japanese
economy.'[27] It is a mastery that leaps the geo-political rims of the island
empire, with banks providing the financing; the *sogo shoshas* providing the
purchasing, marketing, carrying of inventory, and market research; and the
industrial subsidiaries providing the production muscle.

In the case of Japanese oligopolistic capitalism, the bulkheads separating
big politics from big capital have long since vanished. Thus corporate
capitalism becomes, as Chitoshi Yanaga writes: 'the major concern of the
government, and the government's policy becomes the prime concern of
organized business. Today, at least 90 per cent of the work of the government's lawmaking body, ministries and administrative agencies is concerned
with the problem of business and industry. In the conduct of foreign
relations, economic matters virtually monopolize the government's attention,
with the result that diplomacy becomes the means to economic ends. Even
the cultural aspects of diplomacy are used to achieve economic objectives.'[28]
In the shifting cross-currents of oligopoly this remains a constant of Japanese
capitalism.

The perpetual interplay of these forces is further stimulated by power
centralization (in several ways a pre-Meiji phenomenon) in Tokyo, a city of
over 12 million. It is the locus of power not only of the government but of
the *zaikai* (the business leader clique) and 'practically all the major corporations, making it the business, banking, financial, transportation, communications, publishing and mass media center of Japan.'[29]

Foundations

Although the *zaibatsus* were Japan's militant response to the encroachment
of international capitalism in the post-Meiji period, the designation *sogo
shoshas*, many of whom descended from the *zaibatsus*, emerged only in the
mid 1950s. Mitsui was set up in 1876; Mitsubishi in 1889, as the group's
trading arm. Although the Mitsubishi corporation was reborn in July 1957
and Mitsui in February 1959, the House of Mitsubishi was one of the four
zaibatsus which jointly controlled 76 per cent of the nation's total paid-in
industrial capital before the end of World War II. In the euphoric language
of Mitsubishi's 1979 *Annual Report*, 'after forced disbandment Mitsubishi
Shoji makes its dramatic comeback on the business scene by the regrouping
of the dissolved companies and starts winning back its pre-war hegemony'.
The *sogo shoshas* grew symbiotically with the Bank of Japan which, since
its founding in 1882, gave the major stimulus to economic concentration.
The bank's patrons and pursuits were to be harmonized with the rising

Table 3.3
The Sogo Shoshas: Sectoral Breakdown 1974-78 (% of total sales)

Corporation	Metals		Machinery		Chemicals		Foods		Textiles		Fuel		Pulp & Lumber	
	1974	1978	1974	1978	1974	1978	1974	1978	1974	1978	1974	1978	1974	1978
Mitsubishi	34	28	14	18	9	9	14	13	8	5	15	18	6	9
Mitsui	35	31	11	19	14	12	14	14	9	6	–	7	17	11
C. Itoh	18	17	16	20	23[1]	20	14	13	22	19	–	6	7	5
Marubeni	18	24	19	26	–	12	–	14	–	13	–	2	9	9
Sumitomo	–	33	–	25	–	19	–	9	–	4	–	2	–	9
Nissho-Iwai	39	36	20	25	13[1]	11	13	10	8	8	–	3	7	7
Kanematsu-Gosho	23	19	13	12	10	13	22	15	22	28	10	13	–	7
Toyo Menka	23[2]	21	24[2]	19	9[1] [2]	15	17[2]	19	23[2]	20	–	2	4[2]	4
Nichimen	30[1]	22	17	23	10	11	20	15	16	19	–	4	7	6
Total[3]	*29*	*27*	*16*	*21*	*13*	*14*	*15*	*13*	*13*	*11*	*14*	*7*	*8*	*8*

1. Including fuels.   2. 1975.   3. Weighted average.

Source: Company *Annual Reports* and trade sources.

zaibatsus. Apart from the Finance Ministry's holdings, much of its stock was held by the Mitsui, Iwasaki (the owners of Mitsubishi), Sumitomo, Kawasaki, Yasuda Konoike, Okura and Yamaguchi families. In the vigorous economic expansionist phase (1889–1903), which by the latter date was to plunge Japan into the orbit of imperialism, the bank's fortunes were directed by three former Mitsubishi executives.

Two other distinct cliques, the bureaucratic (*kambatsu*) and the military (*gumbutsu*), joined high finance (*zaibatsu*) as the decisive pillars of early twentieth-century Japanese capitalism. Indeed, this island nation had entered the era of oligopolistic conglomeration decades before such conceptual categories had been born.[30] In its interpretation of the consolidation and expansion of *zaibatsu* power, the US Mission on Japanese Combines noted 'that the low wages and concentrated profits which were generated by the zaibatsu clique were inconsistent with the development of a domestic market capable of keeping pace with the increased productivity of Japanese industry . . . this drive for exports and for imports of food and raw materials has been an outstanding motive of Japanese imperialism. Thus the concentration of Japanese wealth and economic power must carry a substantial share of the responsibility for Japanese oppression.'[31]

The early fortunes of the *sogo shoshas* were intimately intertwined with the take-off of Japan's first leading industrial sector in the late 19th Century – cotton textiles. A fourteenfold jump in cotton yarn production between 1882 and 1890 was made possible by Mitsui's massive import of spindles from the British firm, Platt Brothers.[32] By 1897, ten years after Japan became a net cotton importer, Mitsui was pulling in 17-million-*yen*-worth of cotton annually, almost a third of Japan's cotton import totals. Mitsui's early dominance of the industry was rounded out in exports of processed cotton goods; by 1910–13 this leading *sogo shosha* accounted for a third of Japan's annual 10-million-*yen*-worth of exports in this sector.[33]

In its exploration of another facet of *zaibatsu* power – namely its connexions with high finance that bolstered the export drive – the US Mission reported that the governor of the Bank of Japan in the 1930s worked with the Mitsui banks and headed the Mitsui *honsha* (holding company). Similarly, his successor (1937–44) was his predecessor's designee, and a senior executive in the Yasuda banks. Such connections were a boon for the *zaibatsu* commercial banks. Six of them, although accounting for only 59 per cent of all ordinary and savings banks' deposits, received 77 per cent of the Bank of Japan's loans to such banks. Further borrowings by the *zaibatsu* banks were by special loan rather than ordinary lending procedures. 'The significance of all this', stated the US Zaibatsu Mission in its summation, 'should not be missed. The policy of the government of channelling industrial financing into the big banks and of lending such banks the liquid funds necessary for these activities added tremendously to their profits' – and thus to the detriment of the smaller banks.[34]

Although a barrage of anti-trust legislation was foisted on Japan by the American occupation after the Second World War (ie. the 'Anti-Monopoly

Act' and the 'Elimination of Excessive Concentration of Economic Power Act', both in 1947), it did not alter the direction of Japanese capitalism, nor did it serve to check the abuse and non-accountability of concentrated economic power. In the words of the leading anti-trust administrator employed with the Japanese Fair Trade Commission, 'the history of the anti-monopoly law is a history of emasculation'.[35]

Financial Mainsprings and Communications Network

Sogo shosha arrangements with their group banks permit financial techniques not yet deployed in other DCEs. The entire system is run on paper, with only the final consumer paying cash. A manufacturing subsidiary sells its products to the *shosha* in its group against three-month bills that it can immediately discount. Likewise, the *shoshas* use such bills to finance sales to other wholesalers and sub-wholesalers. When the manufacturing subsidiaries buy materials from their related *shoshas,* the latter pays for the domestic portion of the materials with promissory notes, and others down the line stretch their promises out still further.[36] The entire credit machinery is oiled by the policies of the Bank of Japan. The bank permits key Japanese industries (particularly those linked to *shoshas*) to operate at very high debt-to-capital ratios, climbing in the case of steel to as high as 85 per cent (as against an average of 28 per cent for the US).

C. Itoh,[37] with aggregate sales of $38.6 billion in 1979, illustrates another dimension of Japanese finance capital, in the following breakdown of its major shareholders (Table 3.4).

Table 3.4
C. Itoh & Co.: Major Shareholders at 31 March 1977

	Number of Shares Held (000)	*% of Total Shares*
The Sumitoma Bank Ltd.	60,632	8.7
The Dai-Ichi Kangyo Bank Ltd.	60,632	8.7
The Bank of Tokyo Ltd.	32,379	4.6
Nippon Life Insurance Co.	27,649	4.0
The Asahi Mutual Life Insurance Co.	25,900	3.7
Tokio Marine & Fire Insurance Co. Ltd.	24,376	3.5
The Fuji Bank Ltd.	22,700	3.3
The Nippon Life & Marine Insurance Co. Ltd.	22,206	3.2
The Sumitomo Marine & Life Insurance Co. Ltd.	20,747	3.0
The Sanko Steamship Co. Ltd.	17,760	2.5
Total	*314,981*	*45.2*

Source: C. Itoh & Co. Ltd., *Annual Report 1977*, p. 21.

The interrelations of finance and industrial capital are brought out in the highly schematic presentation of the six large industrial groups and their principal members as of 31 December 1979 (Table 3.5). However, this listing does not depict the complex patterns of corporate linkages between these two groups; the Sumitomo Bank, for instance, is also a large shareholder of C. Itoh and a member of its board of directors, but none the less forms part of the corporate network of the Dai-Ichi Kangyo Bank group.[38]

Table 3.5
Principal Members of Japan's Six Major Industrial Groups at 31 December 1979

Mitsubishi group (Kinyo-kai: 28 companies)
Mitsubishi Bank, Mitsubishi Corp., Mitsubishi Heavy Industries, Mitsubishi Mining & Cement, Mitsubishi Chemical Industries, Mitsubishi Petrochemical, Mitsubishi Rayon, Mitsubishi Metal, Mitsubishi Estate and Mitsubishi Electric.
Sumitomo group (Hakusui-kai: 21 companies)
Sumitomo Bank, Sumitomo Metal Industries, Sumitomo Chemical, Sumitomo Corp., Nippon Electric, Sumitomo Electric Industries, Sumitomo Realty & Development, Sumitomo Coal Mining and Sumitomo Bakelite.
Mitsui group (Nimokukai: 23 companies)
Mitsui Bank, Mitsui & Co., Mitsui Real Estate Development, Mitsui Mining, Mitsui Toatsu Chemicals, Toray Industries, Oji Paper, Toyota Motor, Mitsui Construction and Toshiba.
Fuji Bank group (Fuyo-kai: 29 companies)
Fuji Bank, Marubeni, Nippon Kokan, Hitachi Ltd., Nissan Motor, Showa Denko, Kubota, Hodogaya Chemical, Oki Electric Industry and Toho Rayon.
Sanwa Bank group (Sanmoku-kai: 39 companies)
Sanwa Bank, Teijin, Nissho-Iwai, Kobe Steel, Hitachi Shipbuilding & Engineering, Ube Industries, Nichimen, Tokuyama Soda and Unitika.
Dai-Ichi Kangyo Bank group (Sankin-kai: 45 companies)
Dai-Ichi Kangyo Bank, C. Itoh & Co., Furukawa Electric, Fujitsu, Nippon Light Metal, Kawasaki Steel, Kawasaki Heavy Industries, Shiseido, Kanematsu-Gosho, Furukawa Co., Nissho-Iwai and Kobe Steel.

As with the pre-war *zaibatsus,* the grip of the giant 'cotton' traders (Itoh, Marubeni, Toyo Menka, Nichimen, Sumitomo) also ramifies into the textile industry. The percentages of imports handled by these and the four other largest *shoshas* are staggering: textiles, 70 per cent; wool, 95 per cent; and cotton, 75 per cent. Six of them embrace over two-thirds of textile wholesaling.[39]

An outstanding characteristic of the *sogo shoshas* is their control of one of the world's mightiest shipping fleets. Through their specialized fleets, they are positioned to obtain bulk discounts for high-volume shipping. Moreover, by guaranteeing return traffic to their group shipping firm, or to any other shipper, they can 'obtain favourable freight costs from transportation firms eager to fill their shipping capacity'.[40]

A distinctive trait of the general trading companies has been the build-up of a complex intelligence network. Modern communication systems permit the transmission of messages to the most distant points of the globe in a matter of seconds. In their speculative, hedging and other commodity practices, the trading giants monitor 'weather conditions in the main agricultural producing countries in the world and thereby anticipate future price trends for internationally traded agricultural commodities . . . Specialized trading companies in textiles, for example, provide information on international fashion trends to their clients . . .'[41]

An effective intelligence network thus operates in a manner that cannot be duplicated by individual manufacturers. Marubeni, one of the cotton giants, had daily telephone charges in 1977 amounting to $28,000, and telex communications soaring to 880 newspaper-sized pages daily; its total global communications costs were $27 million. Nor is this exceptional. 'Japan's unique business organizations, the nine leading general trading companies', writes *Business Japan,* 'all combined must spend far more than the CIA to support their communications network.'[42] Japanese oligopolistic capitalism has thus reached its definitive and ultimate phase of development.

In the Sogo Shosha's Shadow

Cast in the Japanese mould, conglomerate trading companies are arising in the UCE 'giant dwarfs', exemplified by Samsung Moolsan in South Korea and Pan Overseas in Taiwan. The Samsung group's 1979 revenues exceeded $3.4 billion and its export target for 1981 surpasses 8 per cent of South Korea's total exports. Borrowing its name and philosophy from the *sogo shosha,* Samsung's trading activities serve as a springboard for a wide range of manufacturing subsidiaries. Beginning with sugar refining in 1953, the company swiftly diversified into fertilizer, television, ship-building and heavy engineering. Until former Korean strong man Park Chung-Hee forced Samsung to divest itself of bank holdings, it held a controlling interest (70 per cent) in Korea's largest bank and 30-per-cent stakes in the second and third largest banks.[43] In the 1970s, the government designated Samsung as an 'integrated trading firm', granting it special privileges including tax breaks and preferential loans.[44] Today, the Korean state apparatus works intimately with Samsung, guiding its capital into industries deemed important for the 'national interest', for instance, aircraft and sophisticated weapons manufacture.

While borrowing from the Japanese model, Hong Kong's giant trading houses (or *hongs*) hark back to the roots of empire. Jardine Matheson (1979 sales: $1.2 billion), largest of five conglomerate *hongs*,[45] was set up in 1832 by the Scots, who profiteered in swapping opium for Chinese tea. Excluded from China in 1949, Jardine spread its traders throughout Europe, North America, Africa, the Middle East and the Pacific basin, dealing in multiple lines of raw commodities, consumer and industrial goods. Its 95 major subsidiaries range from sugar refineries to brokerage houses and shipping concerns. With the crumbling of the Cultural Revolution and China's proclamation of an 'open door policy' to foreign capitalists, Jardine has moved in massively to exploit joint ventures and the gains of general trading. At present, about one-fifth of its equity capital is controlled by the Keswick family of the United Kingdom.

Taiwan is the latest entrant into the arena of the giant trading company, with large-scale state assistance. Through a joint venture of 43 Taiwanese and overseas concerns, Pan Overseas was formed in the late 1970s to rationalize domestic trade in textiles, plastics and other products, and to serve as a trading weapon to break into the world market. It is aided by tax and customs breaks, interest-free loans, priority in bank credit, and regulation of competition within major trading areas.

However, the operations of the giant traders cannot be investigated in isolation, but rather must be seen in their relation to, and influence on, all aspects of the world cotton economy. The following sections trace in particular the intrusion of the traders into national marketing circuits around the globe.

The Institutions of Interaction

While the specific impact of the trading oligopoly differs between exporting countries, there are certain features common to all; both at the level of the individual producer of cotton and at that of the economy in general. At the first level, all farmers and peasants are confronted with a price structure fabricated by the oligopoly and other actors on the New York futures market. Not only does the oligopoly determine these prices, which are the foundations for contracts; its extensive intelligence networks command, at any moment, knowledge of prices in all spot markets for a large variety of commodities, some of which have a direct or indirect impact on cotton. In addition, these networks can transmit the latest intelligence on prices being incorporated into long-term contracts at various points on the globe. Clearly neither farmers, *latifundistas,* nor African marketing boards command even a fraction of this intelligence power. The result is a highly unequal relationship which lends itself ideally to exploitative practices.

Even so, there is often an intimate working rapport between certain members of UCE oligarchies and the agents of the trading giants, which can be highly profitable to the oligarchies, but is always harmful to the peasantry and landless labourers.

On the macro-economic level, the oligopoly's practices can also be detrimental to the development plans of UCEs which depend on cotton for a high percentage of export earnings. First, inasmuch as the oligopoly contributes to wide and unpredictable price swings, it renders medium- and long-term resource allocation almost impossible. Second, in many cases, the pressing need for foreign exchange, frequently combined with inadequate warehousing facilities, compels several UCEs to sell their crops immediately after harvesting even if world prices are extremely low. For the giant traders, many with extensive warehouses, no such constraints exist. The following examples describe the various marketing institutions in the leading cotton-exporting countries with which the oligopoly deals.

Cotton Marketing Boards
Originally, agricultural marketing boards were devised by colonial governments in the 1930s and 1940s, to ensure a stable supply of raw materials for manufacturing industry in the metropolitan economies. The marketing board was the joint creation of the corporate boardroom and the colonial office, transplanted to the Gold Coast (Ghana) in 1937. In an attempt to pacify small cocoa farmers who had refused to sell to TNCs (Cadburys and United Africa Company, a subsidiary of Unilever) until they obtained higher prices, the British colonial government set up the West African Cocoa Control Board to purchase directly from cocoa farmers. John Cadbury of Cadbury Brothers was appointed Chairman of the Board. Certain historians, however, have questioned the extent of the gains to the peasant farmer, especially during the pre-Independence period: 'None of the benefits went to Africans', noted Walter Rodney, 'but rather to the British government itself and to the private companies, which were used as intermediaries in the buying and selling of the produce. Big companies like the UAC and John Holt were given quotas to fulfill on behalf of the Boards. As agents of the government, they were no longer exposed to direct attack, and their profits were secure.'[46]

Since that time, cotton marketing boards have been established in several of the major producing and exporting countries, including Egypt, Sudan, Chad, Pakistan, Syria, and India, which together account for over 15 per cent of world exports. Marketing boards have been defined as producer organizations which market commodities ostensibly for the gains of farmers or peasants who have insufficient technical and capital resources to market their commodity themselves. However, it should be underlined that colonial and post-colonial governments have used marketing boards as an effective device for taxing farmers and peasants and for boosting internal revenue. Another of their functions is to stabilize producer prices and incomes by buying from the farmer at pre-arranged prices. The boards have not infringed the principle of private property, since they have not altered the exploitative relationships between landlords, tenants and landless labourers. After purchase, the boards sell the commodity on the domestic or international markets.[47] The fact that as a major stabilization measure, marketing boards are not a substitute for a restructuring of social relations in agriculture was noted in an early United

Nations report: 'Whatever the degree of success enjoyed by these domestic policies they have served only as a buffer between the external market and, in the first instance, the export sector of the domestic economy; in no way was the basic solution of the commodity problem advanced'.[48]

The following four short case studies illustrate the marketing mechanisms of marketing boards in their national contexts: Egypt, Sudan, Chad and Pakistan.

(1) Egypt, the world's fourth largest exporter, nationalized its cotton industry in 1961 and entrusted a marketing board with fixing domestic and export prices as well as the level of subsidies to growers. This involved the take-over of the six major private domestic trading companies, who now act as autonomous, but affiliated companies.[49] The marketing of raw cotton is entirely state-controlled and farmers sell solely to the marketing board (the Egyptian Cotton Authority), which then gins, presses, bales and markets the crop. Export prices are determined by the Ministry of Commerce in concert with the six trading firms (whose former owners continue in a managerial capacity) and other selected members of the business community.

Once a major supplier to the USSR and Eastern Europe, Egypt is now diverting a bigger slice of its exports away from trade agreements into the cash markets of Asia (mainly Japan) and Western Europe. These cash market deals are transacted between the Egyptian big six and several of the multi-commodity trading giants. One feature of synchronized trading that nationalization has not impaired is the intimate business contacts forged between certain giant traders and individual Egyptian firms.

(2) Despite massive diversification, cotton still remains the life-blood of Sudan's external sector. Grown mainly between the two Niles in the Gezira strip, cotton arose in response to the raw material requirements of British imperialism, specifically the cotton textile industry. Gezira, an irrigated farming project started in 1925, now spreads over two million acres farmed by 100,000 tenants. To this has now been added the Rahad irrigation project, which upon completion in the eighties will draw into cultivation over 300,000 acres, primarily in cotton and groundnuts. At present, the central marketing organization for Sudanese cotton is the Cotton Public Corporation (CPC). The CPC, like its Egyptian counterpart, markets its cotton through four former private export companies which have been nationalized.[50] Once again, each company enjoys a large autonomy based on its separate and specialized contacts with the giant traders.[51] Almost all cotton is sold on a forward basis with prices adjusted from New York Cotton Exchange quotations.

(3) Chad exhibits the extreme of cotton export monoculture in the world cotton economy, again created in response to the demands of the former colonial power and its textile interests in France. Cotonchad deviates somewhat from the prototype of the public sector marketing board in that only 75 per cent of shares are held by the Chadian public sector. Of the remainder, 17 per cent is controlled by the Compagnie Francaise de Developpement des Textiles, 3 per cent by the Caisse Centrale de Cooperation Economique

(a French corporate body), and 5 per cent by private Chadian banking interests. All export sales go through Cotonchad's Paris office, which is largely French-staffed, and cotton is transported on a cash basis (in dollars) through giant traders, mainly Ralli and Volkart. It is a part of Cotonchad's normal marketing policy to make pre-harvest sales, often more than a year in advance, with the New York futures market playing a central role in price determination.

(4) A recent entrant into the ranks of public sector marketing boards is the Cotton Export Corporation (CEC) of Pakistan, founded in 1973. It sets export prices in conjunction with the Ministry of Commerce based on the principle of the adjustment mechanism already delineated. About 90 per cent of the nation's cotton is sold through bilateral trade agreements, mainly to India, Bangladesh, Hong Kong, China, Indonesia, and the Philippines. This and the remainder sold on international markets is handled primarily by Ralli, Volkart and Nichimen.

Socialist State Trading Organizations

The USSR has become the world's largest cotton exporter, and is the only CPE that sells cotton on the world market to a significant extent. Exportljon is the exclusive state trading arm of Soviet cotton exports.[52] Roughly half its exports are to other CPEs through bilateral trade agreements signed in Moscow which bypass the giant multi-commodity traders.

The remainder of Soviet exports are sold on the international market, mainly to Japan, Western Europe and South-east Asia. As much as 90 per cent of this trade is dominated by the giant traders, mainly Volkart, Ralli, Bunge, Bambax, Blanchard and certain Japanese *sogo shoshas*. The other 10 per cent is funnelled to large individual textile corporations, e.g. Courtaulds in Britain, Dominion Textiles in Canada, and Dierig AG in West Germany. The bulk of trade with Japan has been carried out through exchange deals for textiles, man-made fibres and machinery. Because cotton is traded at 5–10 per cent below world prices, Japanese traders like Marubeni and Itoh are in a position to re-sell unrequired balances at high profit margins. Another mechanism by which giant traders have boosted their profit margins has been the purchase of Soviet cotton from Eastern European countries at very low prices when their national inventories exceed mill requirements. Giant traders have also been able to escalate their profit margins on the basis of Soviet pricing policy. While Exportljon follows the New York futures prices as well as the Liverpool index, their price adjustments often trail behind these world indicators by three or four days. As a result of these time lags, giant traders are able to use arbitrage techniques to increase their profit margins on Soviet cotton transactions.

National Agriculture and Commerce Departments

Sixty to sixty-five per cent of world cotton exports emanate from countries in which national agriculture and commerce departments are the major channels of cotton marketing. In some cases this means deliberate intervention ranging from the setting of minimum prices to actual buying and selling of the commodity, and this in a set of countries whose overall economic and farm policies are erroneously designated as 'free enterprise'.

The United States is one of the world's top exporters, although its share has shrunk markedly over the last two or three decades. Throughout the postwar period, the bulk of US cotton exports was marketed by a coterie of giant traders, heavily bolstered by AID, Public Law 480 (*'Food for Peace'*) and Commodity Credit Corporation (CCC) finance. Indeed, from the onset of the Marshall Plan, giant traders have been amongst the greatest beneficiaries of US government programmes which were ostensibly designed to aid US farmers. At present, three giant co-operatives export approximately 25 per cent, and the giant traders the remainder. The largest exporters include Calcot,[53] Plains Cotton Co-operative,[54] Allenberg, W.B. Dunavant, Cargill, McFadden, Molsen, Volkart, and Weil. It should be noted that several of these giant traders do business in export markets under different trade names as well as their own, principally in order to seek wider outlets by displaying the semblance of choice to buyers. Another reason for using multiple trade names derives from a marketing policy which aims at retaining consumers loyal to brand names of companies absorbed by the giant traders.

Mexico is the second largest raw cotton exporter in the western hemisphere. Forward contracting (3–4 months) accounts for the bulk of Mexican exports. Japan, the nation's largest cotton importer, buys Mexican cotton exclusively through the giant Japanese traders whose bulk purchases yield them discounts below international prices.[55] Although the auction system is often used in the sale of cotton, certain giant traders have been reported to bid collusively. Ralli and Volkart play an important role, not only in the international market, but also in selling domestically to the Mexican textile industry. In addition, many of the giant traders including Volkart, Cargill, McFadden, Anderson Clayton,[56] Esteve, Nichimen, and Itoh have now integrated backwards into ginning plants.

Brazil, as with Egypt and Mexico, is switching from raw cotton exports toward higher stages of domestic processing.[57] Five firms account for about 70 per cent of cotton exports from Sao Paulo, of which four trading giants are dominant: Sanbra (a subsidiary of Bunge & Born), McFadden, Volkart, and Esteve. Three of them have their own extensive ginning operations.[58] From a wider perspective, ten firms have annexed almost 90 per cent of Brazil's exports: 60 per cent are in the hands of the giant traders, and 30 per cent are handled by firms which are apparently national.[59] However, even these national companies are often largely owned and controlled by the big traders, although precise breakdowns are unavailable.

The giant trading conglomerates which have been the centrepiece of this chapter constitute a unique oligopoly. As against the industrial oligopolies dissected in subsequent chapters, their pricing and marketing policies do not assume the guise of price leadership and posted prices. It is for this reason that the study of several different economic sectors in the global economy provides an insight into the varied manifestations that oligopoly has assumed in 20th Century capitalism.

References

1. This applies not only to the trade between market economies (developed and underdeveloped) but also to trade between centrally planned economies and market economies. It excludes, however, trade between CPEs and trade consummated through bilateral deals. The 1973 shipment of US cotton to the People's Republic of China is an example of the intermediation of the giant traders in this field. China's purchase of approximately 400,000 bales of Texas and Oklahoma cotton with an estimated value of $70–80 million was arranged by Ralli Bros. To meet the commitment, Ralli bought cotton from the Plains Cotton Cooperative at an estimated 35–40 cents per pound; cf. *Business Week,* 10 February 1973. This transaction involved three basic mark-ups by the principal actors: farmers, the cooperative and Ralli. The sizes of the mark-ups, as well as Ralli's final price to China, are unknown to the authors. However, assuming that Ralli's mark-up on this deal was 1 per cent per lb, their return would have been of the order of $2 million.
2. These are Universal Leaf Tobacco Co., Transcontinental Leaf Tobacco Co., Debrill Bros, Export Leaf Tobacco Co. (a BAT subsidiary), Imperial Tobacco Leaf, and Kulenkampff and A.C. Monk. See UNCTAD, *The Marketing and Distribution of Tobacco* (TD/B/C.1/205, Geneva, 1978).
3. These are United Brands, Standard Fruit and Del Monte. See UNCTAD, *The Marketing and Distribution System for Bananas* (TD/B/C.1/162), Geneva, 1974.
4. These include Gill and Duffus, A.C. Israel, General Cocoa, J.H. Rayner and CONTINEF. See T.A. Kofi, 'MNC control of distributive channels: a study of cocoa marketing', *Stanford Journal of International Studies,* Spring 1976.
5. The date of the repeal of the Corn Laws in England and the advent of free trade.
6. A.D. Chandler, *The Visible Hand: The Managerial Revolution in American Business,* (London, 1977), p. 214.
7. From the domestically oriented small merchant houses that controlled much of international cotton trade up to the mid-sixties sprang another link in the cotton marketing chain – the broker. Spinners relied heavily on the advice of brokers, who received a one per cent commission on cotton for sifting through the conflicting views of the many raw cotton salesmen. Present concentration and mergers among the giant traders has been paralleled by the amalgamation of many mills that now deal directly with traders through their own purchasing offices.
8. Another deceptive aspect of these indicators is that it is useless to measure whether commodities trading is barely, reasonably or unreasonably profitable unless one knows the company's actual rate of return on invested capital. For example, US supermarket chains also claim that their sales margins are less than 2 per cent, often less than 1 per cent, and therefore that they are enormously efficient in moving produce from processor to consumer. In fact, though sales margins are

low, turnover is high, and each year supermarket chains report profits on capital as high as 16—23 per cent. In other words, the 1 or 2 per cent margin is utterly meaningless in the absence of comprehensive financial accounting including detailed information on investments of the giant traders.

9. UNCTAD, *Impact of the Fluctuations of Cotton Prices on the Profitability of the Mexican Cotton Industry* (TD/B/IPC/COTTON/L.3/Add. 1) Geneva, 1979, p. 3.

10. Another example of the close links was demonstrated in 1974—75 when Ralli Bros collaborated with private British and Kuwaiti banks developing a financing scheme to stock Sudanese cotton.

11. Union Bank of Switzerland, *Annual Report,* 1978, p. 36. The membership of the Board gives us an insight into the interplay of finance, industrial and trading capital. Board directors include, among others, executives of Sandoz, Hoffman-La Roche, Saurer, Ciba-Geigy, Sulzer, Rieter and Andre. The confluence of the representatives of big capital on the boards of the big banks has far-flung implications, as expressed by a senior executive of the Dresdner Bank: 'It is banks who are in the best position to decide the question of mergers', i.e. the pace and direction of capital concentration. See *Business Week,* 19 April 1976.

12. As an instrument of international cotton sales, the auction system is currently limited to a few exporting nations, notably Uganda and Tanzania, with small amounts auctioned in Mexico as well.

13. A recent MITI investigative report uncovers another way corporations work in concert. According to the report, six of Japan's largest trading firms, having available large liquid funds as of September 1972 and in anticipation of swings in foreign exchange markets, bought very large quantities of cotton, as well as wool, silk, soybeans, lumber, land and securities, in purely speculative deals. MITI concludes that such moves contributed to the rise in prices of cotton and other basic commodities. Cf. USDA, Foreign Agriculture Service, *Developments in the Japanese Textile Industry,* (Washington, DC, May 1975), p.8.

14. This is similar to the pharmaceutical industry, which is dominated by 50—60 firms, but where in any national market 3—4 firms usually account for the vast majority of sales for any given product. See UNCTAD, *Major Issues in Transfer of Technology to Developing Countries: A Case Study of the Pharmaceutical Industry* (TD/B/C.6/4), Geneva, 1975.

15. For a comprehensive account of the big five international grain companies (Cargill, Continental, Louis Dreyfus, Bunge, and Andre), all of which are massive conglomerates, see Dan Morgan, *Merchants of Grain* (New York, 1979), pp. 171—2.

16. B. Tamarkin, 'What-and-who-makes Cargill so powerful?', *Forbes,* 18 September 1978.

17. *Business Week,* 16 April 1979.

18. Morgan, p. 204.

19. *Ibid.,* p. ix.

20. *Ibid.,* p. 222.

21. *Milling and Baking News,* 28 November 1978, p. 29.

22. Morgan, pp. 161—5.

23. Nothing reveals the connexions of big capital — its blood and bones —

more than the profile of the Mitsubishi family in the inter-war years. *'Baron Hisaya Iwasaki* is the head of the Iwasaki family and hence of the Mitsubishi combine . . . A prominent personage in the Mitsui combine is *Seihin Ikeda;* the latter has been managing director of the Mitsui Bank, Governor of the Bank of Japan, Finance Minister, member of the House of Peers, member of the Privy Council, Chairman of the Board of Directors of Mitsui Gomei, formerly the top holding organization of the Mitsui Combine. His daughter, *Toshikio,* is the wife of Takaya Iwasaki. Baron Hisaya Iwasaki's sister, *Masako*, married *Kijuro Shidehara*, the present Prime Minister of Japan. A niece of Baron Hisaya Iwasaki, *Tokiko Kiuchi*, married Viscount *Keizo Shibusawa*. He is head of the Shibusawa family and has been Chairman of the Board of Directors of the Tokyo Savings Bank, President of the Dai Ichi Bank, President of the Finance Control Association, Governor of the Bank of Japan, member of the House of Peers, Minister of Commerce and Industry, Chief of the Wartime Economic Bureau, member of the Wartime Commodity Price Investigation Council. He is at present the Minister of Finance.' The report, known as the US Zaibatsu Mission, continues for another two paragraphs to detail the connexions of the Iwasaki family with the representatives of Japanese corporate capital and the prevailing political personalities in Japan; *Report of the Mission on Japanese Combines* (Washington, DC, 1943), pp. 16—20.

24. Important protagonists of big business, such as Senator Adlai E. Stevenson, have called into question the utility of present anti-trust laws in view of the intensified struggle for world markets. He advocated diluting the laws, arguing, 'if it's necessary to permit us to compete on an equal basis with our competitors, and if that's what's necessary I offhand don't know why Congress wouldn't be happy to go along'. United States, Senate, *Export Policy: Hearing before the Subcommittee on International Finance of the Committee on Banking, Housing and Urban Affairs* (95th Congress, 2nd Session, 9 March 1978, p. 18). Stemming from huge trade deficits in the US balance of payments throughout most of the 1970s, the erosion of the dollar as an international unit of value, the loss of global markets, job losses in import-competing industries, a decelerated rate of job increase in the export sector, and sustained inflationary rates have combined to inspire certain segments of the US ruling class to advocate emulation of the *sogo shoshas*. See also United States Senate, *U.S. Export Policy: A Report to the Committee on Banking, Housing and Urban Affairs,* 96th Congress, 1st session, February 1979.

25. Excerpted from a 1978 Mitsubishi advertisement.

26. John G. Roberts, *Mitsui: Three Centuries of Japanese Business* (New York, 1974), p. 491.

27. *Ibid.*

28. Chitoshi Yanaga, *Big Business in Japanese Politics* (New Haven 1968), p. 3.

29. *Ibid.*, p. 26.

30. The incredible conglomerate web of Mitsui is revealed in the number of different industries it controlled which take up an entire page of *Report of the U.S. Mission on Japanese Combines,* pp. 5—6.

31. *Ibid.*, p. vii. In the words of Barrington Moore, 'Japanese big business successfully resisted attempts to subordinate profits to patriotism. The whole period of military hegemony and fascism was very favourable to business' *Social Origins of Dictatorship and Democracy* (London, 1966), p. 301. For details see also J.B. Cohen, *Japan's Economy in War and Reconstruction* (Minneapolis, 1949). These changes were of course not taking place without vigorous class confrontations; see R.A. Scalapino, *Democracy and the Party Movement in Prewar Japan* (Berkeley, 1953).

32. By 1909, 87 per cent of Japan's 1.8 million spindles had been supplied by Platt. See Gary Saxonhouse, 'Country Girls and Communication among Competitors in the Japanese Cotton-Spinning Industry', in Hugh Patrick (ed.), *Japanese Industrialization and its Social Consequences* (Berkeley, 1976), p. 116.

33. Kozo Yamamura, 'General Trading Companies in Japan – Their Origins and Growth', in *Ibid.*, pp. 174–5.

34. *Report of the U.S. Mission*, p. 67.

35. 'Business links to fight controls', *Far Eastern Economic Review*, March 1975, quoted in Max Eli *et al*, *Sogo Shosha: Strukturen und Strategien japanischer Welthandelsunternehmungen* (Hamburg, 1977), p. 270. See also E.M. Hadley, *Antitrust in Japan* (Princeton, 1970); Fair Trade Commission, *Report on the Investigation of General Trading Companies* (Tokyo, 1974).

36. See the testimony of E.J. Frank, in United States, Senate, *Export Policy* ... p. 95.

37. More recently, Itoh has absorbed the former tenth largest Japanese trader, Ataka, a giant in chemical, iron and steel industries. Itoh's President justified the merger on the grounds that 'we have been co-operating with them in improving their operations in the belief that the maintenance of Ataka's credibility both in Japan and abroad would help bolster the footing of all Japanese trading companies in the international business community', *Annual Report*, 1977.

38. *The Industrial Review of Japan 1980* (Tokyo, 1980).

39. Such control permeates all aspects of marketing and distribution so 'that none of the 30 largest retail corporations in Japan is any longer free of the influence of the General Trading Companies' (Max Eli *et al.*, p. 626).

40. Yoshi Tsurumi and Rebecca Tsurumi, *Sogoshosha; Engines of Export-Based Growth* (Montreal, 1980), p. 13.

41. Japan External Trade Organisation (JETRO), *The Role of the Trading Companies in International Commerce* (Tokyo, 1976), pp. 11, 14.

42. *Business Japan*, November 1978.

43. *Financial Times*, 1 November 1978. Following the bank divestiture, Samsung bought massively into insurance companies.

44. *Korean Herald*, 20 May 1975.

45. *Business Week*, 21 May 1979. The other four are Hutchison Whampao, the Swire Group, East Asiatic Co., and Wheelock Marden.

46. W. Rodney, *How Europe Underdeveloped Africa* (Dar es Salaam, 1972).

47. See Tetteh A. Kofi, 'M.N.C. control of distributive channels: a study of cocoa marketing', *Stanford Journal of International Studies,* Spring,

1976.
48. United Nations, *World Economic Survey* (New York, 1958), p. 111.
49. The big six were the Societe Misr pour l'Exportation du Coton (a trading arm of the Misr cotton and textile empire); Alcotan Cotton Trading and Export Co.; Port Said Cotton Export Co.; Al Kahira Cotton Co.; Eastern Cotton Co.; and Alexandria Commercial Co.
50. Prior to nationalization, there were 16 export companies, whittled down through competitive pressures to the present four: National Cotton and Trade Co., Alaktan Trading Co., Port Sudan Cotton and Trade Co., and Sudan Cotton Co.
51. Although the giant traders brand all their bales, all Sudanese cotton exports carry the Sudan cotton label.
52. 'The Exportljon All-Union Export-Import Association shall be established to carry out operations relating to the export and import of flax, hemp, jute, cotton and wool and their by-products, as well as all kinds of products manufactured from these by-products and all kinds of other goods'; quoted from *Annex to Order No. 265 of the Ministry of Foreign Trade of the USSR*, June 1948.
53. This co-operative handles about half the cotton produced in California, Arizona and Nevada, and exports about one million bales globally each year. Its significant new outlets are Eastern Europe and China.
54. Represents about 20,000 farmers, mainly in Texas and Oklahoma.
55. All cotton imports into Japan are handled by the Japanese trading giants; the spinning mills then buying directly from them. Individual trading firms and spinning mills may, in certain cases, be part of the same large conglomerate. Some trading companies also own subsidiary spinning mills in exporting countries and import yarn, fabric, or made-up articles as well as raw cotton.
56. Anderson Clayton's role in Mexican agriculture has altered significantly in the last decade. In the 1950s, it led all others in cotton marketing, both internal and external. It contracted with growers for their cotton and seed, ensuring availability and quality by providing all necessary materials and assistance: inputs, ginning, financial and technical services, etc. Other international companies now operate in the same manner and have far superseded Anderson Clayton, who now only market around 1 per cent of the total crop. Significant of the changing pattern of corporate structures of the giant trading companies is Anderson Clayton's diversification policy since the mid-1960s. Acquisition of Api-Aba, a mixed venture of American-Mexican capital, gave them access to the animal feed market. They have rapidly augmented their markets in Mexico in this activity, approaching the leader, Purina. Equally important, they are Mexico's market leaders in the highly competitive edible oil and margarine market, as well as in convenience foods, especially pre-prepared flour.
57. Brazil now consumes more cotton in its own mills than any other country except China, the USSR, USA, India, Japan and Pakistan.
58. One of the four manufacturers of cotton ginning machinery in the USA has recently begun operations in Brazil, and is not only supplying the Brazilian market, but is in the exporting business as well.
59. Bolsa de Mercadorias de Sao Paulo. *Relatorio da Directoria Contas,*

Documentos e Parecer da Commissao Fiscal, Assembleia Geral Ordinaria, Sao Paulo, 1976.

4. The Futures Market

Born on 12 September 1870, in the wake of the Union's triumph, the New York Cotton Exchange[1] was the creation *par excellence* of the American bourgeoisie or, more specifically, its trading and financial arm. It was created in response to the demands of the burgeoning world cotton and textile industry. It has now become one of the major institutional determinants of world cotton prices. Recently, allegations of price manipulation, tax evasion, and actions resulting in excessive price fluctuations have been launched against large traders on the futures market. To understand these allegations (which hark back to the Exchange's foundations) and their wider policy implications, an analytical review of futures trading is essential.

The alleged free play of 'market forces' of supply and demand has been severely abridged by the mechanisms of the futures markets and the power relationships between large and small traders in these markets. To focus analysis on the futures markets exclusively in terms of the 'laws of supply and and demand', as has traditionally been done, is to mistake the semblance of movement for movement itself. In essence, as distinct from appearance, the market is subject to the compulsive logic of larger economic units which have outgrown, and indeed are anathema to, the principle of competition between relatively small units characteristic of an earlier epoch.

Traders within the oligopoly engage in widespread and highly profitable speculation, and by controlling a very large volume of futures contracts during delivery months, they can manipulate prices to their advantage. These price manipulations are embodied in price-destabilizing 'long and short squeezes'. Speculators, for their part, heighten and deepen the peaks and troughs in cotton futures prices, and are an integral determinant of cotton price formation. Inherently unstable price quotations from the New York Cotton Exchange, disseminated globally, then act as the barometer for cotton prices in producing countries. While ostensibly operating within a framework of supply and demand, a numerically small complex of giant multi-commodity traders shapes both the contours of global cotton marketing and the pattern of price formation. The producing countries of the underdeveloped and centrally planned economies have historically been cast into a minor role in both domains, and will remain there as long as the existing institutional structures prevail.

Mechanics of the Futures Market

There are three facets crucial to the understanding of futures transactions: futures trading, futures contracts and futures markets. Futures trading in an organized commodity exchange consists of the sale and purchase of a commodity by means of uniform futures contracts. The futures contract is an agreement to buy and receive — or to sell and deliver — a stated quantity[2] of a commodity, at a definite date, at a specified price.

Only a small proportion of futures contracts, however, are settled by the actual delivery of the commodity. Hence futures markets are often referred to as paper markets, since it is possible to deal in futures contracts without ever actually seeing the physical commodity. The futures market provides a central marketplace where actual and potential commodity buyers and sellers make bids and offers for contracts covering delivery in designated later months. Each delivery month in which trading takes place is referred to as a future.[3]

The two major participants in futures transactions are hedgers and speculators and their activities are institutionally enmeshed. The rationale of hedging springs from the price uncertainties endemic in all stages of production and marketing due to the vagaries of nature, wars, economic crises, and so on. *Hedging* is essentially defined as the buying/selling of futures contracts when these transactions are offset, in terms of quantity, by the sales/purchase or ownership of the same cash commodity. *Speculation,* whose practitioners are often also hedgers in other transactions, is motivated by the opportunity to exploit price swings on commodity exchanges for positive gain rather than avoidance of loss as in the basic hedging operation. By definition, speculation is all non-hedging trading activity; speculators do not co-ordinate their buying and selling of futures contracts with actual commodity transactions. Thus, while the same trader can hedge at one time and speculate at another, each specific contract is either a speculation or a hedge. It cannot be both.

The mechanics of futures trading can be illuminated by tracing an actor's movement on the New York Cotton Exchange from initial contract purchase to final sale. The following example of a cotton farmer participating on the exchange is typical of traders who deal in futures in conjunction with their sales of cotton. The same principles also apply to cotton buyers, but in reverse, since their need is to cover real future purchases with hedging long futures contracts.

Let us take the example of a cotton farmer whose annual crop averages 500 bales. In May 1978, after planting his cotton, he decides to hedge 100 per cent of his anticipated crop. He calls a commodity broker, asking him to sell five contracts (of 100 bales each) that will mature in his harvest month, October 1978.

The farmer reads the commodity price listings and sees that on 15 May, when he calls the broker, October futures are priced at 59.80 cents per pound. On 16 May the broker enters the trading ring at the New York Cotton

Exchange and through a series of bids and offers with other traders buys five short contracts at 60 cents/lb.

The farmer immediately pays the broker a commission of $30 as well as $12,000 – an 8-per-cent margin deposit on the five contracts valued at $150,000. The contracts oblige the farmer to deliver 500 bales of cotton to a warehouse in his locality any day during the month of October. He will receive 60 cents/lb. for his cotton upon delivery, but must pay transport costs to the warehouse as well as inspection costs.

The farmer has two options when October arrives: delivery of cotton as prescribed in the contract or offsetting his contracts. As already mentioned, only about 1 per cent of cotton futures contracts are settled by delivery. This farmer decides instead to repudiate his obligation for delivery by instructing his broker to buy five offsetting October long contracts before the delivery date arrives. Now let us imagine further that the October futures price quotation has risen to 65 cents/lb. and that his local spot market price has similarly risen to 65 cents per pound.

The farmer brings his cotton to the spot market and sells it at 65 cents/lb., representing a 5 cent/lb gain over the 60 cents/lb. he expected during May planting. His broker then buys the offsetting five long contracts at 65 cents/lb, representing a 5-cent/lb loss from the short contracts bought at 60 cents/lb five months earlier. The broker's acquisition of offsetting long contracts completely erases the farmer's former obligation to deliver cotton.

It may seem difficult to conceptualize how the farmer can sell something on the futures market in May that does not yet exist. His initial future sale (in the form of buying short contracts) is made possible since delivery is not due for five months. He is merely selling first and either delivering or buying later to cover the sale. In terms of cash transfers, the broker waits until October, when he calculates the sales price versus the purchase price, and in the above case demands 5 cents/lb. – or $12,500 from the farmer. In this instance the broker will keep the $12,000 margin deposit and demand $500 more from the farmer.[4]

Since futures and spot prices were both at 65 cents/lb., the farmer's gains on the spot market were equally offset by his losses on the futures market (minus the cost of the broker's commission). Hedging does not always provide such exact insurance. If the spot price is a trifle higher than the futures price at the delivery date, the farmer will gain. However, if the futures price is a bit higher, as it is after a successful 'long squeeze', then the farmer will lose.[5]

At present, the New York Cotton Exchange is one of more than forty commodity futures exchanges operating in the United States. In the fiscal year 1975–6 alone, the value of contracts traded on these exchanges outstripped $670 billion, with close to $25 billion traded in cotton futures (see Table 4.1). By 1978, this figure had jumped to $1.5 trillion, with Arab petrodollars and European capital playing an influential role.[6] For each of these 40-odd commodities there is a parallel market in which transactions in the actual commodity occur. These markets are referred to as spot, cash, or 'actuals' markets, and trading is not centralized in a specific marketplace. The tremendous upsurge from $9 billion in cotton contracts traded in 1974—75 to $24 billion in 1975—76 is a clear manifestation of the capacity of multi-commodity traders — as well as big speculators — to shift their massive resources rapidly from other commodity operations to cotton. Conversely, they are also capable of shifting just as quickly out of cotton. Hence, the multitude of commodity exchanges serves as insurance to the large multi-commodity conglomerate traders who are thereby shielded from the buffetings of price fluctuations.

Spot and Futures Markets

Two major differences exist between trading in futures markets and trading in spot markets. First, transactions on a futures market are limited to a small paying broker membership of the exchange, which includes representatives of the large traders often concealed under a different name. Mitsubishi, for example, hedges and speculates on the London Metal Exchange through its subsidiary Triland Metals Ltd., organized in the company's Copper Metal and Ore Department. In turn, this subsidiary dovetails its operations with its counterparts on other major futures exchanges, a practice common to all of the big traders. Second, spot market contracts can be designed to meet the specifications of buyers and sellers regarding quantity, location, and time of delivery, whereas futures contracts are more conventionalized in these respects.

While spot prices are important in international trade, most cotton is traded through contracts which specify a predetermined price and month for future delivery. Relatively short-term contracts (three to twelve months)[7] are predominant in international cotton trade, the balance being traded on a spot basis or through longer term contracts covering one to two years. Relative shares traded on a spot and forward contract basis vary from year to year depending on prevailing prices, price expectations and changes in supply and demand.[8] The New York Cotton Exchange's role in forward contracting is central. Sellers, be they plantation owners, marketing boards, or national export companies, sit down with trading giant representatives with only one international indicator for determining what cotton prices are expected to be three, six or nine months hence — the New York Cotton Exchange quotations. Final contract price terms are adjusted from these quotations on the basis of volume traded, quality and staple length, location of crop, season of delivery and relative bargaining strengths of seller and trading company.

Price quotations generated by the interplay of buying and selling on the futures market are instantaneously disseminated worldwide by highly sophisticated communications media. These quotations are picked up by designated spot markets throughout the US Cotton Belt, by national cotton marketing boards and by cotton spot markets globally, who then adjust their

Table 4.1
United States: Total Futures Trading, by Commodity[1]

		Volume of Trading (000 contracts)		Value of Trading ($ million)	
	Contract Unit	*1975/76*	*1974/75*	*1975/76*	*1974/75*
Soybeans	5,000 bu.	4,601.3	3,135.7	133,568.9	102,231.5
Silver	5,000 Troy oz.	5,373.6	3,450.6	125,810.4	82,061.0
Corn	5,000 bu.	4,841.7	4,859.5	77,754.1	79,325.7
Wheat	5,000 bu.	3,959.9	2,873.8	76,319.4	60,249.2
Cattle		2,694.8	2,293.8	45,322.8	36,619.0
Frozen pork bellies	36,000 lbs.	1,325.4	1,097.9	35,755.7	27,659.9
Cotton	100 bales	801.5	416.9	24,445.0	9,395.6
Live hogs		1,619.7	1,183.2	22,786.4	14,791.1
Soybean oil	60,000 lbs.	1,487.5	1,436.3	19,617.0	29,273.7
Soybean meal	100 tons.	1,071.3	824.2	16,974.1	12,031.5
Sugar	112,000 lbs.	888.1	784.7	16,737.9	26,643.2
Copper	25,000 lbs.	942.4	313.2	15,562.9	4,973.7
Gold	100 Troy oz.	837.0	367.8	12,242.8	6,834.4
Foreign currencies[2]		202.4	232.0	11,065.7	19,153.3
GNMA mortgages	$100,000 prin bal.	72.2	–	6,834.2	–
Cocoa	30,000 lbs.	316.5	285.2	6,159.6	6,866.6
Coffee	37,500 lbs.	119.4	76.0	4,727.9	1,660.9
Potatoes	50,000 lbs.	823.0	669.0	4,660.7	1,414.3
Lumber and studs	100,000 Bd. ft.	294.9	249.2	4,651.1	3,395.5
Treasury bills	$1,000,000 FCE Val.	36.5	–	3,423.2	–
Plywood	76,032 sq. ft.	239.0	338.9	2,547.3	2,541.8
Iced broilers	28,000 lbs.	183.9	208.1	2,222.7	2,044.4
Petroleum	5,000 lbs	25.2	30.2	1,460.0	1,592.0
Eggs	22,500 doz.	120.1	255.2	1,430.0	2,891.1
Silver coins	$ 10,000	43.0	113.0	1,360.6	3,709.6
Oats	5,000 bu.	202.1	180.2	1,079.7	1,518.0
Platinum	50 Troy oz.	103.4	149.3	761.2	1,346.8
Frozen juice	15,000 lbs.	74.3	76.4	563.0	595.3
Propane	100,000 gal.	3.2	6.8	86.0	173.0
Frozen boneless beef	36,000 lbs.	2.9	4.2	62.7	75.5
Coconut oil	36,000 lbs.	3.5	6.8	47.7	125.3
Palm oil	36,000 lbs	1.6	1.2	20.9	14.8
Palladium	100 Troy oz.	3.9	.9	19.0	17.8
Rubber	33,000 lbs.	1.7	3.0	18.5	156.0
Wool	6,000 lbs.	.7	1.4	5.5	10.7
Grain sorghums	400,000 lbs.	.3	1.3	4.8	26.6
Butter	38,000 lbs	3	0	0.6	0
Industrial fuel oil	38,000 lbs.	.1	3	0.5	0.1
Eggs	36,000 lbs.	0	3	0	4
Turkeys	36,000 lbs.	0	3	0	0.1
Heating oil	100 metric tons	3	3	4	0.1
Total		*33,318.0*	*25,925.9*	*676,110.5*	*544,419.1*

1. Volume and value figures were taken from the Association of Commodity Exchange Firm, Inc.
2. Contract units for individual currencies were used.
3. Less than 50 contracts.   4. Less than $50,000.

Source: Commodity Futures Trading Commission, *Annual Report, 1976*, (Washington, DC, 1977).

spot prices for different grades, specifications and qualities of cotton.

The result of this adjustment process is a national spot price, which becomes the base line for mark-ups or mark-downs depending, once again, on the volume of individual sales as well as the relative bargaining power of the marketing board *vis-a-vis* the buyer. In this respect, the New York futures price serves a similar role to the oligopolistically determined posted price of synthetic fibres. In both cases, sales are based on mark-ups or mark-downs from a declared price, with greater volumes generating bigger discounts.

Spot prices for standard cotton can never appreciably deviate from the futures price near delivery dates, since this is the period when futures contract holders make or demand actual delivery of cotton to fulfil contracts.[9] The ubiquitous technique for arbitrage provides the mechanism. Arbitrage, in this context, is defined as the simultaneous purchase of futures contracts against the sale of the actual commodity to profit from a difference in price. Conversely, arbitrage also entails the simultaneous purchase of the actual commodity against the sale of futures contracts, once again to profit from price differences.[10]

An example will suffice to illustrate this point. On the assumption that cotton was selling at 55 cents per lb. in mid-September and that the October contract on the futures exchange was selling at 60 cents per lb., holders of the physical commodity would obviously gain five cents/lb. if they sold their cotton through the medium of October futures. The effect of heavy selling of October futures (and buying of the physical commodity) would push the futures price down toward the level of the prevailing spot price.[11] The price manipulations and speculator-induced price movements in the futures market described later are transmitted to spot prices through the same arbitrage mechanism.

Despite the enormous volume of contracts traded, the cotton futures market is not an important arena for actual commodity trading. Data indicates that cotton traded and delivered through the New York Cotton Exchange (as opposed to the amount of cotton futures) is negligible, amounting to a mere 1–2 per cent of the $25 billion traded in 1975–76.[12] To avoid delivery commitments, traders usually offset futures contracts to sell (or buy) cotton by later obtaining contracts to buy (or sell) cotton. The importance of the exchange lies in the interplay between futures and spot prices, and in the services and profits that it yields to commodity hedgers and speculators.

Long and Short Contracts

Of the two groups of participants that deal in cotton futures, hedgers predominate. In November 1977, hedgers controlled 87 per cent of long (buy) contracts and 76 per cent of short (sell) contracts[13] of the large traders[14] on the New York Cotton Exchange. Every futures contract is held simultaneously by two traders: the future buyer of cotton holding the long end of the contract, and the future seller of cotton holding the short end of the contract.

A *long contract* refers to the market position of a futures contract buyer whose purchase commits him to accepting delivery of cotton later unless he liquidates his contract with an offsetting sale. Conversely, *a short contract* refers to the market position of a futures contract seller whose sale commits him to delivering cotton in a future month unless he liquidates his contract with an offsetting purchase. Hedgers (including cotton farmers, traders, and manufacturers) buy or sell futures contracts to offset their actual purchases or commitments in cotton, and thus hedge or insure against adverse price fluctuations in the future.

There are three different groups of hedgers: sellers of cotton, buyers of cotton and the big traders who do both. Farmers constitute the bulk of the first group, bent on ensuring the sale of their future cotton.[15] They enter the futures market through uncertainty that cotton prices at harvest time will cover their production costs. Hedging in this context is a risk avoidance policy, the hedger synchronizing his activities on two parallel markets: the spot market and the futures market.

During the planting season a cotton farmer sells cotton futures that expire in six months, equivalent in volume to his anticipated crop, as we discussed earlier. If the futures price falls during the six-month period, the spot price will tend to decrease correspondingly. The loss that the farmer sustains in accepting a lower spot price for his cotton will be offset by his simultaneous gains on the futures market. These gains result from the farmer's offsetting his original short (sell) contracts by acquiring long (buy) contracts also at lower prices. Likewise, if cotton prices had risen on both futures and spot markets, gains in spot sales would have been offset by losses on the futures market to the farmer. This offsetting mechanism is used in 98–99 per cent of all cotton contracts traded.

The second group of hedgers, those concerned with ensuring their cotton purchases, deploy the hedging mechanism in a similar way, with one important difference — they buy long contracts instead of the farmers' short contracts in the initial period. The cotton spinner, for example, might buy long futures to be offset later, to ensure that he will not be caught out by rapidly rising cotton prices.

The final group of hedgers, and the group which is of paramount importance for manipulative practices, are the giant multi-commodity trading conglomerates. These giants deal simultaneously in long and short contracts in massive trading volumes. While these three groups of hedgers are by definition distinct from speculators, large traders have deployed a myriad of accounting techniques to conceal those contracts which are speculations as distinct from hedges. One technique of concealment springs from the ruling that there is no limit to the number of contracts a hedger can hold as long as they are hedging contracts (i.e. as long as he is dealing with an equivalent or larger amount in the cash market). As the following illustration indicates, there is no assurance that multi-commodity trading activities (on the futures market) are hedging activities. A multi-commodity trader may have 30 million pounds of cotton in his warehouse — the equivalent of 600 futures contracts. The trader may choose not to hedge, and is thus left free at any time to enter the futures market with orders for 600 contracts for purely speculative reasons. The trader can then shift out of the futures market with the same alacrity when prices have swung to his advantage. Both the entry and exit of very large orders can contribute to price-destabilizing forces.

A trader may further decide to hedge only a part of his cash position and, technically, would still be free to speculate with the unhedged portion. Speculative activities by giant traders pass unperceived since the positions of all commodity traders (persons or institutions dealing with the actual commodity) are listed as hedge positions, except for the unusual case where a trader will have a speculative account maintained separately from his other trading accounts. Speculators constitute the other category of traders. However, it should be emphasized that speculation is inextricably and operationally related to hedging, and is complementary to it. The rationale of speculation was clearly spelled out in a brief by the New York Cotton Exchange: 'Since there are not an equal number of hedgers taking long and short positions on the exchange, speculators are invited into the futures market and for an expected profit they act as insurers for those who deal with the actual commodity.'[16] Speculators further provide some of the liquidity essential for futures market operations.

Contrary to the hedging rationale of risk avoidance, speculators risk large sums daily in pursuit of large gains. The speculator is not committed to any commodity deliveries, and thus can follow favourable price trends in other futures markets, and quickly shift his financial operations from one commodity to another. While speculators, by definition, are not concerned with commodity deliveries, the giant cotton trading corporations also employ their highly efficient intelligence networks for speculation, thereby reducing speculative risks to a minimum. By providing these giant traders with both a risk avoidance policy through hedging, and great speculative potential, the cotton futures market is an institution ideally geared to their transnational business operations.

Despite the dissimilar operational mechanisms in the futures and securities markets, there is one overriding similarity: on both the securities and futures markets, trading is carried out through specialized brokers who operate on a commission basis. The following points summarize five significant ways in which speculative activities differ on the two markets:

1) Since a speculator on the futures market can hold contracts for more than one future month, he is positioned to gain on several futures holdings of the same commodity. Such occurrences do not take place on the securities market where stocks do not refer to any time period.

2) In contrast to the securities market, the futures market is characterized by a permanent flow of market data which the giant traders are able to tap

continuously in their speculative activities. The corresponding data flow in the securities market is far more limited.

3) While futures markets have no equivalent to dividends, the futures contract deposit of 5–10 percent is greatly surpassed on the securities market where traders must pay almost the full price in cash for shares.

4) Securities market trading deals in shares that were invariably put on the market at an earlier time. The life-span of the share or shares is not bounded in time. Futures contracts have a specific life-span ranging from one day to eighteen months.

5) In the securities markets almost all persons holding shares gain when prices rise and lose when prices fall. On the futures market traders bet on prices either rising or falling and thus gain or lose depending on whether they hold long or short contracts. There are thus two opposite sides on any futures markets pushing in opposite directions. This is one component which explains the greater instability of commodity prices in futures markets as against stock prices.[17]

The familiar contention that for every gain on the futures market there is an offsetting loss is generally true. What is more interesting, however, is the composition of winners and losers and their relative sizes. An enquiry by the Chicago Mercantile Exchange revealed that small speculators (those trading one or two contracts at a time) lost on four out of every five trading transactions. A 1976 study found 92 per cent of futures traders losing on their investments. Whilst this does not preclude giant traders suffering huge losses, in general they deploy their resources to obtain consistent gains on the market.[18]

This interchange of rapid buying and selling among hedgers and speculators on futures exchanges is often referred to as the closest approximation to the free interplay of 'supply and demand' in modern markets. A more critical analysis proves otherwise.

Manipulative Practices

Manipulative practices are endemic in the cotton futures market. In Alfred Marshall's classic *Industry and Trade* (1918), the widespread manipulation of futures markets had already been the subject of critical analysis. In the United States a definition of manipulation was articulated in 1962 (in *Volkart Bros. Inc. v. Freeman*) by Arthur R. Marsh, former president of the New York Cotton Exchange, who later defined it as 'any and every operation or transaction or practice . . . calculated to produce a price distortion of any kind in any market either in itself or in relation to other markets. If a firm is engaged in manipulation, it will be found using devices by which the prices of contracts for some one month in some one market may be higher than they would be if only the forces of supply and demand were operative . . . Any and every operation, transaction [or] device, employed to produce these abnormalities of price relationship in the futures markets, is manipulation.'[19]

In 1973, some of these practices were exposed by government investigations.[20] In response to unprecedented commodity price turbulence, US consumers were distressed by high prices, and farmers were dissatisfied that they were not receiving an adequate return on these price levels. Suspicion of widespread profiteering once again triggered investigations of the commodity futures exchange. These manipulative practices fall into three categories: hedging, speculation and tax spreading.

Hedging – the Long Squeeze

The most widespread manipulative practice discerned in the futures market is called the 'long squeeze'. A 'squeeze' or 'corner' is said to have occurred when a trader or group of traders controls a substantial segment of the contracts in a maturing future[21] as well as a significant portion of the deliverable cotton supplies[22] and uses control of these two vantage points to alter prices for that particular future. According to a USDA futures analyst, the squeeze 'appears to be one of the most pervasive market forces and one that could weaken the institution of futures trading'.[23]

The anatomy of the 'long squeeze' assumed different characteristics before 1971, when cotton futures trading was small in volume. A large trading company, with its vast financial and trading power, was in a position to acquire the bulk of contracts for a given delivery date. It was possible for a single giant trading company to control as much as 90 per cent of the long (buy) end of all cotton contracts. In those cases where the dominant company also controlled a large share of certified cotton stocks[24] available for delivery, the company was in a position to impose a 'long squeeze'. On the delivery date, holders of short (sell) contracts must either deliver cotton or buy long contracts to offset their position. When one company holds a controlling position over both available cotton and the long contracts, holders of short contracts usually have no option but to buy contracts at the price dictated by the larger trader.

There are legal limits of two cents a pound in either direction with regard to minimum and maximum price changes on a given trading day. The limits are dropped during delivery months on that month's prices, however, and traders who have succeeded in pushing up prices have gained millions of dollars by liquidating their contracts on a delivery day.[25] Prevailing market structures offered no protection against such monopolistic abuses.

The United States Agricultural Act of 1971 was largely responsible for reshaping the ways in which traders imposed 'squeezes'. It makes a historic watershed. Prior to that year, the US Agriculture Department established an annual price[26] at which it loaned money to farmers who pledged part or all of their crops as collateral. At harvest time, the farmer compared cotton spot prices to the loan price. If spot prices were low, he had the option of retaining the borrowed funds and discharging the loan by authorizing the government to keep his crop. Or, if spot prices were high, he could repay the loan plus interest and storage charges, at which point the government returned his crop for sale on the spot market.

By maintaining a loan price above cotton's commercial market price for most years, the Agriculture Department's Commodity Credit Corporation accumulated large price-stabilizing stocks of cotton during the 1950s and 1960s.[27] The Food and Agriculture Act of 1965 was an important precursor of the 1971 Act. In 1965, the government lowered loan rates, making them conditional upon a minimum 12.5-per-cent reduction of cotton acreage. The subsequent years saw the Agriculture Department releasing its cotton stocks, to such an extent that by 1971 government-owned stocks were 3 per cent of their 1964 level.

In 1971, legislation lowered the loan rate again in the face of rising spot prices. Many speculators plunged into cotton futures, realizing that cotton prices less fettered by regulatory constraints would be susceptible to larger fluctuations. Likewise cotton hedgers of all kinds, no longer assured of stable cotton prices, rushed to acquire contracts. The psychological impact of this Act on traders and speculators seeking vehicles for their activities was quickly reflected by the expanding number of cotton futures contracts, which grew from 4,200 in March 1971 to over 15,000 three months later.[28]

The increased number of contracts held by a larger number of traders made it increasingly difficult to effect a 'long squeeze'. Table 4.2 demonstrates the concentrated power in futures of the large traders, with the four largest controlling about 30 per cent of cotton futures contracts and the eight largest 41 per cent. Henceforth, the success of 'long squeezes' may require collusive futures-buying policies among several giant traders.[29]

Collusive action may take the form of traders selecting a particular future delivery day, preferably toward the end of the storage year when there is a paucity of available cotton stocks. They could then co-ordinate buying policies so that as the delivery date approaches they control a substantial number of long contracts. On the delivery date, holders of short contracts would be forced to accept the price dictated by the large collusive traders to offset their contracts.[30] The vulnerability of small traders springs from two sources: first, large traders control the bulk of cotton stocks, which the small traders may buy to fulfil their contractual deliveries; and second, small traders lack adequate marketing intelligence on other potential sources of available, deliverable cotton. The result of these two basic weaknesses is that in offsetting their short contracts on or near delivery dates, the small traders must buy long contracts at the higher price dictated by larger traders.

One of the more recent and effective 'long squeezes' was carried out by a large trader on the exchange in May and July 1972. The case was successfully prosecuted by the Commodity Futures Trading Commission (CTFC).[31] The trader laid the foundation for the 'squeeze' in late 1971. As from December 1971, the large trader bought and accepted deliveries on huge volumes of long futures contracts. Out of a total volume of 36,420 bales of certified cotton delivered on March 1972 futures, the trader received 35,820; out of another 59,963 bales delivered on May 1972 futures, it received 59,078 bales.

Table 4.2
Breakdown of Contracts on New York Cotton Exchange, 30 November 1977

| | Reporting (Large) Traders[1] | | | | | | Non-reporting (Small) Traders: Speculative and Hedging[2] | |
| | Speculative | | Hedging | | Total | | | |
	Long[3]	Short[4]	Long	Short	Long	Short	Long	Short
	Cotton Contracts of 50,000 lbs.							
Contracts (Total= 22,639)	2,216	3,849	14,410	12,313	16,626	16,162	6,013	6,477
	% of contracts held by each group of traders							
	9.7	17.0	63.7	54.4	73.4	71.4	26.6	28.6
	Number of Traders in Each Group							
Traders[5] (Total = 79)	26	40	41	41	55	63	–	–

Incidence of trading concentration, 30 November 1977 (%)

4 largest traders		*8 largest traders*	
long	short	long	short
27.8	33.0	40.8	40.4

1. A large trader is any trader who holds 500 or more cotton futures contracts. Large traders are required to submit reports of their trading activities to the CFTC.
2. Traders holding less than 500 contracts are unaccountable to the CFTC, and thus no breakdown into speculators and hedgers can be attempted.
3. The buying side of an open futures contract.
4. The selling side of an open futures contract.
5. This total does not represent a sum of the sub-categories of traders since many traders hold both long and short positions or are both hedgers and speculators.

Source: Compiled from data in Commodity Futures Trading Commission, *Commitments of Traders* (New York, 1977).

In parallel transactions, the trader bought up large quantities of long futures contracts for the two delivery dates in question. According to the findings of the CFTC (which were not contested), the trader used its dominant position on both the spot and futures markets to 'cause prices of the May 1972 and July 1972 cotton futures contracts and the price of spot cotton to be abnormally and artificially high during the period 15 March 1972 to 7 July 1972'. The big trader accepted a sanction which led to its exclusion from trading on any contract market for a period of one year.[32]

Hedging — the Short Squeeze

A less frequently used manipulative practice is the 'short squeeze', the aim of which is to depress the price of a particular future to the gain of a large holder or holders of short contracts. The mechanics of this squeeze emanate from a defensive posture of large holders of short contracts striving to protect themselves from the long 'squeeze' described above. The defence consists of buying up substantial stocks of deliverable cotton.

The squeeze is effected by either the threat of or by actually making substantial large deliveries early (or by a combination of both). Since the cash market cannot readily absorb this input, holders of long contracts are thrown into a panic, particularly where the 'deliveries fall into weak, unsuspecting hands who must not only redeliver but must sell long positions as well . . . '[33] Deliveries, or the threat of deliveries, force them to liquidate their long positions at increasingly lower prices.

A 1971 case history dramatically demonstrates step by step the staging of a 'short squeeze'. As early as May 1971, the giant trader in question owned 6.6 per cent of short contracts due to mature in December 1971. Through a steady accumulation of December futures he increased his position to 46.3 per cent by late November. This acquisition policy was matched by purchases on the spot market of large quantities of certified cotton also by November.

Just prior to the onset of 'squeeze' deliveries, the giant trader learned that another trader held an equally dominant position in long December futures. An attempt was made to threaten the holder of long contracts with delivery of inferior cotton unless he offset his long contracts by buying short contracts (presumably at a lower price to be dictated by the 'squeezer').[34] In this case the holder of long contracts refused to comply and subsequently accepted deliveries of 70,000 bales.

Thus, the attempt to stage the squeeze failed (in this case) to depress prices.[35] The failure was due to the countervailing power of another giant who at that point did not stand to gain by collusive activities. It should be emphasized, however, that, had the holdings of long contracts been less powerfully concentrated in the hands of one trader, the squeeze would in all probability have been successful.

In short, the cotton futures market has become a trading mechanism whereby large traders, individually or through collusive manipulative practices, can acquire substantial gains and, in so doing, destabilize prices.

One other major factor determining cotton prices should be mentioned at this juncture. In 1979, when cotton traders and speculators managed to drive cotton prices up from 60 to 68 cents a pound in one month, a commodity trading adviser observed that if polyester was rising in price, 'there isn't any reason why cotton shouldn't be selling for 80 to 85 cents' a pound.[36] In this case the chemical fibre oligopoly's pricing policy, not supply and demand, was guiding the manipulations.

Speculation and Straddles

There is a widespread misconception that speculators dominate commodity futures markets. This is not so in the case of cotton where, in November 1977, they controlled under 20 per cent of the cotton futures of large traders (see Table 4.2), a share that seldom rises to 50 per cent. While the more powerful actors on the cotton exchange, the hedgers, can accumulate any number of contracts, the CFTC limits the number that any speculator can hold on the exchange at any time to 300.[37] This is by no means inconsequential, since 300 contracts amount to 15 million pounds of cotton, which represents a very powerful position on the exchange.

As already noted, though there is a marked distinction between the functions of hedging and speculation, the same giant multi-commodity traders are actively involved in both. Their all-pervasive commodity intelligence network makes them the most potent and effective speculators on all futures markets.[38]

Speculators entered the market in large numbers in 1971 when there was a rise in trading activity on the exchange in response to that year's farm legislation. One of the main reasons for their presence was the low-margin deposit demanded by the futures exchange: usually only 5–10 per cent of the value of contracts purchased. Another heavy influx of speculators occurred in 1973 as investors deserted a depressed securities market for the commodities exchanges where prices had begun to swing wildly. Over the last five years cotton has experienced considerable price fluctuations which have encouraged speculative contract activity.

It is, of course, recognized that speculators gear their trading positions to the movements of prices on futures exchanges. Their general response is to deal as if rising prices are likely to rise still further and falling prices to continue to fall. In operational terms, it follows that speculators will tend to react to rising prices by buying futures contracts in the hope of being able to sell them later at a higher price.[39] By the very act of buying these contracts the speculator contributes to lifting prices even higher by boosting demand. Speculative practices, which are an integral part of futures trading, are destabilizing to the extent that they push mounting prices even higher and falling prices even lower.[40]

Manipulative practices have by no means been confined exclusively to the cotton futures exchange. Extensive hearings before the United States House of Representatives in 1973 disclosed instances of wild speculation and manipulation in both soybean and grain futures. In describing a one-month jump in soybean futures prices from $3.31 to $12.90, a former Vice-Chairman of the Chicago Mercantile Exchange testified: 'It is my opinion that the last $5 or $6 of the increase in the July soybeans was the result of the manipulative practices.' He continued that 'squeezing a market unfortunately is a fairly simple affair, all it requires is a great deal of money and brokers who are willing to look the other way'.[41] In the period 1976—79, major scandals erupted over manipulation by traders and professional speculators 'on US commodity exchanges in coffee, meat, potato, and wheat futures'.[42]

In wheat, the futures exchange was actually shut down in March 1979, when four traders amassed futures positions representing 7.4 million bushels of wheat when there were only 2 million deliverable bushels in the Chicago area.[43] According to *The New York Times,* these four, including the Vice Chairman of the Chicago Board of Trade, stood to gain as much as $1.8 million in the deal.[44]

Another example of manipulation or excessive speculation has been described by Congressman Neal Smith, Chairman of the US House Committee on Small Business, who called futures markets a form of 'legalized gambling'. In his testimony before the subcommittee on Livestock and Grains in 1979 he noted: 'As you are all aware, there have been a number of times when radical movements in futures prices could not possibly be explained by cash positions or by changes in supply or demand. The most recent one that attracted attention was during July and August of this year when the closing price of live cattle futures dropped over $12.00 from a high of $69.47 on July 12th to a low of $57.42 on August 6th and then shot back up $11.00 to a level of $68.45 on August 31st. There had to be outside forces because supply and demand simply could not have changed that much in so short a period of time.'[45]

The possibilities for such manipulations are greatly enhanced by the vertical integration of several of the largest corporations dealing in grain, cattle and meat. In the United States, thirteen of the twenty-five largest cattle feeders are owned or controlled by packing or grain companies which are also trading in live cattle futures. Cargill, one of our giant cotton traders, also owns five major cattle feeding lots, one of the nation's biggest meat packers (MBPXL), and its own commodity futures trading subsidiary — the Cargill Investors Service.[46]

The potential for manipulation by large vertically integrated firms is immense, as Congressman Smith pointed out: 'In the period from January, 1978 through April, 1979, grain companies, beef packers, and commercial feedlots held about 30% of the short positions in live cattle futures and had the capacity to control from 50% to 100% of those positions . . . under this situation, the futures market helps the packer-feeder and the packer-feeder-grain companies keep constant downward pressure on the cattle futures contract when it is to their advantage, until they drive feeders, who are not in the packing business out of business.'[47] Thus in certain commodity lines, the futures market not only becomes a forum of price manipulation, but also serves as a catalyst of corporate concentration.

In 1976, CFTC investigations exposed an entirely new area of malpractice on futures markets. The structure of the futures market provides tax loopholes which have given an impetus to additional speculation. In the words of a CFTC official, 'What we are talking about here is not just traders rigging the market for their own profit and to the detriment of the public, but one of the biggest tax rip-offs of all times.'[48] Both hedgers and speculators have been using futures exchanges to carry out what is commonly referred to as tax spreading or tax straddles, by which traders defer their taxes and spread their trading income over a period of years. According to the source quoted above, more than $500 million in taxes have been evaded in recent years in this manner. One of the upshots of this tax loophole is that high-bracket taxpayers have been steered in escalating numbers into commodity tax straddles by their tax lawyers and the accounting establishment. 'These rigged tax straddles appear to have been going on for years, but the IRS [Internal Revenue Service] has lacked the resources or knowledge of futures markets to ferret them out,' points out one CFTC official. 'The amount of taxes being laundered through these trades is staggering. Interestingly, a lot of it ends up flowing to offshore Bahamian and Panamanian trusts beyond the reach of U.S. tax authorities.'[49] The presence of tax-induced speculators also serves to intensify prevailing price-destabilizing activities on the cotton exchange.

The most far-reaching implication of our discussion of the futures market and oligopoly is that international trade in commodities with futures markets is subject to intense price manipulation. Further, it is precisely the same traders of actual cotton who are the price manipulators on the New York futures market. Hence this fusion of functions gives the oligopoly unassailable supremacy in its trading interactions with all forms of institutional marketing, be they based in UCEs or CPEs.

References

1. Cotton futures exchanges also existed in New Orleans (founded in 1871) and Chicago (founded in 1924), although neither experienced the volume of trading of New York. The Chicago exchange closed down after World War II, and the New Orleans Cotton Exchange folded in 1961 (see Frank Richards, *The Marketing of Cotton and the Financing of Cotton Merchants* (New York, 1949). Another cotton exchange opened in Hong Kong in May 1977, but thus far trading has been light, and it looks as though the bulk of trading will continue on the New York market.
2. The stated quantity of a New York Cotton Exchange contract is 50,000 lbs or 100 bales. The prohibitive size and cost of these contracts is

revealed by US cotton farming. In 1973, 300,000 US farmers produced 13 million bales, an average of 43 bales per farm. (cf. United States House Committee on Agriculture, *Review of Cotton Marketing System: Hearings before the Subcommittee on cotton,* 93rd Congress, 2nd Session, 1974, p.10). The 100-bale futures contract is therefore too large for the majority of these farmers. With respect to costs, one contract at 50 cents/lb costs $25,000, of which about $2,500 must be paid as a margin deposit. Many farmers do not have the financial resources, especially at planting time, to make such a purchase.

3. L.L. Johnson, 'The Theory of Hedging and Speculation in Commodity Futures', *Review of Economic Studies,* 27 (1960).

4. Had both spot and futures prices been 55 cents/lb at delivery date, the farmer's gain of 5 cents/lb on the futures market would have been off-set by 5 cents/lb losses on his spot market sales.

5. Gains or losses can be computed by the following simple formula devised by Leland Johnson: 'As an illustration, assume a hedge carried in a future from time t_1 to time t_2 (where the future specifies delivery at time t_3) against x units of inventory purchased at t_1 and sold at t_2. Let S_1 and S_2 denote the spot price and F_1 and F_2 the price of the future that exist at t_1 and t_2 respectively. The hedger will take a total gain (loss) arising from price movements from t_1 to t_2 equal to the positive (negative) value of $x [(S_2 - S_2) - (F_2 - F_1)]$. The hedge is perfectly effective if $[(S_2 - S_1) - (F_2 - F_1)]$ is equal to O.' Johnson, *op. cit.* (Calculation excludes broker's fees and net cost of interest of the margin deposit).

6. *Wall Street Journal,* 9 January 1979 and 6 October 1978.

7. Six months is fairly typical. Contracts commonly stipulate monthly or bi-monthly shipments.

8. US cotton producers sold one-third of their crop on a forward basis in 1972, three-quarters in 1973, and about one-fifth in 1974; USDA, *National Cotton Marketing Study Committee Report* (Washington, DC, 1975), pp. 60–1.

9. The difference between future and spot prices as the delivery date approaches is called the 'maturity basis'. The reader should also be aware of the important relationship between spot prices and prices of futures contracts in later delivery months, referred to as the 'basis'. When futures prices are higher than the spot price in successive months, the basis (futures price minus spot price) is known as 'contango' or 'forward premium'. Conversely, when futures prices are lower than the spot price in successive months, a 'backwardation' or 'spot premium' is said to be in evidence. See J.M. Keynes, *A Treatise on Money* (London, 1930), for a further discussion of this concept.

10. In general, arbitrage is the simultaneous purchase and sale of the same quantity of the same commodity in two different markets. It should be added that arbitrage transactions can also align prices of different futures maturities of the same commodity (i.e. between May and July cotton futures), or the prices of the same commodity's futures in different markets nationally or internationally (i.e. between the Hong Kong and New York Cotton Exchanges). See B.A. Goss and B.S. Yamey, *The Economics of Futures Trading* (London 1976), p. 35.

11. Arbitrage operations will push the futures price down to a level still

above the spot price such that the basis (spot price minus futures price) reflects the storage and carrying charges of the holder of cotton. The profit made in arbitrage is limited by the amount of the contango. As an example of other factors influencing spot prices in developing countries, we give the following testimony of the Syrian Cotton Marketing Organization: 'Our prices are adjusted according to world market movements and New York Cotton Exchange's fluctuations, as well as on the basis of our agents' reports' (quoted from communications to the authors, 27 December 1977). This is indicative of pricing policies of most exporting countries for cotton sold on the international market.

12. In 1974—75, this 1—2 per cent (or 4,169—8,338 contracts) amounted to about 1 per cent of global cotton production of 64.5 million bales. Due to heavier trading in 1975—6, this 1—2 per cent (or 8,015—16,030 contracts) amounted to about 4.5 per cent of 54.6 million bales produced globally.

13. Compiled from data in Commodity Futures Trading Commission, *Commitments of Traders* (New York, 1977).

14. Traders holding more than 300 contracts of 50,000 pounds of cotton are designated 'large' traders by the CFTC and must report their trading activities to the CFTC. In November 1977, these large traders, numbering 79, controlled 72.4 per cent of all cotton futures contracts. The figures of 87 and 76 per cent were derived from this 72.4 per cent. Smaller traders (with 27.6 per cent of the contracts) are not required to file reports that would categorize them as hedgers or speculators.

15. While individual farmers play a relatively small role on the cotton exchange, the big US cotton co-operatives (e.g. the Plains Cotton Co-operative, representing over 20,000 cotton farmers) deal extensively in cotton futures.

16. Quoted from *Volkart Brothers Inc. v. Freeman* (311, F.2d 52 1962), United States Court of Appeals, Fifth Circuit.

17. For further analysis, see C.W.J. Granger, *Trading in Commodities, An Investors' Chronicle Guide,* (Cambridge, 1975).

18. *Business Week,* 11 June 1979, p. 68; and *Special Reports on Major Business Problems,* Business Week Executive Portfolio, (New York, 1978).

19. United States Senate, *Hearings on Senate Resolution 142 before the Subcommittee on Agriculture and Forestry,* 70th Congress, 1st Session (Washington, DC, 1973), pp. 201—202.

20. A series of Congressional hearings in 1973 resulted in the establishment of a new independent regulatory agency with exclusive jurisdiction over commodity futures trading. This organization, the Commodity Futures Trading Commission (CFTC) began work in 1975. Patterned after the Security and Exchange Commission, the CFTC has investigated dozens of allegations of illegal activities on futures exchanges.

21. A maturing future is a contract nearing expiry at one of the five annual delivery dates. For cotton, delivery months are March, May, July, October, and December.

22. Delivery is effected through a written 'notice of delivery' sent through the clearing house by the seller of a futures contract indicating that he

intends to honour the futures contract by delivering the physical commodity.

23. A.B. Paul, for USDA, Economic Research Service, *Treatment of Hedging in Commodity Market Regulation* (Washington, DC, 1976), p. 9.

24. 'Certified cotton' is cotton which has been inspected, weighed and sampled under New York Cotton Exchange supervision, and which has been judged deliverable on futures contracts traded on the New York Cotton Exchange upon classification, review and micronaire test under USDA regulations.

25. In one case in the late 1950s, a giant multi-commodity trader pushed futures prices up on the delivery date by controlling over 120 long contracts out of an available 134.

26. This price is based on the Agriculture Department's 'parity prices', which are theoretical levels at which farm commodities should sell to keep them in relationship to other prices for the same base period.

27. For description of US legislation relevant to futures, see Gerald Gold, *Modern Commodity Futures Trading* (New York, 1968).

28. *Business Week,* 5 June 1971, p. 44.

29. The term 'collusion' should not be construed as implying that all their trading and other activities are centralized, controlled and directed in part or in whole by all members of the oligopoly. Rather, the evidence, fragmentary as it is, suggests that given their close trading relationships, there is scope for collusive buying and selling. Successful consummation of such collusive conduct depends on the strength of regulatory agencies and the specific opportunity afforded by any given commercial transaction.

30. A thorough analysis of the anatomy of 'squeezes' is available in USDA Economic Research Service, *Treatment of Hedging* (Washington, DC, 1976).

31. For further evidence of court actions on price manipulations, see *Cargill Inc. v. Hardin* (452 F. 2d 1154, 1163, 8th Cir. 1971), *cert. denied*, 406 U.S. 932 (1972); *Great Western Food Distributors, Inc. v. Brannan,* 201 F. 2d 476 (7th Cir.), *cert. denied* 345 U.S. 997 (1953). In the case of *Volkart Brothers Inc. v. Freeman* (311 F. 2d 52 1962), the US Court of Appeals for the Fifth Circuit exonerated Volkart of the USDA accusation of manipulating and attempting to manipulate the market.

32. See CFTC Docket No. 75–11.

33. T. Hieronymus, *Economics of Futures Trading* (New York, 1971) p. 309. See also CFTC Docket No. 75–4, p. 22.

34. It should be recalled that each contract has two sides: a short or 'sell' position, and a long or 'buy' position. Price variations of a futures contract affect both sides equally.

35. The Enforcement Division of the CFTC, however, continued to argue that 'the preponderance of the evidence' establishes that the trader 'intentionally acted and traded in a manner calculated to cause the price of December 1971 cotton futures contracts to be artificial, and thus attempted to manipulate the price of a commodity in violation of the (Commodity Exchange) Act' (CFTC Docket No. 75–4).

36. *International Herald Tribune,* 28 June 1979.

37. Notwithstanding this statutory upper limit, there is nothing to stop a

large multi-commodity trader holding 2,000 contracts of which over 300 are speculative. This is so, as already emphasized, since despite the provision that hedgers must support the hedge classification of their positions by filing weekly CFTC Form 304 reports, there are many ways: of concealing which ones are hedging and which ones are speculative contracts. By the end of 1978, the CFTC advocated that all daily limits on speculation in agricultural commodities be dropped. See *Wall Street Journal*, 21 December 1978.
38. As one Commodity Exchange official confirmed: 'Many hedgers, depending on how they set up their positions, end up speculating . . . I would think the Comptroller of the Currency would find that to be true if he looked at what some of the banks are doing' (*Business Week*, 11 June 1979, p. 65).
39. This is an extremely complex area, and the speculative thrusts of the large traders need be neither uniform nor synchronized.
40. Aliber's 1966 study demonstrated a link between the profitability and price instability generated by speculation. The researcher's methodology consisted of devising a test to identify short time-spans within which speculators were deepening the troughs and lifting the crests of prices on the cotton futures market. Using additional data on the profits and losses of speculators, he discovered a definite correlation between speculators' profitability and their price-destabilizing activities. The study is referred to in Goss and Yamey, *The Economics of Futures Trading* (London, 1976, p. 37).
41. This lawyer, a former trader on the exchange, detailed one further mechanism of manipulation: 'Commodity brokers frequently not only trade for themselves but also customers whom they put in the market. The control and direction of their own accounts as well as their customers' accounts is frequently part and parcel of a manipulated market.' For details, see United States, House, Permanent Select Committee on Small Business, *Small Business Problems Involved in the Marketing of Grain and Other Commodities*, (Washington, DC, 1973), pp. 48–9.
42. *International Herald Tribune*, 16 May 1979.
43. *Business Week*, 11 June 1979, p. 68.
44. *The New York Times*, 23 March 1979.
45. See House of Representatives Transcript Record, 'Excerpts from the testimony of Neal Smith before the Subcommittee on Livestock and Grains' (Washington, DC, 30 October 1979), pp. 8, 13. See also United States, House, Permanent Select Committee on Small Business, *Small Business Problems in the Marketing of Meat and Other Commodities* Washington, DC, 1978.
46. G. Richardson, 'A game any number can play', *Livestock*, August 1979.
47. 'Excerpts from the testimony of Neal Smith', pp. 1, 11.
48. 'US Cracking Down on Futures Markets', *International Herald Tribune*, 21 September 1977.
49. *Ibid*. Recent evidence of such activities was disclosed when eleven New York Cotton Exchange brokers were indicted by a U.S. federal grand jury on charges of rigging commodity futures contracts to generate more than one million dollars in short-term losses to evade taxes

and generate kickbacks. This involved setting up fraudulent 'tax straddles', or the deferment of gains on the futures transactions to the following year, to claim losses and thus evade taxes in the current year. See *Wall Street Journal,* 30 December 1980.

5. The International Division of Labour: Petrochemicals and Chemical Fibres

We begin from the principle that a commodity must be understood not only in relation to its own internal structures but in the wider perspective of external forces that inflect its direction and pace. With the rise of petroleum prices — the basic feedstock of petrochemicals and chemical fibres — towards the end of the 1970s, the new elements which have been injected into these two major sectors are recasting the international division of labour for the 1980s and 1990s. The growth of the chemical fibre industry and the petrochemical industry that supplies its raw materials means that the challenge to cotton will continue to be greater than that faced by most other natural primary commodities.

The scale of geographical diffusion of petrochemicals and chemicals to CPEs and leading UCEs has already been matched by clothing, textiles, and the more rudimentary varieties of electronics, shipbuilding, and steel. In the 1980s these manufacturing sectors, long the preserve of the DCEs, will be joined by practically the entire range of industry (with the exception of such high technology export lines as aircraft manufacturing, outer-space technology and the more complex computer product lines). However, this geographical spread of industries is (with the exception of certain CPE deals) in no way synonymous with transfer of ownership. Productive ownership and marketing, not to speak of basic and applied research, will continue to remain largely within the grip of transnational corporations. It will, of course, be increasingly attentuated by joint ventures with the UCE oligarchy, to the extent that their political aspirations coincide. Joint ventures have indeed become the ideal institutional vehicle for the extraction of the actual economic surplus from the underdeveloped capitalist countries, and for the perpetuation of global oligopoly.

There are two important traits of the global market: chronic overproduction and intensified competition. Consequently CPE and UCE industries intending to be export-oriented require a technology that measures up to the DCEs' competitively high levels of capital intensity. They must also acquire marketing capabilities, another crucial prerequisite for breaking into the global market. As a result, the large amounts of capital required to set up industry yield negligible employment in UCEs, already suffering from massive unemployment. Restrictionist measures can only exacerbate this crisis. Thus competition on the global market in the 1980s will be vastly intensified.

This chapter examines the changing geographical location of the petro-chemical and chemical fibres industries, but it also serves as a case study of the effects of the shifting international division of labour. The drama of these two industries is being re-enacted over a wide range of industries: rising industrial exports from CPEs and UCEs (notably from the 'giant dwarfs'); the spread of job-cutting technological innovations; and the prospects of prolonged economic stagnation. Here we are basically sketching in the map whose contours are filled in in the following chapter, where the mechanisms of corporate expansionism are dissected in order to reveal the way in which the oligopolies produce market onslaughts and overcapacities.

Technical Constraints

It is first of all necessary to understand certain technical determinations of the petrochemical and chemical fibres industries. Petrochemicals are the creations of chemists manipulating carbon molecules and another hundred-odd elements. The 7,000 products that comprise the petrochemical industry account for about 30 per cent of the chemical industry's global sales; and (in Western Europe) around 15 per cent of aggregate industrial output.[1] Of this, a quarter is absorbed by the chemical fibre industry. Though only a fragment of the total chemical industry, it has the highest returns on invest-ments.

Six basic chemicals (benzene, toluene, xylene, ethylene, propylene and butadiene) provide the major building blocks in the fabrication of polyamid, polyester and acrylic fibres. With the exception of benzene, obtained from coking coal, all these basic chemicals are derived from crude oil and natural gas liquids through refining or petrochemical processes.[2]

There are several backward and forward linkages between chemical fibres and petrochemicals, and chemical fibres and textiles. The process route from petroleum to synthetic fibres includes the following five major steps: output of intermediate chemical raw materials; production of monomers; formation of high polymers; spinning and stretching of fibres; and finishing. Of these major steps, monomer output constitutes 50–75 per cent of fibre production costs.[3] In a relatively short span of five decades, petrochemicals have bred a mighty array of products: synthetic fibres, plastics, synthetic rubber, deter-gents, dyestuffs, fertilizers and pharmaceuticals. The bulk of output (directly and through licensing agreements) is produced and marketed by the trans-national, multi-product chemical giants, including the petrochemical subsi-diaries of the petroleum majors. Acknowledging the industry's importance, a United Nations report noted:

Among the various industries that may come in for consideration in an accelerated programme of industrialization, some sectors, because of

their particular technical and economic characteristics, the type of
resources on which they are based and the nature of their products, are
of a particular dynamic character. Establishment of industries in these
sectors creates, in addition to the direct economic effects, an impact
which exerts an overall stimulating effect upon the rest of the economy.
The petrochemical industry is an example of such a dynamic industry.[4]

In particular, 'this industry is considered to be of strategic importance in
inducing further industrial development because most of its output goes to
other producing sectors. It shares this characteristic of intermediate manufacture with other industries such as iron and steel, paper and its products,
and petroleum products.'

The chemical industry's growth record is consistently above the average:
between 1950 and 1956 world industrial output tripled; but chemical output
quadrupled. From 1955 to 1969 world manufacturing output grew by 6.6
per cent; chemical output by 9.4 per cent. World petrochemical consumption
leapt from 3.5 million tons in 1950 to 65 million tons in 1965, or an annual
compound rate of over 14 per cent — the highest industrial sectoral rate
within world manufacturing.[5] Concomitant with this aggregate growth has
been the industry's use of economies of scale and technological development.
The first to crack ethylene in the 1950s put out 30,000–50,000 tons
annually, blossoming to 500,000 by the mid-1970s.[6] Yet these larger plants
require no increase in the workforce, and can achieve economies in both
fuel and raw material inputs.

Chemical fibres, our more direct concern, are second only to plastics in
the sprawling chemical industry, which can claim not only aspirin, perfumes,
nylon and valium, but also DDT, napalm and thalidomide. Fibres have
undergone less uniform growth, particularly between the two major
components, synthetics (based on petrochemicals) and cellulosics (derived
from wood-based cellulose). Synthetic fibres, led by polyester (representing
46 per cent of synthetic fibres in 1976), have spurted ahead since their entry
into the global market after World War II; polyamid (33 per cent of synthetic
fibres) and acrylic (about 20 per cent) have grown less swiftly, but continue
to flow into new markets, thus eroding the share of natural fibre. Cellulosic
fibres, sometimes referred to as 'man-made fibres', consist principally of
rayon and acetates. Their production growth peaked in 1969 and has since
tapered off, mainly because of the superiority of synthetics in several end-
uses, particularly clothing and high-strength industrial products. Further, the
high cost of pollution control in rayon and acetates has affected financial
returns and thus discouraged manufacturers.[7]

Petrochemicals Overview

Historically, the highly capital-intensive petrochemical industry has depended
on, and been geared to the supply of, cheap naphtha feedstocks for

production of lower olefines such as ethylene, propylene and butylene – the three most significant groups of base chemicals. To increase their overall sales and profits, the major oil companies are now looking towards the 10 per cent of world oil production slated for petrochemicals. This is a rational aim, since feedstocks derived from crude oil, coupled with natural gas, are the basic inputs for over 90 per cent of overall organic output.[8]

At present, however, overcapacity in petrochemicals is rampant, and still climbing. Plants opened during the 1970–73 period of capacity shortages are still coming on stream, whereas demand has been stagnant or sluggish from 1974 onward. Synthetic fibre plants operated at 60–65 per cent of capacity in 1977, plastics (the major end-use) at around 50 per cent,[9] and the allied dyestuff industry at 60–70 per cent in Britain and only slightly more elsewhere.[10] It would be unrealistic to assume that in such a state of crisis meaningful solutions to overcapacity, as distinct from ephemeral expedients, can be achieved by shifting from one petrochemical end-use to another.

The industry's technical coefficients serve to underline the nature of over-capacity, exacerbated by the industry's lagging demand growth, and aggressive marketing policies. Invariably petrochemical output is large-scale and highly capital-intensive,[11] with high fixed costs and extremely low variable costs. Thus, the larger the output run, the less the fixed cost per output unit. Since variable costs are similar for each unit of output, total unit costs drop with rising output. A polypropylene plant operating at 10 per cent of capacity will have unit costs about five times higher than one running at full capacity. For a petrochemical plant the break-even output level is 75–80 per cent. Since the gains of declining unit costs can only be acquired if the plant works at or near full capacity, there is constant pressure to maintain production levels, even at the cost of reducing unit prices. This is why severe overproduction has plagued the industry since the mid-1970s, and can only be eliminated by a sharp recovery in demand or by wholesale scrapping of older plants.

The first alternative is highly unlikely, as most industry experts envisage that the growth rate in world demand for petrochemical and chemicals will drop markedly by 1990.[12] The decline can be attributed to three major causes. First, stagnation in overall industrial growth hits chemicals particularly hard, as the industry relies more than other sectors on sales to other industries, rather than direct sales to the consumer. Growth in demand for plastics, the major consuming industry, is expected to fall from about 15 per cent per annum in the late 1960s to less than 5 per cent after 1990.[13] Second, petrochemicals' astounding growth has been based largely on the demand for substitutes for natural products, a process which is approaching saturation levels in several chemical industries and which must inevitably decelerate. Finally, new CPE and UCE plants are fulfilling demand previously met by DCE exports.

The global petrochemical industry is rapidly becoming less homogenous, with widely divergent cost structures, size, dependence on imported fuel, chemical stocks and ratios of added value to sales. Japan's dependence on imported fuel and chemical stocks is suggested by the price paid for its basic inputs: up to two-thirds higher for naphtha than its European and US competitors.[14] The price increases, coupled with DCE environmental concerns, are blocking the introduction of several new products and adding to the costs of new plants and processes. In the United States, 10 per cent of research and development funds and 15 per cent of capital spending (in the entire chemical industry) has been absorbed in these concerns.[15]

In OPEC countries and other UCEs, petrochemical projects are being constructed at capital costs invariably higher than in DCEs, although their feedstock costs may well be significantly lower. One enquiry, based on Aramco's experience with such projects in Saudi Arabia, argues that capital costs are two-thirds higher than for similar projects in the United States Gulf Coast.[16] The significance of an emerging OPEC presence in petrochemicals, combined with earlier moves into oil refining, puts the industry

> in the process of joining industries like cars, steel, shipbuilding, textiles and electronics as battlefields on which exporters and importers quarrel over the speed with which non-traditional producers can replace more established ones. The distinctive feature of the two sectors . . . is that they mark the first time that the oil-producing world will find itself seeking markets for its industrial products.[17]

The dynamics of the oil and petrochemical trade war now unfolding follow a regional pattern.

The Developed Capitalist Economies

At the moment the United States is the world's greatest petrochemical power,[18] possessing cost advantages of 30–40 per cent over its Western European and Japanese competitors. In view of the appreciation of the Deutschemark, the yen and the Swiss franc, the competitive cost edge of the United States should be further sharpened. Using around three-quarters of its capacity for most of the late 1970s, the US industry hovered around or below the break-even point. Still, given the dollar's erosion, lower US feedstock prices, and the protection of high tariff barriers, foreign investment poured into the US petrochemical industry at around $1 billion per annum in the mid 1970s. This annual figure skyrocketed to $7 billion in the late 1970s, when corporations laid the foundations of new petrochemical plants virtually at the well-head in Texas and Louisiana.[19] The unanswered question, in view of the multi-billion-dollar investments now being spewed into the industry, is where and whether and by whom such output can be effectively marketed.

Western Europe remains one of the focal points of global overcapacity. Existing petrochemical manufacturers are beset by depressed trading and the large-scale overcapacity makes new financial commitments difficult and imprudent in the light of future surplus flows. According to CEFIC (European Council of Chemical Manufacturers' Federations), overcapacity

will worsen by 1981. It will be accompanied by higher feedstock prices, as
well as the legacy of the USA's historical lead in the industry, which gradually
forced Europe's organic chemical industry to shift from indigenous coal to
oil-derived feedstocks. While world ethylene consumption is expected to grow
between 1977 and 1981 at a rate of about 4.2 per cent yearly, capacity is
projected to rise at around 5.3 per cent.[20] This spectre of overcapacity[21]
is revealed by the 1977–81 ethylene output estimates for Western Europe
(see Table 5.1). Exacerbating the crisis, European peripheral states such as
Spain, Portugal, Greece, Turkey, and Austria have embarked on chemical
and petrochemical industries to lessen import dependency.[22] North Sea
feedstocks are now servicing new facilities in Norway, Scotland, and England.
Major appeals by European banks and the European Council of the Chemical
Manufacturers' Federation for joint government action indicates that the
crisis has been recognized.[23] Efforts at amelioration, however, have largely
failed, and by the onset of the 1980s, plant closures with their attendant
unemployment were well under way.

Japan: In the late 1950s, when Japan seriously turned its attention to petrochemicals, it was a negligible force on the world market. A decade later, it
had shot past all competitors except the United States, and petrochemicals
had become one of its leading domestic and export product lines, behind
only automobiles, oil refining, and steel.[24] Inevitably, overproduction caught
up with this ambitious expansion programme. Despite Japanese conglomerates' ability to cross-subsidize and survive even large petrochemical
losses, their rising costs have forced them to accept overseas orders at prices
far below domestic prices that have themselves been under the break-even
point for some time. Oil import dependence, coupled with Japan's desire
to reduce pollution at home, has led to massive infusions of capital into
petrochemical ventures in South-east Asia and the Middle East. Such export
of petrochemical industries, combined with drastic cutbacks aimed at halving
the number of domestic petrochemical plants, can only lead to mass unemployment in the petrochemical labour force of 200,000.

The Underdeveloped Capitalist Economies
Despite excess capacity in the DCEs, there has been a big drive by major oil-
exporting countries to increase profits from downstream processing, and
by other UCEs to break into the petrochemical field. However, the pace of
output and marketing build-up differs markedly from one country to
another, with OPEC and Mexico clearly in the lead. By the end of the 1970s,
for ethylene alone, over 100 projects were operating or in the development
phase in 55 different UCEs.[25]

A salient feature of this build-up is that most contracts are awarded on the
basis of joint ventures with the petrochemical conglomerates. Such new
directions have roots almost 20 years old, or as a 1960s United Nations
report remarked: 'the international agencies, including the World Bank, would
rather encourage developing countries to appeal to the major international
petrochemical companies to help them not only with transmission of know-

how, but also with provision of funds'.[26]

Table 5.1
Estimated Ethylene Capacity and Consumption, 1977–81 (million tonnes)

						Annual Growth Rate
Effective Capacity	*1977*	*1978*	*1979*	*1980*	*1981*	*1977–81 (%*
Benelux	2,630	2,960	3,140	3,215	3,170	4.8
West Germany	3,905	4,030	4,350	4,400	4,510	3.7
France	2,465	2,685	2,685	2,685	2,685	2.1
Italy	1,990	1,990	2,460	2,550	2,550	6.4
United Kingdom	1,515	1,695	1,815	1,990	2,030	7.6
EEC	*12,505*	*13,360*	*14,150*	*14,840*	*14,945*	*4.6*
Spain	480	645	1,070	1,070	1,070	22.2
Austria	105	105	105	105	105	0.0
Scandinavia	620	805	805	825	845	8.1
Western Europe	*13,710*	*14,915*	*16,430*	*16,840*	*16,965*	*5.5*
Consumption						
EEC	9,300	9,750	10,200	10,650	11,150	4.6
Western Europe	10,370	10,900	11,450	12,000	12,600	5.0

Source: European Council of Chemical Manufacturers' Federations.

State/corporate patterns of ownership, for political reasons, continue to be promoted by certain international institutions (specifically the World Bank) and DCEs in certain oil-producing regions. Japan's MITI reveals another species of interaction between the state apparatus and big corporations:

> The most active single foreign partner is not a company, but the Japanese government, which has spearheaded Mitsui's entry into Iran, gone a long way towards getting Mitsubishi and a variety of other Japanese companies into a couple of Iraqi ventures and been very active in trying to win a Japanese stake in the Saudi plans. (Mitsubishi originally considered one of the Saudi ethylene projects and rejected it, but was forced by the Japanese government into reconsidering it).[27]

This is not merely confined to driving Japanese petrochemical giants much deeper into the area's economies, but holds true for all major petrochemical corporations of the developed economies. The UCEs' aspirations to maximize value added and build up processing industries at the national level meshes with a less pressing concern for environmental protection than that prevailing in Japan, the United States and Western Europe. Further, many of their resources — notably gas — still remain grossly underexploited: as late as 1974, over two-thirds of the gas generated by five major Middle East producers was flared.[28] Since more than 10,000 products can be manufactured from crude petroleum, the push to enter downstream processing has recently acquired a new export-oriented impetus,[29] wedded to strident appeals for national self-sufficiency.

Nineteen Middle Eastern and North African countries alone are expected to allocate over $67.3 billion between 1976 and 1980 on petrochemical and related development, or $13.5 billion yearly,[30] resulting in a considerable build-up of capacity (Table 5.2).

Table 5.2
Middle East: Actual and Potential Petrochemical Buildup (000 tons p.a.)

Product	Present Capacity	Under Way	Likely to Be Built	Under Study	Total
Methanol	20	850	3,572	11,418	15,860
Ammonia	2,200	3,183	3,005	4,578	12,966
Ethylene	160	800	656	3,300	4,916
Aromatics	300	430	410	1,900	3,040
Polyethylene	68	125	348	300	841
PVC	35	75	165	370	645

Source: Estimates of Information Research Ltd, quoted in *Chemical Week,* 23 March 1977.

Petrochemicals and their manufacturing derivatives are thus expected to become one of the drivewheels of UCE industrialization. Yet a drive which depends so much on breaking into the entrenched markets of traditional suppliers will not be without friction and there are already hints of future conflict.

In Saudi Arabia, the home of the world's richest hydrocarbon reserves, petrochemical projects are found in two giant new industrial zones: Jubail (a joint venture with Mobil, Exxon, Dow, and the US subsidiary of Shell) on the Persian Gulf, and Yanbu[31] on the Red Sea. From Aramco's petroleum and natural gas fields on the east coast, feedstocks will flow through trans-peninsular crude and natural gas pipelines to the Yanbu complex, at a cost of roughly $15—20 billion for both projects. The national market, however, is small compared to the gigantic scale of plant operations.[32]

Underscoring the need to break into the world market despite the impli-cations of the current unused capacity, the Saudi Ministry of Industry commented that the Gulf oil-exporting countries 'are determined to set up their own petrochemical industries in spite of threats of a possible trade war with the industrialized states'. Admitting that project costs will be 30 per cent higher than in industrialized countries (other estimates put the figure as high as 50 per cent), he argued that OPEC countries are determined to carve a place for themselves in the global market.[33] It would be absurd to expect the DCEs to sit idly by and accept UCE encroachment on their markets. As a spokesman of the Paris-based International Energy Agency stated, 'Why should they expect that we cut back our petrochemical plants to subsidize theirs?'[34] This is precisely one of the frontiers where the petrochemical battle is unfolding.

The marketing strategy of breaking into the world market (in joint ventures with the oil and petrochemical majors) hinges on large-scale subsidization by the Saudi government. About 60 per cent of each project will be financed by long-term, low-interest government loans and by long-term contracts for crude oil throughout the 1980s. In addition to these state inducements, the 50/50 joint ventures with SABIC (Saudi Arabian Basic Industries Corporation) involve cheaper gas feedstock supplies at present being flared as a by-product of crude petroleum.[35] In this industrial strategy, subsidies to the transnational majors are to be calculated according to plant size. 'We have not finalized the formula,' explained Saudi Arabia's Minister of Industry, 'but the price will be the OPEC price for all companies, irrespective of membership in Aramco. Entitlements will be directly related to the size of each company's investment.'[36]

Iran, whose natural gas reserves are estimated to be second to those of the USSR, set itself the target of acquiring 5–10 per cent of the world petrochemical market by 1983–85, and 10 per cent thereafter. Already chemical and petrochemical complexes are operational in Shiraz, Bandar Khomeini, Ahwag, Abadan and Kharg Island. Among the biggest of the new projects, undertaken as a joint venture with Mitsui, is the $3.3-billion project at Bandar Khomeini. Another major petrochemical complex in the Persian Gulf (involving an estimated $3 billion), producing synthetic fibres, polyvinyl chloride and polyethylenes, is now under way with a Swiss consortium.[37] Iran's National Petrochemical Corporation anticipates that its capital investment will grow by one billion dollars a year over the next decade.[38] If carried out, this would be tantamount to an investment avalanche possibly unprecedented in the annals of petrochemicals. After Iran, the smaller OPEC nations have launched headlong into petrochemicals, for instance Qatar (in joint ventures with France), Libya, Kuwait and Algeria.

Striking rates of petrochemical expansion are also recorded for Venezuela[39] and Mexico and their transformation into net exporters is expected by the early eighties. Mexico,[40] in addition to a 1,200-km. natural gas pipeline, projects substantial investment for the petrochemical industry. At present, 63 plants are producing basic materials for this sector. Petrochemical output, which grew at 20 per cent yearly from 1960 to 1976, is to be tripled by 1982.[41] Backed by the state owned oil monopoly Pemex,[42] Mexico offers private companies a 30 per cent discount on raw materials, fuel and electricity. In return, the companies are expected to sell part of their output abroad, a provision designed to enlist the global marketing capabilities of the petrochemical conglomerates. According to the five-year plan, petrochemicals will grow to a staggering 3.8 per cent of GDP by 1982.[43]

Rapid expansion is also under way in Brazil, a net petroleum importer, involving investments of $2–3 billion between 1973 and 1980, by Mitsubishi, Du Pont, Sumitomo and Hoechst amongst others. Further expansion for the domestic and external market is also envisaged throughout the 1980s as pilot plants to produce ethylene from sugar and maize continue to show encouraging results. Nigeria, with the second largest population (after Indonesia) in the OPEC group (80–100 million), has earmarked billions for refineries, associated pipeline developments and laying the foundations of a petrochemical industry. Similarly, Indian planners allocated around $700 million to petrochemicals for the five-year period ending in 1979. The Baroda complex, one of the largest ever built in India (at a cost of over $470 million), is geared not just for the domestic market but for the global market as well.[44] Apart from the Baroda complex India is planning to spend over $10 billion in the 1980s to exploit gas discovered off its west coast. India plans to use the gas as feedstock for fertilizer and petrochemical plants (the most capital-intensive way of using it), rather than as fuel. Each proposed petrochemical complex is costed at $2.5 billion; each fertilizer plant at $400 million.

Finally, South Korea and Taiwan are leading Southeast Asia into petrochemicals at breakneck speed. The Koreans hope to join the world's top ten producers by the 1980s. An annual growth rate of 21 per cent over the past fifteen years has been abetted by government fostering of research and development to a point where its personnel account for 10 per cent of the industry's work force.[45] The basic component of this strategy has been the State's establishment of three giant unified petrochemical complexes, together with Japanese and American firms. Taiwan's success has been spurred on by $2 billion in petrochemical investments between 1973 and 1979.[46]

The Centrally Planned Economies

Through deals with Western European corporations, the Soviet Union and Eastern Europe loom large on the global petrochemical horizon. Soviet natural gas reserves of 28 trillion cubic metres are believed to be the world's largest, and would provide more than 80 years' output at the 1977 production level of 346 billion cubic metres.[47] In terms of vital feedstocks, only the Soviet Union with its vast oil, gas and coal reserves is self-sufficient. The rest of the Council for Mutual Economic Assistance (CMEA) is heavily dependent on OPEC. Several Eastern European countries have been bartering machinery for oil and intend to enlarge these trading relationships.[48]

Since the early 1970s, petrochemical contracts have been signed mainly in the form of barter or buy-back arrangements, where Western firms accept the commodity rather than cash for at least part of the payments for their engineering expertise and plant and equipment supplies.[49] The usual procedure is for large contracting and engineering firms to buy, under licence, processes developed by the chemical conglomerates. They then contract with Eastern European governments to deliver the plants' products, once on stream, to a Western European trader or chemical corporation. Through the French corporation Technip, the Soviet Union is building petrochemical complexes in Ufa and Omsk to begin production in 1980–81. Technip has agreed to buy back Russian products of equal value to the contracts.[50] A 1973 France–USSR contract for a $100-million styrene and polystyrene complex will be paid back in part with eight and a half years' supply of polystyrene once the plant comes on stream.[51] In view of the expansionary momentum of the petrochemical industries in the CPEs, certain West European industrial leaders have voiced apprehension that products from these plants will soon be flooding into their own already saturated markets.

By the close of the 1970s, there were plans to build some sixty petro-chemical plants under East-West barter agreements; well before their completion, already as much as 30 per cent of CMEA's output has been earmarked for the world market. Together with other chemicals, these petrochemical imports are likely to turn a Western European chemicals trade surplus of $1.8 billion with CMEA in 1977 into a deficit of $1.7 billion by 1985.[52] While in appearance a 'save-capitalism' device in the short run, the buy-back deals will aggravate the crisis of capitalist overproduction in the medium and long run. And to make matters even worse, the UCEs and China, poor in hard currency, are looking increasingly to buy-back deals to propel their industries into the 1980s.

A newer entrant to the world petrochemical arena is China, with considerable bridging finance via Japanese trade agreements. Two recent events have launched China on a future commitment to large-scale, export-oriented petrochemical expansion. Firstly, major oil discoveries in 1977 promised to push China's annual 90-million-ton production well over 100 million in the near future.[53] Secondly, early in 1975, China signed a $20 billion, eight-year trade agreement with Japan embracing modernization and expansion of its petrochemical industry. Two large ethylene plants built largely by Japanese corporations are already on stream, with another under construction in Kirin Province.[54]

New contracts were signed throughout the late 1970s with firms linked to the omnipresent *sogo shosha,* such as the Mitsui Corporation, Mitsubishi Heavy Industries Co., and C. Itoh & Co. Corporate penetration is further revealed in the contracts, typified by a 1979 agreement where Mitsui Petro-chemicals provides production technology and Mitsui Engineering services the equipment. French,[55] German, Italian and British corporations are involved in similar deals. Further, China clearly intends to meet its import requirements by raising exports in the petroleum chain. What remains unclear amidst current political instability is how rapid the growth of import require-ments will be, and at what point in the petroleum chain (i.e. crude oil, refined petroleum, petrochemicals, chemical fibres, yarn, cloth and/or garments) the exports will be selected.

It is clear, as with Eastern Europe, that an export barrage from China will commence in the near future. The swarm of technical and buy-back deals in the face of this contradiction, however, was explained by the General Secretary of Italy's Foreign Trade Department: 'Western producers have no choice but to try to get a foot in the door. The payoff is . . . too great to ignore.'[56]

Chemical Fibre Overview

The output of chemical fibres doubled in volume between the mid-1960s and the mid-1970s.[57] Notwithstanding chronic overcapacity, sizeable growth was recorded in the late 1970s for both non-cellulosic and cellulosic fibres, resulting in a growing gap between output and capacity. Global variations have been marked, with the United States displaying an impressive fibre output increase in the 1970s, while Western Europe output has declined in several years of the past decade.

A marked feature of the world fibre industry has been the shifting geographical spheres in world output portrayed in Table 5.3. The DCEs today account for around 75 per cent of synthetic fibres (non-cellulosics) while the share of the UCEs has risen to around 17 per cent (see Table 5.3). In the other major branch of man-made fibres, cellulosics, the share of the DCEs has fallen to a little over 50 per cent, while the CPEs' share exceeds one-third of total output. At present, per capita world consumption of polyester is around one kilogram; in Western Europe three kilograms, the United States seven kilograms. Price-wise, polyester has been cheaper than wool since the mid-1960s and cheaper than cotton for most of the 1970s.

With the mushrooming of the petrochemical industry, the largest additions to chemical fibre capacity are planned in the emerging UCEs, especially the oil-producers. In the DCEs, capacity expansion is projected for non-cellulosics with a net decline for cellulosics, i.e. rayon and acetate (see Table 5.4). Even in the CPEs, where cellulosics still comprise the bulk of total chemical fibre capacity, non-cellulosics are steadily acquiring bigger market shares. Outside the socialist countries, cellulosics have been reduced to about a quarter of aggregate chemical fibre capacity in both the DCEs and UCEs.

The chemical fibre war of the 1980s is already discernible from the figures in Table 5.4. The struggle for larger market shares must, therefore, be evaluated not only within the context of the industry proper and of pricing policies, but also in the light of its wider impact on all fibres. Hence cotton textile producers can expect little respite, notwithstanding a continuing rise in prices of petroleum feedstocks.

Besides the shifting structural configuration of the chemical fibre industry and the global division of labour, there are other factors that continue to bedevil the industry in both UCEs and DCEs: endemic over-capacity and the pull for greater economic autarchy in certain countries. Overcapacity meshes with growing capitalization to produce a devastating employment picture, especially in DCEs (due to their larger numbers employed in the industry).

111

Table 5.3
World Production of Synthetic and Cellulosic Fibres, 1966 and 1978

| | Synthetic Fibres | | | | | Cellulosic Fibres | | | |
| | '000 tons | | % | | | '000 tons | | % | |
	1966	1978	1966	1978		1966	1978	1966	1978
USA	916	3,253	37.7	32.3	USSR	362	635	10.5	17.6
Japan	450	1,413	18.5	14.0	USA	758	560	21.9	15.6
West Germany	213	746	8.8	7.4	Japan	516	424	14.9	11.8
USSR	96	475	4.0	4.7	United Kingdom	n.a.	217	n.a.	6.0
Taiwan	3	464	0.1	4.6	East Germany	153	163	4.4	4.5
Rep. of Korea	2	433	0.1	4.3	India	88	153	2.5	4.2
Italy	139	403	5.7	4.0	China	38	145	1.1	4.0
United Kingdom	n.a.	402	n.a.	4.0	West Germany	280	133	8.1	3.7
France	109	247	4.5	2.4	Austria	65	107	1.9	3.0
Mexico	14	199	0.6	2.0	Poland	80	93	2.3	2.6
Spain	24	189	1.0	1.9	Italy	180	86	5.2	2.4
Brazil	19	180	0.8	1.8	Benelux	96	75	2.8	2.1
Poland	30	152	1.2	1.5	France	126	74	3.6	2.1
Benelux	71	133	2.9	1.3	Czechoslovakia	72	71	2.1	2.0
East Germany	21	127	0.9	1.3	Taiwan	6	70	0.2	1.9
DCEs	2,183	7,290	89.9	72.4	DCEs	2,467	1,974	71.3	54.8
CPEs	174	1,090	7.2	10.8	CPEs	764	1,212	22.1	33.7
UCEs	70	1,693	2.9	16.8	UCEs	229	414	6.6	11.5
Total	*2,427*	*10,073*	*100.0*	*100.0*	*Total*	*3,460*	*3,600*	*100.0*	*100.0*

Source: Computed from data in International Rayon and Synthetic Fibres Committee (CIRFS), *Information on Man-Made Fibres*, Paris, 1979.

Britain's giant Imperial Chemical Industries (ICI) announced plans in 1979
to reduce employment in its fibres division at a rate of 4 per cent
annually.[58] In the United Kingdom as a whole, the British Fibres Training
Board forecast fibres employment to drop between 4 and 8 per cent from
1979 to 1981.[59] Even in West Germany, which can boast one of the lowest
overall unemployment figures in Europe, the chemical fibres sector
recorded very large figures — between 22 and 28 per cent — from 1975 to
1977.[60]

Table 5.4
World Production of Chemical Fibres, 1971–79 (000 tons)

	Western Europe	United States	Japan	Others	Total
1971	2,882	2,572	1,633	2,238	9,325
1972	3,049	3,032	1,601	2,565	10,247
1973	3,420	3,435	1,818	2,911	11,584
1974	3,171	3,317	1,620	3,202	11,310
1975	2,611	2,983	1,435	3,645	10,674
1976	3,164	3,327	1,616	4,092	12,199
1977	3,016	3,668	1,712	4,405	12,801
1978	3,223	3,869	1,823	4,880	13,795
1979	3,250	4,150	1,822	5,115	14,337

% share

1971	30	28	18	24	100
1972	30	30	16	24	100
1973	30	30	16	24	100
1974	28	30	14	28	100
1975	24	28	13	35	100
1976	26	27	13	34	100
1977	24	29	13	34	100
1978	23	28	13	36	100
1979	23	29	13	37	100

1971 = 100

1971	100	100	100	100	100
1972	106	118	98	115	110
1973	119	134	111	130	124
1974	110	129	99	143	121
1975	91	116	88	163	114
1976	110	129	99	183	131
1977	105	143	105	197	137
1978	112	150	112	218	148
1979	113	160	112	229	154

Source: Computed from data of Enka BV, Netherlands.

In addition to these bleak statistics, demand prospects for fibre consumption are grim. The most recent chemical industry estimates suggest that synthetic fibre growth, which averaged more than 20 per cent per annum in the 1960s, will collapse to less than five per cent after 1990.[61]

The Developed Capitalist Economies

The depth of Western Europe's fibre crisis is manifest in the huge losses estimated by Enka Glanzstoff at $4.3 billion between mid-1974 and 1979. And there are no symptoms of respite for the 1980s, with prevailing capacity utilization hovering around 75 per cent as against the 85 per cent average break-even point of the chemical fibre industry.

Despite several plant closures since 1975, the chairman of the West German firm Hoechst contends that 25—30 per cent of Western Europe's fibre capacity must still be shut down if supply and demand are to balance.[62] Much of the impetus for fibre growth outside Europe (through technology, machinery, capital, construction, management and engineering) originates from the very same corporations now reaping losses because of stagnation in Western Europe.

The shift of the chemical fibre industry out of its traditional orbit, notably to UCEs, is generally geared to market pre-emption[63] and tapping lower labour and raw material costs. Europe's relatively high costs put the fibre industry not only at a disadvantage *vis-a-vis* UCEs, but, as an Akzo spokesman asserted, wages of fibre workers in the Netherlands and Germany in 1975 were already 30—50 per cent higher than in the United States. The gap has widened, in fact, with the accelerated depreciation of the dollar since 1978.[64] Higher petroleum and petrochemical prices in Europe in 1973 and again in 1979 have only aggravated the problem.

In large measure, the power of the United States in the chemical fibres sector is based upon relatively greater energy independence than Europe and Japan. It is this price/cost advantage which explains the fact that certain US chemical giants had annexed almost a third of the British polyester filament market by 1980. According to CIRFS, estimates of United States corporations' cost advantage stemming from cheaper feedstocks is $250 for each $1,500-worth of polyester staple, which works out to a US cost advantage of 17 per cent. Reverberations of the uninterrupted global fibre crisis are thus by no means uniform among the chemical giants. To speak of a homogeneous 'fibre crisis' among all the major economic actors would be to ignore the casual factors of unequal growth which, in all likelihood, will deepen the antagonisms in the 1980s. Du Pont's fibre sales, for example, have systematically been pushed from $2.6 billion (1975) to $3.4 billion (1978) to $4.1 billion (1979). Structurally this growth is mirrored in the shifting commodity composition of consolidated sales and net income, with fibres chalking up profits of $286 million in 1979 (Table 5.5).

European fibre capacity has risen markedly since the onset of the 1970s despite the relatively small volume of new investment; it is innovations which are responsible for boosting output. However, these relatively minor innovations have also raised the unit volume produced per worker, thereby contributing to increasing overcapacity. While there have been certain official and quasi-official statements on the urgency of submitting to market forces, national governments and the trade union movement have proved largely unresponsive to these appeals.

Table 5.5
Du Pont: Consolidated Sales and Net Income from Fibres

	1975	1977	1979
% of Consolidated sales	36	33	33
% of Net income	2	11	31

Source: *Annual Report* 1979.

Chemical corporations are themselves reluctant to cut back in a marketing area that absorbs about 25 per cent of their petrochemical output. The expiry of patents on nylon, polyester and acrylic fibres has touched off an investment boom based on the expectation that chemical fibre output would grow at the 1960s rate of 15 per cent.

Whereas in the early 1970s Western Europe's trade was roughly in balance, imports have now outpaced exports, and are equivalent to around 14 per cent of the region's fibre output. The cost-price gap of certain basic fibres would suggest that plants are being operated at well below long-term break-even point (see Table 5.6). This milieu of cost-price squeeze renders the survival of the small and medium-sized corporate entity, with no recourse to cross-subsidization, almost impossible.

Table 5.6
Cost-Price Gaps for Selected Chemical Fibres, Western Europe, 1977

	Nylon 6	Polyester	Acrylic
Labour	11	17	11
Raw materials	65	47	50
Energy and utilities	4	3	13
Other current costs	4	7	10
Capital costs	16	26	16
Selling price	100	100	100
Price necessary to stay in business	116	119	147

Source: Enka Glanzstoff

With the run-up in cotton prices in recent years, textile producers have resorted to mini-blends, i.e. cotton mixed with a 5 to 35 per-cent content of polyester staple. In several cases, sheeting cloth, now equally divided between cotton and polyester, is anticipated to be adjusted to 65-per-cent polyester. In industrial textiles, polyester staple and warp-knit fibres have also begun to erode the still dominant market share held by cotton cloth as a base for coating.[65]

On an industry-wide basis, the United States is a global leader in chemicals, encompassing 45 per cent of the world's top 200 companies' output in 1976.[66] This primacy is mirrored — though to a lesser degree — in synthetic fibres, where the USA's slice of 32 per cent of world output (1978) is more than double the 14 per cent held by the second-ranking producer, Japan. Even in the distinctly secondary and apparently declining cellulosic man-made fibre industry, only the Soviet Union has greater capacity.

To a large extent, United States chemical power resides in its relatively greater energy independence compared to Europe and Japan. Internal oil production meets about 60 per cent of petrochemical needs, which is translated into a cost advantage for polyester of 30–40 cent/kg over the rest of the DCEs.[67] In the economic crisis of the late 1970s, this price differential was responsible for an outburst of inter-imperialist rivalries between the United States and the European Economic Community. Contending that US fibres have captured major shares of their domestic markets, EEC countries threaten to revive anti-dumping legislation and invoke GATT (General Agreement on Tariffs and Trade) rules to beat back this onslaught.[68] This is but one outgrowth of the oil price hikes in a climate of economic crisis threatening widespread protectionism and intensified crises in the 1980s.

The record 9 billion pounds put out by United States chemical fibre producers in 1977,[69] however, was not based on rising US fibre consumption, which hovers around 1973 levels. Nor is it explained by rising exports, for these still represent about 6 per cent of output. Rather, chemical fibre's success rests simply on its steady erosion of cotton's share of US fibre end-uses, which have slipped from 70 to 30 per cent in the two decades since 1954.

Japan ranks third in the world's chemical fibre industries after the USA and Western Europe, although the fact that it also owns much of the non-Japanese output means that Japan's productive capacity is effectively higher than that of the United States. The expansion of the Japanese chemical fibre industry should therefore be examined from the vantage point of ownership and control and not in terms of traditional international trade analysis which assumes that national location equals ownership. Japan is the major inspirer of UCE exports to developed countries, which in large part stem from its overseas investments.

Japan's chemical fibre industry began in 1951 when Toray bought a Du Pont licence and commenced nylon production. During the immediate years of reconstruction, nine companies produced polyester under licence from the United States and Europe. With a swiftly expanding domestic market, chemical fibre output surged from 54,000 tons (1955) to 380,000 (1965). By 1970, it was second only to that of the United States.[70] Closely allied to these developments was the sweeping integration of fibre producers with manufacturing mills, clothing producers and the *sogo shosha*. Unhampered by anti-trust legislation or labour activism, the top seven Japanese fibre makers responded to the fibres crisis by cutting their payrolls. Number two fibre maker Teijin, for example, simply sacked 2,600 employees in late 1978; a production cartel, formed in April 1978, has aided its rationalization. Overseas expansion is focused in Asia: Thailand, Hong Kong, South Korea, the Philippines, Taiwan, Malaysia, Singapore and Indonesia, with corporations showing interest in the Middle East and Latin America in the second half of the 1970s. A more detailed sectoral breakdown indicates that, although Latin America had played a negligible role in the early 1970s, by 1976 it was the second major region, receiving one-fifth of Japanese foreign investments in the textile industry. It is precisely these corporate structures,[71] partially and wholly Japanese-owned, in South East Asia and elsewhere that are now competing with Japanese domestic output to a point where protectionist measures for domestic producers are being sought and granted.

The Underdeveloped Capitalist Economies

The shift in the international division of labour in the chemical fibre industry towards the UCEs has not reached the proportions of the textile, clothing, or petrochemical industries. However, UCE participation is dominated by the now familiar group of countries. Two of the four largest chemical fibre producing UCEs are not oil producers: South Korea and Taiwan. Of the other two, Brazil is still a net chemical fibre importer and only Mexico is a net exporter. Brazil's textile fabric expansion has been so out of proportion that cotton exports are being drastically curbed to meet internal demand, and this marketing trend seems likely to be followed by several cotton producing countries. Symptomatic of Brazil's textile ascendancy has been the unrelenting expansion of chemical fibre output, which soared eleven-fold between 1963 and 1973.

Mexico's expansion has been even more stunning. Chemical fibres have been the vanguard of the entire Mexican chemical/petrochemical industry, chalking up a 23-per-cent annual growth rate (by volume) from 1970 to 1976.[72] Affiliates of such companies as Du Pont, Monsanto, Celanese, and BASF have used cheap feedstocks from Pemex to set up a variety of chemical fibre operations. Yet Mexico, like other UCEs with export-oriented sectors, has not escaped the overcapacity crisis of the DCEs. With the notable exception of fertilizers, there are no end-uses into which Mexico could shift petrochemical production without facing glutted markets (see Table 5.7). And, in the case of fertilizers, the time lag between a decision to undertake a major expansion and eventual commissioning of the plant is five to eight years.

South Korea's advances in synthetic fibre output have been no less

117

impressive: from 16 million square metres in 1962 to 541 million in 1976.[73] One of its leading synthetic fibre manufacturers spelled out the technological implications of being a late starter: 'We came into nylon manufacturing well after the United States and Japan. But at least that gave us the advantage of being able to install the most modern plant. At present, South Korea's total synthetic fibre output is one-sixth of Japan's, but we have a third of Japan's population and one-sixth of Japan's *per capita* income.'[74] Sixty per cent of this growth is destined for the world market.[75]

Table 5.7
Mexico: Petrochemical End Products, 1978

Chemical End-Uses	Installed Capacity (tons/year)	Used Capacity (%)
Artificial and synthetic fibres	291,840	62.0
Synthetic fibre polymers	273,880	61.5
Resins[1]	340,660	68.7
Plastifiers	73,130	40.4
Fertilizers[2]	1,820,500	89.3
Pesticides	29,499	55.2
Elastomers	95,125	72.4
Rubber-related products	83,444	59.6
Diverse products	272,800	61.3
Intermediate products	881,218	72.3

1. Does not include polyethylene; this is accounted for in the basic sector.
2. Does not include direct usage ammonia; this is accounted for in the basic sector.

Source: UNIDO, *Development and Outlook of the Petrochemical Industry in Mexico,* ID/WG.268/3 (2 February 1978), p.9.

Taken together with Taiwan, South Korea's fibre capacity is rapidly approaching Japan's in several areas. According to the Japan Chemical Fibres Association, 'production capacity of Korea and Taiwan combined for polyester filament came to 90 per cent of Japan's 1,531,200 lbs/day as of July 1976; polyester staple 93 per cent of Japan's 1,672,000 lbs; acrylic staple 43 per cent of Japan's 2,032,800 lbs. Asian countries are making increased efforts to become self-sufficient in the supply of fibres, and Korea and Taiwan in the supply of raw petrochemical materials.'[76]

In other Asian countries too, notably Thailand, already by 1977 synthetic fibre capacity (built almost entirely with Japanese capital) exceeded domestic demand. Thus, rising surpluses of chemical fibre capacity are seen to be not a unique feature of DCEs, but of UCEs as well. The quest for export markets will not be easy, since UCEs are obstructed by a panoply of restrictionist measures in all major regions.[77]

The Centrally Planned Economies
A sustained chemical fibre build-up in Eastern Europe since the early 1970s gives an indication of the disparate growth rates within the overall European regional economy as a whole (see Table 5.8). The extent of growth is due primarily to unadapted transfer of DCE technology, a process more obvious in chemicals than in any other manufacturing sector.

Table 5.8
Europe: Output of Cellulosics and Synthetics, 1970 and 1978

	Eastern Europe	Percentage of total	Western Europe	Percentage of total	Total
		(in 000 tons)			
Cellulosics					
1970	851.5	43	1,119.1	57	1,970.6
1978	1,067.3	53	950.3	47	2,017.6
Annual growth rate	2.9	–	–2.0	–	0.3
Synthetics					
1970	361.4	19	1,506.5	81	1,867.9
1978	1,010.0	29	2,438.1	71	3,448.1
Annual growth rate	13.7	–	6.2	–	8.0

Source: Computed from data in International Rayon and Synthetic Fibres Committee (CIRFS), *Information on Man-Made Fibres*, Paris, 1979.

Until recently, CPEs were an important market for chemical fibres from Western Europe, but this is now changing as self-sufficiency rises. The export capacity of the socialist world has been aided by their willingness when dealing with UCEs, to barter chemicals for primary commodities as well as to promote UCE user industries. The impact of increased CPE exports is strengthened by the shift from cellulosics into synthetic fibres which have grown from 26 per cent of chemical fibre output in 1970 to almost half at present.[78]

China, while still importing some synthetic fibre and fabric from Japan, is well on the way to chemical fibre self-sufficiency. Since the acreage available for new cotton plantings is limited, China intends to meet rising per capita fibre demand by a rapid boost in chemical fibre. By 1985, chemical fibres' share of total fibre consumption is planned to reach 40 per cent, a huge figure for a population that is likely to surpass one billion by that year. This would not have been possible without close collaboration with the chemical fibre oligopoly, in terms of technology and licensing agreements.

In our examination of two industries whose rapid global expansion in the 1970s led to a crisis of overcapacity by the close of the decade, we have described what is becoming a characteristic of several industrial sectors. The extension of these industries to CPEs, OPEC, Mexico, and the giant dwarfs has generated exports which are intruding onto the national markets of the very corporations which originally built them. Now, within this framework of crisis, inter-imperialist rivalries are erupting not only in fibres but in a proliferation of industries such as television and textiles. Exacerbating this overcapacity and these antagonisms are the TNCs, which by definition transcend national frontiers in their pursuit of profit. We turn in the following chapter to the mechanisms deployed by transnational oligopoly in its quest for market aggrandizement and the inherent crises which are its concomitants.

References

1. *Financial Times,* 17 January 1978.
2. See UNIDO, *The Petrochemical Industry* (New York, 1973).
3. *Wool Record,* 30 November 1973.
4. United Nations, *Studies in Petrochemicals,* (New York, 1966).
5. UNIDO, *World-Wide Study of the Petrochemical Industry* (Vienna, 1978).
6. *The Economist,* 20 November 1976.
7. Cf. ICAC, *Annual Review of the World Cotton Situation, 1975/76.* A possible resurgence of cellulosics is foreshadowed by the diversification programmes of several major oil corporations into forest products, supported by large-scale research efforts.
8. Cf. M. Quinlan, 'Planning for 1980s feedstocks', *Petroleum Economist,* November 1977. There appears to be substantial potential in commercially marketing coal-based petrochemicals, and several of the oil majors already control extensive coal deposits.
9. The upshot has been that bulk plastic prices, for example, tumbled by 30–40 per cent between June 1976 and October 1977; cf. *The Economist,* 25 February 1978.
10. *Chemical Week,* 8 February 1978.
11. The capital-labour ratio ranges from $20,000–$100,000 for each new job created in the mid-1960s, figures that have risen considerably since then. Cf. C. Mercier, *The Petrochemical Industry and the Possibilities of its Establishment in the Developing Countries* (Paris, 1966). In DCEs, the battle to slash production costs is leading to increasingly large manufacturing units whose annual output is beyond the domestic requirements of many UCEs.
12. Cf. forecasts by the Chemical Industries Center, quoted in *Chemical Week,* 28 March 1979; Eurofinance findings quoted in *Financial Times,*

25 April 1978; and UNIDO, *First Consultation Meeting on the Petro-chemical Industry Report,* Mexico City, 12—16 March 1979.

13. Figures from Chemical Industries Center at SRI International, in *Chemical Week,* 28 March 1979.
14. *The Economist,* 18 March 1978.
15. *The Economist,* 7 April 1979, p. 3. of 'Chemicals: A Survey'.
16. D.M. Wallace, 'Saudi Arabia building costs', *Hydrocarbon Processing,* November 1976. It has also been suggested that the estimate of the operating cost in Saudi Arabia of a world-scale petrochemical complex could run between 60 and 80 per cent above that in DCEs. Such estimates, note Turner and Bedore, 'may be too pessimistic, but we certainly assume that for the first wave of Iranian and Saudi Arabian export-oriented projects, both capital and operating costs will be distinctly higher than those of the industries they are trying to replace elsewhere in the world' (L. Turner and J. Bedore, 'Saudi and Iranian petrochemicals and oil refining: trade warfare in the 1980s?', *International Affairs,* (London, October 1977).
17. *Ibid.*
18. The industry originated in the United States in the 1920s. Although it expanded during the 1920s and 1930s, it was not until the onset of the Second World War that it became a major supplier of organic chemicals.
19. *Forbes,* 2 October 1978.
20. *Financial Times,* 24 February 1978.
21. The divergence between production capacity and consumption was clearly manifest in certain companies before 1977. This is seen in the 1977 loss of DM124 million by Deutsche BP, more than double the losses in 1976. For Deutsche Shell these losses rocketed from DM 186 million in 1976 to over 400 million in 1977.
22. Symptomatic of this are the millions of dollars being poured into a 10-unit petrochemical complex at Sines, Portugal's huge and controversial industrial complex south of Lisbon; cf. *Financial Times,* 2 February 1979.
23. *Financial Times,* 25 April 1978.
24. *Chemical Economy and Engineering Review,* February 1978, p. 46.
25. *Financial Times,* 22 January 1979.
26. United Nations, *Studies in Petrochemicals,* (New York, 1966), p. 130.
27. Turner and Bedore, 'Saudi and Iranian petrochemicals', p. 579.
28. *Petroleum Economist,* July 1976. Even in Kuwait, which has one of the more sophisticated petrochemical industries in the Middle East, 'about 50 per cent is still being flared, a record unequaled elsewhere in the Mideast', although plans are already afoot to utilize the remainder in new facilities, *Chemical Week,* March 23, 1977.
29. By the same token, it will acquire an import substituting character. Although South Korea's current five-year plan (1977—81) does not concentrate on petrochemicals as earlier plans did, a very significant import substitution build-up is now underway. An equally vigorous Korean export drive entails an outlay of one billion dollars for petrochemical expansion and new plant construction, and constitutes part of a $10-billion industrial development plan aimed at doubling

exports to $20 billion. Crucial to this plan are the two major petro-
chemical centres at Ulsan and Yochan (built as joint ventures with the
Mitsui Corporation) which will slash petrochemical imports by one
billion dollars annually.

30. *Chemical Age,* 7 January 1977.
31. Undertaken also as a joint venture with C. Itoh, Mitsubishi Methanol,
and W.R. Grace.
32. One of the Yanbu complexes (due on stream in 1981) will operate
as a 50/50 joint venture by SABIC (Saudi Arabian Basic Industries
Corp.) and Shell International. The latter will be the exclusive marketing
agent for the project in the USA, South-east Asia, Japan, and Europe.
33. *International Herald Tribune,* February 1978, special number on OPEC.
Underlining this point, OPEC's Secretary General Mohamed Ali Jaidah
stated that 'OPEC countries are tired of hearing about the problems
of surplus petrochemical capacity while new plants are continually
being constructed in the developed countries'. To achieve this goal of
technology transfers and access to new markets, he added (with reference
to OPEC's success in raising oil prices), 'I must say in all seriousness
that unless greater progress is made in redressing the imbalance our
member countries will have no recourse but to adopt collective
strategies to achieve their aims'.
34. *International Herald Tribune,* 27 November 1978.
35. It is reported that ethane will be priced at US$0.43−0.53 per million
BTUs − i.e. one quarter the cost in Western Europe and the US
(International Herald Tribune, February 1978 special number on
OPEC).
36. Quoted in *Business Week,* 13 March 1978.
37. *Chemical Week,* 10 August 1977.
38. *The Economist,* 2 July 1977.
39. Its petrochemical arm is the Instituto Venezolano de Petroquimica.
40. Pemex (Petroleos Mexicanos) is the state monopoly for the production
of basic petrochemicals. The corporation is empowered to grant licences
to private industry for the output of secondary petrochemicals with
the proviso that they are 60-per-cent owned by Mexican nationals.
41. *Union Bank of Switzerland Reports, Mexico* (May, 1978), p. 4; and F.
Manzanilla, *Development and Outlook of the Petrochemical Industry
in Mexico,* (Vienna, 1978).
42. *Financial Times,* 15 November 1978. In 1978, assets exceeded $11
billion, sales hovered around $5.4 billion, and the number of employees
passed the 100,000 mark.
43. *The Economist,* 7 April 1979.
44. For the impressive global targets of the Baroda Complex, an important
component of which includes synthetic fibres, see *Chemical Age,* 26
August 1977.
45. *Financial Times,* 2 May 1979.
46. *Financial Times,* 11 May 1979. Certain Taiwanese corporations are
exporting, under the impetus of state export promotion policies, as
much as four-fifths of their total output.
47. *International Herald Tribune,* 16 August 1978.
48. Both Hungary and East Germany have large reserves of natural gas.

49. Before this time, DCE engineering and construction corporations usually demanded cash since most lacked the expertise required to trade in the commodity. Now, several corporations have set up commodity trading groups to fulfil marketing functions.

50. Four-fifths will be paid in diesel fuel and naphtha and the remainder in xylenes and benzene, *Chemical Week,* 17 August 1977.

51. *Chemical Week,* 17 August 1977.

52. *Financial Times,* 6 November 1978.

53. *European Chemical News,* 16 September 1977.

54. Toyo Engineering and Mitsubishi Petrochemical built the first two, and Ishikawajimi Harima Heavy Industries is supplying materials for the third; *Chemical Week,* 22 March 1978.

55. A 'turn-key' contract with the French firms Technip and Specitrim for a petrochemical complex in 1976 was worth 1,200 million French francs, the largest contract China had ever signed with a Western country at that time; *Textile Asia,* March 1976.

56. *Chemical Week,* 20 December 1978.

57. International Rayon and Synthetic Fibres Committee, *Information on Man-made Fibres* (Paris, 1978), and *Chemical Week,* 15 March 1978. There are also wide variations in the advance of certain specific fibres. While non-cellulosics are expected to grow at 7.5 per cent by the end of 1979 in the USA, the biggest gains are expected in nylon carpet yarn (16 per cent), polyester textile filament (10 per cent), and polyester staple (8 per cent).

58. *Financial Times,* 10 April 1979.

59. *Financial Times,* 25 October 1978.

60. Calculated from Eurostat, *Employment and Unemployment: 1971– 1977,* (Statistical Office of the European Economic Community, Brussels, 1978).

61. *Chemical Week,* 28 March 1979.

62. *Chemical Week,* 25 January 1978.

63. A prime example of this is the recent setting up by United States chemical and financial interests of a major polyester plant in Costa Rica, which is expected to meet the needs of the five-nation Central American Common Market.

64. *Chemical Week,* 4 June 1975.

65. *Financial Times,* 21 December 1977.

66. *Chemical Age,* 24 June 1977.

67. *Chemical Age,* 3 December 1976. This advantage eroded slightly as the United States continued to import higher percentages of their oil needs towards the end of the 1970s.

68. See *Financial Times,* 17 October 1979; and *The New York Times,* 1 August 1979.

69. *Chemical Week,* 29 March 1978.

70. Exports grew rapidly as well, accounting for a third of output as early as 1965. See M.Y. Yoshino, *Japan's Multinational Enterprises* (London, 1976), p. 64.

71. Within this framework is the $2.5–3.0 billion petrochemical complex led by the Sumitomo Chemical Corporation and financed by 23 Japanese companies, plus the Overseas Economic Co-operation Fund, as a joint

venture with the Singapore government. It is the biggest investment to
date in South-east Asia. *Financial Times,* 1 November 1977.

72. UNIDO, *Development and Outlook of the Petrochemical Industry in Mexico* (ID/WG.268/3; New York, 1978), p. 11.
73. *Business Week,* 12 December 1977, p. 37.
74. *Ibid.*
75. A more or less similar policy and strategy of overseas expansion is observable in South Korea's shipping industry.
76. *Daily New Record,* 24 January 1977. With the chemical fibre industry firmly entrenched, Taiwan is integrating backwards into petrochemicals. The state-owned Chinese Petroleum Corporation brought its third naphtha cracker on stream in 1978 and is planning a fourth; *International Herald Tribune,* 14 June 1978.
77. In its comment on export growth obstacles, *Japan Textile News* (August 1977) commented that Thailand has no coherent production flows from petrochemical complexes through the synthetic fibre industry and it must import feedstocks and raw materials. The few favourable marketing conditions stem from its marketing contiguity to such countries as India, China and Bangladesh.
78. United Nations, Economic Commission for Europe, *Market Trends for Chemical Products 1970–1975 and Prospects for 1980* (CHEM/GE.1/R.3/Add. 6, Geneva, 16 May 1977), p. 3. The 1980 Soviet plan expects synthetic fibres' share of chemical fibre output to increase from 40 per cent to over 50.

6. The Enmeshed Oligopolies: From Oil to Chemicals

The dramatic shift in the international division of labour in the petro-chemicals, fibres, and textiles industries has further synchronized the technological and marketing interrelationships of what we have designated as the enmeshed oligopolies. In this chapter we describe the interactions between the oil and chemical giants in the production, research and marketing of petrochemicals and chemical fibres – interactions which are crucial to the future course of the whole fibres and textiles industry. There are in fact no such entities as petrochemical or chemical fibre corporations. Petro-chemicals are produced by the oil and chemical giants or in joint ventures between them; chemical fibres fall within the domain of the chemical giants, although certain big corporations designated as textile majors (e.g. Courtaulds) are significant forces in chemical fibres.

Our first section describes some characteristics of the big corporations in the chemical, oil, and petrochemical industries, and the forms of inter-action between companies. This outline is followed by a number of specific case studies of major corporations of the chemical fibre oligopoly, which illuminate the origins and evolution of certain aspects of corporate reality, such as the relationship of the state apparatus and capital. Thirdly, we describe seven specific strategies of corporate annexation, ranging from research and development to transfer pricing. The final section dismantles the myth of prices as the unique behavioural determinant of major economic actors.

The multiple strands of chemical corporate power extend far beyond their own product lines. It is a truism that innovations in medicine, nucleonics, electronics and engineering, would have been utterly inconceivable without the creation of new materials by modern chemistry. In themselves, how-ever, inventions, innovations, and the permanent revolutionizing of scientific discovery are insufficient to explain the *modus operandi* of economic change. Rather, applied science in the service of corporations is implacably related to, and rooted in, the logic of capitalism's evolution over the last century, as spelled out by Professor David Noble (the argument is relevant not merely to the United States):

> As the first science-based industries in the country, the electrical and

chemical industries set the pattern of production and management for modern industry as a whole. Moreover, they produced the people — industry-minded physicists and chemists and, especially, the electrical and chemical engineers — who would carry the scientific revolution into the older and the new industries: extractive, petroleum, steel, rubber, and, most important of all in terms of American economic development, automotive. In all of these industries the systematic introduction of science as a means of production pre-supposed, and in turn reinforced, industrial monopoly. This monopoly meant control not simply of markets and productive plant and equip-ment but of science itself as well. Initially the monopoly over science took the form of patent control — that is, control over the products of scientific technology. It then became control over the process of scientific production itself, by means of organized and regulated industrial research. Finally it came to include command over the social prerequisites of this process: the development of the institu-tions necessary for the production of both scientific knowledge and knowledgeable people, and the integration of these institutions within the corporate system of science-based industry.[1]

Chemical Corporations

Without exception, all members of the world chemical oligopoly are horizon-tally and vertically integrated. Of the leading twenty-five corporations, those whose sales topped $174 billion in 1979, 10 were American; 3 West German; 3 Swiss; 3 Dutch; 2 Japanese; 1 French; 1 Italian; 1 Belgian; and 1 British. The big three German firms led the pack with combined sales of over $46 billion.[2] These 25 chemical corporations dominate all chemical end-uses, including plastics, paints, fertilizers, pharmaceuticals, dyestuffs, and synthetic rubber, and chemical fibres.[3] Within this overall chemical oligopoly, specific product lines are often dominated by a handful of firms. In the case of dyestuffs,[4] to mention but one oligopoly within the oligopoly, four German conglomerates have annexed more than two-fifths of world trade, four Swiss companies about one-third, and ICI 10 per cent.

Global price fixing; setting up of protected spheres of influence through cross-licensing; patent pooling and market allocation deals; individual or collusive action to deter the entry of newcomers; parallel and predatory pricing; and, above all, cartel arrangements have long been the hallowed practices of this oligopoly. National cartels blossomed shortly after the world economic crisis of 1873 in several chemical lines, producing, for instance, the Fertilizers Manufacturers' Association (1875) and the Sulphate of Ammonia Federation (1885) in Britain; the Alizarin Convention (consisting of three German firms which controlled 90 per cent of the global dyestuffs market) in 1881; and a Swiss dyestuff cartel in 1895.[5]

It was only a matter of time before competition-minimizing and risk-reducing cartelization transcended national boundaries, and the formal 1901 agreement between the United Alkali Company (UK) and a German syndicate of alkali producers ushered in an age of global cartels.[6] By 1939, the pace of inter-corporate linkages had reached such a tempo that an ICI historian could write that the

> long-established cartel system in the world chemical industry was at its ultimate pitch in labyrinthine complexities . . . I.C.I. business was governed by 800 agreements . . . Three cartels regulated world trade in nitrogen, in dyestuffs and in the process of hydrogenation. The alkali business was governed by agreements between I.C.I. and Solvay, Alkasse (U.S.A.) . . . Underpinning the whole was the Patents and Processes Agreement between I.C.I. and Du Pont, dated in 1929 and renewed in 1939.[7]

Today, all DCE governments authorize domestic export cartels, and with the exception of the United States and Japan, all confer their benediction on international cartels. By the mid-1970s, fifteen of West Germany's export cartels centred on chemicals, resorting to price restrictions, fixed quotas or sales syndicates. Likewise, 21 out of 167 Japanese cartels and four out of 38 US cartels were specifically concerned with chemical markets.[8]

Only rarely does such cartel activity reach the public eye. After what appeared to be widespread collusion in the international aniline dyestuff market, the EEC commission charged ten European firms with fixing prices between January 1964 and October 1970. Even after the imposition of fines, cartel members were able to continue to control prices within national markets.[9]

In certain chemical lines, one firm predominates, e.g. Courtaulds in rayon and ICI in methanol.[10] Likewise, in many national markets, one or two of the giants predominate. Montedison alone controls more than 60 per cent of Italy's chemical output, ICI[11] more than half of the UK output, and Solvay around 37 per cent of Belgian chemical sales.[12] West Germany's big three, Bayer, BASF and Hoechst, manufacture two-fifths of its chemical output, and in Japan chemical affiliates of the *sogo shosha* produce the bulk of chemical products. In the United States the industry, while led by Du Pont, Union Carbide, Dow Chemical and Monsanto (all with 1978 sales exceeding $5 billion), has seen the intrusion of such conglomerates as General Electric, ITT, Tenneco, and Eastman Kodak.[13] The vast reaches of conglomeration are glimpsed in an extremely limited listing of a few of the giants' other product lines: Montedison in electronics; Bayer in fashion; Hoechst in building materials; Dow Chemicals in banking; Rhone Poulenc in audio-visual aids; Ciba-Geigy in seeds; and Shell in retailing. Concentration in all chemical industries has been intensified by three pressing concerns: rising raw material costs, pollution clean-up devices, and costly new safety regulations in most DCEs.

Another major trend in chemicals has been increasing forays into overseas

127

markets. The total overseas sales figure (from foreign plants and exports) as a percentage of aggregate sales (1976) is extraordinarily high for several members of the oligopoly: 88 per cent for Akzo; Hoechst, 67 per cent; and ICI, 61 per cent.[14] Export success is further glimpsed in the list of leading US corporate exporters, where four fibre giants (Du Pont, Monsanto, Allied Chemical and Celanese) rank prominently among the top 35.[15] This globalized vision of the corporate chemical boardroom is aptly described by ICI's Chairman of the Board: 'The old distinction of looking at the manufacturing divisions as the UK and the continental Western Europe as the export area, is becoming inappropriate. There is no longer any territorial division with a Channel in between.'[16]

The Oil Majors

While our principal concern with the petrogiants derives from their massive push into petrochemicals and chemicals, it is mandatory to examine briefly the techniques by which they have acquired hegemony in all segments of the petroleum industry. As with other oligopolistic industries, the conglomerate thrusts of the petrogiants accept no limits to the momentum of the accumulation engine. In doing so, they obey the laws of motion of oligopolistic capitalism in its totality. Oil differs from other oligopolistic industries, in terms of sheer size, with industry sales now at the level of tens of billions of dollars. Joined to the OPEC oligarchy, the petrogiants clearly exhibit the morphology of oligopolistic structures.

In 1979, the 'sorocracy', or the 'seven sisters', as they are familiarly known (the top seven companies in Table 6.1), had total sales of $349 billion.[17] Not surprisingly, they fill seven of the eleven top slots in the list of the world's largest industrial corporations. These staggering surges in sales are related to the very structures, processes and mechanisms of the marketing and distribution channels controlled by big corporate oil. The tenfold boost in oil prices in the 1970s has contributed not only to an OPEC current account surplus now outstripping $115 billion, but no less crucially to the exponential growth of the petrogiants owing to the inextricable marketing interconnections between them and OPEC. Moreover, the marketing strides of the oil majors are measurable by their swiftly changing share of aggregate profits in US manufacturing: from 15 per cent in 1972 to 40 per cent in 1980. No less important is the fact that these massive profit flows are not imputable to an upsurge in aggregate corporate sales and profits, but in part have been siphoned off from the global manufacturing sector as a whole through higher prices.

The petrogiant oligopoly markets 75–80 per cent of global oil. The following section examines the techniques whereby the petrogiants became ensconced in the oil industry.

Table 6.1
World Petrogiants' Sales, 1978–79 ($ billions)

	1978	1979	1978 = 100
Seven Sisters			
Exxon	60.3	84.3	140
Royal Dutch/Shell	44.1	73.9	168
Mobil	34.7	47.9	138
British Petroleum	27.4	48.2	176
Texaco	28.0	39.1	140
Standard Oil (California)	23.2	31.8	136
Gulf Oil	18.0	23.9	133
Total	*235.7*	*349.1*	*148*
Others			
Cie Francaise des Petroles	13.5	18.3	135
Atlantic Richfield	12.3	16.2	132
Total	*25.8*	*34.5*	*134*
Grand total	*261.5*	*383.6*	*147*

Source: *Annual Reports* and trade sources.

Vertical Integration

The petroleum industry can be divided into four basic areas: crude oil exploration and production, refining, transportation,[18] and marketing. The overriding trait of the industry's leading firms is vertical integration, that is, corralling under one corporate roof the diverse operations through which the raw material is transformed into refined products for the final market.

Vertical integration in the United States reached its apotheosis with the Standard Oil Trust, which refined and marketed petroleum, and undercut its rivals by cheaper transportation. 'So long as it is possible,' wrote Ida Tarbell in her classic work on Standard Oil at the turn of the century, 'to own the exclusive carrier on which a great natural product depends for transportation, and to use this carrier to limit a competitor's supply or to cut off entirely that supply if the rival is offensive, and to always make him pay a higher rate than it costs the owner, it is ignorance and folly to talk about constitutional amendments limiting trusts.'[19] Dissolution of the Standard Oil Trust in 1911 meant that monopolistic domination was now to pass from a monopoly to an oligopoly of the integrated majors. Eight decades later, a Senate source could write: 'Since then, most petroleum pipelines have been continuously controlled by a handful of Standard Oil successor companies and a small number of other powerful integrated oil companies. Control of pipelines has enabled these companies *to entrench their position throughout the industry*, to earn monopoly profits, and to stifle competition from smaller companies.'[20] Over the years pipelines have become the major strategic device for maintaining control of the production, refining and marketing segments of the industry. And, of course, lower real costs of pipe-

line transportation have not been translated into lower consumer prices, but
into higher oil profits for the petroleum oligopoly. A torrent of anti-trust
legislation and the vast corpus of regulations in nine decades have in no way
impeded the oligopoly from restricting pipeline throughput capacity, when
expedient, to maximize downstream profits.

Concentration in pipeline transportation is higher than all other segments
of the industry. In 1973, the top four petrogiants controlled 48 per cent;
the top eight, 69 per cent; and the top 20, 96 per cent of the industry. In
1975, one company, the Colonial Pipeline Company (a joint venture owned
by ten major integrated companies) alone accounted for 44 per cent of total
barrel-mile pipeline movements of petroleum products in the United
States.[21]

Pipelines run to and from refineries, which are virtually the only
purchasers of crude oil and which again are almost the exclusive domain of
the petrogiants. They are complex, synchronized units for transforming the
hydrocarbon mix of different crude oils into a wide range of products from
the 'top of the barrel' — gasoline, propane, butane, and petrochemical feedstocks, such as benzene, xylene, and propylene; through the middle distil-
lates — home heating oil, diesel, jet fuel, and kerosene; down to the heavier
end of the barrel — residual fuel oil, petroleum coke, and asphalt. Given its
high capital intensity and its economies of scale, average unit costs dip
precipitously as capacity utilization rises. It is at this juncture once again
that we come to grips with the impact of technology on capitalism. Profitable
refinery operation demands full plant utilization, with a high premium on
availability of crude supplies. Here we perceive how 'barriers to entry'
becomes a battering ram of the oligopoly.

Pervasive vertical integration in the petroleum industry places the majors
in a position to foreclose markets to non-integrated competitors, denying
them access to raw materials or marketing outlets. By charging all customers,
including themselves, a high price for inputs or raw materials, while maintaining a stable output price, the vertically integrated firms are in a position
to make it difficult for non-integrated firms to compete. Moreover, vertical
integration reinforces the oligopolistic structure by diminishing the impact
of price instability. By internalizing cost adjustments in the form of transfer
prices, the destabilizing pressures on market prices may be minimized.

Other Characteristics
Oligopolistic pricing has long been a dominant trait of the industry, as neatly
summarized by Senator Edward Kennedy:

> The major oil companies continue to protest that the crude market is
> really competitive right now, and that the Government need not worry
> about protecting their independent brethren. In a competitive market,
> however, we would expect to find similar grades of crude to be sold
> at the same prices. But we do not. In a competitive market we would
> expect to find price differentials to be eroded. But we do not. In a

competitive market we would expect to find all buyers having equal
access at equal prices. But we do not. And, in a competitive market,
we would expect to find sales of lower-priced crude to expand in
response to higher demand. But we do not.[22]

At present eight petrogiants control two-thirds of the United States oil
industry's assets, and appropriate three-quarters of its profits. And yet
consistently the libations to 'free enterprise' flood the glossy coloured pages
of their annual reports. The pace of concentration continues unabated.
According to the Federal Trade Commission, the eight largest petrogiants
in 1955 produced 36 per cent of US crude, while the 20 largest grabbed 56
per cent; by 1970 these shares had leaped to 49 and 69 per cent
respectively.[23] United States census data[24] pinpointed that by 1975 the big
eight had further annexed 53 per cent, with at least 75 per cent in the bag
of the biggest twenty.

The industry's leader has long been Exxon, whose sales, from its more
than 400 subsidiaries, now outstrip $84 billion. The majors' awesome finan-
cial power, now far greater than at any time in their history, confers on them
an annexation potential possibly unrivalled in any other industry. 'The
prospects of big pools of incoming cash', writes *Business Week,* 'presents oil
industry strategists with a compelling need to find outlets for that cash —
either within energy or, if need be, outside energy. For no company is the
need greater than Exxon . . . Its long term debt grew from about $3 billion
in 1973 to about $4 billion last year, but its cash rose from $3.1 billion to
$5.2 billion in the same time. And the company plans no new debt to finance
an ambitious $27 billion capital investment programme over the next five
years.[25] It is this avalanche of accumulation which led Senator Kennedy to
declare before the US Senate Anti-Trust Committee that 'the potential for
mergers and acquisitions is staggering: Exxon, for example, could tomorrow
buy J.C. Penney, Du Pont, Goodyear, and Anheuser-Busch, using its accumulated cash and liquid assets.'[26]

Global annexation is being spearheaded by specially designed holding
companies — in the case of Exxon, Exxon Enterprises Incorporated. The
holding company has helped usher in the petrogiants' transition from horizontal and vertical integration to conglomeration. The case of coal in the
United States indicates the scale of conglomerate encroachment. Today,
thirteen petrogiants own one-fifth of all outstanding Federal coal leases,
containing 46 per cent of total recoverable coal. Yet in 1976 they
accounted for only 5 per cent of coal production on Federal lands, a
strategy aimed at propping up oil and gas prices until the majors find it
profitable to release the coal. Fourteen of the top twenty holders of coal
reserves are now oil giants or their subsidiaries; annexation began between
1967 and 1974, when the oil and gas giants boosted their coal reserve holdings by 141 per cent.[27] It seems now more than likely that the oil majors
are positioned to control — unless there are countervailing political forces to
impede them — the price and pace of development of virtually all energy

forms.

Of the massive incursion into energy fields ranging from nuclear to solar to fusion, the deepest in recent years has been into uranium. In his testimony on Gulf Oil (part of the Mellon empire), the Commissioner of the Pennsylvania Utilities Commission pointed out that 'it is an acknowledged fact that in combination with the British owned Rio Tinto Company, Gulf Oil is a major owner and supplier of nuclear fuel. You can imagine our surprise at learning that Consolidated Coal Company, the second largest in the nation was owned by these same Mellon interests. Recently, the control of the Consolidated Coal Company was merged by Mellon into Continental Oil Company, one of the nation's largest oil interests.'[28] Joining in the uranium race, Gulf Oil has bought out General Atomic; Arco has acquired Nuclear Materials Equipment Corporation; and Getty, Nuclear Fuels.

In other commodities, Shell produced and marketed $1.2 billion worth of aluminium, copper, zinc and nickel in 1978, sufficient to earn it a place in the *Fortune 500,* even without oil. Without exception all the oil conglomerates produce farm chemicals, and Tenneco has long been an agribusiness giant. Recent multi-million dollar mergers include Mobil Corporation's acquisition of Marcor Inc., the giant retailer and papermaker (1976); and Atlantic Richfield's acquisition (1977) of first Anaconda, one of the world's biggest copper corporations and later the British newspaper, *The Observer.* Diversified product lines that have been penetrated include electronic subsystems, computer software, almond and tomato growing, word processing equipment, advanced batteries, fasteners, medical equipment, etc.

Joint Ventures
The frontal assaults of Big Oil — by no means exclusively limited to the United States — have been buttressed by pervasive exchange agreements and the omnipresent practice of joint venturing. Joint ventures, notably in pipeline construction, mushroomed in the 1920s as a means of circumventing anti-trust laws. Most, if not all, modern large-diameter pipeline systems are joint ventures.[29] These agreements continue to confer on individual major participants veto power over pipeline expansion, and preserve downstream product prices while stabilizing market shares of participants.

For the oligopoly, joint ventures, apart from the economic demands of profit maximization, serve other political imperatives. 'The frequency of inter-company exposure and participation', noted one expert, 'unquestionably provides opportunities for exchanges of information, a discussion of marketing practices, perhaps some production planning, and perhaps a general forum of unanimity with respect to such problems as scarcity, prices, political associations and other pertinent affairs . . .'[30] The community of interests that welds the petrogiants together is also seen in their joint operations in oil nations (of which Aramco is the clearest incarnation on the international level), joint bidding on Federal and State lands, and their common banking ties.

Political Power

Corporations with the economic power of the oil majors inevitably tend to use that power in the form of bribes (payoffs) for political purposes. 'After all,' acknowledged one of the top executives of Big Oil before Senator Church's committee on multinationals, 'ten million dollars is small change, given what we are involved in.' Indeed only the scale of payoffs has changed since the comment of William Demarest-Lloyd at the turn of the century 'that the Standard Oil Co. has done everything with the Pennsylvania Legislature except to refine it.' But the payoff complex is only one aspect of political power wielded by big oil companies. Another is the capacity to conceal and distort information to an unprecedented degree:

> Until recently, almost every bit of information that we had about energy came from the corporation, often collected by their trade associations, like the American Gas Association, the American Petroleum Institute, with no questions asked about methodology, nobody challenging the organization of the figures . . . The National Petroleum Council launders (the information), puts it into a fancy new volume with some more statistics at a cost of millions, we are told, and the President of the United States will get on the air and talk about taxation, rationing, controls, embargoes, arms policy, survival, war and peace, based on figures which he hasn't the foggiest notion of their validity.[31]

A recent example is Exxon's persistent refusal to communicate to the Federal Trade Commission what it labels 'proprietary information'.

Such demonstrations of political muscle may be considered relatively innocuous. Others have been less so. The 1953 CIA/British Government/oil consortium collaboration to oust the Iranian Mossadeq regime showed glaringly that the force of the integrated majors need not be in opposition to the state. It mattered not at all whether the state apparatus working in conjunction with the petrogiants advertised itself as Democrat or Republican (in the United States), or as Labour or Conservative (in the United Kingdom).

The need for the strategic use of power by the oil companies proved in no way incompatible with unscrupulous profiteering at the expense of governments and the consumer. The meshings of the state apparatus with the drives of corporate capital were not always harmonious. In its onslaught on big oil pricing policies, the Brewster Committee (1948) of the US Senate lamented that the companies were not playing the rules of the game. 'The oil companies have shown a singular lack of good faith, an avaricious desire for enormous profits, while at the same time they constantly sought the cloak of United States protection and financial assistance to preserve their vast concessions.' But, then as now, the 'rules of the game' meant something different to corporate oil interests, whose ultimate and overriding goal is accumulation.

Petrochemicals: The Oil-Chemical Nexus

The oil majors are now a permanent feature of the petrochemical industry, with five of their number amongst the top fifteen petrochemical producers (see Table 6.2). The oil giants' involvement in chemicals predates the Second World War, and their incursions into petrochemicals, alone and in joint ventures, is on a sharply rising curve. While for the moment traditional members of the chemical oligopoly are paramount, almost the entire productive capacity (particularly in the United States) for olefines and their polymer derivatives are manufactured by the chemical subsidiaries of the petrogiants.

The meshing of chemical and oil oligopolies in this industry has assumed a myriad of forms. There are six giant joint ventures between oil and chemical concerns in the United States and another four in Western Europe.[32] Toward the end of the 1970s, looser forms of cooperation such as common purchasing arrangements for raw materials, cross-licensing, licence-pooling, and sharing of marketing facilities, have become more prevalent. Such agreements have blurred the petrogiants' traditional practice of investing in the lower petrochemicals, leaving the chemical end-products for the chemical oligopoly. By the close of the 1970s, Big Oil's share of bulk plastics was over one-third of world markets. British Petroleum has emerged as the decisive leader, with backward and forward linkages, and has become one of Europe's premier plastics producers, with interests in every major plastic material save polypropylene.

Table 6.2
Sales of the World's Leading Petrochemical Producers, 1976 ($ millions)

	Petrochemical and Plastics Sales	Total Sales	Petrochemicals as % of Total Sales
Shell	3,752	36,087	10.4
Exxon	3,238	48,631	6.6
Union Carbide	2,801	6,346	44.1
Dow Chemical	2,617	5,652	46.3
Montedison	2,523	5,826	43.2
Hoechst	2,188	9,333	23.4
ICI	2,064	7,465	27.6
Amoco[1]	1,403	11,532	12.2
Phillips	1,400	5,696	24.6
BP Chemicals	1,300	19,103	6.8
DSM	1,284	3,523	36.4
Du Pont	1,200	8,361	14.4
Veba Chemie	1,132	3,337	33.9
Sumitomo Chemical	1,076	2,057	52.3
Monsanto	1,075	4,270	25.2

1. Subsidiary of Standard Oil of Indiana.
Source: *Chemical Insight,* August 1977.

More recently, food, tyre, and steel corporations have joined the petrochemical race. On the eve of the 1980s, US Steel, in the chemical business
since the early 1900s, signed contracts for a spate of petrochemical joint
ventures. While this was clearly motivated by a desire to lessen its dependence
on steel (having acquired a quarter of the US market),[33] it indicates that
petrochemicals have become a major confrontation point for some of the
most powerful corporate forces in the world.

Chemical Fibres: Corporate Histories

This growing corporate power in petrochemicals has been concomitant with
escalating concentration in the global chemical fibre industry (see Tables
6.3 and 6.4).

Table 6.3
Annual Growth of Fibre Majors, 1974—77

Corporation	Annual Capacity (000 tons)		Annual Growth Rate	Dependence on Overseas Production (%)[1]	
	1974	*1977*	*1974–77*	*1974*	*1977*
Du Pont	1,030	1,876	22.1	28	21
ICI	630	898	12.5	64	76
Akzo	280	712	36.5	85	85
Celanese	330	681	27.3	9	27
Monsanto	340	603	21.0	21	17
Hoechst	210	567	39.2	21	43
Rhone-Poulenc	300	562	23.3	57	52
Toray	270	348	8.8	5	30
Courtaulds	150	266	21.0	22	24
Teijin	160	240	14.5	10	43
Total	*3,700*	*6,751*	*22.2*		

1. i.e., overseas capacity as percentage of global capacity for each corporation.

Source: Computed from data of the Japan Chemical Fibre Association.

While concentration is not a new phenomenon, as the following eight
corporate histories indicate, the nature of its impact has shifted in recent
years. As evidenced in Chapter 5, levels of concentration have contributed to,
and become more marked as a result of, the growth of over-capacity and the
huge financial losses in the second half of the 1970s. Western European fibre
giants responded to big post-1974 losses with average annual growth rates
of 22 per cent; while for Akzo and Hoechst, fibre growth jumped to nearly
40 per cent annually (see Table 6.3).

135

Table 6.4
World's Fifteen Leading Fibre Producers by Sales, 1979 ($ millions)

	Approximate Fibre sales	% of Total Fibre Sales of top 15	Total Corporate Sales	Fibre as % of Total Corporate Sales
Du Pont (US)	4,161	19.0	12,572	33.1
Akzo (Neth)	2,121	9.7	6,349	33.4
Celanese (US)	1,816	8.3	3,146	57.7
Toray (Jap.)	1,702	7.8	2,138	79.6
Rhone-Poulenc (Fr.)	1,607	7.4	8,415	19.1
Courtaulds (UK)	1,413	6.5	3,924	36.0
Teijin (Jap.)	1,310	6.0	1,793	73.1
Hoechst (FRG)	1,162	5.3	15,704	7.4
Asahi Chemical (Jap.)	1,113	5.1	2,409	46.2
ICI (UK)	1,105	5.0	11,887	9.3
Monsanto (US)	1,069	4.9	6,195	17.2
American Cyanamid (US)	960	4.4	3,187	30.1
Allied Chemical (US)	940	4.3	4,539	20.7
Unitika (Jap.)	740	3.4	872	84.9
Kuraray (Jap.)	642	2.9	847	75.8

Source: Computed from data in *Chemical Week*, 23 April 1980 and 2 July 1980; Company *Annual Reports;* and trade sources.

Data on the overspill effects of this prodigious growth into UCEs dispel any misconceptions that their nationals control the industries located there. The Latin American fibre industry reveals sector after sector of near-total domination by transnationals (see Table 6.5). Further concentration, and the overseas forays of the fibre oligopoly, thus present a dual force of immense power. Wedded as it is to the state apparatus in the major DCEs, the oligopoly's power becomes incontestable.

IG Farben
No sector of Germany's economy so richly depicts the historical meshing of corporate capital and political power as the chemical industry. From 1856, when the pioneer discoveries of the eighteen-year-old English chemist, William Henry Perkins, laid the foundations of the dyestuffs industry, strides in applied chemistry were partnered by economic concentration. By the end of the century, the giants, BASF, Bayer, and Hoechst and the lesser Agfa, Cassella, and Kalle dominated an industry which in its scale of operations, research and marketing capabilities moved beyond the frontiers of imperial Germany.[34]

The Great War gave new impetus to enhanced co-operation,[35] as did the

Versailles treaty, finalising the debacle of imperial Germany and redividing its empire among its imperialist rivals. Under the benign gaze of the Weimar Republic, IG Farben was born (25 December 1925), destined to become Europe's biggest corporation and the world's largest chemical giant. Immediately, this new manifestation of BASF, Bayer and Hoechst swiftly triggered mergers within the British and French chemical industries that created Imperial Chemical Industries (ICI) in 1926 and Rhone-Poulenc in 1928.[36] The birth of IG also cleared the road for the annexation of of certain segments of the armaments industry: Dynamit AG, Rheinische-Westfalische Sprengstoff AG, and Koln-Rottweil AG, thus vertically integrating IG's nitrate plants with what had been their chief customers.

Table 6.5
Latin America: Transnational Ownership of Chemical Fibre Capacity, c.1975 (%)

	Viscose	Acetates	Nylon 6	Nylon 66	Acrylic	Polyester
Brazil	58	50	54	100	66	84
Argentina	75	100	38	100	100	80
Colombia	100	100	50	–	100	75
Venezuela	–	100	40	–	–	75
Peru	100	100	33	–	100	100
Mexico	100	100	33	–	75	44

Source: B. Bolton, *The MNCs in the Textile, Garment and Leather Industries,* Brussels, 1976.

A labyrinth of cartel arrangements ensued, connecting IG with Du Pont, Dow Chemical, Mitsui, Montecatini, ICI, Czechoslovakia'a Aussiger Verein, Poland's Boruta, and Ugine Kuhlmann of France. IG's pathbreaking invention of the hydrogenation process (coal and oil into gasoline) brought it into a direct and cosy technical, financial, marketing and, of course, political relationship with Standard Oil of New Jersey, the dominant force in the US and world oil industry.[37] The former received minority ownership in Standard's equity in exchange for the rights to the hydrogenation process. The El Dorado of synthetic oil and petrochemistry was now in the grips of the IG/Standard axis.

In the political sphere, a tenuous relationship grew with the Weimar politicos who, even in their extreme bourgeois manifestation, had always been the object of implicit contempt by IG's oligarchy. Without IG Farben, pontificated Gustav Stresemann, Chancellor and Foreign Minister during the Weimar period, 'I can have no foreign policy.'[38] With Hitler's ascendancy in 1933, IG Farben, having earlier bankrolled his political activism, espoused his political ideals. By 1937, IG Farben's Nazification was complete, with all leading members of the board transformed into Nazi party activists. In return, Hitler's New Order was to ensure its profits, power and markets. Between 1933 and 1945, IG grabbed more than 85 per cent of Germany's chemical industry — around 400 domestic firms — to which could be added subsidiaries and shareholdings in more than 500 foreign enterprises.[39]

IG Farben was not merely a lavish financial contributor to Nazism, a fact it flaunted for public relations purposes. More crucially, its organizational power furnished the techno scientific blueprints of Nazi expansionism. 'Without IG's immense productive facilities,' commented a team set up by General Eisenhower, 'its far-reaching research, varied technical experience and overall concentration of economic power, Germany would not have been in a position to start its aggressive war in September 1939.'[40] In his story of IG's involvement with Hitler, Joseph Borkin writes: 'Even a partial list of products IG produced for German rearmament demonstrates clearly that IG was indispensable: it produced almost all the synthetic oil (direct and by license), synthetic rubber, poison gases, magnesium, lubricating oil, explosives, methanol, sera, plasticizers, dyestuffs, nickel and thousands of other items necessary for the German war machine.'[41] Never before in the history of war had senior executives played such a seminal role. Fittingly, when Karl Krauch, Chairman of IG's Supervisory Board and architect of the IG Auschwitz project, was made a Knight of the Iron Cross by a grateful Goering, the citation exulted that he had 'won marvellous victories on the battlefield of German industry.'[42]

The nearest replica of this vast 'military/industrial' complex was that of the Japanese state and its *zaibatsus*. Together, the IG/Nazi team rooted out the trade union movement and reinstated slavery as a viable economic proposition. In Borkin's poignant words:

> The construction of IG Auschwitz has assured IG Farben its unique place in business history . . . for it was able to depart from the conventional economics of slavery in which slaves are traditionally treated as capital equipment to be maintained and serviced for optimum use and depreciated over a normal life span. Instead, I.G. reduced slave labour to a consumable raw material, a human ore from which the mineral of life was systematically extracted. When no usable energy remained, the living dross was shipped to the gassing chambers and cremation furnaces of the extermination center at Birkenau, where the S.S. recycled it into the German war economy — gold teeth for the Reichsbank, hair for mattresses, and fat for soap. Even the moans of the doomed became a work incentive, exhorting the remaining inmates to greater effort.[43]

IG Farben's dismemberment in 1945 led to the re-emergence of its predecessor companies: Bayer, Hoechst, BASF and Casella (now a Hoechst subsidiary) to corporate autonomy in 1951–52. By 1962, each of the big three successor companies had posted sales matching those of the pre-war IG Farben. The massive thrust of the capital accumulation engine is best evaluated in the aggregate sales (1979) of the big three, topping $46 billion, almost 60 times the pre-war figure.[44] Corporate independence has not, however, severed their interlocking interests in former IG Farben holdings..

ICI and Others

A similar expansionist course was followed by the United Kingdom's Imperial Chemical Industries (ICI) on 25 September 1926. ICI was the outcome of one of the two largest mergers in the United Kingdom's history (the other was the formation of the Imperial Tobacco Company at the turn of the century). It involved the fusion of four chemical giants: Brunner-Mond, Nobel Industries, United Alkali Company and the British Dyestuffs Corporation.[45] ICI's birth signalled its transnational ambitions as proclaimed by Sir Alfred Mond (one of ICI's founders): 'The company has, of deliberate purpose, been given the title of Imperial Chemical Industries Ltd. The British Empire is the single greatest economic unit in the world . . . and it will be the avowed intention of the new company, *without limiting its activities in foreign overseas markets,* specially to extend the development and importance of the chemical industry throughout the Empire.'[46]

The innovative surgery which the British chemical industry had now undergone was a radical departure from the prescribed therapy of an earlier, and idealized, competitive order. As an ICI official recently noted, Sir Alfred Mond 'preached the necessity of "rationalization" – and claimed to have invented the industrial application of the term – and the virtues of cartel agreements and managed markets. Unregulated competition was not to his liking at all, nor to that of Sir Harry McGowan' (the other ICI founder),[47] nor was it to the liking of other leaders of the world chemical oligopoly in that era or ours. Over a span of more than fifty years, ICI was to fashion a marketing network (in which chemical fibres now account for less than 10 per cent of aggregate sales) that spans the world's continents.

New technologies have multiplied the product range of the chemical oligopoly, involving ever deeper penetration into the world market through a highly complex distribution network. By the mid-1960s, over 60 per cent of ICI's total sales were funnelled into the world market. Ten years later, more than a third of its assets were overseas via wholly- and partly-owned subsidiaries and associate companies.[48] In one decade (1966–76), sales grew five-fold from £885 million to £4,135 million.[49]

The history of the second British chemical fibre producer, Courtaulds (1979 sales: $3.9 billion), has followed a pattern similar to that of several of the larger chemical conglomerates: fabrication of a wide range of fibres.[50] Courtaulds' initial emphasis, however, and its continuing area of concentration, is in cellulosics, in which it has a monopoly (with its subsidiary British Celanese, over 95 per cent of the market) within the United Kingdom (see Table 6.6). By 1974, it operated 500 manufacturing units in 230 different industrial locations. More than a hundred of its plants were outside the United Kingdom, notably in the former British colonies, and included several major subsidiaries in North America, Australia and

South Africa.

Table 6.6
Courtaulds' Market Share of Cellulosics, 1920–62 (million lb)

	Courtaulds	UK	% of UK market
1920	6.2	6.5	95.4
1930	23.5	45.1	52.1
1939	53.6	111.0	48.3
1950	103.0	190.2	54.2
1960	145.8	186.5	78.2
1962	164.2	176.8	92.9

Source: Monopolies Commission, *Man-Made Cellulosic Fibres*, (HMSO, 1968), Appendix 3.

Hard on the heels of massive vertical integration in the 1960s, Courtaulds has become a mammoth textile corporation, figuring amongst the top ten in the world.[51] Characteristic of its extension over the marketing chain is that its US manufacturing operations straddle yarn spinning and processing, weaving, warp knitting, bonded fabrics, dyeing, printing and finishing, and clothing manufacture: all hooked into its global wholesale network.[52] Courtaulds and ICI together engulf 50–55 per cent of the British chemical fibre market, the rest being divided among subsidiaries of Du Pont, Monsanto, Hoechst and Enka.[53]

Rhone-Poulenc, France's biggest chemical and textile producer and the world's ninth largest petrochemical company,[54] reveals a comparatively low conglomerate profile, inasmuch as 27 per cent of its $8.4 billion 1979 turnover is in man-made fibres and yarns, and the rest in allied chemicals or textiles. Yet it produces 85 per cent of all French man-made fibres and employs about three-quarters of all workers in this sector.[55]

Rhone-Poulenc was founded in 1895 and grew mainly as a textile corporation until the 1960s, when the chemical fibre market boomed. In attempts to rationalize the French chemical industry, Presidents de Gaulle and Pompidou singled out Rhone-Poulenc to lead the concentration drive. The company expanded at a headlong pace, buying out two major chemical companies, Progil and Pechiney-Saint-Gobain, in 1969. Between 1967 and 1973, sales tripled.[56]

Since the onset of the crisis, Rhone-Poulenc's losses have been large ($400 million in the chemical group from 1975 to 1977),[57] but restructuring has proved difficult. As in Italy, attempts to shut down plants have been met by stiff worker (and government) resistance. Another thorn in Rhone-Poulenc's side is reduced demand in the clothing industry, its largest client.[58] Further cutbacks in French clothing production will bite deeper into the company's sales. Since 1977, it has been considering acquisitions in fertilizers and high technology areas such as chemicals for the electronics and data processing industries.

It is indicative of the new petrochemical orientation of the oil majors that Rhone-Poulenc's heavy chemicals divisions have now been taken over by France's second largest oil corporation: Elf-Aquitaine. Its directions for the 1980s are symptomatic of emergent corporate chemical strategies marked by a shift to highly sophisticated chemicals in which the raw materials component is a minor segment of total cost, e.g. fine chemicals, rare earths, colourants, etc. Already it is France's biggest pharmaceutical company, and the scope for corporate annexation is considerable, since France's 332 pharmaceutical companies are expected to be cut by half over the next decade with four majors being the decisive economic actors: Rhone-Poulenc, Sanofi (heavily financed by Elf-Aquitaine), Roussel Uclaf (a subsidiary of Hoechst) and Synthelabo, a subsidiary of L'Oreal, the nation's biggest cosmetic company.

Nowhere is one chemical company so dominant in a national economy as Montedison in Italy (1979 sales: $8.2 billion). In 1976, this fibre giant's sales were equivalent to 3.5 per cent of Italy's GNP; exports were 4.5 per cent of the national total; and its labour force numbered 144,000.[59] Montedison's crucial position is buttressed by chemicals and fibres, which are Italy's foremost industrial sector. The conglomerate was forged out of a 1966 merger between Montecatini, a chemical company, and Edison, a former electrical utility corporation. The management diversified into retail stores, car distribution, drug companies, and other concerns that led to losses approaching half a billion dollars by 1971. In subsequent management reshuffles 300 subsidiaries were sold for $565 million,[60] narrowing the company's focus back to chemicals, fibres, and retailing.

The onrushing crisis has further accelerated capital centralization. Montedison, which traditionally accounted for 70 per cent of Italian fibre output, has now annexed Snia Viscosa, which brings their combined share of the Italian market to more than 85 per cent of chemical fibres. Snia complements Montedison's synthetic fibre predominance with major cellulosic plants. With continuing investment in new plants in the United States and Europe, the combined company is a major actor in the present drama of over-capacity.

Excessive fibre dependence has reached critical levels with the Dutch chemical giant Akzo (1979 sales: $6.3 billion), with its labour force of 88,000. Recent heavy losses sustained by its fibre division (which accounted for 33 per cent of Akzo's sales in 1979) emphasized the marketing consequences of over-reliance on fibres. Akzo only recently entered the ranks of the chemical giants as a result of the 1969 merger of AKU (at that time West Europe's biggest fibre producer) and AZO (salt and speciality chemicals, pharmaceuticals, and foods).

The 1974–75 economic crisis precipitated a major restructuring, and all fibre operations outside the United States centralized under the Enka-Glanzstoff management. As one unit, Enka became an international leader in a vast array of fibre products, buttressed by three research institutes which work in close co-operation with Akzo Research and Engineering. Closing down several rayon and nylon yarn plants, Enka is shifting more into industrial fibres and carpet yarns, which have much greater new end-use potential. Akzo is banking equally on its profitable US-based Akzona unit and on expansion in pharmaceuticals to pull it through the continuing fibre crisis.

Japan
Japan produces almost a sixth of the world's synthetic fibres, second to the USA. It is a highly concentrated industry with four companies controlling the bulk of output and with the top nine appropriating over 90 per cent of output. Several of the nation's chemical and petrochemical giants are the descendants of the pre-war *zaibatsu*. Of these, both Toray and Teijin are amongst the world's top ten chemical fibre producers. Toray industries,[61] set in motion in 1926 by Mitsui, had by 1971 produced 36 per cent of the nation's nylon, 30 per cent of its polyester, and 15 per cent of its acrylics, and this in only one of its chemical subsidiaries. All the leading Japanese producers reacted quickly to the crisis of the 1970s. Toward the end of 1977, the president of Teijin proposed that Japan's eight major fibre firms fuse into four groups. Within a year Toyobo and Mitsubishi Rayon established a joint acrylic textiles sales company. Teijin and Unitika, both in the same financial group, signed extensive co-operation agreements covering both sales and production. Asahi and Kanebo agreed to begin a joint sales company for all their chemical fibres. The remaining two, Toray and Kuraray, have also agreed to co-operate. All these shifting patterns have been achieved through the state apparatus, MITI.

These far-reaching rationalization measures within the fibre industry are being matched by no less impressive diversification strides into other major sectors, notably electronics. Indicative are advances in fibre technology via such products as polyester films for magnetic video tapes by Toray. Teijin has extended its electronic research capability to new fibre applications, notably optical fibres and the pharmaceutical industry.

Du Pont
When the family of Eleuthere Irenee Du Pont arrived in America on 1 January 1800, they were not in the common run of immigrants. They had with them 241,000 francs, and a million more on the way. The process of capital accumulation that was on an exponential curve by the turn of this century thus had its modest origins in revolutionary France, in one gunpowder factory.

The Du Pont de Nemours family enterprise[62] was built on black powder and remained largely in the explosives field until the end of the First World War, when it made the transition to chemicals[63] and automobiles — with a major holding in General Motors.[64] By then it had become one of the world's largest corporations, and a trail-blazer in the domain of industrial conglomeration. The family biographer, Gerald Zilg, tells us that 'the Du

Ponts own more personal wealth and control more multimillion dollar
corporations than any one family in the world. They employ more servants
than Britain's royal family, own more yachts, cars, swimming pools, planes
and estates than any other family in recorded history.'[65] Of some 1,600
living Du Ponts, a mere 250 are the inner circle. Of these, only about fifty
make up the all-powerful inner core of the family. Together these fifty Du
Ponts control over $150 billion worth of assets, a figure larger than the
national income of most states.

Just as a drop of water gives us a clue into the chemical composition of the
sea, the Du Ponts provide us with profound insights into the nature and
mechanisms of economic power; remembering, of course, that the Du Ponts
were from the start rather more than a drop in the ocean of American
capitalism. From gunpowder-making the Du Ponts ramified their power to
chemicals and beyond. Few people realized that this family had controlling
interests at certain stages in such well-known multinationals as Coca Cola,
United Fruit, First National Bank, Remington Arms and scores of other
celebrated companies. The main catalyst behind successive moves of technical change and enhanced market power was an unrelenting commitment
to research pursued even in the great Depression of the thirties. Zilg tells us:

> Few companies in the world [in the 1930s] spent more on research
> than Du Pont. Every day Du Pont's experimental research center near
> Wilmington buzzed like a beehive as thousands of scientists and
> assistants busily searched for new products at cheaper costs. From here
> came 'Dulux' enamels, Orlon, Dacron, and neoprene, the artificial
> rubber which revolutionized the tire and hose industries. From here
> came moisture-proof cellophane, which revolutionized the baked goods
> market, and Lucite, the symbol of the new age of plastics. And from
> here came Du Pont's greatest money maker, nylon.[66]

The interaction of science and capital has been one of the major well-
springs of Du Pont, which ploughed back $1 billion yearly from 1974 to
1977 on new plants and equipment. Du Pont's fibres segment, a relatively
small but important part of its total operations, consists of five distinct
sectors: fibres for the domestic clothing market and for home fabrics, comprising about half of the company's fibre sales; carpet fibres, with 18 per
cent of fibre sales; industrial fibres, with 12 per cent; spunbonded and other
specialty fibres, around 7 per cent; and fibre manufactures in Europe, 13 per
cent.

The world-wide pattern of sales and investments is suggestive of the size
and scope of its corporate operations (see Table 6.7). Sales outside the United
States by Du Pont and its consolidated subsidiaries comprised 32 per cent of
the aggregate sales,[67] effected through three major marketing circuits: consolidated subsidiaries, which are wholly or majority owned; non-consolidated
affiliates, in which Du Pont's equity is 50 per cent or less; and other export
sales, including those made through independent distributors abroad.

Table 6.7
Du Pont: Sales and Investment, 1979 ($ million)

	Sales	Percentage	Investment	Percentage
USA	8,590	68.3	12,867	79.3
Other regions				
Europe, Africa, Middle East	2,060	16.4	1,757	10.8
Canada	672	5.3	801	4.9
Latin America	710	5.6	492	3.0
Far East	540	4.3	311	1.9
Total	*3,982*	*31.7*	*3,361*	*20.7*
Grand Total	*12,572*	*100.0*	*16,228*	*100.0*

Source: Du Pont, *Annual Report,* 1979.

Mechanisms of Corporate Power

While corporate histories give an insight into an individual corporation's strength, transnational oligopolistic power perhaps can best be understood by studying the vast marketing and engineering weaponry deployed in order to increase market shares. Since the Second World War, chemical corporations — engulfing plastics, synthetic fibres, detergents, fertilizers, paints and pharmaceuticals, and so on — have perfected many of these techniques and penetrated a huge number of markets traditionally restricted to natural commodities (e.g. metals, natural rubber, cotton, wool). In its practical contempt for neo-classical economic theorizing, which preaches the primacy of price in the kingdom of supply and demand, the chemical oligopoly has systematically eroded demand for competing primary commodities, irrespective of price. Take, for example, the chemical fibre corporations' massive intrusion in the 1960s into a world fibre market, previously dominated by cotton producers. During that decade, all major chemical fibres swelled their shares of the fibre end-use market (apparel, domestic and industrial), despite prices approximately three times higher than those of cotton. The mechanisms described below are clearly part of an oligopolistic marketing structure which is a far cry from neo-classical notions of 'inter-fibre competition' in a free market.

Research and Development
The pervasiveness of scientific and engineering breakthroughs is one of the constants of contemporary chemical technology and the outgrowth of the creative energies of tens of thousands of research technicians and scientists, funded by astronomic outlays of money. Knowledge creation and control has become one of the pre-conditions for aggressively sustaining markets, inventing new product lines, and shaving manufacturing costs. An index of

the dimensions of such knowledge creation is the ratio of research and development to sales in selected chemical firms (see Table 6.8).

In the United States alone, the work of nearly 50,000 scientists and engineers took up over $4 billion in chemical research and development funds in 1978, 90 per cent of which was corporation-sponsored, with the remainder coming from the State.[68] In both the United States and Britain, research and development expenditures in chemicals are second in importance only to electronics and aerospace. A barometer of the magnitude of these outlays is seen in the rising percentage of US patents related to chemicals, which rose from 14 per cent of all patents in 1953 to 26 per cent by the onset of the seventies.[69] The sheer volume of formal research expenditures, however, masks the self-reinforcing nature of the research thrust of the chemical giants, indicated in IG Farben's research on polymethyl methacrylate plastic, which led to nitrile rubber and, in turn, to acrylic fibre.

Table 6.8
Research and Development Expenditure of Selected Chemical Corporations, 1978 ($ million)

	Sales	*R & D*	*R & D as % of sales*
Hoechst	12,599.5	559.4	4.4
BASF	12,111.4	432.0	3.9
Bayer	11,893.8	310.9	2.6
Du Pont	10,584.0	377.0	3.6
ICI	9,247.3	335.0	3.6
Union Carbide	7,869.7	155.9	2.0
Dow	6,887.6	231.5	3.4
Montedison	6,851.3	162.5	2.4
Rhone-Poulenc	5,812.3	250.9	4.3
Ciba-Geigy	5,133.3	437.9	8.5
Akzo	5,079.0	224.0	4.1

Source: *Chemical Age,* 20 July 1979.

A hallmark of research and development has been the advent of new products from proprietary technology with rapid scientific responses to changing technological environments. To ensure the meshing of research, development and effective marketing, manufacturing processes have been constantly adjusted to vary the properties of established product lines. At the same time, cost reduction methods have been unrelentingly pursued to enlarge market application on a national and global basis.

To achieve these marketing goals an advance on four major fronts has been necessary. Big research thrusts have been directed to gradual improvements in existing product lines which have demonstrated a high and sustained earning capacity, as well as expanding such products tailored to specific end-uses, as in the automobile industry. Secondly, new product lines emerge from corporate proprietary technology which, in the words of one corporation, 'complement an established line of industrial fibres on the growing edge of existing markets'[70] incorporating innovations in, for example, strength-to-weight ratios. A third research direction leads to trimming labour and raw material costs without impairing quality. Fourthly, manufacturing costs are cut by innovations in process technology, notably for large-volume products such as polyester fibre. Here research and development process technology is geared to an intimate collaboration with textile machinery producers.

The cumulative result of these various lines of research and development has been new, previously unmarketed, product lines.[71] When clothing makers announced the wrinkle-free, permanent press, 100-per-cent cotton shirt in the late 1970s, Du Pont and ICI responded with polyester surface treatments that overcame the major drawbacks. Adding only 2–4 cents/lb to clothing items the new finishes have reduced static, increased absorbency, and are easily added in the dyeing process. ICI's new fibres and finishes are now being developed in a colossal, totally integrated marketing and research structure, whose successes may prove a model for other chemical majors. ICI carefully researches consumer preferences to see whether they can be met with existing fibres or through development of new characteristics. It then directs its engineers and its basic fibre research toward the development and modification of yarns. Other products of this consumer-oriented policy include a moisture-absorbent acrylic fibre and acrylic staple products for year-round use. Akzo has also produced a new fibre, Arenka, which is as strong as steel but seven times lighter. Such centralized configurations of applied scientific research contrast markedly with the paltry and fragmented research efforts in cotton; these are non-existent in most underdeveloped capitalist countries, and of minor consequence in the developed ones.[72]

Blending
One of the effective techniques deployed in 'inter-fibre competition', which accounts for the decreasing use of cotton, has been the blending of fibre components of various properties to meet more complex and demanding cloth formations and diversified fibre end-uses. Since no one fibre as yet combines all properties, the blending of fibre components with varying properties to meet diverse requirements for texture, colour, dyeability, tensile strength and durability involves complex operations invariably leading to a cutback in the amount of natural fibre in the input mix. Members of the fibre industry have forecast that, following the lead of the 65 per cent polyester/35 per cent cotton shirt, over nine-tenths of all clothing will contain polyester by the early 1980s.[73] Further strides have been made by one of the world's largest cotton spinners and cellulosic manufacturers, producing a modified form of rayon eliminating many of the problems of blending rayon with polyester. Thus in certain blended goods rayon may be

used in place of cotton.

Blending different fibres alters the effect of each, but all contribute to the character of the final product. As a result, there is now no fabric impervious to the continuous onslaught of blending techniques. Even denim (once an exemplar of 'a pure cotton product'), is now being reshaped by the intrusion of chemical fibres. In fact, one senior ICI executive recently proclaimed that the next denim boom will be a polyester one.[74]

Marketing Techniques

As with most major manufacturing products, advertising has come to play a decisive role within the chemical empire and in 'inter-fibre competition'. Chemical corporations are aided in advertising and promotion by textile manufacturers, wholesalers and retailers. The imbalance in research and development expenditures between natural and chemical fibres is matched by the equally awesome difference in advertising outlays. The fatter advertising budgets for chemical fibres, and the ideological power of the increasing influence of the media, have come to play a vital part in pricing policy and consumer response.

No world fibre advertising breakdowns are available, although estimates suggest that they run as high as 1 to 2 per cent of total sales. The struggle for enhanced shares of the market has seen brand names assume an ever greater effectiveness over the last two decades. Hoechst could claim by the end of the 1960s that more than 90 per cent of West Germany's population had reached 'a high level of brand awareness'; its Trevira brand[75] is the envy of all chemical giants. But once the market, i.e. processors and consumers, were psychologically conditioned to brand recognition, a switch in marketing strategy — toward fashion — was called for.

> With its fashion studios, which were introduced to garment makers in many places in Germany and abroad, Hoechst demonstrated to the clothing industry that highly fashionable garments can also be produced from man-made fibres and that, moreover, it is precisely these fibres which as a result of their adaptability to changing consumer requirements are excellently suited for utilizing fashion as an instrument of marketing. These studios had become a genuine stimulating influence in the textile sector so that eventually they were taken over by the garment makers and utilized for their own sales promotional campaigns.[76]

Advertising is geared not only to the clothes-buying public, but also to the textile industry. Less concentrated than the chemical industry, it is thus more subject to 'market guidance' from the chemical industry. Once again in the words of Hoechst, 'the main factors in favour of a closer co-operation with the textile industry were the generally limited market strength of its individual members, the greater technical and marketing knowhow of the fibre producers and, last but not least, the fact that since the beginning of the

147

sixties consumption of natural fibres in Western Europe had been stagnating'. Here is the rationalization for the fibre producers' claims 'that individual corporate growth was now only possible through the use of synthetic fibres'.[77]

Transfer Pricing

Cotton's diminishing competitiveness does not derive only from such direct corporate strategies. A boundless source of profit maximization for the giant oil and chemical corporations, as well as all transnationals, is the widespread technique of 'transfer pricing'. Prices are assigned by TNCs to the transfers of goods, services, technology or loans between their related enterprises in various countries. The prices charged for such transfers, as explained by a recent OECD report, 'diverge considerably from the prices which would have been agreed upon between unrelated [corporations] .'[78] This is possible because any transnational will gear its pricing policies between affiliates to serve the overall profit-maximizing interests of the corporation as a whole.

Different national tax structures provide a golden opportunity for enhancing profits through transfer pricing. TNCs can minimize their overall tax payments by manipulating the prices of transactions within the corporation, shifting profits from countries with higher tax rates to those where taxes are lower. In countries with government price controls prohibiting corporations from posting retail prices above a fixed percentage of prices of imported goods or the cost of production transfer pricing is also an effective counter. Oil and fibre corporations inflate import costs from their own subsidiaries and can therefore legitimately impose much higher retail prices on their products. Thirdly, transfer pricing has also been used to switch profits and cash balances out of countries with repeated currency devaluations.

On a larger canvas, as Professor Robin Murray notes, all species of intra-firm relations — advisory services, blueprints, factoring, insurance, general management, capital goods servicing, the loan of money — can be categorized as transactions and thus assigned a price. Moreover, lump sum charges can be made for brand names, head office overheads, future research and development, or simply good will. Each transaction, each phone call, letter, meeting attended, etc., can be given a price. In other words, any aspect of normal intra-corporate interchange can be treated as a normal market transaction. Thus any transnational conglomerate firm (not only the chemical and oil oligopolies) can shift its resources between affiliates for the purpose of tax avoidance and other corporate goals.[79]

Since as much as one-third of world trade is conducted between affiliates of transnational corporations, the space for gain through transfer pricing is prodigious. The evidence indicates that intra-firm transactions rose as high as 40 per cent of US imports in 1974, 50 per cent of US exports in 1970, and 59 per cent of Canadian exports in 1971.[80] For chemicals specifically, 1977 data for the United States reveal that intra-firm trade accounted for over one-half of imports in organic chemicals (50 per cent), plastics and resins (55 per

cent), dyestuffs (85 per cent), and synthetic rubber (87 per cent).[81] A survey
of the Indian dyestuffs industry in 1970—71 demonstrates the impact of
transfer pricing on a UCE.[82] There is a marked difference in prices paid by
domestic and transnational firms for imports of similar inputs (see Table 6.9).
Overpricing varied between 124 and 147 per cent, indicating a prodigious
shifting of corporate resources, to India's disadvantage.

Table 6.9
TNC Overpricing of Imported Raw Materials in India

Product	Extent of Overpricing (%)
Dinitrochlorobenzene	347
Sodium Nitrate	328
Paranitrotoluene	271
Orthotoludine	249
Bromine	124

Source: *Economic and Political Weekly* (Bombay), 30 October 1976.

Widespread abuses of transfer pricing have also been uncovered among
chemical subsidiaries dealing in pharmaceutical products. The Swiss corporation Hoffman-La Roche was caught paying 90 times the Italian price for the
active ingredient in valium, and 47 times the price for the active ingredient
in librium.[83] Investigations of transnational pharmaceutical enterprises in
Spain disclosed unit price differentials of up to 18 times for raw material
imports.[84] The foreign exchange losses through overpricing imported
chemicals by chemical TNCs are immense; in Greece, for instance, they
amounted to $1.8 million in 1975.[85]

These manipulative price transfers in both UCEs and DCEs have been
facilitated by the active collaboration of the accounting establishment.
Increasingly over the last two decades such balance-sheet manoeuvres have
become an integral component of global marketing and distribution. In view
of the spread of transfer pricing techniques, a recent UN study warned that
'the potential for such manipulation is likely to increase as a result of the
continued concentration of economic power in the hands of transnational
corporations and the increasing importance of intra-corporate transactions
in their total trade, and in particular, on account of the continued diversification of their activities on a horizontal, vertical and conglomerate basis'.[86]

The intricacies of transfer pricing are not unlike the cross-subsidization
practices of the chemical majors. Needless to say, most of the industry
leaders could not have sustained the enormous losses on the glutted petrochemical, fibre and plastic markets of recent years without heavy cross-subsidization from drug, fertilizer and speciality chemical profits. The crisis
has thus provided a further impetus to conglomeration.

State Aid

The importance of the petrochemical and chemical industries to DCEs completely dwarfs the cotton producers and explains the massive state intervention on their behalf. The British government's support to the chemical industry is an example: the government assisted ICI in renegotiating its long-term contract with the British Gas Corporation, whose cheap methane supplies enabled ICI to produce ammonium nitrate fertilizers at prices that undercut competitors and boosted its already firm hold (over 55 per cent) on the nitrate market.[87] State aid has also become a means of enhancing concentration within the chemical oligopoly, as can be seen within all major political centres of the industry, particularly Japan, where MITI oversaw the recent reduction of major fibre giants from eight to four.[88] Tariff mobilization has also been used, with EEC governments negotiating the exemption of sensitive products designated by the chemical giants from tariff reductions in the Tokyo round of GATT talks.[89] Though tariffs and cheaper raw materials are among the more explicit manifestations of state aid, no less significant has been the encouragement — and at times the compulsive pressure — by governments for economic consolidation and corporate ties between apparently competitive giants. Thus in 1972, Toray and Teijin, Japan's two major synthetic textile producers, were prodded by MITI to share their synthetic yarn-making patents.[90] Due to MITI's efforts, the nation's three largest synthetic fibre producers also concluded formal agreements on sales, exports and output of polyesters, nylon and acrylic fibres. Finally, these measures were reinforced by the establishment of a synthetic fibre cartel, designed by MITI to avoid competitive practices by setting floor prices and export quotas.

The consummation of MITI's triumph was that, by the end of 1979, at a time when the West European fibre industry continued to be battered, Japan's leading fibre producers were chalking up impressive sales and output records highlighted by the 65-per-cent upsurge in Toray's 1979 profits. One of the mechanisms behind this dramatic turnaround was MITI's meticulous preparation of quarterly demand data harmonized with the fibre giants submitting their output plans to MITI. Such inter-meshing between the state apparatus and corporate power was hammered out over a six-year period in the aftermath of the 1973 oil crisis. This meant in practice that a 50-per-cent increase in fuel and raw materials costs in 1979 was offset by higher fibre prices and far-reaching rationalization measures. Such solutions were predicated on new levels of corporate concentration made feasible by a special MITI public corporation engineered to liquidate productive capacity of small amd medium-sized firms.

The French state also continues to proffer massive financial handouts to its big three, Rhone-Poulenc, CdF-Chimie and Pechiney Ugine Kuhlmann, in order to 'eliminate overlapping operations so that they will be better able to compete on an international scale'.[91] According to the Chairman of the Union des Industries Chimiques: 'The companies now want to complement each other rather than get involved in abnormal competition.'[92] Such policy utterances are echoed throughout the industry. 'There are impediments in the market today,' says a senior ICI executive, 'that make it difficult to adhere simply to the principles of open competition.'[93] In the Netherlands, chemical fibre manufacturers, along with the steel and furniture industries, received restructuring grants of almost $300 million in 1978. To help the chemical industry, the state gave additional investment premiums, particularly for research efforts on environmental controls.[94]

Perhaps the most graphic illustration of state intervention — in this case supported by the trade union movement — is the proposed restructuring of the Milan-based conglomerate Montedison, after heavy financial losses in recent years. Such restructuring involves harmonizing antagonistic chemical corporate structures (or attempting to do so) into one group, thereby rationalizing existing plants and investment flows. Blatant in this picture of oligopolistic capitalism in crisis is the state's repudiation of its role as custodian of an idealized competitive market (viz the Anti-trust Division of the US Justice Department) in favour of capital concentration. Here in this working relationship is demonstrated the reality of the current global economic war, corporate expansion of overseas investment, and the annexation of larger market shares. What are the ideological currents that coalesced to re-float Montedison in the 'national interest'? The trade union movement, the ruling political parties and the private sector.

The Crisis Cartel

The proposed creation in 1978 of a European crisis cartel was an attempt to de-activate the lethal effects of long-term overproduction. It was indicative of the depth of the crisis, and the inability of national and corporate bodies to find solutions. However, with its cartel the EEC is striving to solder into a workable alliance the thirteen leading producers who together control over 90 per cent of its output. Its aim: to slash output, chop inventories, and boost profit margins. The EEC's blueprint envisages the banning or considerable cutback of all state aid to fibres for two years and urges the big thirteen to slash capacity by up to one-fifth through plant shutdowns.[95]

The crisis cartel, viewed in historical perspective, is but one link in a long chain of corporate collusion and cartelization in the fibre industry. As early as 1920, the seven leading rayon producers were all associated, either through interlocking capital or joint subsidiaries. By the 1960s, three associations were set up, comprising all large Japanese and European fibre producers, which urged specific minimum export prices and export quotas.[96] Regional cartels have even worked out mutual arrangements as seen with the tie-up of UNICEL, (an 'export club' of Western European producers that fixed prices for viscose yarn and staple) with Konjestaple (a Japanese cartel dealing with the same commodity).[97] International cartelization through patent licensing of certain specific fibres has also been deployed to repel non-holders of the license by means of market allocation arrangements, supply restrictions and price fixing.[98]

Two years after the so-called 'crisis cartel' achieved some negligible capacity cutbacks, the agreement was resurrected as the Common Market Fibre Agreement, on foundations no less rickety than those of its precursor. Even assuming that the EEC were able to monitor and enforce an agreement holding the big thirteen to a coherent and combative marketing posture, it would encounter a formidable phalanx of outsiders: the USA, Japan, the socialist countries, and the non-traditional OPEC producers, representing a massive productive capacity that could breach a cartel-controlled European market.

The Banking Circuit

Chemical fibre power is also buttressed by the intimate links with the transnational banking structure and hence a privileged access to the world's capital markets. Notwithstanding the traditionally high level of self-financing by the chemical majors, over the past hundred years such connections have been forged in many areas.

In 1976, ICI's balance sheet indicated that 88 per cent of its financial requirements were met by self-generated funds. Finance is planned for the group as a whole, including borrowing from capital markets. Rapprochement with the centres of finance capital is facilitated by ICI's central borrowing policy, which can shift relatively easily to specific finance markets where capital costs are lowest. According to an ICI financial planner. 'London suffers from the drawback that there is virtually no long-term debt market for companies any longer, and that any medium-term sterling finance raised can be used only in Britain; elsewhere it is a question of building up and maintaining one's position in New York and in the national or semi-national markets, such as those in Swiss francs, Deutschemarks and Dutch guilders as well as using the Eurobond market to maintain the right mix of currencies, costs and maturities'.[99]

This is an almost perfect representation of how most transnational industrial structures tap the capital resources of both developed and underdeveloped capitalist countries, via the transnational banking structures. There are also cases where certain chemical giants have themselves penetrated bank and insurance structures to the point where they exercise a controlling interest, as the findings of Professor Zilg suggest for Du Pont: members of the Du Pont clan are representatives on the boards of directors of six US banks and insurance firms.[100]

Equally, the penetration by big banks into some of the chemical majors was borne out in a US Senate study. Banks not only manage huge blocks as trustees, but also supply large amounts of capital to them. 'While banks are generally not permitted to invest in common stocks for their own account', notes the Senate report, 'they have become major holders of common stocks as trustees or in other fiduciary capacities and, most importantly, in their role as trustees of corporate pension funds. While banks do not own the beneficial interest in these securities which they hold in these capacities, they often have the power to exercise voting rights either solely at their own discretion or with the concurrence of others'.[101] Banks were prominent amongst the major shareholders of Union Carbide, Dow, and Monsanto. Chase-Manhattan, for instance, had 7.4 per cent of Monsanto's stock and 5.2 per cent of Union Carbide in 1974.[102]

In Italy, the banks are the only thing standing between a barely surviving fibre industry and total bankruptcy. In 1979, a consortium of eleven state-owned and private banks took effective control of the Societa Italiana Resine (SIR), which trails Montedison and ANIC in chemical and fibre output. SIR's $3.5 billion debt was not helped by allegations in 1979 that the company's Chairman had been embezzling part of SIR's bank loans and funnelling them to the ruling Christian Democrat Party as a kickback for easy government-backed credit. But SIR represented only the tip of a rapidly melting iceberg, as stated by the governor of the Bank of Italy: 'A process of industrial and financial reorganization cannot be further delayed if we are to keep the crisis from involving the banks.'[103]

What has been designated as 'the universal banking system' in West Germany harks back to the time of Bismarck, when the state lent a major impetus to 19th Century German industrialization and concentration. No legal difference exists in West Germany between credit, business and equity dealings and, in contrast to the United States, there are no legal restraints deterring the banks from enlarging their stake in industry. The German Monopoly Commission's findings indicated that the credit banking sector (i.e. the commercial banks, including the big three – the Deutsche, Dresdner and Commerz) supplied between 50–66 per cent of credit to all manufacturing sectors by the mid-1970s.[104] The top three banks had 6.1 per cent of the equity capital in the big industrial corporations in 1974–1975. They controlled, through proxy power, 34.9 per cent of the votes of annual general meetings, a share which has increased since then (see Table 6.10).[105]

Table 6.10
Bank Holdings in the 74 Largest West German Companies, 1974–75 (%)

	Share of Equity Capital	Share of Voting Right at AGMs	Share of Supervisory Board Membership	Share of Supervisory Board Chairmanships
Beutsche Bank	3.5	18.6	5.3	24.3
Deutsche Bank	1.6	11.8	2.7	8.1
Commerzbank	1.0	4.5	1.9	1.4
All three above	6.1	34.9	9.9	33.8
Other banks and investment companies	3.0	27.8	8.0	16.2
Total Credit institutes	9.1	62.7	17.9	50.0

Source: Gessler Commission Report, 1979.

Pricing Policies

So far we have demonstrated that the mechanisms of corporate power are major determinants of chemical fibres' inroads into cotton's share of the world fibre market precisely during a period when chemical fibre prices were much higher than cotton's. To recognize this fact is not to ignore the role of prices in inter-fibre competition – a role which is growing as blending techniques give textile producers increasing leeway in choosing to substitute small increments of natural for chemical fibres or vice versa on the basis of price swings. The role of pricing, however, must be understood within the framework of oligopolistically determined prices.

A major aspect of pricing policies has been 'posted' or 'administered' prices. Posted prices are little more than first appearances, since chemical fibre market prices are subject to both high levels of discounting in particular markets and variation over time. Posted prices do give an order of magnitude, normally above real prices, and permit comparisons from one market to another. It is useful to compare these prices with the oligopolistically dominated pricing structure on the New York Cotton Exchange for cotton. In both raw cotton and chemical fibres, price guidelines are basically the starting point of a complex price adjustment process: actual fibre sales are made on the basis of mark-ups or mark-downs from this basic price, depending on volume traded.

The existence of such price guidelines is in no way incompatible with widely divergent price structures within national markets. In both Japan and the United States, polyester sold at $1.00/lb. in 1964. A decade later a Japanese polyester was domestically marketed at $0.90, which was by then more than double the US price. Despite lower labour costs in UCEs, over-all synthetic fibre costs tend to remain much lower in developed market economies. As can be seen in Pakistan, UCE capital and depreciation costs are as a rule much higher than in DCEs (see Table 6.11). Cost data do not, however, necessarily bear any relation to selling prices. India's price for domestic chemical fibres is $3.13/lb due to heavy taxation, a price that is competitive on the Indian market only because of the tariffs on fibre imports.[106]

Differences within national units are matched by no less important differences between the major chemical fibres themselves; nylon, for instance, costs almost twice as much as acrylic to produce.

The steady fall in polyester prices throughout the 1960s was due in large part to a series of cost-cutting innovations (see Table 6.12). By 1972, United States polyester prices were only one-quarter of 1955 levels. While the cost curves of polyester and cotton crossed in 1972, what should be noted was that it was precisely in the 1960s, when there was still a sizeable price gap between cotton and polyester, that polyester made its significant break-through into textile markets.

In the battle of 'inter-fibre competition', the 'energy crisis' which erupted in 1973 did not diminish the market credibility of synthetics, as was widely predicted at the time. Rather, the evidence demonstrated that it was cotton which was more adversely affected by the oil price boost. Despite the central role played by petroleum, a doubling in oil prices precipitates less than a 10 cent increase in the cost of producing a pound of synthetic fibre. Thus, between October 1973 and May 1974, for instance, price rises of 400 per cent in crude oil and 350 to 400 per cent in naphtha led to rises of 35 to 40 per cent in the price of acrylics and 30 per cent in polyamids and polyesters. As against these synthetic fibre price hikes, between January 1973 and May 1974 Pakistani cotton prices rose by 60 per cent, Mexican by 54 per cent, Egyptian by 162 per cent, and Ugandan by 84 per cent.

Table 6.11
Britain and Pakistan: Comparative Polyester Costs, 1976 (US cents/lb.)

	British Producer	%	National Fibres Ltd of Pakistan	%
Raw material	31.36	56.0	47.35	55.0
Labour	7.84	14.0	1.30	1.5
Services, energy, etc.	5.60	10.0	7.29	8.5
Maintenance	2.24	4.0	0.32	0.3
Depreciation	3.36	6.0	10.50	12.2
Capital costs	5.60	10.0	19.40	22.5
Total manufacturing cost	56.00	100.0	86.16	100.0
Sales and distribution costs	18.00		2.64[1]	
Total costs	*74.00*		*88.80*	

1. Cost of transportation by National Fibres Ltd apparently not included.

Source: ITC, *Marketing of Pakistan Polyester Products in International Markets,* March 1977.

In the face of the overcapacity and flagging demand that began in 1975, the price leadership prevailing since the Second World War momentarily broke down. Two years later, acrimonious inter-corporate recriminations of dumping fibres below cost became widespread, with Du Pont clamouring for the US Treasury Department to investigate Rhone-Poulenc and then Toray and Kanebo for selling nylon yarns at up to 30 per cent below costs.[107] That very year even posted prices (already higher than real prices) dipped below costs in most countries: by 6 cents/lb. in Japan, 3 cents/lb. West Germany and the Netherlands, and 2 cents/lb. in France and the UK.[108] The upshot was what one chemical industry analyst termed 'a rash of temporary allowances on prices that breaks the industry discipline'.[109]

New UCEs and CPEs breaking into chemical fibre markets also produced a steady downward pressure on prices, thereby threatening cotton even more, until the 'seven oil sisters' and their OPEC collaborators capitalized on the Iranian revolution to send oil prices skyward. Still the petrochemical and chemical fibres oligopolies' ability to soften the blow of the oil hikes was another demonstration of their power. Many chemical conglomerates' upstream properties allowed them to buy oil-based feedstocks cheaply from themselves; furthermore they were able to produce the details of decade-old energy conservation programmes that dazzled their opponents. In the United States, synthetic fibre producers slashed average energy use per output unit by 56 per cent from 1967 to 1976.[110] ICI cut its energy consumption by 18 per cent between 1971 and 1977.[111] In fact, in the wake of the oil price increases petrochemical producers argued that oil-based synthetics of all sorts had reaped comparative gains against all competitors, from energy-intensive metal producers to fertilizer- and pesticide-addicted cotton growers.[112]

Table 6.12
Cotton, Rayon and Polyester Prices, 1955–77 (US cents/lb.)

	Cotton[1]	Rayon[2]	Polyester[2]
1955	37.2	33.7	160.0
1960	29.7	28.3	126.0
1965	28.8	27.4	85.2
1970	30.7	25.0	40.7
1971	35.5	26.8	37.0
1972	37.5	31.0	34.5
1973	63.1	33.1	36.7
1974	66.2	50.8	46.0
1975	55.9	51.5	47.8
1976	79.3	55.0	53.0
1977	73.9	58.0	55.0

1. Mexican SM 1–1/16"
2. US prices.

Source: IMF, *Staff Papers,* July 1977; and UNCTAD *Monthly Commodity Price Bulletin,* various issues.

As has been seen, variations in cotton and chemical fibre prices are intricately enmeshed with and dependent on price structures fabricated by yet another oligopoly, the seven petroleum majors. While the price hikes of both 1973 and 1979 were triggered by OPEC, the subsequent spiralling of these prices was due to the pricing strategies of the majors and made possible by their extensive control of all stages of processing, marketing and distribution. The upshot is that, for any given unit price boost by OPEC, the ultimate retail price is multiplied several-fold by the oligopoly.

Oligopolistic oil pricing has had two major consequences: it has fanned the fires of world inflation and thereby intensified the economic crisis; and related to this, it has exacerbated inter-imperialist rivalries. With respect to the global capitalist crisis, the DCE state apparatus has, in general, responded by supporting the beleaguered larger corporations (e.g. Montedison, British Leyland, and Chrysler) to the detriment of medium and smaller enterprises. Thus the crisis, induced by the oligopoly, finally benefits the oligopoly. Inter-imperialist rivalries have meant that the oil price boosts have had a varying impact on the major imperial centres. Western Europe and Japan, with smaller oil and natural gas resources than the United States, have been hit considerably harder. Once again, however, the larger European members of the chemical oligopoly (e.g. ICI, Bayer, and Hoechst) have largely out-manoeuvred higher prices, with their access to relatively cheap US feedstocks via their corporate operations in North America.

In sum, it is the interactions of these enmeshed oil and chemical oligo-polies — and not the unfettered operations of supply and demand — which largely determine the fibre mix that is fed into the textile web.

References

1. David Noble, *America by Design: Science, Technology, and the Rise of Corporate Capitalism* (New York 1977), p. 6.
2. *The Economist,* 7 April 1979, p.5; and company *Annual Reports.*
3. The great diversity in chemicals of some of the giants is epitomized by Hoechst, which is not only a global leader in several fibre lines, but also launched more new drugs (46) in 1978 than any other competitor in the pharmaceuticals industry. See *The Economist,* 23 June 1979.
4. Concentration in dyestuffs is perhaps more clearly delineated in the United States, where half the national market is accounted for by four US firms, 30—40 per cent by three non-US firms (ICI, Sandoz, Ciba-Geigy) and the remaining 10—20 per cent by US and foreign-owned companies.
5. United Kingdom, Board of Trade, *International Cartels 1944,* Vol. I (London, 1976).
6. L.F. Haber, *The Chemical Industry During the Nineteenth Century* (Oxford, 1969), pp. 225—7.
7. W.J. Reader, *I.C.I.: A History,* Vol. II (Oxford, 1975), p. 413.
8. OECD, *Export Cartels: Report of the Committee of Experts on Restrictive Business Practices* (Paris, 1974).
9. *The Economist,* 9 September 1972.
10. Recently, the Federal Trade Commission charged that Du Pont accounted for 40 per cent of all US output of titanium dioxide pig-ments, exploiting its dominant position, size and economic power to monopolize the market. Four companies alone account for over four-fifths of titanium dioxide output, *Financial Times,* 12 April 1978.
11. *Chemical Economy and Engineering Review,* April 1978, p. 19.
12. Shell International Chemical Co., *Chemicals Information Handbook 1978—79* (London, 1979).
13. See *Chemical Week,* 25 April 1979 for a complete list of United States

conglomerates in chemicals production. Increased merger activity in US chemicals is best exemplified by the 1978 marriage of Celanese and Olin to create the fifth largest chemical group in the United States.

14. *Chemical Insight,* October 1977.

15. *Fortune,* 22 September 1980.

16. *Financial Times,* 31 March 1978.

17. In the United States the industry is usually broken down into majors and independents. According to the US Department of Energy, 18 firms are considered as the 'majors', led by Exxon Corporation, Texaco, Shell Oil Company, Standard Oil (Indiana), Gulf Oil, Atlantic Richfield, Getty Oil, Union Oil of California, Sun Oil, Phillips Petroleum, Continental Oil, and Cities Service.

18. Transportation is another vital link in the industry; its elements are pipelines, tankers, barges, railroad tank cars and tank trucks. Pipelines have certain absolute cost advantages over other modes of transportation and are of central importance to the industry. There are three categories of pipeline: crude gathering, crude trunk and petroleum product pipelines. For details, see United States, Senate, *Oil Company Ownership of Pipelines,* 95th Congress, 2nd session (Washington DC, 1978), pp. 2–3.

19. Ida M. Tarbell, *The History of the Standard Oil Company* (Gloucester, Mass., 1904), p. 283.

20. United States, Senate, *Oil Company Ownership of Pipelines,* p. 1. Our italics.

21. In its report on the oil industry, a 1933 Congressional Enquiry discovered that of 42 pipelines, only 11 were not owned by the oil industry. The full impact of such oil company ownership, however, was obscured since independents accounted for a mere 0.58 per cent of total capitalization, and 5.63 per cent of gross investment. To cap it all, eight of these independent pipelines were controlled by the Rockefeller interests. See US Interstate and Foreign Commerce, *Report on Pipelines,* 72nd Congress, 2nd session (Washington, DC, 1933), p. xxvii.

22. United States, Senate, *Competition and Public Policy in the Petroleum Refining Industry: Hearing before the Senate Judiciary Committee,* 95th Congress, 2nd Session, (Washington, DC, 1978), pp. 1–2.

23. Federal Trade Commission, Bureau of Economics, *Concentration Levels and Trends in the Energy Sector of the U.S. Economy,* (Washington DC, 1974), p. 40.

24. Bureau of the Census, *Annual Survey of Oil and Gas,* 1975. Conversely, outside the charmed circle of twenty, the drop in producers' shares was from 44 to 25 per cent in those two decades. Such precipitous declines had little to do with efficiency, but rather with the massive scale of annexations. The twenty giants, between the mid-1950s and 1970, had made 147 acquisitions — roughly ten a year. The pickings in the 1970s have proved equally lush, as should those of the 1980s.

25. *Business Week,* 24 April 1978.

26. United States, Senate, *Mergers and Industrial Concentration: Hearings before the Subcommittee on Antitrust and Monopoly,* 95th Congress, 2nd session (Washington, DC, 1978), p.2.

27. El Paso Natural Gas increased its coal holdings during that time from zero to 11.8 billion tons; Shell from zero to 5.1 billion; Mobil from zero to 2.6 billion and Texaco from zero to 2.5 billion.
28. United States, Senate, *Mergers and Industrial Concentration*, p. 135. The findings of the Commissioner on the Mellon holdings indicate that they are not of recent vintage. As early as 1932, 'Mr. Mellon and his associates were busily engaged in putting together a gigantic purchase of mining rights . . . And it is estimated that each acre foot can yield 1,000 tons of coal. The royalty payments on this coal being collected by the Mellons, when spread over the 27 million acres, produces the almost incredible sum of $486 billion. This becomes all the more amazing when it is reconciled with the fact that Mr. Mellon actually paid $1 an acre for these 27 million acres.'
29. No less important is the mode of financing which links big oil with the big banks. Owners in joint ventures subscribe to shares of stock, in proportion to their expected throughput. There are adjustment provisions to provide for changes in actual throughput. Financing is based on the throughput commitments of the owners; that is, long-term debt is provided by banks in return for the oil companies' commitment to ship sufficient oil through the system to cover all costs.
30. S.H. Ruttenberg *et al., The American Oil Industry: A Failure of Anti-Trust Policy* (Washington, DC, 1973), p. 57; also N. Medvin and I.J. Law, *The Energy Cartel: Big Oil vs. The Public Interest* (Washington, DC, 1975).
31. See the testimony of Robert Engler, *Hearings before the Subcommittee on Anti-trust and Monopoly,* 95th Congress, 1st Session (Washington, DC, 1978), p. 64.
32. *The Economist,* 7 April 1979, p. 24. Another form of co-operation has been outright merger, epitomized by BP's 1979 acquisition of the oil refining and trading units of Veba, the large West German energy, mining, chemical and trading company.
33. *Business Week,* 9 October 1979.
34. The present big three of West Germany arose almost simultaneously in the 1860s. The Badische Anilinand Soda Fabrik (BASF) was set up in Mannheim in 1865. Its transnational character became marked in the period 1873–1900, when affiliates were set up in Russia, the United States, the United Kingdom and France. Bayer was set up in 1863 and between 1876 and 1908 dyestuff offshoots were established in a number of overseas countries. A central research laboratory in Ludwigshafen started in 1889, and was a landmark in the history of research and development. In 1863, Hoechst was founded; already by the 1880s it had developed overseas affiliates. By 1881, the dyestuffs convention embracing BASF, Bayer and Hoechst, four other German dyemakers and one English company, specified output, sales and minimum prices. Although it proved abortive, it set the course for future consolidation of the German dyestuffs industry.
35. On the impact of the war economy in stimulating concentration, see G.D. Feldman, *Army, Industry, and Labour in Germany, 1914–1918* (Princeton, 1966); and W. Manchester, *The Arms of Krupp, 1587–1968,* (Boston, 1968).

36. It represented the merger of Poulenc Freres in Paris and Usines de Rhone in Lyon.

37. For the connexions of Standard and IG Farben during the inter-war years, see G.S. Gibb and E.H. Knowlton, *The Resurgent Years: History of the Standard Oil Company, 1911–1927* (New York, 1956); H.M. Marson, E.H. Knowlton, and C.S. Toptle, *New Horizons: History of Standard Oil Company, 1927–1950* (New York, 1971).

38. Joseph Borkin, *The Crime and Punishment of I.G. Farben* (London, 1978), p. 2.

39. See the work of the Nuremberg chief prosecutor, Josiah Du Bois, *The Devil's Chemists: 24 Conspirators of the International Farben Cartel Who Manufacture Wars* (Boston, 1952) and *Trials of War Criminals Before the Nuremberg Military Tribunals, Under Control, Council No. 10* (Washington, DC, 1953).

40. US Group Control Council, Finance Division, Germany, *Report on Investigation of I.G. Farbenindustrie,* 12 September 1945.

41. For a masterly account, see Borkin, *op. cit.,* p. 75. The author was the chief of the patent and cartel section of the Anti-trust Division of the US Department of Justice.

42. *Ibid.*

43. Quoted in Borkin, *op. cit.,* p. 126. Such practices were justified in the name of anti-Bolshevism. And it was not surprising that Krauch's legal defence cited Hitler as a prophet, 'How right Hitler was in this outline of his policy . . . might be confirmed by the political situation [i.e. the Cold War] which has developed in recent months.' Moreover, the indictments were said to have been misplaced by Krauch's counsel, who contended that the IG defendants were mere businessmen, like their counterparts in other countries. 'Replace IG by Imperial Chemical Industries for England, or Du Pont for America, or Montecatini for Italy,' Krauch's lawyer declared before the Nuremberg Tribunal, 'and at once the similarity will become clear to you.' Quite. See Borkin, *op. cit.,* p. 149. The Nazi effusions of Krauch were not isolated from the representatives of international capitalism as a whole. An exuberant spokesman of Nazi theory and practice was Director-General Sir Henri Deterding of Shell, who by the 1930s was 'convinced that the Nazis were the only solution to the communist menace'. Appropriately, at the time of his death, 'Hitler and Goering both sent wreaths to the funeral'; Anthony Sampson, *The Seven Sisters* (London, 1976), p. 96.

44. Company *Annual Reports.*

45. Architects of this merger were Sir Alfred Mond, later Lord Melchett (1868–1930) and Sir Harry McGowan, later Lord McGowan (1874–1961); see Leslie Hannah (ed.), *Management Strategy and Business Development: An Historical and Comparative Study* (London, 1976) and W.J. Reader, *Imperial Chemical Industry, 1900–1930* (Oxford, 1970). The authorized capital of the new company was £65,000,000, 'the biggest initial capital of any company hitherto registered in this country'.

46 *ICI at Fifty,* (a company publication, London), p. 7. Our italics.

47. *Ibid.*

48. *Ibid.,* p. 24. The official spokesman added that 'interestingly enough,

the existence of these plants does not reduce export sales, for they
have the effect of 'priming the export pump' and give rise to additional
opportunities for exports from the UK'.

49. ICI, *1976 Annual Report,* p. 4. Excludes Carrington Viyella Ltd and its
subsidiaries.

50. See D.C. Coleman, *Courtaulds: An Economic and Social History* (2
vols; Oxford, 1969); L. Briscoe, *Textile and Clothing Industries of the
United Kingdom* (Manchester, 1971); Counter Information Services,
Courtaulds on the Inside (London, 1977).

51. These aspects of Courtaulds' textile operations are examined in Chapter .7.

52. At the beginning of the 1970s, Courtaulds' market power was
summarized as follows by *Management Today:* 'So powerful a
company, with control over its own fibre supplies at one end, and
guaranteed outlets all the way down the line to the other end, is in a
perfect position to call the tune if it wishes. And the old history of
Courtaulds never revealed any abnormal reluctance about calling tunes.'

53. *Management Today,* April 1978, p. 57.

54. *Business Week,* 30 April 1979.

55. Bolton, The *MNCs in the Textile, Garment and Leather Industries,*
(Brussels, 1976), p. 13.

56. *Ibid,* p. 116.

57. *The Economist,* 24 December 1977.

58. *Financial Times,* 17 June 1978.

59. *Business Week,* 25 July 1977.

60. *Chemical Week,* 25 May 1977.

61. Its marketing directions and technology transfers in the period between
the wars and the aftermath of the Second World War indicate the path of
the conglomerate's growth. Anticipating the future of synthetic fibres,
Toray succeeded in synthesizing Nylon 6 through its independent
technology. Although research and development was suspended during
the war, in 1951 nylon output was activated on a large scale under a
Du Pont licence. In 1958, Toray concluded a licence agreement with
ICI for polyester fibre. By 1963, following its own extensive research
build-up, it pioneered its own acrylic fibre and shifted out of rayon.
Parallel with the growth of synthetic fibres, it successfully moved into
plastics, as well as backwardly integrating into the petrochemical
industry. European Chemical News, *Booklets on Japan,* July 1972.

62. See the following works for the corporation's growth and
diversification: G.C. Zilg, *Du Pont: Behind the Nylon Curtain* (New
York, 1974); A.D. Chandler and S. Salsbury, *Pierre D. Du Pont and the
Making of the Modern Corporation* (New York, 1971); W.H. Carr, *The
Du Ponts of Delaware* (New York, 1964); P.K. Winkler, *The Du Pont
Dynasty* (New York, 1935); E.I. Du Pont Co., *The Chemical Industry*
(New York, 1935).

63. Du Pont's entry into the chemical industry, notably dyestuffs, was
facilitated by US entry into the First World War, when in 1918 the
Congress passed the Trading-with-the-Enemy Act, whereby all German
patents fell under the jurisdiction of the Office of the Alien Property
Custodian. Approximately 5,700 German patents were sold for
$271,000, many falling into Du Pont hands. For the close ties with IG

Farben, see Zilg, *op. cit.,* pp. 259–335; and a wider setting, United States, Senate, Committee on Military Affairs, *Economic and Political Aspects of Military Cartels,* Monograph 1, (Washington, DC, 1944).

64. In 1965, Du Pont completed its divestiture of GM.
65. Zilg, *op. cit.,* p. 2.
66. *Ibid.,* p. 347. Nylon was the first chemical synthetic fibre, emerging from the seven years of research by Dr Wallace Carothers at the then unprecedented cost of $27 million. According to the company's estimates, nylon sales topped more than $2 billion in net earnings from fibres, plastics and related products since 1939. The marketing implication of this revolutionary innovation is that it spawned the 450 types of nylon fibres and resins being marketed today. The potential of this innovation is far from exhausted; see *Du Pont Annual Report, 1976.*
67. Acceleration of overseas corporate investment between 1965 and 1976 indicates that total plant investments more than quadrupled from $345 million to $1.5 billion. One of the biggest is the joint polyester and acrylic venture with Iran that came on stream in 1978.
68. *Chemical Week,* 18 April 1979.
69. American Chemical Society, *Chemistry in the Economy* (Washington, DC, 1975), p. 515.
70. *Du Pont Annual Report,* 1976, p. 15.
71. Approximately one-third of Hoechst's present sales derive from products which did not exist a decade ago.
72. With reference to one of the major UCF fibre-producing countries, one technologist noted that 'in India, the fibre manufacturers have limited testing and research facilities and have not so far undertaken any worthwhile research work' due to small production units and restricted end-uses, in most cases producing fibres for apparel end-uses only. Cf. J.G. Parikh, 'Research and development in man-made fibres in Europe', *Indian Cotton Mills Federation Journal,* February 1977.
73. *Knitting Times,* 24 July 1978.
74. *Financial Times,* 18 September 1978.
75. Herman Zwick, 'Man-made fibre marketing at Hoechst', International Federation of Cotton and Allied Textile Industries publication, Vol. 15, 1974.
76. *Ibid.,* p. 52.
77. *Ibid.* The advertising organization which this involves is exhibited in Du Pont's Textile Marketing Division strategy with dacron and its multiple variants. More than 300 sales outlets were mobilized towards the end of 1977 in retail promotions, and 60 television commercials were run during peak viewing times; see *Textile World,* April 1977.
78. OECD, *Transfer Pricing and Multinational Enterprises: Report of the OECD Committee on Fiscal Affairs* (Paris, 1979), p. 7.
79. Robin Murray, *'Transfer Pricing and the State',* unpublished thesis presented to the Institute of Development Studies, University of Sussex, 1978.
80. United Nations, *Transnational Corporations in World Development: A re-examination,* (New York, 1978), p. 43.
81. UNCTAD, *The Structure and Behaviour of Enterprises in the Chemical*

Industry and their Effects on the Trade and Development of Developing Countries (Geneva, 1979), p. 20.

82. K.K. Subrahmanian and P. Mohanan Pillai, 'Implications of technology transfers in export-led growth strategy', *Economic and Political Weekly*, 30 October 1976.

83. OECD, *Restrictive Business Practices of Multinational Enterprises; Report of the Committee of Experts on Restrictive Business Practices* (Paris, 1977), paras 76–7.

84. UNCTAD, *Major Issues Arising from the Transfer of Technology: A Case Study of Spain,* (TD/B/AC.11/17), Geneva, 1979.

85. UNCTAD, *The Control of Transfer Pricing in Greece* (TD/B/C.6/32), Geneva.

86. UNCTAD, *Dominant Positions of Market Power of Transnational Corporations: Use of the Transfer Pricing Mechanism* (UNCTAD/ST/MD/6/Rev. 1) 30 November 1977, p. 1.

87. *The Economist,* 17 December 1977.

88. Ostensibly, the major impetus behind MITI's push for rationalization and consolidation stems from the alleged impact of South Korean fibre imports (originating from industries spawned by Japanese capital in the 1960s and early 1970s) embracing about one-half of Japanese fibre imports.

89. Tariffs on EEC chemical products tend to vary from 8 to 15 per cent. For certain chemical lines, however, they escalate as high as 16 to 18 per cent.

90. This was done by MITI to rationalize research and development efforts, and because of the costs involved in lengthy patent litigation. The understanding covers 6,500 fibre and textile patents; 5,000 by Toray and 1,500 by Teijin; *European Chemical News,* 1 September 1972.

91. *Chemical Week,* 30 October 1974.

92. *Ibid.;* see also *Chemical Week,* 18 May 1977.

93. *Business Week,* 27 March 1978.

94. *International Herald Tribune,* special issue, December 1978.

95. Du Pont and Monsanto (the two American majors in the EEC) have indicated their concurrence with the cartel's plans, but have avoided direct involvement for fear of US anti-trust action.

96. United Kingdom Monopolies Commission, *Report on the Supply of Man-made Cellulosic Fibres* (London, 1968).

97. UNCTAD, *The Structure and Behaviour . . .* , p. 41.

98. By the end of the 1970s, terylene and Du Pont's Nylon 66 were covered by such agreements.

99. A. Clements (ICI Secretary), 'Financing a Multinational: A Case Study', *Chemical Age,* 24 June 1977.

100. Zilg, *op. cit.* pp. 549–56. The representatives are: Chemical Bank New York Trust, Lammot du Pont Copeland; First National City Bank, Charles B. McCoy; Florida First National Bank, Willis H. du Pont; Liberty Mutual Insurance Co., Willard A. Speakman, Jr; Life Insurance Co., Irenee du Pont; Wilmington Trust Co., Lammot du Pont Copeland.

101. United States Senate, *Disclosure of Corporate Ownership,* p. 7.

102. *Ibid.,* p. 52.

103. *Business Week,* 2 July 1979.

104. *Financial Times,* 8 March 1978.
105. See *Bericht Bundeskartellamt,* (Mehringdamm, West Berlin, 1979–80) p. 13–21.
106. R. Evans, 'Manmade fibres gain more markets in '77', *Foreign Agriculture,* 30 January 1978.
107. *New York Times,* 6 January 1978; and *Financial Times,* 21 November 1977.
108. International Trade Centre, *Marketing of Pakistan Polyester Products in International Markets,* (Geneva, 1977), p. 18.
109. *Business Week,* 12 December 1977.
110. *Chemical Week,* 28 March 1979.
111. *Financial Times,* 22 June 1979.
112. *Chemical Week,* 28 March 1979. In this period, US members of the chemical fibre oligopoly benefited more than their competitors, protected by tight federal price controls on oil, and by their use of natural gas, rather than oil, for the bulk of their feedstocks.

7. The Textile Crucible

The textile industry is the crucible in which the world's fibres are transformed. Though one industry in the global economy which is common to all countries, it reaches its highest technological expression in a small coterie of DCEs. At present, control of textile processing is in the hands of a loose oligopoly, with approximately 35 to 40 large textile corporations exerting a paramount force on world markets. In general, these are horizontally-integrated firms, although vertical integration and conglomeration, as in the cases of Courtaulds, Agache-Willot, Burlington, and Japanese members of the textile oligopoly, will gather momentum in the 1980s. This oligopoly continues to be one of the major forces behind the gigantic shift in textile output and exports from DCEs to an elite group of UCEs. This chapter analyses the forces which are reshaping the topography of textile manufacturing and, by extension, also influence other sectors of the world economy.

World textile exports hovered around $34 billion in 1977 (reaching an estimated $60 billion by 1980), 3 per cent of all world trade.[1] As one of the leading industries in the changing international division of labour, textiles is the major battleground within and between the UCEs and the DCEs. The 1970s Multi-fibre Arrangement stands as a model of some, but by no means all, of the DCEs' strategies of economic warfare. With large areas of the world already staked out by the oligopoly, the cut-throat scramble for markets amongst different UCEs has intensified. The clear leaders are South Korea, Taiwan, and Hong Kong, which had over 39 per cent of UCE textile exports between them in 1977 (see Table 7.1). Worse, in 1965 these 'big three' predators (plus India) had already grabbed 54 per cent of the UCEs' clothing exports; a decade later they had gobbled up almost four-fifths. In the light of this competition, the notion of a unified 'Third World' working in solidarity towards some equally mythical 'New International Economic Order' is little more than a slogan.

By centring in this chapter on the corporate and technological stimuli that are transforming the textile international division of labour, these larger issues are raised. Beginning with an overview of the contours and concentration in the industry, we then trace the paths of the oligopoly and other allied actors in the leading DCE, UCE and CPE producers. For the DCEs, this entails an analysis of the combined impact of technical change and the

Table 7.1
Exports of Textile Materials and Clothing, 1965 and 1977

	Raw Material Value of Exports ($ billions)	Textile Fibres Share in World Total Exports (%)	Share in Total UCE Exports (%)	Textile Yarn and Fabrics Value of Exports ($ billions)	Share in World Total Exports (%)	Share in Total UCE Exports (%)	Clothing Value of Exports ($ billions)	Share in World Total Exports (%)	Share in Total UCE Exports (%)
1965									
DCEs	3.37	56.6		6.32	78.8		2.47	67.5	
CPEs	0.45	7.6		0.35	4.4		0.51	13.9	
UCEs	2.13	35.8	100.0	1.35	16.8	100.0	0.68	18.6	100.0
Hong Kong	—	—	—	0.18	2.2	13.3	0.32	8.7	47.1
Taiwan	—	—	—	0.05	0.6	3.7	0.02	0.5	2.9
S. Korea	0.01	0.2	0.5	0.03	0.4	2.2	0.02	0.5	2.9
India	0.05	0.8	2.3	0.58	7.2	43.0	0.01	0.5	1.5
World	*5.95*	*100.0*		*8.02*	*100.0*		*3.66*	*100.0*	
1977									
DCEs	7.78	57.2		24.58	72.7		12.07	50.9	
CPEs	2.00	14.7		2.64	7.8		2.96	12.5	
UCEs	3.83	28.2	100.0	6.57	19.4	100.0	8.70	36.7	100.0
Hong Kong	0.01	0.1	0.4	0.57	1.7	8.7	2.92	12.3	33.6
Taiwan	0.03	0.2	0.7	0.92	2.7	14.0	1.32	5.6	15.2
S. Korea	0.09	0.7	2.5	1.08	3.2	16.4	2.06	8.7	23.7
India	(0.10)[1]	0.7	2.5	0.81	2.4	12.3	(0.40)[1]	1.7	4.6
World	*13.60*	*100.0*		*33.79*	*100.0*		*23.73*	*100.0*	

1. Estimate.
Source: Various United Nations Trade Yearbooks.

flood of UCE imports on the crisis enveloping their industries, and the response of the state apparatus. But we also analyse the growing market power of this DCE oligopoly in their battles for the reconquest, retention, and aggrandizement of world market shares.

The several operations involved in textile processing fall basically into two groups: yarn spinning, and fabric manufacture through knitting and weaving. The first consists of ordering and cleaning natural fibres by drawing, roving, winding, twisting, warping and the extrusion of man-made fibres. At the second or fabric-forming phases, over four-fifths of output is woven and the balance is knit. However, an upsurge in knitting since the early 1960s has resulted in knit goods climbing from about 10 per cent of all textiles produced in 1960 to 18 per cent in 1970, with projections for 1985 suggesting a further boost to 30 to 50 per cent.[2]

Despite the textile industry's size and ubiquity, textile producers (unless vertically integrated) are not the decisive protagonists in inter-fibre competition. Rather, the industry is caught between the demands of two smaller (in terms of output) but more powerful and dynamic industries in the chain: chemical fibres and textile machinery. It is these two industries who invariably work in tandem on new fibre specifications, while clothing producers and the wholesale/retail establishment often specify fabric and fibre content to textile producers.

Development of the Textile Industry

Throughout the 19th Century Britain was the centre of world textile power. As Thomas Carlyle wrote in 1839, 'English Commerce stretches its fibres over the whole earth; sensitive literally, nay quivering in convulsion, to the farthest influences of the earth.'[3] Although by 1913 its universal dominance was tarnished, Britain was still the world's leader in textile production, with two-fifths of global cotton spindleage. However, its pre-war status was further eroded in the inter-war period, and the process has continued unabated since the Second World War.

The geographical diffusion of the textile industry was matched by marked productivity gaps, symptomatic of the different stages of capital intensities. This would be grossly misrepresented, however, as a shift from a labour-intensive to a capital-intensive industry. After all the textile industry was the apotheosis of the Industrial Revolution. Equally today, its labour/capital ratios must be gauged in relation to other industries, notably the newer, science-based, industries of the last quarter of the 20th Century, whose capital requirements per worker are generally much higher.

The impressive strides in spinning and weaving productivity are evident in West Germany, where textile productivity rose by 57 per cent in the first seven years of the 1970s as compared with a 27-per-cent increase for industry as a whole. Between 1963 and 1978 British output per textile employee rose by 80 per cent, compared to 54 per cent for the rest of manufacturing.

Such productivity has in many cases been made possible by the strides in synthetics, as noted by ICI's Deputy Chairman for Research:

> Another example of the textile industry seizing the opportunities offered by synthetics is the rate of picking at weaving. This used to be 150 picks/minute in a Lancashire loom, now it is 600 picks/minute in water jets [a speed at which cotton begins to disintegrate] and a recent British invention is aimed at picking rates in excess of 2,000. This spectacular speed increase (and even the actual figures) closely mirrors developments in aircraft speeds, 600 mph jets having replaced 100 mph DC3s and Concorde just beginning at 1,400 mph. With a record like this the textile industry has every right to feel proud of its achievements and to boast of developing technically as fast as the aerospace industry.[4]

UCE textile muscle in the world market, on the other hand, is in some measure due to the subsistence wages enforced by the oligarchy in the absence of a militant trade union organization. This is not an overwhelming threat to DCEs since technical innovations, partnered by continuous managerial rationalization of work methods, have boosted their productivity to a point where the competitive disadvantages of higher wage levels are being partially trimmed or neutralized.[5] Even among developed countries there are marked productivity divergences. According to a study by the Werner management consultants, the United States has the world's highest average textile productivity, with West Germany's textile plants roughly 73 per cent as high as that of the USA; France 57 per cent; and the United Kingdom less than 50 per cent as high. Moreover, the average unit size of West European textile firms is about one-tenth the United States average, with US mill costs in certain sectors (e.g. carpets) 25 to 30 per cent below those of West Europe. The prime rationale behind West European modernization and concentration is that the wage content of textile items produced in Western Europe (whose labour force, in contrast to the United States, is almost entirely unionized) is around a third higher than in the United States. The US industry is composed overwhelmingly of non-unionized women, blacks and Hispanics whose wages are less than half of workers in the automobile industry. There is an enormous gap (distorted to a certain extent through the prism of foreign exchange rates) in wage rates between DCEs and UCEs, and between different UCEs themselves (see Table 7.2). Comparisons between 1970 and 1978 can be highly misleading in view of the precipitous fall in the value of the dollar during the 1970s.

The unrelenting crisis which has battered the world textile economy since the early 1970s is symptomatic of the pervasiveness of the world economic crisis, in which overall productive capacity outpaces demand. The crisis has dovetailed with massive automation and rationalization to curtail employment sharply in most DCE industries. It is generally expected that EEC textile employment will be halved during the first half of the 1980s, which would amount to an additional 2 million workers joining the unemployed, now over 6.5 million. In Japan, the textile labour force shrank from 1.1 million to 0.8 million in just six years during the 1970s.

Undoubtedly, this movement will be speeded up in the 1980s. In the case of synthetic fibre production, plans have already been blueprinted in certain DCEs for the full integration of spinning, stretching, crimping, setting and cutting.

Table 7.2
Estimated Hourly Wage of Production Workers in Clothing and Textile Industries, 1970 and 1978 (US$)

	1970		1978	
	Textiles	Clothing	Textiles	Clothing
	(US = 100)		(US = 100)	
Netherlands	58	56	170	146
Sweden	112	111	160	167
Belgium	46	39	146	135
West Germany	57	52	142	141
Italy	33	26	104	101
Canada	92	80	104	98
France	49	44	103	100
United States	100	100	100	100
Japan	32	26	76	61
Ireland	46	52	66	52
United Kingdom	56	56	64	56
Hong Kong	16	17	23	23
Rep. of Korea	7	6	13	12
Taiwan	10	6	13	14
India	5	5	4	4

Source: Computed from data in ILO, *Yearbook of Labour Statistics; The US Dept. of Labor, Office of Productivity and Technology,* February 1980, and national sources.

The high-speed devices being developed for all these single operations have engendered certain socio-economic consequences. A leading textile technologist at Hoechst stated: 'In the field of staple fibre production as in the case of filament spinning and texturing process we have to expect an increasing mechanization and automation of the individual process steps. This rationalization will lead to increasing capital investments parallelled by further personnel reductions. For such an automation large-scale plants are especially suited . . .'[6]

It must be re-emphasized that such strategies of labour liquidation, combined with the accelerated concentration of capital, are already in evidence in the leading textile DCEs and must also be implemented by those UCEs desiring to break into or retain their global market shares of textile and clothing output. World Bank figures make it clear that the number of industrial jobs wiped out by UCE imports has been minuscule compared to the layoffs stemming from technological innovations and faltering demand.[7] In West Germany, 50 times more jobs were lost from 1962 to 1975 through labour productivity deals than from UCE imports. For the DCEs as a group, over five million jobs disappeared in 1975 as demand crumbled — a loss 20 times greater than that due to UCE imports in any year in the 1970s.

Concentration

Faced with constantly changing demand and swift engineering innovations in a highly competitive field, textile producers have three options: to invest substantial capital in advanced machinery; to accept liquidation in favour of (or takeover by) those better placed to introduce technical innovations swiftly; or to merge with chemical fibre producers or larger textile corporations. In other words, taken jointly or separately, the trend is towards vertical integration and concentration.

EEC findings show that in the cotton textile industry the need for long production runs in spinning and weaving means that vertical integration is economical only for large firms capable of combining economies of scale with product differentiation.[8] The future size of the cotton industry depends upon forging links with the final market through forward integration, since such control over weaving and knitting plants tends to counteract the unpredictable and rapid changes in fashion. Before such consolidation occurs, traditional modes of marketing weaken the bargaining power of textile manufacturers, leaving them vulnerable to: demand fluctuations due to inventory adjustments of wholesalers and retailers; the ability of retail clients to dump small textile suppliers and switch to imported fabrics, marketing them under the same brand labels as domestic fabrics; a weak bargaining position in marketing relations with large scale retailers dominating certain segments of the consumer textile market; severe limitations in the use of advertising and sales promotion; inability to influence the choice between knitted and woven fabrics for household textiles and apparel.

Another major factor promoting mergers has been the chemical fibre giants' desire to bolster the position of their major end-users. The rather weak user firms could often be salvaged only by consolidation and refinancing, which in turn was feasible only if the chemical fibre firms first acquired a dominant stake. Thus the pattern of vertical integration has been more a defensive operation to preserve purchases rather than an offensive action to acquire new profit centres.

The emergence of excess capacity has also heightened the need for integration. With their greater access to finance capital in general, and the transnational banking structure in particular, larger units are in a better position to elaborate long-term investment plans and to attract and retain a more highly skilled labour force. Furthermore, the larger textile units (as with their allies, the chemical fibre giants) are also better placed to pursue product research and to utilize modern marketing techniques, advertising, and brand promotion. Advocates of concentration see it as allowing two contradictory aspects to be reconciled: enhanced specialization in pecific product lines, and spread of marketing risks through product differentiation.[9]

Concentration is nowhere more clearly exemplified than in the sales of the British 'big three', Courtaulds, Carrington Viyella (an ICI subsidiary) and Tootal. At present, the big three represent 70 per cent of spindle hours; Courtaulds alone takes 50 per cent. Likewise, in loom hours worked they account for almost 50 per cent; and in finishing, for roughly one-half of total employment.[10] Hence, in the wake of the takeovers, a huge gap still persists between the largest and the medium-sized firms. And in a smaller DCE, Finland, a single private sector textile corporation, exporting a third of its output, has succeeded through the leverage of state power in annexing four-fifths of total textile output.

The Transnational Textile Oligopoly

As in the case of chemical fibres, DCE penetration of the international textile market since the early 1960s has been led by transnational textile corporations. While most oligopolistic firms are horizontally integrated, several of the 35 to 40 leading textile corporations are segments of conglomerates that embrace a wide range of textile and non-textile activities. The giant traders, particularly the Japanese, figure prominently in this sub-category.

Although formally autonomous, these 35 to 40 textile transnationals dominate global textiles in both UCEs and DCEs through a complex interlocking marketing network centred in five countries: Britain, the United States, France, West Germany, and Japan. Corporations from these five countries alone account for 94 per cent of the top 100 firms' turnover (see Table 7.3). This power structure is strongly reinforced by a network of interlocking directorships, the forging of common policies with respect to certain governments on specific issues, joint stockholdings, and joint ventures. The latter are manifested in specific operations of Toray and Unilever, Toray and Jardine Matheson, Dollfus-Mieg and Coats Patons, Courtaulds and Snia, Monsanto and Mitsubishi, Courtaulds and United Merchants, Tootal and Unilever, and others.

Whether the major textile groupings have carved out specific spheres of influence must remain a matter of conjecture. Historical connections, notably the colonial nexus, have undoubtedly determined plant location and marketing dependency. United States textile power is centred primarily in the Americas and Western Europe; the United Kingdom and France have both largely retained their primacy in their former colonies, with Britain holding extensive interests over a wide range of textile sectors in Latin America. Although the Japanese have stepped up their encroachments on

Africa and Latin America in the last decade, they remain essentially confined
to the East Asian perimeter.

Clearly, there is no global policy co-ordinator of all the TNCs in any
formal sense; on the contrary, economic warfare in specific markets and
products is common. At the same time there are no cases in which all 35 to
40 compete in the same product or market. The normal market situation
in any one product involves either a monopoly (smaller UCEs), a tight
oligopoly (larger UCEs, some smaller DCEs), or a somewhat loose oligopoly
(large DCEs).

This oligopolistic expansionism is not without its contradictions. Although
answering the short-term need for outlets for capital accumulation, overseas
investments have increased productive capacity which now returns to DCE
markets in the form of low-priced imports. This has led to aggressive state
protectionism through tariffs, subsidies, 'voluntary' export agreements,
greater access to credits, supportive mergers and research grants. The late
1970s saw this assistance reach a new peak with the EEC Commission blue-
printing plans to harmonize state aid to textiles and co-ordinate research and
export promotion.[11] By looking at the five leading DCEs we can see the
similarities and dissimilarities within this pattern for the nations that
headquarter the textile oligopoly.

The British textile industry vividly illustrates the post-war drive to concentration and mergers. Originally operating under the mantle of *laissez-
faire* the industry has, for many decades, been shaped by government intervention. Disparate pre-war groupings coalesced into a few giant spinning
combines. The 1959 Cotton Industry Act speeded up the rationalization
of the industry with large-scale subsidies for scrapping old machinery and
buying new equipment. However, it can be argued that such state intervention goes back not only to the inter-war years,[12] but even earlier, to the 19th
Century.

Between 1958 and 1963 the number of textile firms engaged in spinning
and/or weaving cotton and/or man-made fibres fell from 482 to 289; and
total employment from 261,000 to 186,000. At the same time, net output
rose from £149 million to £154 million. The five-firm concentration ratios
in the period 1958–77 display the cumulative impact of government legislation.[13] The steady movement toward greater concentration in most sectors
in the 1960s accelerated in leaps and bounds in the 1970s (see Table 7.4).
In certain specialized textile branches in the UK, an upper limit to concentration has almost been reached, three corporations having over 90 per cent of
output in rope fibres, and another three over 80 per cent (including the
American multinational Johnson & Johnson) of medical textile output.

The highly integrated structure of the five major textile groupings
(Courtaulds, Carrington Viyella, Tootal, Coats Paton and Vantona)[14] in
Britain constitutes an oligopolistic structure marked by interlocking directorates and minority holdings; high product-differentiation across a wide
spectrum of fabrics; inter-group sales accounting for a large fraction of total
output; and a large slice of world sales from overseas affiliates. This must be

evaluated in the context of an industry of national importance which, combined with clothing, provides jobs for more than 800,000 persons, and an output exceeding £2 billion by the end of the 1970s. It thus constitutes one of the top half dozen major industrial sectors.

Table 7.3
Distribution and Ranking of World's 100 Largest Textile Corporations, 1977

	% of Total Turnover of Firms	No. of Firms	Rankings
USA	39.4	33	2, 4, 8, 11, 13, 14, 15, 16, 18, 19, 21, 22, 24, 26, 30, 31, 35, 39, 43, 45, 46, 47, 50, 60, 62, 64, 67, 70, 81, 85, 97, 99, 100
UK	17.9	15	1, 6, 17, 20, 28, 51, 57, 58, 59, 65, 80, 87, 90, 91, 93
Japan	17.9	16	3, 5, 10, 32, 33, 37, 40, 41, 44, 55, 56, 68, 75, 77, 89, 96
West Germany	6.9	14	42, 48, 49, 53, 54, 61, 69, 71, 72, 74, 78, 82, 83, 88, 95
France	8.1	7	7, 12, 27, 29, 34, 76, 79
Italy	1.1	3	73, 86, 94
South Korea	3.4	2	9, 25
Argentina	0.8	1	36
Hong Kong	0.8	2	63, 92
Netherlands	1.0	2	52, 66
Canada	1.2	1	23
Belgium	0.4	1	84
Sweden	0.8	1	38
Switzerland	0.3	1	98

Source: Computed from data in *Textil-Wirtschaft*, 1 February 1979.

The largest textile company in this group is Courtaulds, whose role in chemical fibres was analysed in Chapter 6. Although an ICI takeover bid failed in 1961, the activities of both corporations have intersected at various points both before and after the Second World War. 'In some cases', noted an EEC report, 'Courtaulds co-operated with ICI during the period 1963–68 in providing funds to support major textile groups. In 1963, Courtaulds and ICI both acquired minority holdings in English Sewing Cotton (now Tootal) and in Carrington and Dewhurst, though the 10 per cent holding of Courtaulds in the latter was sold to ICI in 1968.'[15]
ICI's annexation of Carrington Viyella (as with takeovers by Courtaulds) was designed to secure outlets for its fibre output. A big company's need for

a bigger cut of the national market is matched by implacable opposition to foreign imports, so lucidly articulated by Courtauld's Chairman of the Board: 'With modern capital-intensive equipment the productivity of our activities and hence our competitiveness depends upon running plants at or near their full capacity. Any further erosion of our U.K. markets would damage our export competitiveness, any domestic expansion would enhance it.'[16]

Table 7.4
UK Five-Firm Concentration Ratios[1]

	1958	1963	1968	1972	1977
Man-made fibres	n.a	100	100	95	98
Finished thread for sewing, etc.	n.a.	82	88	88	86
Underwear/shirts	25	40	53	50	59
Woven man-made fibre cloth	21	36	52	64	n.a.
Single cotton or man-made fibre spun yarn	35	37	50	76	79
Doubled cotton or man-made fibre spun yarn	35	42	47	64	70
Socks, stockings, etc.	21	20	43	46	56
Knitted fabrics	30	35	43	45	55

1. Combined sales of five largest firms as percentage of total sales of selected products.

Source: UK *Census of Production* data.

The transnational character of the oligopoly is evident in Coats Paton, the world's largest manufacturer of sewing threads. Coats operates 160 manufacturing units in 30 countries, employing over 66,000 people. Almost 75 per cent of its sales are outside the United Kingdom, of which 65 per cent are supplied by its subsidiaries. Overseas expansion has to a large measure been prompted by higher profit margins. Average return on capital over the years 1968–73 stood at 6.3 per cent in the United Kingdom, as against 16.6 per cent overseas.[17]

Although the movement to concentration in the textile industry has gathered speed in the United States in recent years, it has been achieved only by constant battle with US anti-trust laws. This obviously contrasts with the state-aided integration of the UK. The sales of the top ten publicly-held US textile corporations in 1978 varied from $640 million to $2.7 billion

for Burlington, which ranks with Courtaulds as one of the world's biggest
textile corporations.[18] It comprises a few giants 'and a number of relatively
small companies more than 90 per cent of which have sales of less than
$10 million annually'.[19] Due, however, to what has been portrayed 'as a
growing flood of cheap foreign imports, a powerful union organizational
drive and relentless pressure from the Federal Government to spend billions
on new safety equipment, [the textile industry] is entering one of the most
critical periods in its recent history.'[20] Or in the words of *Business Week*
in 1979: 'fragmentation, overcapacity, and cut-throat competition are
bleeding the life out of the US textile industry'.[21]

By the end of the 1970s, the flood of foreign imports had reached unprecedented levels, contributing in 1977 to a textile clothing trade deficit
of $3.4 billion.[22] A set of convergent pressures on the US textile economy
must inevitably exacerbate the cost/price squeeze: the pressure to
unionize, and government legislation on safety, noise, dust, and the environment (not to speak of the mounting fuel and water bill) will involve costs
that should surpass $7 billion in the early 1980s.[23] In addition, require-
ments, such as large scale re-equipment involving massive capital outlays
amounting to an estimated $2 billion in the 1980s, are forcing many of the
family-owned textile groups to sell out or close down. But, despite such
deterrents, the industry has continued to annex larger sectors of the global
market. Textile corporations have scored some successes in breaking into
foreign markets, with roughly 50 per cent of their exports going to DCEs,
20 per cent to lower cost processing plants in UCEs, and the final 30 per
cent to UCE domestic consumption. In addition to tough measures
against countries that try to restrict US textile exports, other stimuli to the
textile industry are envisaged, such as changing depreciation provisions, thus
cutting back the periods in which company expenditures can be written off.

For the American textile worker the battle for unionization has
historically been bedevilled by repressive state legislation and corporate
power. In the 1920s, when the predominantly northern textile industry was
becoming at once politically militant and unionized, corporations shifted
their plants to the more congenial and better policed labour markets of the
South. By the end of the 1970s, repression had paid off and at present only
a trifling 7 per cent of hourly paid workers in US textile plants are
unionized.[24] Growing working-class pressures for unionization, however,
again jeopardize textile capital, spearheaded by a co-ordinated union and
consumer strategy against number 2 textile giant J.P. Stevens. As we turn to
the 1980s, mounting working-class pressure will tend to be countered by job-
displacing, capital-intensive technology spawned by oligopolistic capitalism,
which could well prove to be the most implacable enemy of the labour movement in all DCEs.

In the 1980s, it is anticipated that one-third of textile corporations and
7,000 plants will either have been closed down or gobbled up.[25] The big
fifteen in the United States, with one-quarter of aggregate output by the
end of the 1970s, will have appropriated two-fifths of total output by 1990.

No less noteworthy is that this allegedly 'labour-intensive' industry, with its 910,000-strong labour force (already chalking up an impressive 15- to 20-per cent unemployment level), is predicted to liquidate a further one-third of its workers.[26]

Anti-trust policy seems to have been reversed. By the mid-1970s the Federal Trade Commission had backed down on its earlier criticism of the 1960s that a few giants had acquired an over-dominant market position. What is more, the lines are opening up for conglomerate as well as intensified merger traffic in textiles.[27] Though traditionally laggards in the realm of conglomeration, several of the giants had gone into new consumer lines by the end of the 1970s: frozen foods, kitchen utensils, shampoos, cosmetics, among others.

In France, the 1960s witnessed the emergence of new corporate consolidations and their overseas extensions. Two of the leading French textile giants have been the Agache-Willot Group and Dollfus-Mieg (1979 sales: $1.1 billion). Yet in this era of the publicly owned company, the French transnational enterprises remain atypical, family enterprises, even after the demise of the once dominant Boussac family textile empire.

> An examination of Dollfus-Mieg reveals not only some amazing tie ups with other multinational corporations, which are to be expected, but also some interesting interconnections with the rest of the French textile industry. The Bureau Intersyndical d'Etudes de l'Industrie Textile had already shown the substantial collusion of interests between Dollfus-Mieg and Pricel Gillet, largely through the interest of the Gillet and Thiriez families. Again it is practical to consider these as an entity, for they appear to complement one another. It is also worth noting that the Gillet family is the major group of shareholders in Rhone-Poulenc. They are thus able to direct some 95 per cent of French fibre production and spinning and some 50 per cent of total mill capacity. . . This represents a far greater degree of control by one group over a national textile industry than we have discovered elsewhere and most definitely in one of the world's major textile producers.[28]

This major textile group, linked through equity participation with the Schaeffer Corporation, has numerous subsidiaries, mainly in Africa and Latin America.

'The Agache Willot Group', notes one of its corporate brochures, 'has grown within a framework inspired by state power and at times at their prodding.'[29] The history of the four Willot brothers includes a conviction in 1974 by a French court for share manipulation and fraud connected with their takeover of Bon Marche, France's fifth largest department store chain. Subsequently, they extended their control to France's leading furniture store chain, the Belgian Galeries Anspach, and the United States chain Korvettes. Their annexation of the Boussac empire, in the world's largest textile takeover ($160 million), indicates the pace of French capital concentration and centralization.[30] As with Courtaulds, their marketing policies have been directed to forward integration via the clothing industry and onward into department stores, fashion and textile engineering. In addition to extensive European and North American holdings, they have vast trading and industrial operations in Africa.

Due to the activities of these two major groups, concentration in French spinning and weaving escalated to a point where, in 1975, the top three firms accounted for around 29 per cent of spindleage and looms.[31] Anti-trust activities have not hampered concentration, as they have in the United States. Rather, as in Britain, state intervention has stimulated takeovers.[32]

West Germany is unique amongst world textile producers. Even though it is the world's largest textile exporter, it has no textile concern comparable to the top eighteen (in 1977 sales) US textile firms. Rather, the industry is dominated by a large number of medium-sized firms: 33 German corporations are listed among the world's second 100 largest textile firms.[33] And the winnowing out of smaller firms continues: their number has fallen from 4,381 in 1962 to 2,765 in 1976.[34]

Germany's export strength largely derives from extensive interlocking with banking structures on a scale comparable only to Switzerland and Japan. Banks often assume very high equity as well as loan positions in large corporations. This makes them much more concerned than other DCE banks to ensure their borrowers' survival, and they are more apt to intervene directly with financial, managerial and other supportive action. Often, it is only the power and money of the banks which keep companies solvent during recessions. A bank consortium of three giants — Deutsche Bank, Commerzbank, and Westdeutsche Landesbank — and two German state governments collaborated in an attempt to salvage Germany's version of the French Boussac empire, the vast textile holdings of industrialist Hans Gloggler.

Despite its recent buffetings, the Japanese textile industry was once the most powerful in the world. Indeed, the 'Tragedy of Lancashire', the decline of the British cotton spinning industry from 1933 to 1941, stemmed in large part from the body blows delivered by Japanese textile imperialism (an offensive which nonetheless was infinitely milder than Britain's textile policy towards India in the preceding century). High in quality and low in price, Japan's cotton fabrics penetrated into its Korean colony, China's treaty ports, and then to every corner of the world. The resurgence of Japanese expansion since the late 1950s has been characterized 'by headlong efforts to produce and export at all costs, and textiles have been no exception.'[35] In addition to the Asian big three, South Korea, Hong Kong and Taiwan, Japan galvanized the textile industry in Singapore, Malaysia, Indonesia and Thailand, draining off domestic capital resources from these countries via the Japanese conglomerates and transnational banks.

From the beginning of the 1970s, a concatenation of events battered the industry. In 1971, Japan lost the bulk of its lucrative American market. Simultaneously, the years of overseas investments and consequent overproduction began to take their toll on the home front. In the 1960s, the Mitsui subsidiary Toray, for example, had invested over $200 million in 23 manufacturing joint ventures and 27 other affiliates abroad. While jobs in Toray's domestic textile firms fell by 15 per cent, those abroad quadrupled to over 29,000 by 1970.[36] By 1973, Japan became a net importer of textile products.[37] Low-priced imports speeded up domestic concentration, led by the Mitsui, Mitsubishi and Sumitomo complexes. By the mid-1970s, nineteen textile firms, many of them interlaced through marketing organizations, had staked out 75 per cent of the nation's domestic spindleage,[38] and their affiliates were responsible for an even higher percentage of Japanese-linked offshore production.

This co-ordinated expansion was by no means exclusively due to the efforts of individual corporate groups. It was underpinned and co-ordinated (as with chemical fibres) by MITI's unceasing sponsorship of 'recession cartels' and promotion of inter-firm collaborative efforts — for instance, the MITI-backed rapproachement of Toyobo, Kanebo and Unitika in overseas textile investment and marketing programmes. MITI is clearly trying to prevent a crisis of the kind that battered Lancashire in the 1930s. What is notable is that, with the compliance of the *sogo shosha,* Japan is the first DCE to de-emphasize textiles in favour of more and more capital intensive industries. Whether other DCEs can and will follow this route in the 1980s seems doubtful; despite losses of close to a million jobs in textiles and clothing in the 1970s,[39] the EEC still depends on these two sectors for 10 per cent of industrial employment.[40] Equally pressing are the important links between textiles and clothing, chemicals and engineering. As the EEC Commissioner for Industry warned: 'The textile and clothing industry is essential for maintaining a balanced economic structure in the Community.'[41] What this means is that oligopolistic capitalism and its allied state apparatus will not, and cannot, relinquish the textile and clothing industries. In the 1980s, therefore we can look forward to a continued avalanche of protectionism, subsidies, and rationalization, with their implications of crisis for the future course of capitalism.

Growth Strategies of the Developing Countries

Increasingly the UCEs are becoming stratified into three major groups: 1) a rapidly industrializing group consisting of Hong Kong, South Korea, Taiwan, Brazil, Mexico, and India (to which could be added Singapore); 2) a middle group of countries that have managed to break into a few markets by processing primary commodities; 3) the vast majority of UCEs, which remain dependent on DCE manufacturers for their survival. As the first group — the 'giant dwarfs' — realize annual growth rates of real GDP from 7 to 10 per cent in the 1960s and early 1970s,[42] the gap between them and the third group has grown perceptibly larger and now far exceeds that between most DCEs and the giant dwarfs. By the late 1970s (see Table 7.5), the giant dwarfs (plus Singapore and Yugoslavia) dominated almost three-quarters of all UCE manufacturing exports.[43]

The growth strategies of the giant dwarfs and their transnational protagonists have proved as effective (thus far) on the world market as their political policies at home: 'political stability' has been achieved by eliminating organized labour and imposing subsistence wage rates. Following and co-operating with certain international organizations, the oligarchies of the UCEs moved to undervalue their currencies, restrain already stricken consumption levels and pump investment funds into a massively subsidized export-led growth. Crucial to their growth strategy has been concentration on a limited basket of manufactures, primarily clothing, textiles, electronics, machinery, footwear, steel, chemicals, and leather.[44] In any one of these industries (see Table 7.6), the top three giant dwarfs control as much as 74 per cent of all UCE exports of that commodity. And, despite a phalanx of tariff and non-tariff barriers, over 70 per cent of UCE-manufactured products find their way into the DCEs.[45]

Table 7.5
Leading UCE Exporters of Manufactures, 1965 and 1978

	1978 ($ millions)	1965 %	1978 %
Taiwan	10,700[1]	4.1	18.0
South Korea	10,588	2.3	17.9
Hong Kong	8,339	21.5	14.1
Singapore	4,358	6.5	7.3
Yugoslavia	3,849	13.4	6.5
Brazil	3,760	2.7	6.3
India	3,500[1]	17.6	5.9
Mexico	1,300[1]	3.2	2.2
Total	*46,395*[1]	*71.3*	*78.2*
All UCEs	*59,300*[1]	*100.0*	*100.0*

1. Estimate .

Source: Computed by the UNCTAD secretariat.

The intermediate group of UCEs consists of countries which are processing more and more of their primary commodities for the domestic and export market. In the case of textiles, this includes Turkey, Pakistan, Egypt and three of the giant dwarfs whose export strength derives from processing their own cotton: India, Mexico and Brazil. For the vast bulk of UCEs trying to penetrate the world market, the future is dark, a choice between the clutches of two predatory groups: the DCEs and the export-oriented giant dwarfs.

Table 7.6
Share of Leading UCE Exporters in Selected Manufactures, 1968 and 1976
(% of Total UCE Exports)

	1968		1976	
	Leading Three	*Leading Six*	*Leading Three*	*Leading Six*
Clothing	77	89	74	83
Textiles	47	58	42	59
Electrical machinery	72	84	60	88
Other machinery	48	63	52	80
Footwear	63	77	73	91
Iron and steel	52	70	49	69
Chemicals	27	40	21	32
Leather	63	69	66	73

Source: Computed by the UNCTAD Secretariat.

In this view of the underdeveloped world, the United Nations Industrial Development Organization's 'goal' of UCEs' acquiring 25 per cent of global manufactures by the year 2000 is wishful thinking.[46] First, even were this 'goal' to be achieved, the gains of industrialization will trickle down only to a tiny number of countries, with no hope that workers and peasants will share the fruits. Second, control of much of the industrialization will remain in the grip of TNCs, where policies of profit repatriation and transfer pricing will minimize the positive impact of industrialization on living standards. This much is already clearly discernible.

For an examination of textiles, we must adjust somewhat our three categories of UCEs, since South Korea, Taiwan and Hong Kong so clearly dominate UCE textile and clothing that they must be considered separately. The Asian big three have created industries specializing in the upper end of the processing chain, i.e. in clothing and high-quality textiles. The other major textile producers, which we have designated as 'intermediates', have centred their industrial strivings on the first stages, i.e. yarn and to a lesser degree fabric production. Of this group, India has moved farthest out of yarn into fabrics. Most of the other UCEs are still at the stage of building up their textile industry to meet national demand and are blocked from breaking into the international market to any appreciable extent.
extent.

The Asian 'Big Three'
The textiles strength of the big three has its roots in the major overseas push of Japan's textile oligopoly in the 1920s and 1930s and in the aftermath of the Second World War. Because of labour cost advantages. Japanese

capital moved primarily into the more labour-intensive clothing industry, although with a substantial secondary focus on textiles. The imprint of its Japanese origins can be gauged by glancing at the South Korean machinery: 64 per cent of cotton spindles, 66 per cent of worsted spindles, 93 per cent of woollen spindles, and 80 per cent of synthetic fibre machinery are from Japan.[47]

A decade of headlong development in the 1960s continued unabated throughout the 1970s. By 1978,[48] the textile labour force numbered 700,000, double the 1972 figure. Over the same time span, textile exports were catapulted from $700 million to around $4 billion, which Korea intends to boost to a fantastic $10 billion in 1986.[49] However ambitious these plans for textiles, Korea nonetheless is hoping to shave textiles' present one-third share of exports by shifting from light consumer goods into heavy industry and chemicals in the 1980s.

The absence of an organised trade union movement has been a boon to the industry. While 22 per cent of South Korea's 700,000 textile workers are 'unionized', they 'are weak and ineffective. Strikes and collective bargaining are outlawed under the National Defence Act of 1971. Labour activism of any kind is nipped in the bud by the massive security apparatus. The Korean Central Intelligence Agency harasses Christian groups that advise workers on their right under the Labour Law and on how to deal with unions.'[50] Such repression, however, is by no means confined to 'Christian groups' but to all working-class and trade union militants, as the national uprising in 1979 (and the subsequent KCIA elimination of President Park) amply demonstrated. Certainly, sustained repression has proved a bonanza to the five conglomerates that dominate the $60-billion South Korean economy. According to the Republic's Commerce and Industry Department, textiles generated about $12 billion, or about 20 per cent of the nation's GNP, in 1979. More than half of the textile industry is dominated by the fifteen largest textile companies or conglomerate groups, led by Samsung, the Republic of Korea's oldest conglomerate.[51] In 1954, Samsung set up the Chiel Wool Textile Company, from which the Chiel Synthetic Company split off, with a third of its equity controlled by Mitsui and its textile arm, Toray. The other leading conglomerates are: the Hyundai Group ($3.7 billion in 1979 sales); the Lucky Group ($2.2 billion); the Daewoo Industrial Group ($2.0 billion) and the Hanjin Group ($1.1 billion).

Taiwan's economy mirrors South Korea's in its textile export supremacy in export earnings. In the face of overcapacity and what they considered their own weak international competitiveness, the state Industrial Development Bureau has promoted a spate of mergers to absorb thousands of small, financially beleaguered firms. Cuts in import duties on high productivity machinery plus various tax concessions facilitate mergers.[52] Spurred by the competitive pressures of the world market, state inducements have also included outright government grants, tax holidays, and interest-free loans accorded primarily to export-oriented corporations.

In 1978, the government pushed five synthetic fibre-makers into consolidation, a mere portent of things to come. As the General Secretary of the Taiwan Man-Made Fibre Industries Association revealed: 'Under ideal circumstances, we would end up with one big integrated company for each of the synthetic branches.'[53] This could well be necessary if Taiwan is to survive the onslaught of neighbouring China, whose estimated labour costs are only a fifth of Taiwan's.[54]

In Hong Kong it was the spinning industry which set off industrialization in the early 1950s, originating in Shanghai. One of the main bastions of its textile power, showing clearly the fusion between foreign capital and its export-oriented salients, is the integrated Textile Alliance Group. The Group's major shareholders are Toray (50 per cent), Itoh, Jardine Matheson and the Lee family (a scion of one of Shanghai's pre-revolutionary textile dynasties).[55] Geographically, it has now ramified its operations into Singapore, Thailand, Malaysia, and as far west as Mauritius. In Malaysia, it has set up, through a wholly-owned affiliate, the country's largest single integrated textile operation. [Over the last decade's intensified trade war among the Asian textile producers, Hong Kong has borne the brunt of competitive pressures because of its higher wage levels. However, Hong Kong does not intend to relinquish its textile dominance, and thus will have to make drastic cutbacks in the labour force. At present, textiles and clothing account for about half the manufacturing labour force. Mergers are moving at such a rapid pace that between 1973 and 1976 the three largest establishments increased their share of total wool spinning from 55 per cent to 70 per cent, and in synthetic fibre spinning from 44 to 84 per cent.[56] In addition to consolidation, Hong Kong is moving into more expensive fabrics (to meet European standards of finishing), and into higher quality yarns. In this way it can bypass DCE protectionist barriers which, for the moment, are less restrictive on specialized textiles.

By the end of the 1970s, the big three's textile offensive suffered its inevitable backlash. On the grounds of alleviating the increasingly violent trade confrontations, not least on the Japanese market itself, proposals were made for regional co-operation between South Korea and Japan, and eventually Taiwan and Hong Kong.[57] This is symptomatic of the depth of the crisis: according to the findings of Japan's Long Term Credit Bank, competitiveness on the international market has been whittled away by South Korea in certain sectors such as textiles, shipbuilding and overseas construction. Whether this 'co-operation' will ever be translated into effective institutional forms and guidelines remains open. It is highly unlikely that the big three and Japan, as major exporters, can reduce competition among themselves, but even supposing they could, the creation of an economic bloc would merely direct their predatory policies elsewhere. Indeed, 'co-operation' is little more than a disguise for economic warfare.

The Intermediates
Besides the Asian group falling largely within the Japanese extended economic sphere of influence, there exists another major UCE group with a

different development trajectory: India, Pakistan, Turkey, Egypt, Brazil and Mexico. These six countries, all major cotton producers, are expanding textile processing from lower to higher stages. Together, they present a formidable phalanx on the world textile market, with 57 per cent of UCE exports and almost 9 per cent of global exports of textile yarn and thread in the mid-1970s.[58] They have carved out similar shares in other textile categories. They are thus increasingly at daggers drawn with the Asian big three as well as with the DCEs, which are finding that markets, once lost, are almost impossible to re-penetrate.

The state has played a vital role in supporting all the 'intermediates' for instance in the import substitution-based industrialization drives of the 1930s and 1950s which generated indigenous textile mills and later helped facilitate concentration. Today the state often protects and subsidizes industries which otherwise would seldom be internationally competitive. In addition the textile oligopoly markets a substantial share of the intermediates' textiles, as well as participating in production, either through technology licences or investment and managerial contracts.

India has invested massively in its textile industry since independence and now ranks among the world's largest producers. As with other Asian UCEs concentration has surged ahead over the last two decades, with 26 firms having over one-fifth of total spindleage, and 184 firms having 86 per cent of the country's loom capacity.[59] To maximize employment opportunities and circumvent the DCEs' heavier restrictions against power loom goods, the Indian Government decreed in mid 1978 that all additional cloth production must come from handlooms.

Although foreign capital figures prominently in Indian chemical fibres, it is far less marked in textiles − notably cotton textiles.[60] India has a well-entrenched indigenous capitalist class dating back to the pre-independence period and reinforced since then by its own internal capital accumulation. Further, the pattern of industrial development in relation to population size is such that foreign capital from a single provenance seldom gets a chance to acquire a monopolistic position in output or expertise.[61] Last, and perhaps most critical, the bulk of output is domestic-oriented − precisely the opposite of South Korea, Taiwan and Hong Kong.

Of the giant Indian trading and industrial companies, Birla is perhaps the prime exemplar. It has expanded its interests beyond India, and has overseas investments in textile plants in South-east Asia and some African countries. Its trading arm (by no means limited to textiles) bears some similarities to that of Jardine Matheson, through numerous joint ventures and collaborative agreements in textiles, synthetic fibres, and pulp and paper production, to name but some of its major deals. Birla's scope as a trading corporation is seen in its dominance in the marketing of India's cotton yarn and cotton piece-goods. (In the marketing of Indian textiles, Courtaulds and Hoechst have also acquired an important niche in the non-cotton sector.)

In the early 1970s Pakistan exported almost 60 per cent of its textiles (as against less than 20 per cent for India). Yarn accounted for roughly one-

eighth of both national export earnings and UCE yarn exports. The current
six-year plan (1977–83) continues to place emphasis on further expansion,
with the planned installation of 800,000 spindles – 40 per cent in the public
sector, and 60 per cent in the private. This will raise spindleage to roughly
4.4 million,[62] producing 1.2 billion pounds of cotton yarn, of which almost
half is expected to be marketed abroad. The entire external marketing
operation is handled by the Staflex International Trading Corporation, based
in the tax haven of the Netherlands Antilles. Hence, 'with imports, exports
and sewing thread controlled multinationally', as one marketing specialist
notes, 'it is hardly necessary for [foreign] companies to penetrate the
industry to any extent.'[63]

As with many UCEs, the Turkish textile industry underwent a metamor-
phosis in the first half of the 1970s, due to massive investment injections. In
this case, the state was the primary source of the one-billion-dollar five-year
(1972–7) textile expansion programme for spinning and weaving, raising
spindleage to four million (as against 3.3 million in 1971). Large-scale yarn
processing is coupled with a cutback in raw cotton exports. Domestic cotton
processing as a percentage of output rose from 39 to 66 per cent between
1969 and 1979. The overpowering realities of global competitive power,
however, have undercut the projected target of exporting about 45 per cent
of yarn produced domestically in the 1970s and 1980s. These plans have
either been scrapped or drastically scaled down as 'the stagnation of the
world economy and the difficulties in marketing have resulted in shortfalls
in investment for cotton yarn. The economic policy of encouraging such
investments has been discontinued. In the future no increase in yarn production is foreseen by the business community.'[64] Such afflictions are not
unique to Turkey, but are a foretaste of the 1980s for the majority of UCEs.

Africa's textile industry is comparatively recent, largely coinciding with,
or trailing in the wake of, independence (and protective tariffs). A
conspicuous exception, however, is Egypt, whose textile industry is anchored
in decades of manufacturing experience dating from the 1920s. For over a
century, Egypt's economy has revolved around cotton, and the ascent of
textile manufacturing was a natural outgrowth. By the 1950s, output
surpassed domestic demand and several mills became export-oriented. By
1978, the industry absorbed almost two-thirds of domestic cotton, a drastic
rise from 27 per cent only a decade earlier.[65]

The Egyptian industry is one of the most concentrated in the world, with
12 firms (in yarn) having 91 per cent of spindles, and 18 firms (in fabric)
with 80 per cent of loom capacity. A notable feature of the industry is the
absence of foreign ownership and cont ol, stemming from nationalizations
in the late 1950s and early 1960s. This, however, is likely to change with the
current oligarchy's economic liberalism. The Misr complex, located on a 640-
acre tract in Mehalla, was already by 1975 the world's biggest textile plant,
employing 35,000 workers and vertically integrated from fibre through to
finished product.[66] The complex included 300,000 spindles, 5,000 looms
located in thirteen weaving departments, plus texturing, finishing and

garment-cutting facilities. Additional investment programmes of $100 million are expected to modernize and boost spindleage to 380,000.[67] Still, productivity differences with US plants remain large. Average Egyptian productivity is 3.75 lb/man-hour, compared to 39.7 lb/man-hour in the United States. Egypt's lower labour costs are thus offset by political pressures to accept high employment levels, a factor common to many UCEs.[68]

Brazil and Mexico, which have already made marginal inroads into the world market, possess Latin America's two biggest populations as well as its largest textile industries. As with synthetic fibres, foreign ownership in textiles is pervasive and the trend is toward units vertically integrated from spinning through to finishing. Expansion of Brazil's industry into global markets has been stimulated by certain tax concessions on exports, such as the elimination of corporate income tax, abolition of sales and other taxes amounting to 15 to 18 per cent of the product's value, and export credit rebates.[69] In Mexico's case, billions of pesos have been pumped into the industry at an annual rate of 8.2 per cent since 1970, inducing a structural change that clipped cotton's share in textiles from 64 to 33 per cent in the first half of the 1970s.[70]

The Minors

In almost all other UCEs, the major preoccupation is with consolidating national textile markets and curbing foreign imports. Many of these hundred-odd countries are still in the midst of breaking colonial ties, with their familiar trade flows of raw cotton exports and the import of finished products. Several European members of the textile oligopoly still dominate African markets, through both contraband and legitimate imports. The British giant Tootal, for example, floods West African markets with exquisitely dyed cloth incorporating African designs and motifs.[71] Other corporations break into the UCEs through joint ventures and wholly-owned subsidiaries, often marketing their negligible exports through other trans-national conglomerates such as Lonrho.

Within this large group of UCE minors, two different trends have emerged. Certain UCEs, epitomized by the Ivory Coast and, to a lesser extent, the Asian UCEs within Japan's orbit, have evolved as ideal neo-colonies. They offer generous inducements to foreign investment and provide politically stable, labour-cheap zones for production and export. Kenya and Nigeria provide variations on this theme. At the other end of the UCE spectrum, a few countries, for instance, Tanzania and Algeria, have shaped a textile development strategy relying on a powerful public sector.

Expansion of textile capacity for the global market in the Ivory Coast hinges on transnational corporations and joint ventures, many of which should be launched in the early 1980s. In line with its average of 68 per cent foreign ownership of overall manufacturing companies, Ivory Coast textiles are 65 per cent under foreign control.[72] Cotton production burgeoned from 3,000 tons in 1960 to 23,000 in 1975, and by 1980 is expected to shoot up to 40,000 tons. The Ivory Coast's attempted push into the world market is through vertically integrated units spearheaded by four projects. The first group (Sotoxi), formed by the Japanese, Dutch, French and Ivorian private sector, envisages the creation of an annual cotton weaving capacity of 12,500 tons by 1981, two-fifths of which is intended for export. A second project (Cotivo), promoted by United States and French interests, will put on stream by 1980 a cotton yarn plant of 7,500–9,000 tons' capacity, destined as a major supplier to an Abidjan Blue Bell jean subsidiary, which exports its whole output to Western Europe.[73] A third transnational French project is already operating with 12 per cent of its output entering the French market in spinning, weaving, and dyeing, and is expected to be wedded to a mass-production apparel industry by 1980, the bulk of which it is also hoped will be exported. A fourth transnational textile project, a polyester complex of 10,000 tons, is also linked to the clothing industry and will be operative by the early 1980s. This experiment in the processing and upgrading of the fabrication process, however, highlights the limitations of breaking into the international market, since it is based on small runs inappropriate to mass merchandizing, unless handled by TNCs which can amalgamate production runs from several plants. And, in 1979, it was still importing twice as many textiles from the EEC as it exported.[74]

Integrated into the production apparatus are francophone Africa's variants of the transnational trading corporations. These include the CFAO (Compagnie Francaise de l'Afrique Occidentale), a general import/export/ wholesale firm linked to a loose grouping of French maritime, financial and manufacturing firms; and the CFDT (Compagnie Francaise pour le Developpement de Fibres Textiles), a firm specializing in cotton plantations and marketing of yarn and textiles within Africa and abroad. To these textile traders could be added Niger France, a subsidiary of the British conglomerate Unilever, the United-Africa Company, another wholly-owned Unilever sub-sidiary, which straddles French- and English-speaking Africa, and Otorg. These firms virtually control the entire chain of Ivorian textile distribution domestically and abroad.

Kenya and Nigeria are typical of most African nations, whose textile ambitions are less global. In contrast to the export orientation of Ivorian textiles, Kenya's production also combines foreign[75] with state and domestic private ownership but produces largely for the home market. Its overall development strategy is aimed first at textile self-sufficiency, and second at widening the employment market. From an entrepreneurial perspective, such natural employment policies swell labour costs, thus lessening Kenya's competitiveness on national and international markets. 'We need two workers to one in Europe for the same output', comments an executive of an expatriate textile group. 'This is because the government wants labour-intensive industries to provide more jobs.'[76]

Similarly, Nigeria emphasises import substitution for the large and rapidly growing internal market. Certain transnational majors have played a role in its expansion. The nation's modern textile industry came into being in the mid 1950s under the impetus of transnational corporations

such as Mitsui. Joint ventures are a feature of the industry, such as Kaduna
Textiles, Arewa Textiles and Nigerian Teijin Textiles, in which both Itoh and
CFAO have important stakes. The Hong Kong-based Textile Alliance
operates the General Cotton Mill at Onitsha, which is a joint venture of
Toray and Unilever's United Africa Company (UAC). Likewise, UAC has
joined forces with Tootal to set up the West Africa Thread Company.

In Algeria, the textile industry barely existed at independence, supplying
less than 10 per cent of domestic consumption. Since then, it has become a
major industry, whose activities are centralized through Sonitex (Societe
Nationale des Industries Textiles). Some of the large French textile corporations still operate within Algeria. They include Dollfus-Mieg, Agache-Willot
and Schaeffer. The setting up of the giant $115-million textile plant will
modernize the industry rapidly, and it could be a major thread exporter
by 1980. This plant will employ a total workforce of 1,400, representing
an investment of $82,143 per worker − one of the highest textile industry
capital/labour investment ratios in the world.[77] Thus, the capital intensity
imperatives of the international market, shaped by the oligopoly, apply not
only to the private sector but to the public sector as well.

While national ownership remains the stated ambition of most African,
Asian and Latin American countries, the transnationals are present in most of
them. The ramifications of control are, however, even more pervasive in
marketing and distribution than in processing, both at the national and
international level.

The Multi-Fibre Arrangement
In the wake of the Second World War, the DCEs established a myriad of institutions to protect their interests. One of these was the General Agreement
on Trade and Tariffs (GATT), through which the United States, Western
Europe, and Japan have guided global trade (largely through tariff manipulation) to their advantage. Often under GATT's tutelage, new forms of protectionism have sprung up whereby 'orderly' or 'voluntary' marketing agreements are used by various DCE and UCE state apparatuses to harmonize
their conflicts. At first only in textiles (in the early 1960s), these have spread
to embrace footwear, steel, transport equipment, mechanical and electrical
engineering goods, electronics, and ball bearings. A leading capitalist mouth-
piece commented on the 'voluntary' agreements: 'talks are usually conducted
with a pistol on the table in the form of a threat by importing countries to
cut off access to their markets'.[78]

GATT's Multi-Fibre Arrangement (MFA) has become the forum where
conflicts between DCEs and UCEs find their highest institutional expression.
International agreements have regulated trade between the two groupings
since 1962, culminating in the MFA's 1977 renewal. Originally, the agreements' scope was confined to cotton goods.[79]

Reflecting the surge in chemical fibres and blends in the 1960s, the MFA's
ambit was broadened in 1973 to include all categories of textiles and
clothing. Its official rationale was to ensure 'the orderly and equitable

development of this trade and avoidance of disruptive effects in individual markets and on individual lines of production in both importing and exporting countries'.[80] Fifty-one nations (including several CPEs) representing 85 per cent of world textile trade signed the agreement, whose main purpose was to limit annual trade growth in most items to 6 per cent or less.

By 1977, the ensuing crisis had cast a pall over negotiations. The renewed MFA is based on bilateralism and global ceilings. While in principle the agreement is multilateral, the EEC declared that their acceptance was contingent on bilateral arrangements concluded with exporting nations. These bilateral agreements singled out Taiwan, the Republic of Korea and Hong Kong for absolute cutbacks in exports.[81] Hong Kong, supplying 15 per cent of EEC imports at a value of $1.3 billion in 1976,[82] has been hardest hit. Quotas for the colony fell below actual 1976 performance,[83] with growth so limited in major categories that there is little prospect of regaining 1976 trade levels by 1982. Giving his version of the intensified rivalries, the Chairman of the Hong Kong Spinners Association noted that 'the atmosphere in Brussels at the time of negotiations was charged with flashes of veiled threats; and tactical leverage was used by an over-powering nine-nation trade combine to the fullest extent against a freeport which has no instrument of effective retaliation'.[84] At the other end of the fence, the United Kingdom received extensive protection, especially for its clothing sector.

That textiles are now subject to a corset of controls on global markets tighter than any other manufactured commodity should not mask the impact of the MFA on driving wedges between different UCEs. The DCEs have succeeded in blunting the export offensive of the four major UCEs (Hong Kong, Taiwan, South Korea and India), by slashing their quotas and allocating them to other developing countries. Consequently, these 'big four' are compelled either to reduce textile output, shift to new product lines or seek new markets, primarily in other UCEs. However, all three options only intensify competition among UCEs who are confronted with entrenched competition from DCE subsidiaries that have already carved out sizeable UCE market shares.

Other 'illegal' responses have also cropped up in the attempt to market textiles and apparel. Hong Kong-made clothing bearing the label 'Made in Indonesia' has been seized in the United Kingdom. More recently, numerous textile firms with headquarters in Hong Kong, the Republic of Korea and Singapore have set up operations in the newly established Sri Lanka Export Processing Zone. From this marketing vantage point they are positioned to take advantage of Sri Lanka's export quotas as well as a female work force vaunted by the Government as 'the cheapest labour in Asia'. As in most Asian free trade zones, the foreign companies obtain highly advantageous land prices, tax holdings and exemptions from duty payments. It has become common practice for the Asian big three to buy portions of unused UCE quotas for textile and clothing exports to the EEC and continue the export barrage through false labelling.[85] South Korean firms have even used Japan, whose exports are not subject to quotas, for trans-shipments with fresh certificates of origin. Certain Asian producers have also traded textiles through African member nations of the Lome Convention, which offers almost tariff-free entry of manufactured goods into France and the United Kingdom. Others have skirted MFA restrictions by classifying power-loom items as handloom products (which face fewer restrictions), a subterfuge which is almost impossible to detect. Thus, the minimal protection offered to DCEs by the MFA has only served to heighten antagonism. The roots of the crisis remain untouched.

The Centrally Planned Economies

Although the CPEs rank among the world's textile leaders, their share of world exports is negligible. Thus, the development of their textile industries affects oligopolistic capitalism only marginally, as they are largely able to satisfy their vast and growing textile needs domestically or through trade via the Council for Mutual Economic Assistance. Only in such specialty items as denim is it likely that the CPEs will serve as a textile market for the oligopoly. In turn, the only CPE that threatens to become a major force on world textile markets is China, which may well approach the Asian big three in the 1980s. The Soviet Union, the world leader in output of yarn, cotton, wool and several categories of fabrics,[86] may also begin to break into world markets, but to a far lesser degree.

The mainstays of China's exports, which should continue unaltered into the 1980s, remain crude oil and petroleum products, agricultural raw materials, farm-processed goods, and textile products. Textiles are second only to petroleum products as the nation's most rapidly growing manufacturing export. In the turbulent aftermath of the Cultural Revolution, China is a conspicuous example of a CPE that has aligned its export sectors with international capitalism and the prescriptions of the world market.

Chinese textiles hark back to the 1880s when the industry was set up in the treaty ports of Shanghai, Tsingtao and Tientsin. By the mid 1920s, it had become China's leading manufacturing industry, with 118 cotton mills (3.8 million spindles and 24,000 looms); at the inauguration of the People's Republic of China on 1 October 1949, it had 247 cotton mills, five million spindles and 67,000 looms.[87] The nation already has more than 4,500 modern fibre, textile and textile machinery plants. Textile and apparel now embrace around one-fifth of China's global exports. This modernization drive also uses the mechanisms of buy-back deals, with the foreign party providing advanced manufacturing equipment and China reimbursing with the final products. Shanghai remains the hub of textile modernization, with 48 specialized export factories, including 1,300 professional designers and increasingly computerized operations. Today, the industry boasts around 15 million spindles and a dazzling array of machine novelties, and mills have been spread throughout the country.[88]

Of pivotal significance has been the shift, born of necessity and aided by

China's vast deposits of natural gas and oil, from natural to synthetic fibres. This shift has been furthered by increasing pressures on arable land and a steady population growth, with the result that areas allocated to cotton have dropped or at best remained stagnant over the last decade. By the mid 1980s, it is anticipated that more than two-fifths of fibre consumption will emanate from synthetic fibres. This shift to synthetic fibres has been partnered by, and is related to, a no less spectacular return to capitalist relations of production, based on joint ventures largely (though not exclusively) between the giant traders and the textile and chemical oligopolies.

The new economic policy, particularly obvious in textiles and clothing, has been formally sanctioned by the present rulers on the grounds of bureaucratic incompetence, economic inefficiency (Hua Guo-Feng has acknowledged that 'one-quarter of the country's government-run enterprises have been operating at a loss'),[89] and their inability to satisfy simultaneously the basic demands of the Chinese people and the need for foreign exchange. The model being used is that of the giant dwarfs in general, and Hong Kong in particular. Indeed, Hong Kong textile capitalists are already quietly managing plants in various areas of China. Joint ventures with foreign capital are now being pushed to the foreground, in which China provides a heavily subsidized infrastructure including fuel and raw materials, public utilities, factory buildings, and a low-wage labour force. The new policy has already yielded fruit. Because of the growing cost squeeze in Hong Kong the colony's capitalists are farming out ever larger quantities of textiles and apparel to be processed and finished in China. 'For all intents and purposes', observed Sir Lawrence Kadoorie, Chairman of the China Light and Power Co., 'Hong Kong has become the free zone of China under British management.'[90] Business deals of this kind are by no means confined to Hong Kong. In line with the Sino-Japanese economic *entente*, 'special districts' in China are being opened up to produce for the export market.[91]

Ironically, Chinese products are now replacing Korean and Hong Kong textiles in Japanese supermarkets, with the transportation and marketing assistance of the *sogo shosha*. *Textile Asia* writes:

> How much longer can those Korean factories that had been supplying the Osaka supermarkets compete as wages and industrial costs generally in Korea continue to rise? If they cannot compete in the Japanese market then it is likely that they are ceasing to compete in world markets generally, and will have to upgrade their production or go out of business — the same problem as faces textile producers everywhere, more and more urgently. The Osaka supermarkets are not the only ones in Japan that are taking advantage of the new opportunities offered by China. Fukusuke is discussing possible joint production of underwear and stockings in China and Wacoal, the quality women's underwear and foundation garment maker, is also negotiating a joint venture for underwear.[92]

These are precursors of a much larger movement. China's redirection of its economic policies therefore implies that important sectors of its export trade have come under the increasing control of external forces. Whether this will remain a permanent fixture in China's economic policy, and in what ways it may develop, is for the moment unpredictable.

Lower wage rates are, however, not incompatible with the drive to modernization in the textile industry, with its emphasis on open-ended spinning, rapier looms, air jet looms, warp knitting, etc. Indeed, labour-related stimuli are pushing in the direction of automation. As an expert from the China Textile Engineering Society observed:

> The idea that China could never be short of labour was mistaken. This was not always the case, especially in the textile industry. In fact many newly set up mills were having difficulty in recruiting workers partly owing to the lack of skilled labour and partly to the relatively heavy workload on the average textile worker as compared with other industries. To solve this problem it was urgent for China to use more automated equipment. Such equipment will also increase the productivity of our industry. At present, for what you in Hong Kong can produce with 3.25 workers, and the U.S.A. with 1.25 workers we have to employ six.[93]

The importance of material incentives, plus a panoply of rationalization measures, have now become a part of a familiar landscape: productivity bonuses and premiums, speed-up, piece work, and tightened work discipline. Entering the euphoric embrace of the world market, however, involves a political decision, as the textile designer Pierre Cardin jubilantly noted after an official tour of China: 'They are looking toward the American life, the Japanese life. I think they will become a Western democracy.'[94] Whether this will ever happen remains to be seen. It is indisputable, however, that these new market orientations, as they are now designated, are not unrelated to a choice of political direction.

In the last analysis, the success or failure of a policy of joint ventures will depend on the absorptive capacity of the world market (not to speak of the internal political battles now raging within China itself) and the business acumen of the current political class, who aim to match, and possibly surpass, the market conquests of the giant dwarfs in the 1960s and 1970s. Intrusions of this size into the global market, exacerbated by spiralling costs and economic slowdown, can only intensify antagonisms in the 1980s. On this score, the balance sheet is sufficiently explicit. 'The explosive growth of textile imports from China', comments *The New York Times,* 'has come about even though China has had to absorb from 50 per cent to 600 per cent higher tariffs than most other suppliers to enter the United States market ... The domestic textile industry, which considers the competition from China a mounting threat, has heavy influence on Congress.'[95] In other words, the short-term profit-maximizing thrust of the textile oligopoly has helped create

191

a Chinese spectre that has already begun to haunt them in their industrialized lairs.

In the unfolding global textile war that we have depicted, the jagged battle lines for the 1980s are already discernible. Retention and aggrandizement of market shares is the major objective.

Wedded to state power, the extremely powerful DCE oligopoly has succeeded to a large extent in keeping its hegemony over world markets despite the mounting onslaughts of the giant dwarfs, the intermediates and China. As we move to the battle front of clothing, the same alignment of forces is visible — with the notable exception of a DCE clothing oligopoly. Here the fortunes of battle have been more favourably tilted towards the UCEs in the 1960s and 1970s. But the current technological advances in clothing indicate a movement towards oligopolistic capitalism.

References

1. Extrapolated from Economist Intelligence Unit, *World Textile Trade and Production* (EIU Special Report No. 63, London, 1978), pp. 40–3.
2. Cotton did not share proportionately in the phenomenal growth of the knitting industry. Once again, the major strides have been in the field of non-cellulosic man-made fibre yarns, which compete not only with cotton but with other natural fibres. In 1960, yarn consumption by Western European knitters topped 759 million lbs; by 1971, it had reached 1.56 billion lbs. Whilst cotton had 40 per cent at the beginning of the 1960s, its share fell to 23 per cent by 1971. In contrast, use of non-cellulosics soared from less than 16 per cent (1960) to 55 per cent in 1971; that is, their total sales rose about sevenfold and accounted for over nine-tenths of additional yarn output in the knit sector. See B.M. Hornbeck, *Knits in Western Europe – Their Impact on Cotton* (USDA, Washington, DC, July 1973).
3. See his essay on 'Chartism' (1839) in *English and Other Critical Essays,* (London, 1915), p. 185.
4. K. West, 'The Future of Synthetic Fibres: Opportunities and Problems', *Opportunities for Man-Made Fibres* (11th Shirley Institute International Seminar, Manchester, 4–6 September 1979), p. 5.
5. Illustrative of the 'aggressive capital investment program to modernize production in those areas where good long-term market opportunities are expected to exist', and 'to improve productivity, increase flexibility and enhance product quality' (in the words of its 1978 *Annual Report*), Burlington invested over $420 million in 1977 and 1978.
6. Alexander Dahmen, 'New developments in the field of polyester fibres', *Opportunities for Man-Made Fibres,* p. 8.
7. *World Trade and Output of Manufactures: Structural Trends and Developing Countries' Exports,* World Bank Staff Working Paper, No. 316, (Washington, DC, 1979), pp. 51–2.
8. EEC, *A Study of the Evolution of Concentration in the United Kingdom*

Textile Industry (Brussels, 1975).

9. See ILO, Textiles Committee, *The Effects of Structural and Technological Changes on Labour Problems in the Textile Industry* (Geneva, 1968). A barometer of these changes is West Germany, where the number of textile mills was axed between 1970 and 1977 from 2,700 to 900. In Japan (1972–78), the closures of textile and apparel plants were even greater from 121,000 to 10,000. The litany of woe reverberates throughout the DCEs.

10. J.A. Blackburn (managing director of the Vantona Group), 'The new textile industry – a 25 year revolution in the U.K.', *Textile Month*, November 1976.

11. *Financial Times*, 18 May 1979.

12. Before 1939–45, legislation had been introduced to give legal enforcement to the Yarn Spinners Price Agreement, which set common prices, and to empower spinners' organizations to purchase compulsorily excess spindle capacity.

13. This merger movement was sectorally far from uniform. Neither the woollen textile, hosiery, nor knitwear industry was subject to the same concentration drive as the cotton textile industry. All three sub-sectors were considerably more fragmented than manufacturing industry as a whole. This contrasted with what has been called 'the virtual duopoly already existing in the supply of man-made fibres'. Cf. EEC, *A Study of the Evolution . . .* , p. 29.

14. ICI has a 63 per cent holding in Carrington Viyella. To these five could be added Illingworth Morris (a family enterprise), the Nottingham Manufacturing Company, one of the major suppliers of Marks and Spencers, with whom it has family and financial ties, and Dawson International Ltd.

15. EEC, *Study of the Evolution . . .* , p. 189. Courtaulds and ICI each hold around 8 per cent of Tootal's equity.

16. Statement by Courtaulds' Chairman, Sir Arthur Knight, 20 July 1977, p. 6.

17. EEC, *A Study of the Evolution . . .* , p. 207; and *Financial Times*, 31 May 1979.

18. *Business Week*, 9 April 1979.

19. *New York Times*, 15 May 1977.

20. *Ibid.* The industry, which is the backbone of the Southern economy, employs one out of every five industrial workers. It ranks among the lowest-paying manufacturing industries in the United States, with profit rates also among the lowest.

21. *Business Week*, 9 April 1979.

22. *Textile Asia*, December 1978.

23. *Textile Asia*, December 1978. In the lugubrious prognostication of the

24. Vice-President of the number 9 US textile corporation: 'The cotton-dust standards are a death knell for some smaller mills. I see a lot of consolidation in our industry';*New York Times*, 5 June 1979.

24. *Business Week*, 9 April 1979.

25. *Ibid.*

26. *Textile Asia*, August 1978; and *Business Week*, 9 April 1979.

27. Machinery costs will accelerate mergers. It was estimated that the typical

small mill of 15,000–30,000 spindles and 100–200 looms was running spinning frames that probably cost, and were depreciated at, something between $12 and $28 per spindle, and looms between $500 and $2,000. But already by 1975 (machinery costs have escalated up to 50 per cent since then), spinning frames were roughly $60 per spindle, and open end spinning $500–$1,000 per rotor. At that time shuttleless looms were costed at $20,000. As one analyst noted: 'If the total tax depreciation written off on the existing equipment had been set aside for replacement, the fund would be no more than a small down payment on the cost of the new machines needed' ('Small Mills to Merge?', *Textile Asia*, August 1975).

28. Bolton, *The MNCs in the Textile, Garment and Leather Industries.*
29. *L'Humanite,* 25 October 1979.
30. See *Le Monde,* 19 August 1978, for details of the takeover.
31. IFCATI, *The Structure of the Cotton and Allied Textile Industries, 1975,* Zurich, 1977.
32. State aid is geared to consolidate and further the advance of what it considers viable industrial groups. The Boussac Group, for decades one of the leading textile concerns, did not fall outside this category of viability until several successive years of heavy deficits.
33. *Textil Wirtschaft,* 9 February 1978.
34. *L'Industrie Textile,* December 1977.
35. B.M. Hornbeck, 'Developments in the Japanese textile industry', USDA, Washington, DC, (FAS M-267) May 1975.
36. Its foreign ventures have proved profitable with a recorded $4 million in dividends from overseas subsidiaries and royalties of roughly $15 million; *The Economist,* 4 April 1978.
37. Imported textile products often retailed at prices 20–30 per cent lower than similar Japanese items.
38. IFCATI, *The Structure of the Cotton and Allied Textile Industries, 1975,* p. 7.
39. *Textile Asia,* February 1979.
40. *Financial Times,* 24 October 1978.
41. *Ibid.*
42. *The Economist,* 10 June 1978.
43. See also UNCTAD, *Dynamic Products in the Exports of Manufactured Goods from Developing Countries to Developed Market Economies, 1970 to 1976,* UNCTAD/ST/MD/18, (Geneva, 1978).
44. *Ibid.* The UNCTAD study revealed that the top ten industrial groupings accounted for 44 per cent of UCE manufactured exports.
45. *The Economist,* 10 June 1978.
46. In appearance this 'goal' or 'target' may seem logical, but it is not. As it stands, it is little more than a public relations exhortation which abysmally fails to define what it means by the so-called 'developing world' and from there move on to explore the exploitative class relations of power in the global economy. The UNIDO 'goal' is, of course, not unique, but is patterned after such irrelevant statistical numbers games as the United Nations 'development decade targets'.
47. *Textile Asia,* April 1979.
48. *The Economist,* 1 July 1978.

49. *Ibid.* and *Textile Asia,* April 1979. Attendant concentration and rationalization can be seen in Korea's two members of the World's top hundred textile corporations (see Table 7.3, p. 173). Both Daewoo (number 9) and Sunkyong (number 25) are newcomers to the list, having been formed by state-aided mergers in 1977, and exemplify the thrust of oligopolistic capitalism within the giant dwarfs.
50. *International Herald Tribune* (special issue, South Korea), May 1978.
51. Note the expansionary euphoria of Samsung's Vice-Chairman: 'I want to make sales of $16 billion by 1983.' With 1979 sales outstripping $3 billion, this means that 'with a fifty per cent growth rate the next couple of years, we'll be able to ease up a little thereafter to reach our target.' See *The New York Times,* 28 October 1979.
52. For details of incentives, see *Far Eastern Economic Review,* 14 October 1977.
53. *Far Eastern Economic Review,* 14 October 1977.
54. *Textile Asia,* February 1979.
55. *The Financial Times,* 9 January 1978.
56. Figures supplied by the Hong Kong Census and Statistics Department.
57. For details of the dialogue between the chief policy-maker of Japan's Liberal Democratic Party and Korean President Park Chung Hee, see *Far Eastern Economic Review,* 13 October 1978.
58. Figures computed from data in UNCTAD, *Handbook of International Trade and Development Statistics* (New York, 1979).
59. IFCATI, *The Structure of the Cotton and Allied Textile Industries, 1975.*
60. This does not exclude the presence on the Indian market of textile majors like Courtaulds, Coats Paton, and Tootal. Cotton textiles made up the overwhelming majority of Indian fabrics in the 9.3-billion-metre 1974 budget, outnumbering man-made fabrics by a ratio of ten to one. Cf. H.C. Aiyer, *Economics of Textile Trade and Industry in India* (Bombay, 1977)p. 30.
61. Bolton, p. 48.
62. This amounts to an output of 1.2 billion lbs. of cotton yarn consuming 3.8 million bales of raw cotton.
63. Bolton, p. 48. Around two-thirds of its consumption of man-made fibres are imported.
64. UNCTAD, *Consideration of International Measures on Cotton: Contribution from Turkey,* TD/B/IPC/COTTON/L.4, 17 September 1979.
65. *Financial Times,* 30 July 1979.
66. *Textile World,* September 1976.
67. Understandably, the importance of textiles for the Egyptian economy is that more than half of industrial employment is in textiles. They account for a fourth of total industrial output and over 60 per cent of foreign exchange earnings from manufactures.
68. One feasibility study indicated that the Misr complex, freed from the national employment policy, could operate its spinning plants with 20–25 per cent fewer workers. *Textile World,* November 1976.
69. This has led to charges that Brazilian manufactured yarn is being offered to U.S. knitters, freight paid, at prices lower than U.S. mills can sell the

yarn and at even lower prices than in Brazil. Cf. *Textile World*, March 1976.
70. R.R. Encinas, 'The Textile Industry in Mexico', *IFCATI*, 18 (1977).
71. *Financial Times*, 12 March 1979. Tootal is aided in its African markets by an associate company based in Zaire.
72. World Bank, *Ivory Coast: A Basic Economic Report*, Report No. 1147b–IVC (Washington, DC, February 1977), p. 14.
73. The Blue Bell Corporation manufactures Wrangler jeans and is second in the world after Levi. Blue Bell Cote d'Ivoire is 51 per cent owned by the parent company, 30 per cent by the Ivory Coast Government, and 19 per cent by the US Riegel Textile Corporation, see Business International SA, *Ivory Coast: Strategic Base for Developing West Africa* (Geneva, 1977).
74. *Financial Times*, 25 May 1979.
75. Both Japanese and Indian interests are deeply embedded in the industry. See National Christian Council of Kenya, *Who Controls Industry in Kenya?* (Nairobi, 1968).
76. The tribulations of Kenya's textile industry lie in the fact that 'the ten major mills are facing an inexorable flood of dumped imports, including factory rejects and second hand clothing, garnered from the jumble sales of the U.K. and the U.S.A. Thousands of tons of textiles are being smuggled into the country.' Such contraband, however, is not limited merely to Kenya. Responses have been uniformly ineffective as 'recent government protection measures, raising duty on imported woven fabrics from 45 to 55 per cent, raising duty on other competitive fabrics by an average of 10–15 per cent and slapping a 100 per cent duty on second hand clothing, did not seem to slow down the flood.' ('Kenya Textiles: Dumping threatens a young industry', *Financial Times*, 21 December 1977).
77. It is interesting to observe the scope and comprehensiveness of the project involving Sonitex and General Impiati. When completed, the Algerian project will be completely self-sufficient, endowed with its own training programme and power generator. Important also is the composition of output, which is related to Algeria's burgeoning petrochemical industry, since in addition to thread spun from medium and long staple cotton it will also produce 100 per cent polyester sewing thread. See *Textile Month*, September 1977.
78. *Business Week*, 9 May 1977.
79. In October 1962, countries controlling over 90 per cent of global cotton yarn exports, 70 per cent of cotton fabric exports, and 80 per cent of cotton clothing signed a long-term arrangement (LTA) on cotton textiles with the aim of checking import quotas imposed on UCE textiles and promoting orderly trade growth. A decade later, in place of trade liberalization, the LTA had become the vehicle for imposing quotas and very low export growth rates on UCE yarn, textile and garment producers.
80. GATT, *Arrangement Regarding International Trade in Textiles*, GATT/ 1974–2, article 1, paragraph 2.
81. Global ceilings involve limits to each EEC country on 41 of 114 categories of goods. Quotas are allocated to exporting countries on the basis of five groups of 'sensitive products' and related to the degree of market

penetration which imports had already achieved. Growth rates accorded each product were lowered far below the original 1973 6 per cent levels and tied to base levels below actual 1977 trade.

82. *Business Week,* 5 December 1977.
83. The 1978 cotton fabric quota represents a 30 per cent cutback from 1976; 18 per cent for shirts (*Far Eastern Economic Review,* 23 December 1977).
84. *International Herald Tribune,* 30 May 1978.
85. See *Textile Asia,* April 1979; *Far Eastern Economic Review,* 25 May 1979; *Time,* 25 June 1979; and *New York Times,* 12 November 1978.
86. *IFCATI Newsletter,* No. 1, 1977.
87. Cf. Kayser Sung, 'The Development of Mainland China's Textile Industry with Special Reference to the Changing Pattern of its Foreign Trade', *IFCATI,* Vol. 16, 1975.
88. The major feature of successive overall plans has been decentralization of the industry from the coastal areas to the hinterland. Whereas in 1949, 87 per cent of China's spindles and 92 per cent of its looms were in coastal areas, by 1956, these dropped to roughly 73 per cent. This proportion has continued to slide with the expansion of the modern textile industry to areas contiguous to cotton farmland.
89. *International Herald Tribune,* 30 July 1979.
90. *The Times,* 4 August 1980.
91. *The Guardian,* 8 September 1979.
92. *Textile Asia,* February 1979. The breakneck growth of this trade is seen in the value of Chinese textile products imported into Japan through the Sogo Shosha, rising by 50 per cent in 1978 alone.
93. *Textile Asia,* April 1979.
94. It is expected that the Chinese will export 90 per cent of its Cardin-linked products, keeping the remainder for the home market. Cardin's business is a part of the French conglomerate Agache-Willot.
95. *The New York Times,* 8 December 1978. The same hostile reactions are to be seen in Western Europe and presage intensified battles on the global market. See *Le Monde,* 7 April 1979, where one of the spokesmen of the European Economic Community declared that no concessions should be granted to China without reciprocity.

197

8. Textile End-Uses and Distribution

Textile products flow into three major channels of manufacture: clothing, household furnishings, and industrial end-uses. The focus of this chapter is on the current manifestations and directions of oligopolistic capitalism in each of these channels, as well as in wholesaling and retailing, which are the terminal points of the textile chain. Compared to the oligopolies that dominate the processing stages, all end-uses and distributive networks are fragmented. This relative fragmentation, however, has not precluded the emergence of a few traditional giants: Levi Strauss, Blue Bell, and Courtaulds in clothing; Firestone, Goodyear, and Goodrich in tyres; and Sears Roebuck, C. & A. Brenninkmeyer, and Karstadt in retailing. It can be expected, however, that in clothing and retailing these giants, which operate amidst a multitute of smaller concerns, will be joined in the 1980s by a select group of rapidly growing firms. In this sense, both sectors are in the pre-stages of oligopoly.

In each sector, the motive forces of concentration and conglomeration differ. In apparel, the major end-use, a barrage of UCE imports has wreaked havoc on DCE industry. Since home furnishings are produced primarily by textile corporations, the same forces that are reshaping the textile oligopoly affect this sector. In industrial end-uses, concentration within the tyre industry has already reached oligopolistic proportions, and is being propelled by the general crisis, which has been especially brutal for the automobile industry in the wake of economic stagnation and the renewed petroleum price hikes of 1979. Finally, the massive retail chains that have gouged out sizeable segments of that sector are being fed by the rapid growth of urban populations the world over, and by newer and more effective modes of transportation and communications. It is here, at retailing, that the journey ends, about six months after fibres (making up between 2 and 5 per cent of a garment's price) first entered the textile mill.[1]

The clothing industry has a world-wide labour force of several million. It uses over 75 per cent of fibres in most UCEs, compared to about 50 per cent in DCEs. Whereas Chapter 7 glanced at UCE strengths in textiles, this chapter analyses and describes those state and corporate clothing strategies which are designed to combat the crisis, but are in fact accelerating concentration. From this point, our discussion moves to home furnishings and

198

industrial end-uses and thence to wholesaling and retailing. Our enquiry into retailing looks into the ever-widening marketing margins that the giant retailers have acquired in recent years.

Examination of production and distribution of these three end-uses depicts the corporate battle lines in the cotton-chemical fibre relationships.[2] The confluence of the strategies of the chemical, oil, and textile oligopoly can be seen in the shifting fortunes of major fibres in each end-use (see Table 8.1). Notwithstanding variations between end-uses, the rise of synthetic fibres occurred at the expense of cotton, cellulosics and wool. In particular, the dethroning of 'King Cotton' occurred at a dramatic pace, its share dropping (from 1961 to 1976) between 13 and 29 per cent for all end-uses in both the United States and the EEC. Similar shifts are discernible elsewhere, particularly in the CPEs and oil-producing UCEs.

Of the big three synthetic fibres, polyester made major inroads into apparel, with its characteristics of easy care (crease-shedding properties), durability and low stretch. Nylon followed as the leader in carpets and certain clothing lines such as hosiery, women's nightgowns and clothing linings. Acrylics continued to dominate specialized uses such as upholstery and carpet pile, as well as some clothing items where stretch is important (e.g. sweaters and dresses). Overall, the highest expression of chemical fibre hegemony is seen in the geographical focal point of the chemical oligopoly, in the United States, where by the late 1970s over two-thirds of all end-use markets were of synthetic origin.

Clothing

Although contemporary oligopolistic capitalism is at its least developed in the clothing industry, two major forces are reshaping the industry amongst the DCEs and giant dwarfs that continue to dominate the $40-billion 1980 world export market.[3] Once again, as with chemical fibres and textiles, the general economic crisis is battering the industry as demand for new housing (and thus home furnishings) and automobiles (and thus tyres) is dramatically reduced, and as clothing markets are oversaturated. To add to the malaise, UCEs have transformed the world market, increasing their share of clothing exports from 19 to 37 per cent between 1965 and 1977.[4] This is seen in the shift from 1961, when four women's and children's garments were imported into the United States for every 100 made domestically, to 1977, when 34 out of 100 were imported. Except for petroleum, the massive 1976 $6 billion (up to $9 billion in 1978) clothing flow from UCEs to DCEs is unmatched by any other commodity (see Table 8.2).

These two pincer movements — crisis and UCE imports — have provoked various responses from the larger DCE and giant dwarf clothing corporations. With massive assistance from the state, they have adopted, varying with local constraints, any one, or a combination, of four basic survival strategies: relocation of more labour-intensive phases of production to UCEs;

automation; ever larger advertising budgets, with emphasis on brand names; and co-ordinated state and corporate attempts to shift output from domestic to export markets. The success of these intermeshed strategies increasingly depends on the speedy liquidation of the small producer, which raises the level of concentration. This convergence of strategies on a speed up in concentration, as the ultimate and overriding response to the all-encompassing crisis, has produced the groundwork of the expansionary entrenchment of clothing oligopolistic capitalism in the 1980s.

Table 8.1
Changes in Shares of Fibres in Major End-uses, 1961–3, 1970 and 1978

	Clothing			Household			Industrial		
	1961–63	1970	1978	1961–63	1970	1978	1961–63	1970	1978[2]
United States									
Synthetics	14	38	59	12	34	71	30	52	73
Cotton	62	41	32	58	47	22	49	37	17
Cellulosics	12	14	6	22	17	6	21	11	10
Wool	12	7	3	8	2	1	–	–	–
Total	*100*	*100*	*100*	*100*	*100*	*100*	*100*	*100*	*100*
EEC[1]									
Synthetics	12	33	47	6	25	49	6	28	36
Cotton	44	35	26	59	47	30	43	32	30
Cellulosics	23	16	10	20	17	10	46	36	34
Wool	21	16	17	15	11	11	5	4	–
Total	*100*	*100*	*100*	*100*	*100*	*100*	*100*	*100*	*100*

1. Since 1973, the EEC also includes Ireland, the United Kingdom and Denmark.
2. EEC figures are for 1976.

Source: GATT, *Study on Textiles,* 1972; *CIRFS*, 1978; *Textile Organon,* November 1979.

Outward Processing
In outward processing (or geographical relocation of certain processing operations), one of two strategies for reducing production costs, manufacturers fragment the production process by contracting the most labour-intensive apparel phases to UCEs with lower wage rates. Fabric is designed and cut in the home country and then shipped to a UCE for sewing. The partially-processed items are then re-imported for finishing and packaging. In the major West European DCEs and the United States this strategy has become widespread. In the latter it has been encouraged by a special tariff exemption[5] whereby outward processing corporations pay duty

only on the value added to the garment abroad. Consequently, by the end of the 1970s, over a quarter of a billion dollars' worth of apparel annually was flowing from the USA to Puerto Rico, Costa Rica, Honduras, and Mexico.[6] Similarly, Western European corporations have sucked into their processing vortex the Mediterranean periphery states, principally Portugal, Spain, Tunisia, Cyprus and Malta. Even some giant dwarfs have swung into this strategy, such as Hong Kong, which now contracts with Chinese plants to sew large quantities of apparel.

Table 8.2
Textile and Clothing Trade Flows, 1978 ($ billion)

Region	Textile Exports	Apparel Exports	Region	Textile Imports	Clothing Imports
DCEs	7.35	1.78	DCEs	5.64	10.16
to UCEs	5.92	1.40	from UCEs	4.48	9.03
to CPEs	1.43	0.38	from CPEs	1.16	1.13
UCEs	4.93	9.20	UCEs	7.14	1.81
to DCEs	4.48	9.03	from DCEs	5.92	1.40
to CPEs	0.45	0.17	from CPEs	1.22	0.41
CPEs	2.38	1.54	CPEs	1.88	0.55
to DCEs	1.16	1.13	from DCEs	1.43	0.38
to UCEs	1.22	0.41	from UCEs	0.45	0.17

Source: Computed from data in *UN Monthly Bulletin of Statistics,* May 1980

Technical and marketing operations of this kind have influenced the formation of oligopolistic capitalism in a variety of ways. Outward processing demands that a given firm must possess a dynamic marketing network and the ability to carry sizeable inventory. All this is beyond the resources of small and medium-sized corporations. In other words, outward processing by larger corporations in countries with lower wage rates becomes an engine for annihilation of the small and medium-sized firms. The larger corporations underprice small domestic clothing firms by importing lower-cost outward-processed merchandise. In the UCEs, this subcontracting leads to the setting up of 100-per-cent export-oriented sewing sweatshops in several of their free trade zones. This process is obviously at odds with the conception of indigenous industrialization as embodied in the Lima target.

Automation
A mere ten years ago, it was often said that the clothing industry was not amenable to the grip of automation beyond the sewing state. Today's revolutionizing of clothes-making machinery was unimaginable then. Although the details of that revolutionary process will be studied in the next chapter, for the moment we can say that its immediate and cumulative impact on

concentration is similar to that of outward processing. With many of the newer machines now costing over $200,000, it is obvious that only the biggest firms can automate. To the extent that this technology becomes more widespread so will unemployment rise, coupled with the disappearance of smaller firms whose wobbly capital and marketing foundations effectively prohibit them from entering the realm of such technology. Automation thus becomes another drivewheel of concentration. There is yet a third.

Brand Names and Advertising
One of the latest and potentially most powerful corporate clothing strategies is the promotion of brand names through gargantuan advertising outlays, much of which is concealed through transfer pricing techniques. Consumer manipulation via brand names has been a feature of oligopolistic capitalism for decades, but only in recent times have certain clothing firms had the financial and marketing leverage to realize its potential. The techniques deployed are most visible in denim, where three corporations dominate the world market through exports and licences, each carving out its share by massive brand promotion: Levi Strauss (Levi),[7] Blue Bell (Wrangler) and the Vanity Fair Corporation (Lee). This trinity, in their production of denim and corduroy, embodies cotton's major end-use,[8] and the first two of them are the largest American clothing producers.

Levi Strauss (1979 sales: $2.3 billion), is the world's largest apparel corporation, with 31 overseas plants contributing 35 per cent of its aggregate sales, as against Blue Bell's 27 overseas plants accounting for two-fifths of total sales (1979 sales: $1.1 billion). Levi's success is mirrored in its consolidated profit margins (1976–79) of 36 to 38 per cent. Their brand is sold on all continents. 'Levi's have become a world symbol of U.S. culture', writes the *Financial Times*. 'Such is their fame that the brand name has entered most American dictionaries, a pair hangs in the Smithsonian Institution, and trucks carrying them are frequently hijacked by rag-trade bandits.'[9] Levi is a five-generation dynasty that began producing trousers for California gold-miners in the mid-19th Century, and became a public corporation only in 1971.[10] The company began its huge advertising outlays and brand marketing in the 1970s, triggering what has since been labelled the 'jeans revolution'. By the end of the 1970s, the US jeans retail business alone exceeded $5 billion, and Levi's total advertising budget outstripped $50 million, or well over 3 per cent of sales.[11] An important segment of that $50 million has been spent overseas through a Brussels-based European branch, a Hong Kong location for all of Asia, and plant and marketing outlets in dozens of other countries. Confident in the company's rapidly swelling cash flows, Levi's chief operating officer could well exclaim: 'We only have 15 per cent of the jeans market internationally, but we can get 25 per cent of it – which is still well below our domestic market penetration.'[12] Nor are the centrally-planned economies exempt from this expansionary momentum, for they have now become plugged into the global transnational circuit. Notably, Levi's strategy has cracked the Hungarian market wide open. Despite an immense local demand, the nation's planners were initially prepared to import directly standardized, low-priced jeans which were not part of Levi's product range. Levi's strategy, based on an intensive marketing and precise profitability study, has been neatly summarized by *Business Eastern Europe:*

> Levi argued that a co-production arrangement would save the Hungarians' foreign exchange and cover a large measure of domestic demand, thereby also cutting down extensive black marketeering in jeans products. Equally important, it would enable the Hungarians to obtain know-how and to learn the most modern production and organization methods in the textile industry. Levi's motivation was also spurred by the fact that joint production of jeans in Hungary would give it a permanent entry on an important East European market, and it would also receive running royalty payments. In addition, such a venture would open the door wider for increased sales of Levi models not produced jointly, and it would provide the company with another production source.[13]

And, of course, entry into one nation of a common market such as the CMEA means easier access to the entire market.

Levi has recently introduced a new feature to clothing brand marketing, detailed consumer marketing surveys to identify non-jeans markets amenable to the Levi brand. In so doing, Levi identified women's wear and sports wear as lucrative targets and, through expansion and acquisitions, the Levi brand is already amongst the leaders in those items. Levi's major jeans competitor, Blue Bell, has also imposed its Wrangler brand on several varieties of shirts, sports coats, and trousers. Explaining his company's diversification policies, a Blue-Bell vice-president stated: 'We are after clothes of a standard design that the masses buy and that can be produced in volume through mechanized assembly and marketed with the Wrangler brand. We have spent $75 million on the Wrangler name, and we are cashing in on that now.'[14] It was also estimated that 'designer jeans manufacturers', who captured 5 to 10 per cent of the US jeans market in the late 1970s, spent an unprecedented 10 per cent of revenues on advertising and promotion.[15]

Thus price competition and its corollaries are no longer the only means to acquire larger market shares. And, given that only the biggest can afford this barrage of advertising firepower, a further impetus to conglomeration is introduced, which goes beyond the other corporate strategies of outward processing and automation.

No less crucial is the fact that the world advertising industry is itself an oligopoly dominated by a handful of big firms. In Japan the largest agency, Dentsu Inc., controls a quarter of advertising expenditure, the top ten firms about half, and the top 20 about two-thirds. In the United States, by contrast, the biggest advertising agency has a 3-per-cent market share.

Export Forays

The traditional dependence of DCE clothing corporations on domestic markets is now changing. To crack export markets, the bigger clothing manufacturers honed their strategies (outward processing, automation, and brand promotion) in collaboration with their state apparatuses, and with their substantial support. State tax incentives for exports exist in all DCEs, often including low taxation rates on the income of corporations' foreign subsidiaries.[16] Likewise, in varying degrees, all DCEs provide some form of official export financing. In the United States, for example, the Export-Import Bank provides loans, guarantees, and insurance for exports of goods and related services. DCEs also spend significant sums on export promotion, as seen in the promotional allocations per million dollars of manufactured exports:[17] for the United Kingdom, $2,500; Italy, $1,400; France and Japan $600; and the US, $340. Other state-aided export thrusts have included trade missions, subsidies, state-engineered mergers,[18] and active promotion of *sogo shosha*-like companies.

The best example of state assistance to a beleaguered clothing industry may well be the United Kingdom, clearly detailed in a 'White Paper' by the National Economic Development Council (NEDC).[19] Proclaiming a 1980 goal of £1 billion in apparel exports, NEDC proposed aid along the following guidelines: 'manufacturing firms should consider establishing export marketing companies on a co-operative basis'; 'the Government should press for the elimination of barriers to U.K. clothing exports'; 'the Government should extend its store promotion scheme to include shops and stores in overseas territories wholly-owned or controlled by British retailers or wholesalers'; 'clearing banks should be encouraged' to increase their understanding 'of the specialized nature, problems, and financial needs of clothing manufacturers', particularly in the area of export financing.

Similarly, Swiss clothing specialists have advocated that Switzerland should enhance its export capability by boosting average firm size from the present 44 employees to 100–200 employees.[20] This would amount to a drop from the present 695 firms to about 200. In other words, export success equals concentration.

Thus, the unfolding global battle sees the giant dwarfs attempting to enlarge their present one-third of the world market, but running headlong into vigorous DCE corporate efforts to enlarge their salients. The panoply of state and corporate strategies can only mean escalating 'beggar-my-neighbour' policies to protect crisis-ridden industries in the 1980s.

Concentration: Case Studies

The four strategies used by large clothing corporations in their domestic and overseas operations have already yielded a handsome payoff: the big have simply become bigger. This growth has, however, injected qualitative changes into the world clothing economy with spinoffs in other sectors. These multiple effects reach their high point in the United Kingdom, followed by the United States. Amongst export-oriented UCEs, Hong Kong continues to be the concentration pace-setter. The following overviews of these three countries' clothing industries are not just isolated case studies, but also omens for any countries wishing to retain their power within the global market in the 1980s.

In Britain, there are no large corporations solely devoted to clothing. Eight companies control over half Britain's clothing sales, all of which are horizontally or vertically integrated, or conglomerates. Courtaulds' estimated market share is 15–20 per cent, trailed by the Burton Group,[21] Coats Paton, Imperial Chemical Industries, Raybeck,Selincourt, and two large-scale retailers (Great Universal Stores and United Drapery Stores). To these should be added the remaining two of the four biggest European textile groups, Tootal and the ICI-controlled Carrington Viyella, clearly demonstrating the total interdependence of the textile and apparel industries.[22]

Uniquely in the United States, a handful of giants coexists with a multitude of midget firms in the clothing industry. At one end of this extraordinary spectrum are the thousands of sweatshops in Miami, in several cities in Pennsylvania, and in New York's lower Manhattan. These predominantly small-scale Jewish and Italian firms employ mainly blacks, women and hispanics at minimum wage rates. At the other end stands a heterogeneous group of giants that are the advance units of a concentration drive (see Table 8.3). In the early 1970s, there were 22,700 producing units averaging 59 employees per unit; at the end of the decade this had fallen to 15,000.[23] Data for the mid 1970s indicate that the top five corporations comprised 11 per cent of industry sales, and the top 10, 15 per cent.

Credit and finance play a crucial role in the elimination of small and medium-sized firms. Clothing is an industry largely based on credit transactions, not 'cash and carry'. It is therefore a high-risk industry, as seen in factoring, a common financial practice in the industry. This is the purchasing of receivables by a creditor whose financial charges can run several percentage points above the prime rate. Given the small financial leverage of the medium-sized firms, clothing producers have paid as much as 25 per cent on short-term borrowings. In 1980, however, the average mark-up on a garment was 20–25 per cent. In many cases the financial charges exceeded this sum. These firms' position was made even more precarious when the factoring creditors' usual 60-day repayment period was slashed in 1980 to 40–45 days. This practice, however, is but one element in the impetus to concentration.

Perched on the apex of this corporate pyramid (excluding the denim kings Levi Strauss, Blue Bell and Vanity Fair Corporation), is Gulf and Western, the epitome of conglomerate power (see Table 8.3). In two decades it has rocketed from being a single-product Midwestern manufacturer with an annual sales volume of $8 million into the status of 52nd largest US industrial corporation, with 1979 sales topping $5.5 billion. The composition of its major business groups reveals its conglomerate ramifications, which comprise the clothing products group (producing and marketing a wide variety of textiles, clothing, and shoes) through its wholly-owned subsidiary

Kayser Roth, with no less than 55 proprietary brand names; a consumer and agricultural products group housing the Consolidated Cigar Corporation (engaged in the manufacture and sale of cigars, smoking tobacco and smokers' accessories); the leisure time group, which encompasses, amongst others, Madison Square Garden Corporation, the Paramount Pictures Corporation and Simon and Schuster, one of the biggest book publishers in the United States; the natural resources and mining group, with interests in the United States and abroad covering zinc and coal mines, titanium, iron ore, crude oil, natural gas and coal; the paper and binding products group; the automotive replacements parts group; and the financial services group, engaged in direct instalment loans, sales financing, wholesale financing, underwriting, casualty and life insurance.

Gulf and Western's conglomerate power also extends into agriculture. It is one of the largest corporate land-owners in the Americas, owning slightly more than 11 per cent of the arable land area of the Dominican Republic.[24] In addition, it is a big-time speculator on the New York futures market.[25]

Of the rest of the big ten, seven are also conglomerates, including two of the largest US food companies, General Mills and Consolidated Foods, while the other two, Cluett Peabody and Oxford Industries, are well on their way to becoming conglomerates. Cluett has even purchased its own machinery company and is a forerunner in the race to supplant sewing by automated processes. A stage has now been reached where this corporate elite (these big ten and the denim three) are rich enough to buy up smaller companies at an unprecedented rate. This torrent of mergers and acquisitions, now in its initial stages, will be facilitated by the loosening of anti-trust legislation, and the growing realization of how effective such mergers can be in beating back the import barrage.[26]

Absence of homogeneity among clothing producers explains the actual and potential conflict between the small to medium-sized industries and the large producers. Whereas the first are fierce protectionists confining their activities to the US market, the second not only have their own overseas plants but are able to maintain a high degree of flexibility through outward processing. This is why the bulk of the 'big name' clothing brands in Europe are owned by United States transnationals beginning to domesticate the European market because of their capability of exploiting the possibilities of European integration. The European Common Market, and indeed all regional common markets (including those in Eastern Europe), offer encouraging vistas to boost sales and exploit economies of scale by the US clothing giants, helping to beat back the medium and smaller producers within the US economy. Hence the Common Market becomes one more device for speeding up the concentration and centralization of capital within the clothing sector in the United States.

Specific items in the clothing sector already indicate the extent of product concentration: in men's underwear, five companies have over 50 per cent of the market; in jeans, the big three plus two department store brands, Sears and J.C. Penney, control over 65 per cent of the market; in women's bras, five groups have already carved out two-thirds of the market, and in men's shirts four brand names dominate, Arrow, Van Heusen, Sears and J.C. Penney.

Table 8.3
United States: Major Clothing Corporations ($ million)

	Approximate Sales		Total sales		Clothing Sales as % of total	
	1977	*1978*	*1977*	*1978*	*1977*	*1978*
Interco	640.5	731.3	1,666.7	1,851.5	38.4	39.5
Gulf & Western	629.6	725.2	3,647.5	4,312.0	17.3	16.8
General Mills[1]	403.9	534.2	2,782.8	3,243.0	14.5	16.5
Cluett-Peabody	486.6	495.4	589.4	575.6	82.6	86.1
Northwest Industries	416.3	454.0	1,876.5	2,359.7	22.2	19.2
Consolidated Foods[2]	255.0	283.0	2,932.8	3,535.6	8.7	8.0
US Industries	311.4	266.8	1,333.6	1,370.5	23.4	19.5
Hart Schaffner & Marx	221.5	231.2	568.0	606.6	39.0	38.1
Genesco	197.8	227.6	1,014.8	1,048.4	19.5	21.8
Manhattan Industries	191.3	224.5	300.5	349.4	63.7	64.3

1. Includes some non-clothing sales.
2. Includes some home furnishing sales.

Source: Chase Manhattan Bank, *An Analysis of Chemical Fibre, Textile and Apparel Companies* (New York, 1979).

Hong Kong, whose output is overwhelmingly linked to the global market, displays the dimensions involved in the giant dwarfs' ascent to concentration. Its mainstay has been the clothing industry, which accounts for 45 per cent of its 1975 exports, and has undergone an impressive transformation from little more than a cottage industry in the early 1950s[27] to the biggest single industrial employer in Hong Kong, with a workforce of 240,000. The economic crisis and its ramifications throughout the global market have produced pressures for rationalization measures to consolidate the industry. In general, concentration has tended to be higher in spinning, bleaching, dyeing, textile stencilling and printing, but lower in the less mechanized clothing industries (see Table 8.4).

More recent census data indicate that these concentration ratios remained fairly stable until around 1976, after which they rose again. Using the latest Japanese sewing machines, the bigger plants are gaining ground due to their lower average unit labour costs and discounts from large orders from European and US retailers. Concentration has likewise spurted ahead in Taiwan, South Korea, and other giant dwarfs.

Table 8.4
Hong Kong: Concentration Ratios for Textile and Related Sectors, 1973[1]

		Concentration Ratio (%)		
	Value of Sales and Work Done ($ million)	*Largest 3 Establish-ments*	*Largest 6 Establish-ments*	*Largest 9 Establish-ments*
Textiles				
Textile stencilling and printing	371	75	90	95
Wool spinning	394	55	90	100
Bleaching and dyeing	526	52	68	74
Man-made fibre spinning	587	44	65	79
Cotton spinning	1,455	35	55	69
Cotton weaving	2,077	17	29	37
Clothing				
Manufacture of shirts	1,148	25	38	46
Manufacture of made-up textile goods	229	21	34	44
Manufacture of underwear and nightwear	234	18	31	42
Manufacture of trousers, jeans and shorts	1,515	18	31	40
Manufacture of dresses, blouses and skirts	661	16	24	33
Manufacture of suits, coats and overcoats	845	13	22	29
Manufacture of knit outerwear	1,646	12	19	24

1. Reporting establishments employing 20 or more persons.

Source: Hong Kong, *1973 Census of Industrial Production,* quoted in *Hong Kong: Monthly Digest of Statistics,* October 1977.

Fashion
A final, but crucial, factor influencing the direction of the clothing industry is the corporate world of fashion, which influences as much as 75 per cent of the entire spectrum of the textile industry.[28] Together with corporate brands and promotional onslaughts it is a crucial determinant of consumer choice of fabric and apparel, simultaneously manipulating and satisfying consumer taste. The multi-million dollar fashion industry is based on two constants with their shifting permutations: colour and design.

Contrary to the widespread misconception, fashion is not an autonomous entity subject to the whims of consumer sovereignty or any of its current euphemisms. Rather, it represents the confluence of the major corporate sectors in the textile industry. Several chemical fibre giants initially attempted to set up their own fashion houses, but some have altered course to operate within the more conventional marketing channels. This entails working with designers to produce fabric and clothes that encourage consumer acceptance of new or modifications of older fibres.

It is no paradox to claim that there is no fashion 'industry' as such. Rather, it has several institutional embodiments. Seasonal and annual fashion shows and designer collections are the most celebrated, where stylists and designers mesh with our aforementioned corporate forces[29] to launch fashion trends, producing such 'new looks' as the 'natural look', the 'military look', the 'aviator look', the 'Annie Hall look', and so on. Another fashion area where corporate powers meet is in semi-public, semi-private institutions, such as the British Textile Colour Group, where ideas and suggestions on colour and shading function as the industry's barometer. The Group includes ICI, Monsanto, Courtaulds, the International Wool Secretariat, the International Institute for Cotton, Tootal, Burlington's retailer, Klopman and the Clothing Export Council. In France, the Comite de Co-ordination des Industries de la Mode is a similar and decisive moulding forum of consumer 'preferences'.

Such corporate combinations do not preclude the deployment of individual corporate leverage to influence colour and design. Big textile manufacturers distribute samples to a small number of their larger clients. Tootal, for example, spent £150–£200,000 in 1978 on the initial sampling of merely eight of its new piece-dyed fabrics.[30] Thus, jointly or individually, the largest corporations have taken control of the fashion industry, using it to enhance market power, once again to the detriment of smaller producers, in chemical fibres, textiles, and apparel.

Other End-uses

Home furnishings are largely the products of the textile oligopoly and a few specialized carpet companies. They comprise carpets (their biggest component) and rugs, sheets and pillowcases, quilts, towels, draperies, decorative fabrics, and furniture. Carpets[31] are the most conspicuous growth point, increasingly being used in areas traditionally covered with hard surface materials: bathrooms, kitchens, shopping malls, hospitals, etc. This has been aided by builders shifting from high-quality wooden floors (meant to remain exposed) to low-grade wood covered with a moderately priced carpet. New plateaux in technology have contributed to a further concentration in the field, as instanced by a computer-controlled $4-million continuous dyeing machine capable of dyeing a piece of carpet with several colours and patterns, including Oriental designs. And almost exclusively, these gains are redounding

to chemical fibres, notably nylon.[32] Apart from cotton's traditional mainstay in towelling, chemical fibres are gaining in almost all other items.
Drapery, or decorative fabrics, follows carpets as the second largest sector in
volume in home furnishings. In general, unlike upholstery and drapery, the
curtain market is dominated by relatively few big manufacturers. In the
past, home furnishings offered certain of the largest textile producers
(such as Burlington) an easy outlet for cross-subsidization when housing
demand was high and clothing demand low.[33] Beginning in the late 1970s,
however, the crisis also hit housing construction (and by extension household furnishings) in most DCEs. The upshot of the recession is that many
small-scale producers of home furnishings have been axed because they are
unable to market their products. This is but one more stimulus to further
consolidation of the textile oligopoly.

Whilst the field of industrial applications represents the smallest fibre end-
use segment, it has an almost inexhaustible growth potential. Cotton's
traditional invulnerability from man-made fibre assaults was presumed to
lie in its inherent natural properties: breatheability, moisture absorbency,
softness. In addition to the partial breaching of cotton's defences by the
chemical fibre corporations, these attributes are in any case inappropriate
to industrial end-uses, where strength and durability are demanded, especially
in civil engineering and space technology. Hence, industrial end-uses have
been almost completely annexed by the chemical fibre oligopoly, whose
research and development is generating either new fibres or modifications of
existing ones to meet more exacting consumer specifications. Though new
industrial vistas are opening up, at present tyres comprise around one half
of industrial end-uses. The tyre industry is a highly concentrated one: in the
United States, seven corporations (led by Goodrich, with a 28-per-cent share)
control 84 per cent of the market. The corporations are all conglomerates
and several have big holdings in chemicals.[34]

Viewed through another prism, tyres, reveal the morphology of
corporate power and its ability to modify fibre end-use shares. The most
significant component in a tyre is the textile reinforcement which forms the
skeleton of the tyre. Over the years, this textile reinforcement was gradually
shifted from its original cotton fabric to rayon, nylon and polyester, with
its strength steadily rising. A dramatic modification in strength and modulus
occurred between 1969 and 1971 with the advent of Du Pont's new class
of high-strength organic textile aramid fibre, which more than doubled the
maximum specific strength of a tyre textile fibre. In addition to its inherent
properties of resistance to flames and temperatures in excess of $250°C$,
Kevlar (Du Pont's brand name for its aramid fibres) is, cord for cord, five
times lighter than a textile fibre made of steel, its major competitor.[35]

Both home furnishings and industrial end-uses illustrate the different
oligopolistic power structures in operation at various key points in the
fibre/textile/end-use chain. It is within this overall corporate arc of power
that the general and specific role of oligopoly must be sought.

Wholesaling and Retailing

Textile and clothing sales account for 10–20 per cent of global retail sales, outstripped only by foodstuffs. Wholesaling and retailing, as a specific link in the chain of textile oligopolistic capitalism, is, however, radically different from the other links. It is the world's biggest business, and the largest component of GNP in every country save perhaps the big oil exporters. Thus, despite the awesome size of some retail corporations (Sears' 1979 sales surpassed $17 billion), an oligopoly, in the sense that we have used it, does not prevail. Collusive pricing policies of the big retailers do not, in general, exist nor has evidence surfaced to justify such an assertion. However, because of their size, strategic market locations in urban and rural areas, and colossal inventories and sales turnover, they are ideally positioned to squeeze their suppliers. As one analyst noted of one of the world's largest retailers (Marks and Spencer), it 'becomes involved in every aspect of its 600-odd suppliers' operations, dictating not only the number of stitches and the width of hems but also the profit margins of those from whom it buys'.[36] It is therefore not fortuitous that wholesaling/retailing is the largest segment of the textile chain, appropriating in many cases as much as half of the clothing retail price.

Millions of relatively small retail outlets exist worldwide; but already by the 1870s giant retailers were beginning to emerge in several developed countries. Mass retailers and department stores grew up to exploit growing urban markets and by the turn of the 20th Century large mail-order houses had begun selling to significant segments of rural populations. By the mid 1970s, twenty-eight European and American textile and apparel retailers had sales outstripping $1.7 billion (see Table 8.5). Of these, some are power-houses in clothing retailing (e.g. C. & A. Brenninkmeyer), while others market thousands of products with clothing a relatively small part.

Also, while traditional food retail giants such as Migros in Switzerland (for whom textiles and clothing represented under 10 per cent of their $4.8 billion 1979 sales)[37] were not included in our top twenty-eight, they and other 'food' retailers will inevitably appropriate larger shares of clothing retailing by their increasing command of the overall marketing chain. Family concerns such as the devoutly Roman Catholic C. & A. Brenninkmeyer do not publish even a superficial balance sheet of their operations. Hence, estimates of their total sales vary considerably. *Textil Wirtschaft* puts C. & A.'s 1978 sales as high as $3.8 billion, which would have made it the leader in Europe.[38] All these giants use advertising and advanced marketing techniques not only to annex ever larger national market shares, but also to open international markets.

A profile of the five major textile and clothing sales outlets in DCEs reveals variations in concentration (see Table 8.6). These sales categories should not be considered autonomous, since retailers in one category may, and often do, have proprietary interests in others.[39] A crucial element in the movement to concentration has been the strides made by multiple retailers, i.e. department or variety chains of eleven or more stores. In almost all DCEs (including all those in Table 8.6), the market shares controlled by the multiples have grown since the beginning of the 1970s, most strikingly in the United States, where they sky-rocketed from 13 to 31 per cent of textile and clothing retail sales.[40]

Table 8.5
Sales of World's Largest Retailers of Textiles and Clothing, 1979 ($ billion)

Europe		*United States*	
Karstadt (West Germany)	6.4	Mobil Oil	47.9[2]
Kaufhof (West Germany)	4.6	Sears, Roebuck	17.3
Schickedang (West Germany)	4.1[1]	K Mart	12.6
Hertie (West Germany)	3.7	J.C. Penney	11.1
Marks & Spencer (UK)	3.6	F.W. Woolworth	6.6
Coop (Switzerland)	3.5	Federated Department	
Carrefour (France)	3.5[1]	Stores	5.7
Vroom and Dressman		Household Finance	5.3
(Netherlands)	3.4	Dayton-Hudson	3.3
G B-Inno (Belgium)	3.3	May Dept. Stores	2.7
C. & A. Brenninkmeyer		Rapid American	2.6
(West Germany)	3.0	Carter Hawley Hale Stores	2.4
Great Universal Stores (UK)	3.0	Allied Stores	2.2
Edeka-Zentral (West Germany)	2.2[1]	R.H. Macy	2.1
Horten (West Germany)	1.9	Gamble-Skogmo	2.0
NK-Ahlens (Sweden)	1.7		

1. 1978.
2. Mobil's retailing subsidiary, Montgomery Ward, had 1978 sales of $5.0 billion.

Source: Compiled by the UNCTAD secretariat from trade sources.

One marketing phenomenon which has been a major factor in the speedup of concentration has been the intrusion of giant shopping malls in the late 1960s and 1970s into Western Europe, Japan, the United States and certain UCEs (e.g. Brazil, Mexico, and Venezuela). Large mall developers prefer the bulk of their tenants to be large retail chains which can guarantee regular rental payments, have low bankruptcy rates, and enjoy widespread name/ brand recognition. This is related to their big volume of advertising and, in many cases, to their extensive geographical spread in regional and national markets. Consequently, via restrictive lease arrangements, preferential treatment is given to the giant retailers, who sometimes have several of their subsidiaries in the same mall. Such practices are further entrenched by certain of the largest retailers, for example, Sears, actually own or are in joint ventures with mall development corporations. Thus, difficulty in gaining access to preferred mall sites becomes a deterrent to entry for smaller independents and non-diversified retailers.

Table 8.6
Clothing and Textile Outlets, 1977 (%)

	Multiple Retailers	Department and Variety Stores	Cooperatives	Mail Order	Indepen- dents	Others
UK[1] [2]	53.2	16.9	6.3	8.0	8.7	6.9
USA[1]	31.4	38.0	–	3.9	–	27.7
Netherlands	22.3	10.7	·–	2.0	48.5	16.5
Switzerland	19.7	9.9	11.4	2.5	32.5	24.0
Belgium	13.5	11.0	0.5	3.0	72.0	–
West Germany	12.9	20.0	5.2	7.3	25.8	28.8
Italy	7.5	8.0	0.4	1.3	80.8	2.0
France	5.2	9.8	0.7	4.2	70.3	9.8

1. Clothing only
2. 1976

Source: *Retail Trade International*, 1977.

The United States: A Case Study
The US textile and clothing retail market is dominated by two corporate species: the multiple department store chain and the multiple variety chain, of which the prime examples are respectively Sears and Woolworths. The 1860s and 1870s saw the beginnings of the big department stores in the United States, and by 1914 they had acquired much of their present marketing format. In this respect, big-scale merchandizing followed the lines of the transformation of capitalism. Founded in 1886, Sears' sales had reached $3 million by 1905 and the company had embarked on a wide range of manufacturing of consumer durables such as stoves, firearms, furniture, farm implements, shoes, etc., according to the price and marketing specifications of Sears.[41] Today Sears stands at the retailing apex of the capitalist world, a transnational conglomerate and a model of big merchandizing for the 1980s. Its merchandizing tentacles reflect its retail turnover: 850 department stores and thousands of outlets at 3,800 locations in every state of the American union, and in Europe and Latin America.[42] Its global labour force hovers around half a million, and alone it represents one-tenth of US department store sales. Almost a quarter of all merchandise is purchased from suppliers in which they have equity holdings, for instance Kellwood Co. (with 22 per cent of its equity), one of the biggest US clothing concerns,

which in fact supplies the bulk of its clothing and textile requirements. With a 1977 advertising budget of $650 million, the fattest for any corporation in the world,[43] Sears is leading the march to retail concentration which undoubtedly will gather strength in the 1980s. Sears' major competitor is K Mart (1979 sales: $12.6 billion), the fastest growing retail chain in the US, its merchandizing prowess due to an adeptness in marketing women's clothes, their traditional high gross margin. K Mart now has about 7 per cent of the US general merchandise, clothing and furniture market, and is a runner-up to Sears, whose 1980 market share was 9.3 per cent.

F.W. Woolworth has been in the forefront of the other major US retailing outlet, the variety store, since its foundation over one hundred years ago. Its basic merchandizing innovation ('the five and ten cents store') was the sale of low-priced, simply packaged mass consumer items involving small mark-ups on high turnover.[44] Today, with 5,600 stores, it has global sales in excess of $5 billion. Although its advertising outlays are smaller than Sears, its consumer-luring campaigns have included circulars distributed to twelve million American homes through newspapers and the mail. These techniques are rapidly narrowing the marketing circuit of the small-scale retailer.[45]

Japan

The leverage exercised by giant retailers to squeeze domestic suppliers (which, of course, is vastly more effective against suppliers in developing countries with little or no countervailing power) was recently dramatized by the Fair. Trade Commission's indictment of Mitsukoshi, Japan's foremost department store chain. The FTC charged that the chain, which is part of the larger Mitsubishi and Mitsui groups, was 'pushing suppliers' to buy its products, and coercing them to pay 'co-operation money'. Commenting on Mitsukoshi's refusal to comply with the FTC injunction, *The Japan Economic Journal* noted that it was not the principle of the squeeze that was at issue, but rather that its operation was too blatant, and the Japanese victims too numerous. 'Although "pushing" suppliers and using other pressure tactics are considered a "just" custom by a part of Japan's department store and supermarket industry, the FTC ordered Mitsukoshi specifically to desist from such conduct as it felt that it was too extreme, with those complaining of being victimized running high.'[46]

The tie-up between the top Japanese retailer, Daiei (1979 sales: $4.7 billion, which it plans to quadruple by 1985) and K Mart illustrates the attempt of big-scale retailers to establish global commodity procurement systems to enhance, in the words of one of their spokesmen, 'their bargaining power with manufacturers'. The large retailers have profit rates as high as 43 per cent on direct imports, more than double those on their domestically produced goods. Japanese corporate retailing power reveals more or less the same expansionist patterns as its allies and rivals at home and abroad: Daiei and its rivals, for example, are rapidly diversifying. Its corporate blueprint calls for a boost in non-retailing sales from 11 per cent to almost 33 per cent by 1985, with the bulk of this diversification coming from operations abroad.

Britain and West Germany

In the United Kingdom, the clothing retail market is also dominated by multiple retail chains, the largest being Marks & Spencer, which accounts for 29 per cent of clothing sales and 18 per cent of household textiles. By the mid 1970s, more than two-fifths of its aggregate sales were in food which, like textiles and clothing, are marketed under its brand name 'St. Michael'. Its international network now encompasses 250 stores with 1979 retail sales exceeding $3.6 billion. Undoubtedly the 1980s will see the emergence of new corporate strategies, particularly among the giants. The tie-up between Marks & Spencer and Daier, involving marketing the former's food and clothing brands, is suggestive. Indeed, it demonstrates how different transnational retailers, while not resorting to takeovers, can become self-reinforcing without eroding each other's market shares. Such a merchandizing approach, however, is feasible only between giant retailers in different countries, since within national markets, competition to retain and enlarge market shares remains fierce.

Three other giant retailers, British Home Stores, Debenhams and Little-woods, account for an additional 10 per cent of the British clothing retail market. Certain large retailers like Debenhams, Austin Reed, and Selfridges have enhanced their market hegemony by joining in co-operative advertising efforts with certain giant fibre producers including Courtaulds, ICI, and Hoechst.

West Germany represents what might be seen as an intermediate stage between Britain and the still highly fragmented France and Italy. In recent years the movement towards concentration shows itself in the growing strength of multiple chain stores and department/variety stores, particularly Karstadt, Kaufhof, Hertie, and Horten.[47] Karstadt, Western Europe's largest retailer, is more than 50 per cent owned by two of the big three German banks.[48] Together these four stores have annexed over 80 per cent of West Germany's department store sales.

One of the key German textile and clothing retailing corporations is C. & A. Brenninkmeyer, possibly one of the most secretive family concerns in the world. The foundations of this family empire lay in the 17th Century Dutch linen trade. It was at this time that 'the first hint of the shroud of secrecy which was to encloak the future business activities of the Brennik-meyers was manifested in their "secret language" which was evolved to conceal their business methods and transport routes from rival traders and others. In fact, C & A buyers still use a secret code to this day.'[49]

Today, over 200 male family members (in groups of six to ten) manage subsidiaries in West Germany, the Netherlands, Britain, Belgium, the USA, France and Switzerland, with its share of clothing sales reaching as much as 15 per cent of the national market in some cases. In the Netherlands, it is the fifth or sixth largest corporation, following in the wake of such corporations as Shell, Unilever and Phillips. Like many other large retailers it is also integrated 'backward' into clothing manufacturing.[50] As is to be expected, it is one of the world's biggest advertisers, and the largest in the Netherlands, Belgium and West Germany.

The Netherlands (pop. 14 million), along with Switzerland, represents perhaps the highest expression of concentrated retail power in a small country. The operations of Vroom and Dressman (V & D) illustrate another family department store group that has been transformed into an international retailing and service conglomerate with aggregate sales exceeding $3 billion. Not only does it have an overwhelming presence in a limited national consumer market, but it already has stakes in four large American retail groups with stores in most of the fifty United States. In services, it has diversified into employment agencies, security operations, computer software, catering and estate agencies. It moved into banking with the 1978 acquisition of the Rotterdam-based merchant bank Staal Bankers. It was with good reason that Chairman of the Board Anton Dreesman exultantly declared that 'we have a high degree of internal financing and do not need the stock exchange'. Easy access to finance capital combined with its massive marketing clout has intensified its annexationist thrust, so that Vroom and Dreesman now controls almost a quarter of the equity capital of its large scale competitor, the P & C Group.

This is one more example of the pressure of corporate power in one sector contributing to modify the pattern of capital accumulation in yet another. The Dutch retail giants, via their global procurement network in combination with their massive domestic marketing leverage, have outmanoeuvred the still fragmented clothing industry by new marketing techniques that can be expected to become even more powerful in the 1980s. V & D has linked up with Uny, one of the biggest Japanese retailing groups, to set up home centre chains, combining joint purchases of foreign products and the development of joint brands. This partially explains how eight textile spinning companies, accounting for nine-tenths of Dutch capacity, could be welded into one new company, Spinnerij Nederland, with a 49-per-cent state holding.

The rest of the DCEs are incubating large retail chains and should, to varying degrees, follow in the footsteps of the USA, Britain and West Germany.[51] UCE retail establishments likewise vary considerably from one country to another and from one region to another. There are, however, certain common denominators, most notably among the former British, French, Belgian and Dutch colonies, where the large metropolitan wholesalers/retailers are still important. To this well-entrenched marketing force in many African and Asian countries may be added Asian and Middle Eastern expatriates working as independent retailers, or in conjunction with large metropolitan firms. Symptomatic of this thrust is the multi-million-dollar South Korean-owned department store Renovation in Gabon, marketing a wide range of South Korean textiles and clothing.

The Retailer's Mark-Up
There is a direct relationship between mounting concentration in retailing and

the big retail chains' ability to gouge out ever larger profit margins. Over the last two decades, the proportion of the retail breakdown appropriated by wholesalers/retailers has grown steadily to a point where in most DCEs they now appropriate roughly one-half. In the United States, retailers' margins have shot up from 37 per cent two decades ago to 40–42 per cent (1961) and on to the present 50 per cent, or 'keystone mark-up', as it is now designated in the trade. This means that for each clothing dollar, only half is distributed amongst: the wool, cotton or chemical fibre producers, all handlers and processors through the yarn producer, dyers, knitters or weavers, garment makers and transporters. At the end of the product line, the retailer alone obtains the other half.[52]

The retailer's gain has been at the expense of consumers through higher prices, and the textile, apparel and wholesale establishments who supply them. Smaller clothing and home furnishing producers are particularly afflicted. Here is one more example of an external force, the retailer's fatter mark-ups, becoming a catalyst in escalating the concentration of capital in those two sectors. The contrasted movement of wholesale and retail prices in one segment of US women's and children's clothing illustrates the retailers' bigger bite: since 1947, retailers have pushed up their prices (in real terms) by 58 per cent, whereas wholesalers achieved a 27-per-cent increase (see Table 8.7).

Table 8.7
USA: Mark-Up in Women's and Children's Clothing (1947 = 100)

	Wholesale Prices	*Retail Prices*
1947	100.0	100.0
1968	101.5	117.9
1969	104.7	124.4
1970	108.1	129.1
1971	109.3	133.7
1972	110.9	137.0
1973	114.2	141.8
1974	121.1	150.2
1975	123.3	153.8
1976	126.8	158.0

Source: *Knitting Times,* 23 May 1977, p. 47.

Among the more widespread techniques of aggrandizement is that of retailers making deductions from suppliers' invoicing – a practice which most manufacturers are powerless to resist. Likewise, the extension of private brands by giant retailers replacing producer trade-marks opens lucrative vistas for higher mark-ups, since the purchaser can no longer compare different clothing brand prices. By dealing in mammoth volumes the biggest retailers are able to extort higher discounts from clothing producers afflicted by undercapacity working. Invariably most of the largest retailers are positioned to squeeze these discounts to their limit, due to their precise knowledge of suppliers' production costs and operating margins.

Another marketing strategem used by the giant retailers is the play-off of low-cost clothing manufacturers in UCEs against their own national clothing producers or against transnational marketing companies. This marketing strategem calls for higher mark-ups on cheaper imported clothes which large retailers are positioned to price at around the same level as domestic clothing. Different cost structures for a South Korean and US shirt reveal the retailer's scope for profitability by putting his own brand name on both shirts and selling them at the same price (see Table 8.8). Examples of these sales techniques were recently spelled out in a US House of Representatives Hearing: 'A suit from Korea which lands f.o.b. California at $45 is sold for $125 in a department store in this country; that same suit would cost us to make about $65 to $70. It is immediately apparent why the retailer would very much favour rising imports. He is making an extra $20 to $25 per suit.'[53]

Table 8.8
Comparative Manufacturing Costs for a Shirt in the United States and South Korea ($ US)

	S. Korea	USA
Overhead	1.60	1.60
Labour	0.41	2.72
Materials	2.49	3.36
Total[1]	4.50	7.68

1. Data suggest that with transportation, tariff and quota charges to the USA, the cost differential would be reduced from the 71 per cent here to between 20 and 30 per cent.

Source: ACTWU, *The Impact of Imports on the Men's Clothing Industry*, (New York 1976), p. 39.

In most UCEs, huge aggregations of retailing power are less in evidence because of the more fragmented nature of retail structures, reflecting the stage of capitalist underdevelopment. In consequence, as we saw earlier in the case of Mexico, retail mark-ups are lower. Likewise in India, another UCE where figures are available, retail margins hover around 25–30 per cent.[54] These margins will probably grow as wholesaling and retailing transnationals secure and enlarge marketing beachheads in urban centres of a number of UCEs, particularly in Latin America and some West African states.

References

1. *Wall Street Journal,* 24 July 1979.
2. In Western Europe, for example, 55 per cent of fibres end up in clothing, 30 per cent in household furnishings, and 15 per cent in industrial end uses; see Societe de Banques Suisses, *Le Mois,* 7–8 (1979), p. 11.
3. Extrapolated from Economist Intelligence Unit, *World Textile Trade and Production,* p. 43.
4. See Table 7.1 p. 166.
5. See Section 807 of the Tariff Classification Act of 1962.
6. *Business Week,* 14 May 1979.
7. Almost all Levi Strauss' fabric originates from Burlington, reinforcing the dominant position each exercises in its respective realm. Levi's other major supplier is Cone Mills, one of the largest US textile producers, who together with Burlington exercise considerable control over US denim prices; see *The New York Times,* 11 June 1978.
8. In the face of this incursion into clothing markets, chemical fibre producers have not been neutral. Behind such advertising slogans as 'Cotton loves Dacron', certain chemical fibre giants have launched successful blending campaigns that push chemical fibres' shares in denims as high as 25 per cent, with a lower proportion in corduroys.
9. *Financial Times,* 15 February 1979. The article goes on to point out: 'In the US, the FBI says Levi jeans rank third after liquor and cigarettes as the most frequently hijacked commodity in the country.'
10. The Haas family still owns 50 per cent of Levi's stock.
11. *Business Week,* 14 May 1979.
12. *Forbes,* 21 August 1978. By 1978, international sales represented 35 per cent of Levi's sales.
13. *Business Eastern Europe,* 8 September 1978.
14. *Business Week,* 14 May 1979.
15. See *New York Times,* 25 June 1979. These jean lines, sold under the names of Sassoon, Calvin Klein, Gloria Vanderbilt, etc., are produced either by the designers' own jean divisions, or licensed out to the big clothing companies.
16. For details of this and other state aid, see United States Senate, *U.S. Export Policy,* pp. 8–19.
17. *Ibid.,* p. 10.
18. In the UK, the establishment of two institutions financed by the government is aimed at enhancing export market shares by internal consolidation of the industry. The first is the Clothing Industry Productivity Resources Agency, concerned with raising levels of productive efficiency; the second, the Clothing Industry Joint Council, which brings together various associations representing specific clothing sectors.
19. National Economic Development Council, *Clothing EDC: Progress Report 1979,* London, 1979.
20. Societe de Banques Suisses, *Le Mois* 7–8 (1979), pp. 12–13.
21. The Burton Group, long the dominant power in men's wear retailing (selling one-third of all UK suits at one stage), erupted into the women's wear market in the late 1970s. Each sector has around 400 shops and sales of £90 million. See *Financial Times,* 4 September 1979.

22. In Britain, employment in the clothing industry is around 300,000, and cutbacks in any clothing line would exacerbate the overall level of unemployment (over 1.5 million in 1978). In clothing, this impinges precisely on those regions with above-average unemployment rates. Moreover, job losses in the industry hit the female workforce especially hard as they have limited opportunities for alternative employment. The rationale behind this policy of close state support with large scale clothing corporations was formulated as follows: 'The decline of the clothing industry was also considered serious because of the effect on other sectors. Clothing is a major customer of the U.K. textile industry which employs a further 480,000 people, and any major rundown could eventually work its way back through textiles to the chemical industry which provides the raw material for much of the textile industry's fibre output', *Financial Times*, 27 January 1978.

23. *Business Week,* 14 May 1979, and United States, Department of Commerce, *U.S. Industrial Outlook, 1975: with Projections to 1980* (Washington DC, 1976), pp. 224–5.

24. See UNCTAD, *The Marketing and Distribution of Tobacco* (Geneva, 1978.

25. According to the Securities and Exchange Commission in its proposed lawsuit against Gulf and Western for financial malpractices, Gulf and Western's Chairman of the Board 'made a secret oral agreement with high officials of the Dominican Republic Government . . . to speculate in sugar futures in 1975, but did not deliver the Dominican Republic's $38.7-million share of the profits of the successful speculation.' *The New York Times,* 17 August 1978.

26. It is not by chance that in the USA both Du Pont and the trade union movement have joined in the battle against what they deem as unjustifiably high levels of clothing import penetration by lower-cost producers. It is one of the nation's biggest industries, with shipments of more than $30 billion. National income originating in the apparel industry averaged an annual compound growth of 5 per cent (1967–72) scaling $9.6 billion, or 4 per cent of all manufacturing income. Clothing employment in 1975 averaged 1.3 million, 7 per cent of all manufacturing employment. Around 87 per cent are production workers, with women comprising 81 per cent of the labour force, compared with 29 per cent in all manufacturing. Further, a high proportion of workers 'are members of disadvantaged minority groups'. See United States, Department of Commerce, *U.S. Industrial Outlook,* 1975, pp. 224–31.

27. Hong Kong made a major push onto the global market from 1954–6 to 1964, when its share in world exports increased from 9 to 14 per cent (and has since remained roughly at that level). See A. Maizels, *Exports and Economic Growth of Developing Countries* (Cambridge, 1968), pp. 415–16.

28. 'Fashion's role in marketing', *Ciba-Geigy Review,* No. 1, 1975.

29. An illustration of this is ICI's launching of its new terylene fibre, which it markets under the name 'Soft-Finish'. This has involved close working relationships with finishers, designers and a vast range of clothing producers, and even the International Wool Secretariat, to create new blends and designs that embrace the fibre. For a more detailed breakdown of these relationships and specific blends, see *Textile Month,*

June 1978.

30. *Financial Times,* 20 June 1978. Other corporate initiatives include the recruitment of design specialists, for instance Courtaulds' hiring of Sir Paul Reilly, a past director of the British Design Council.

31. Carpets represent the main outlet for non-acrylic synthetic filament yarns (46 per cent of total consumption in Western Europe), and staple yarns (61 per cent). Cf. J. Bonus, 'Man-made fibres and natural fibres: competition in end-uses in Western Europe', paper presented at the Shirley Institute, 29–30 November 1977.

32. Today, wool carpets have dropped to 3 per cent of US output. See *New York Times,* 20 June 1979.

33. For certain of the largest textile producers, such as Burlington, household furnishings account for over a third of sales; see Burlington Industries, *Annual Report,* 1978.

34. *Business Week,* 28 August 1978.

35. For an amplification of these points, see the paper by G.B. Redmond (Dunlop Research Centre, Birmingham), *Aramids in Tyres,* August, 1979. Kevlar's advance is suggestive of the swift inroads that can alter end-use shares: in 1972, Du Pont was producing 250 tons annually; in 1979 this soared to 6,500 tons; and by 1982 it is expected to triple to 20,000 tons.

36. *International Herald Tribune,* 1 September 1980.

37. Computed from Migros, *Annual Report,* Zurich 1979.

38. *Textil-Wirtschaft,* 15 March 1979. This has been converted from DM 7 billion.

39. Department stores are establishments employing 25 people or more, with sales of clothing and soft goods combined amounting to 20 per cent or more of total sales, and selling each of three product lines: furniture, home furnishings, appliances, radio and TV sets; men's, women's and children's clothes; household linens and dry goods. Variety stores are primarily engaged in retail sale of a multitude of low-priced merchandise. Co-operatives include co-operatively owned retailers; and mail order houses sell merchandise promoted through catalogues and advertisements in newspapers, magazines, radio and television. Independents comprise smaller, privately owned establishments.

40. *Retail Trade International,* 1977.

41. See Alfred D. Chandler, *The Visible Hand: The Managerial Revolution in American Business* (London, 1977), p. 231. Gordon L. Weil, *Sears, Roebuck, USA: The Great American Catalog Store and How it Grew,* (New York, 1977): 'At least once every year, three out of four American adults enter a Sears store . . . Just about the only thing that is obvious to anybody, whether a customer or not, is that Sears is the largest advertiser in the United States. Everybody is regularly exposed to Sears' commercials on television, magazine ads, and a veritable blizzard of newspaper supplements. In 1975, not including spending for catalog sales and Allstate, retail advertising cost Sears $378 million. Some 40 advertising agencies were kept busy churning out the copy to sell Sears' products' (p. 146).

42. For details, see Sears, *Annual Report,* 1977; *Retail Trade International,* 1977, p. 250; and *Business Week,* 14 May 1979.

43. *Financial Times,* 14 October 1978.
44. They held to a 10-cent price limit per item for their first 53 years. See *The New York Times,* 18 February 1979.
45. Even Woolworth's was almost swept up in the takeover drive in 1979, when Brascan Ltd of Canada offered $1.1 billion to buy up 100 per cent of Woolworth's shares.
46. *The Japan Economic Journal,* 1 May 1979.
47. This corporation is 25-per-cent owned by the British American Tobacco Company.
48. These are Deutsche Bank and Commerzbank. Kaufhof is similarly over 50 per cent owned by the Deutsche Bank and the Dresdner Bank. See *Business Week Executive Portfolio,* op. cit.
49. For details, see International Textile, Garment and Leather Workers' Federation, *The Leading Multinational Companies in the Textile, Garment and Leather Industries* (Amsterdam, 1972), p. 62.
50. Its sustained opposition to trade unionism is similar to the second largest US textile concern, J.P. Stevens.
51. Although textile and clothing sales will continue to rise, a discernible trend in both DCEs and UCEs is their relative decline as a proportion of total sales in the face of rising expenditures on housing, transportation and communications. This is also reflected in textile and clothing's declining share in sales of three of the four largest German department stores. For Karstadt, between 1960 and 1976, the share dropped from 54 to 35 per cent; Kaufhof from 54 to 38; and Horten from 62 to 33 (Institut des Deutschen Textileinzelhandels, *Der Marktfuhrer im Textileinzelhandel, 1977*).
52. *Knitting Times,* 23 May 1977.
53. United States, House Committee on Ways and Means, *Library of Congress Study on Imports and Consumer Prices,* 95th Congress, 1st Session (Washington, DC, 1977).
54. H.R. Aiyer, *Economics of Textile Trade,* p. 61.

9. Technology: The Permanent Revolution

The forces of concentration characteristic of oligopolistic capitalism reach their culmination in textile machinery. At present, a mere seven DCEs control four-fifths of world exports in this sector. More importantly, 25–30 highly product-differentiated DCE corporations exercise oligopolistic power that overspills the boundaries of textile machinery. By virtue of being transnationals, they are the determinant actors in five key dialectical relationships: corporate concentration and company fragmentation; employment and unemployment; natural and chemical fibres; knitting and weaving; and relations within and between UCEs and DCEs.

The medium through which the oligopoly controls the pace and direction of these five relationships is largely the permanent revolutionizing of technology in conformity with the compulsive logic of profit maximization. The dynamic behind these innovations is provided not only by the large research-intensive textile machinery producers, but also by the chemical fibre oligopoly, the integrated textile and apparel manufacturers, and electronics corporations. The confluence of these innovations has led to extremely high standards of precision engineering and the growing use of microprocessor control (with the advent of the silicon chip), which for the moment remains beyond the reach of most UCEs. These, in turn, are underpinned by scientists in government research institutions, universities and foundations, who have together mounted a research offensive of staggering dimensions, best seen in the high development of open-end spinning, to a point where 'the ring frame will soon be ready to join the jennies, water frames and mules in our museums of industrial history';[1] the advent of high-speed shuttleless looms; dominance of jet dyeing machines for fabric dyeing; circular- and warp-knitting machines, which have evolved so swiftly that machine speed doubled between 1975 and 1977;[2] and a panoply of transfer printing techniques. Fibre-making developments have centred on boosting the scale of operations, increasing speeds, integrating multiple processes into single steps (a trend which will contribute in the 1980s to a further attrition of the workforce), and shaving other input costs. This integration of processes is particularly highly developed in chemical fibres, whose ever-widening range of end-uses has been exploited by chemical fibre, textile and textile machinery producers to introduce a broad array of textile products.

223

One example among many is the increased speed at which textured yarns can be made. In the 1950s, Crimplene yarn was textured at 50 metres/minute; now, the current speed is around 800 metres/minute. This has been made possible by the integration of separate processes.[3] The original process consisted of six operations: low-speed spinning, drawtwisting, untwist-set. setting, drawtwisting, and stabilizing. The current process involves only two: POY spinning, and a sequence draw-twist-set-untwist set.

Demonstrating the symbiosis of yarn and machinery, the creation of a totally new type of yarn such as Crimplene made it possible to knit a new easy-care fabric on double jersey machines. The further development of the double jersey machine itself was in turn encouraged by such yarns. There are other technical variables which pull together the machinery and chemical fibre oligopolies. Dyeability and texturing are just two of them, which not only inflect cotton/chemical fibre relationships, but ultimately global oligopolistic power relationships as well. The pace of change has been quickened by technical applications conceived in other industries, though often under the same corporate roof: principally in electronics, aerodynamics and chemical technology.

These cumulative and self-reinforcing innovations are being directed towards three goals: lifting individual unit productivity; trimming labour and raw material costs in particular processes; and enlarging the application of automatic transfers between operations.[4] In short, the capital composition of the industry is shifting dramatically in the direction of greater capital intensity. Breakthroughs of differing significance have sprung both from incremental and more radical innovations away from what may be considered as historically conditioned labour-intensive techniques in the major textile sectors: spinning, weaving, knitting and clothing.

The cumulative effect of these changes on the five relationships which are the subject of this chapter can be summarized as follows. With respect to concentration and fragmentation, the scale of financial and marketing leverage required to survive in the face of these innovations is incompatible with small-scale machinery production. Secondly, unemployment will be increased in two ways: in the liquidation of the more labour-intensive small-scale producers, and in the textile and clothing industries which are the repository of this labour-cutting machinery. In fibre choice (natural versus chemical), the newer technology is overwhelmingly oriented towards chemical fibres, for two reasons: machinery producers often work closely with chemical fibre corporations; and the increasingly high operating speeds of knitting and weaving machines are incompatible with natural fibres. In the realm of fabric formation, technical innovations have pushed knitting speeds far beyond those of weaving, with repercussions on intra-oligopoly rivalries. Finally, technological imperatives are hastening the polarity between DCE machinery producers and all but four UCE producers (who are themselves dominated through subsidiaries and licenses of the oligopoly).

DCE dominance is clearly spelled out in the accompanying table, where West Germany and Switzerland together encompass two-fifths of world exports (see Table 9.1). Among CPEs, Czechoslovakia has emerged as the clear leader, with around 5 per cent of global exports in both textile and sewing machinery. Although marginalized as producers, UCEs remain vital as machinery buyers, with annual purchases of more than $2 billion, representing over a third of world exports.

Table 9.1
World Textile and Sewing Machinery Exports, 1977

	Textile Machinery			Sewing Machinery	
Country	Exports ($ million)	Share of World Exports (%)	Country	Exports ($ million)	Share of World Exports (%)
West Germany	1,444.6	28.0	Japan	360.2	30.3
Switzerland	782.4	15.2	West Germany	304.9	25.7
Japan	501.6	9.7	United States	95.4	8.0
Italy	381.2	7.4	Italy	88.2	7.4
United Kingdom	368.7	7.1	United Kingdom	68.0	5.7
United States	314.8	6.1	Switzerland	64.1	5.4
France	293.6	5.7	Czechoslovakia	57.1	4.8
Czechoslovakia	269.6	5.2	Sweden	37.4	3.2
Belgium-Luxembourg	196.1	3.8	Brazil	21.6	1.8
			South Korea	17.6	1.5
USSR	133.5	2.6	Netherlands	16.8	1.4
Poland	100.9	2.0	France	15.2	1.3
Netherlands	92.4	1.8	Belgium-Luxembourg	9.4	0.8
Spain	75.4	1.5	Spain	6.7	0.6
India (1976)	15.9	0.3	USSR	5.5	0.4
Brazil	6.6	0.1	India (1976)	1.3	0.1
Hong Kong	5.8	0.1	Hong Kong	0.3	0.01
South Korea	4.6	0.1	Others	17.5	1.6
Others	175.3	3.4			
Total	*5,163.0*	*100.0*		*1,187.2*	*100.0*

Source: Computed from data in United Nations, *Bulletin of Statistics on World Trade in Engineering Products, 1977* (New York, 1979).

The battle for market shares has already bloodied certain DCEs to the advantage of others. A striking casualty is the United Kingdom, whose one-third world market share in 1954 was slashed to under a tenth by 1977. Conversely, the strident West German offensive pushed its conquest from one-fifth to three-tenths of world markets over the same time span.

In the four sections that follow, the movement of our five relationships, viewed as interacting historical processes, will be brought out. Beginning with an overview of corporate structures, we move to detailed portrayals of technical innovations in each major textile and clothing process. The causes of the United Kingdom's debacle will then be briefly examined, since it provides an illuminating precedent to all UCEs bent on cracking the world textile machinery market and, by extension, is applicable to all engineering export product lines. The final section charts UCE textile machinery efforts to date, with prospects for the 1980s.

Corporate Structures

As with the chemical fibre giants, a simple inventory of the leading producing countries can be grossly misleading. Transnational corporate structures have penetrated into all areas of the world market — DCEs and UCEs — through their exports, technology transfers, patent and marketing arrangements.

The dominant corporate trait of these transnational textile machinery procedures is that, to an extent comparable to chemical fibre manufacturers and far-greater than textile producers, they are highly concentrated on the national and global level. In Switzerland,[5] for example, machinery production for the three major processing stages is dominated by five giants in spinning, weaving and knitting — Rieter, Saurer, Ruti, Dubied, and Sulzer; in Britain by Platt-Saco-Lowell and Bentley; in the United States by Platt-Saco-Lowell; in Japan by Toyoda, Howa and Nissan (a division of the automobile corporation); in Czechoslovakia by Investa; in Spain by Jumberca; in West Germany by Schubert and Salzer, Sulzer, Zinser, Mayer, Schlafhorst (a subsidiary of Deutsche Babcock), Stoll and Terrot; in France by SACM and ARCT; and in Belgium by Picanol. Clothing machinery's major component, sewing machines, was long dominated by Singer (1979 sales: $2.6 billion) but of late its hegemonic position has been cut down by the Japanese, whose Brother Industries, Janome Sewing Machine, and Ryccar are now the major corporate entities both in domestic and global markets.[6] Singer, whose sewing-machine sales still represent about a half of its aggregate sales, is further faced with the whittling away of its sewing-machine markets by Japanese conglomerate subsidiaries, which have set up operations in low-wage Asian UCEs. Its profitable operations in power tools and aerospace systems are thus financing a corporate sector (sewing) chronically besieged by more powerful assailants in the textile engineering industries, notably through foreign subsidiaries in certain Asian countries. Finally, recent breakthroughs in computerized clothing machinery have been made through the corporate laboratories of other engineering sectors, notably aerospace (e.g. Hughes Aircraft).

In any given sector, only a handful of corporations are dominant: in knitting, for instance, Monarch, Bentley, Mayer and Jumberca. Indeed few if any firms are across the board leaders in machinery for all production phases and all fibres. Their overriding common denominators are: the sheer dimension of their research expenditures, which reaches as much as 15–20 per cent of total sales in certain cases; close links to engineering industries, of which they are often integral components; export levels of more than three-fourths of total output; extensive overseas affiliates and marketing networks shaped over the last 100 years; specialization on a range of models; and massive financial leverage through suppliers' credits.[7] The textile machinery oligopoly is best perceived in the corporations that dominate each of the major sectors (see Table 9.2).

Table 9.2
World's Leading Textile Machinery Corporations[1]

Spinning	*Weaving*	*Knitting*	*The Big Nine*
Rieter (Switzerland)	Sulzer (Switzerland)	Mayer Albstadt	Sulzer
Schubert u. Salzer	Saurer (Switzerland)	(West Germany)	Investa
(West Germany)	Ruti (Switzerland)	Mayer Obertshausen	Platt-Saco-Lowell
Zinser (West	Picanol (Belgium)	(West Germany)	SACM
Germany)	Nissan (Japan)	Monarch (Japan)	Nissan
Schlafhorst (West	Investa	Jumberca	Toyoda
Germany)	Dornier (West	Stoll (West Germany)	Bentley
Platt-Saco-Lowell	Germany)	Bentley (UK)	Schlafhorst
(UK/USA)	SACM	Terrot (West	ARCT
Toyoda (Japan)	Somet (Italy)	Germany)	
Howa (Japan)	Jumberca (Spain)	Dubied (Switzerland)	
SACM (France)		Sulzer Morat (West	
Investa		Germany)	
(Czechoslovakia)		Fuhuhara (Japan)	

1. Rankings based on estimated market shares.

Source: Trade sources.

By the mid 1970s there was an estimated world total of 3.4 million conventional looms, as against 200,000 shuttleless machines, a proportion that will radically shift in the early 1980s with shuttleless machines nes expected to appropriate half of world output. Already just one corporation, Sulzer, has staked out around one-fifth of the global market for shuttleless looms, either directly or through licences. In certain lines, such as wool weaving, Sulzer machines have attained a hegemonic position, and in West Germany, about two-thirds of the annual output from shuttleless looms comes from Sulzer machines.[8] Although the dominance in weaving machinery is attributed to the Ruti/Saurer/Sulzer triumvirate, Swiss corporate capitalism boasts another world leader in a more specialized niche: the Maschinenfabrik Jacob Muller AG of Frick,[9] with its high-speed narrow-fabric loom.

This highly specialized expertise, so characteristic of Swiss capitalism as a whole, owes much to its interactions with the textile industry. 'Without the help and very close collaboration of the domestic manufacturers', comments one Swiss textile machinery spokesman, 'we would find it extremely difficult, if not impossible, to maintain our lead in world markets. We are able to work with virtually anyone and everyone in the trade and not only that, but we get immediate and constant feedback when we are attempting to perfect or introduce something new.'[10] This comment dramatizes the warning of a British textile analyst concerning the symbiotic decline of these two industries in Britain, one of Switzerland's major competitors: 'There is a danger that Britain, unless it can develop a stronger textile and textile machinery industry, could by the end of the century find itself without either.'[11]

In West Germany, the equally highly concentrated textile machinery ery industry (as distinct from the textile industry) exhibits many of the traits of Swiss industry, notably its heavy export orientation (over 85 per cent of total output) and its mode of specialization. The 'Karl Mayer Textilmaschin-enfabrik' claims to have appropriated 85 per cent of the world market for tricot and Raschel knitting machines — again a case of dominance in a limited and highly specialized range of machinery. The Schlafhorst corporation, a subsidiary of one of Europe's biggest industrial concerns and a textile machinery producer for over a century, is also a specialized producer of warping machinery and various automatic and non-automatic winders. It illustrates the prevalence within the powerful group of machinery producers of high specialization geared to the international market.

The Czech textile machinery industry is unique not only as an example of a CPE cracking the world market, but as a pre-eminent innovator in three important technologies: open-ended spinning, air-jet and water-jet weaving, and multi-shed weaving. Although the Czech textile machinery industry — like that of other leading producers — is over one hundred years old, the basic innovations currently underpinning it are outgrowths of more than £100 million pumped into research and development since the late 1950s. The organizational anatomy behind the spinning breakthroughs was depicted by the Director of the Cotton Industry Research Institute (CIRI) at Usti nad Orlici:

> A considerable contribution to success was close co-operation with research institutes of other industrial branches. Likewise, co-operation with the future builder of the machine, the Kovoslav National Corporation, and above all, a rapid removal of mistakes and overcoming of difficulties in the development phase, which necessarily accompany any big work, helped considerably to cut down the realization period. Primarily, however, the extraordinary interest and financial support provided by the state authorities . . . helped most to speed up the reconstruction, re-equipment and extension of the Institute, which now employs about 400 workers.[12]

These technical innovations have certainly been spurred on by membership in CMEA, which has delegated to Czechoslovakia since the fifties the job of servicing a market of tens of millions. Long-term planning, partnered by long-term reciprocal delivery contracts, has buttressed such colossal investments in research and plant outlays. Investa pioneered open-ended spinning in 1967, to become the leader with about 70 per cent of world open-ended spinning capacity, either through direct exports or licensing agreements.[13] Czech licences for weaving machines have also been granted to Enshu, Nissan and Toyo Menka in Japan, Draper and Crompton and Knowles in the United States, and Mayer in the Federal Republic of Germany. By 1980, this rapidly burgeoning industry plans to export a full 90 per cent of its output, up from 75 per cent in the mid 1970s.[14]

The New Prometheus: Textile Technology

Clothing technology in the 1980s stands poised on the threshold of unprecedented revolutionary breakthroughs; and textile machinery to a slightly lesser measure can also be expected to chalk up impressive technical strides that will further modify the chemical and natural fibre relationship — to the detriment of the latter. Certain major technical milestones, ranging from modifications of conventional machinery to a radical conceptualization of technology have markedly affected productivity (see Table 9.3). Lower unit manpower requirements, particularly for semi-skilled and unskilled workers, has been the cumulative upshot of these developments.[15]

Spinning
Striking developments for processing staple fibres into yarns have been achieved in manpower cutbacks related to higher machine productivity. Machines have been engineered to higher technical specifications to satisfy demands for higher product quality, and to boost operational speeds. Open-ended spinning (or OE spinning) is undoubtedly its most revolutionary expression, subsuming in one process what conventional spinning accomplishes in three.

From the Napoleonic era until 1970, mule and ring spinning techniques dominated the industry. It took approximately half a century for ring spinning to assert its primacy over mule spinning, and by 1970, after a spurt of rapid productivity growth, this technique had reached the summit of its innovational potential (see Table 9.4).

OE spinning is mushrooming at a pace that suggests it will oust ring spinning in a much shorter time than that required for the superseding of the mule: perhaps as early as 1990 in DCEs, CPEs and export oriented UCEs. It differs basically from ring spinning in that it employs a rotor instead of spindles, with speeds varying from 23,000 — 100,000 rpm,[16] three to six times faster than ring spinning. It also does not require corresponding additions to the labour force, and it reduces floor space and energy requirements. Indeed, in a recent sale of OE rotors by Toyo Menka Kaisha to China,

it was revealed that they would save 40 per cent of manpower over ring
spinning.[17] In addition, some of its major technical advantages include
superior dyeing and printing performance, fewer yarn faults, and ability to
use lower grades and shorter fibre staple lengths. OE machines are the
exclusive production preserve of sixteen corporations of unequal size and
marketing power: three from the CPEs, two from Japan, one from the USA,
and the remainder from Western Europe.

These innovations have altered inter-fibre proportions in several ways,
since any major technical innovation has widespread repercussions on raw
materials procurement policies. At present, chemical corporations are engineering new fibres specifically to withstand increases in yarn take-up speed in
OE systems. In juxtaposition to chemical fibres, attempts to engineer
specific cotton properties (via genetic engineering and plant breeding
programmes) to withstand higher speeds and heat have already encountered
several deterrents, both financial and physical.[18]

In contrast to natural fibres, higher spinning speeds have enhanced the
textile and mechanical properties of the filaments. Already spinning tests
on polyester with take-up speeds of up to approximately 7,500 metres/
minute have been reported. Moreover, super-high-speed spinning lends itself
to the production of filament with vastly superior dyeability properties.
Over the last decade, the spinning of polyester (the major synthetic fibre)
has been conditioned by the colossal strides in texturizing (the process
which adds bulk to chemical fibre yarns) speeds. A pioneer in this field has
been the Coats Paton subsidiary, John Heathcoat, which after eight years
of research developed a new process which raises the texturizing speed from
600 metres per minute to around 5,000. ICI, Hoechst, and other chemical
giants have likewise begun to encroach on this traditional preserve of the
textile industry. Productivity gains in this domain will also adversely affect
cotton yarn through lower chemical fibre production costs.

Weaving

Since classical antiquity the basic principles of weaving have not altered
appreciably.[19] Increased loom widths (or multi-width weaving), larger warp
and weft packages, higher operating speeds, a vast diversity of weft insertion
systems, and multi-shift weaving have all been catalysts in boosting unit
output. Machine designs and operating capability — more than any other
factor — have been dictated by mechanisms of weft insertion.[20] Speed of
weft insertion first experienced large leaps during the industrial revolution of
the 18th Century,[21] and more recently, during the last thirty years.

Four phases of innovation are discernible over the last three decades:
first, the rapier loom, which dispensed with a shuttle carrying its own yarn
supply and replaced it with a weft carrier that transmitted only one pick
length at a time from a stationary supply at the side of the loom. This first
species of shuttleless loom operated at slightly higher speeds than most recent
shuttle looms. In the 1930s, Sulzer commenced development of the projectile loom, which was not marketed until the 1950s. Higher speeds were

achieved by propelling through the warp a metal projectile that gripped pre-measured lengths of weft yarn at each end of the weaving shed. From this original prototype, over 30 models have now been bred.

Table 9.3
Major Technology Changes in the Textile Industry since 1960

Technology	Description and Impact
Texturizing	Heat sets a crimp in synthetic fibre to provide bulk, an additional process on specialized machines. Stimulated growth of knitting sector.
Direct-feed carding	Eliminates picking process and associated manpower.
Open-end spinning	Integrates roving, spinning, and winding. Can produce 2 or more times the output of the conventional spindle.
Spinning attachments	Automatic doffing (unloading) machines reduce unit requirements for doffer operators. Automatic devices for piecing (tying) broken yarn reduce unit requirements for spinners.
Winding attachments and integration	Automatic creeling (loading) of machines; automatic tying-in of yarn ends. Reduces unit requirements for operators. Integration of filling winding with weaving. Eliminates separate process and associated handling.
Shuttleless looms	Operate at faster speeds and require fewer auxiliary operations than shuttle looms. Can produce about 50 per cent more cloth than the average shuttle loom per hour.
New knitting machines	New machines operate at faster speeds and are more automated. Electronic patternmaking devices reduce pre-knit time. Reduce unit labour requirements and permit greater flexibility in design change.
Continuous computerized finishing	Integrates dyeing and finishing techniques and incorporates computerized instrumentation. Reduces unit labour costs and improves quality.

Source: United States Department of Labour, *Technological Changes and Manpower Trends in Six Industries,* Bureau of Labour Statistics, Bulletin 1817 (Washington, DC, 1974).

Table 9.4
Production Increases through Technological Advances in Spinning
(1813 = 100)

	Pounds per Spindle Hour	Index
1813	.002	100
1850	.009	450
1900	.017	850
1920	.018	900
1940	.019	950
1950	.023	1150
1960	.026	1300
1965	.033	1650
1970	.065	3250

Source: Saco-Lowell Division of Maremont Corporation, Greenville, South Carolina.

By the mid 1950s Czech technology had introduced the first water- and air-jet looms, where weft yarn is transmitted across the weaving shed by air or water pulsed from a nozzle. The processes and high velocities attained by these machines have far-reaching implications on inter-fibre proportions. Not only are natural fibres ill-adapted to the tensile requirement of high speeds, but they cannot be employed in water-jet looms, which disintegrate them.

These first three innovational stages are single-phase weaving systems (in which only a single weft insertion is made at a time). Multi-phase weaving,[22] the latest stage, is once again revolutionizing speeds, inasmuch as the performance limit of the single phase system is about 1,700 metres per minute.[23] While multi-phase machines are making brisk inroads in bridging the productivity gap between weaving and knitting, the inhibiting element still remains the inability of fibres (particularly natural fibres) to withstand the stresses and strains of these machines.[24]

World imports of weaving machinery (Table 9.5), now topping 65,000 looms, almost doubled between 1978 and 1979, more than half of aggregate imports going to Asia and Oceania. A no less vital facet of the trading pattern is the unequal distribution between the two major categories of looms. Higher productivity shuttleless looms are overwhelmingly geared to the processes used in developed countries. The upshot of this divergent movement will further help to enlarge the productivity gap between developed and developing countries.

Notwithstanding hundred-fold productivity increases since the first mechanical loom, the fastest shuttleless loom produces only one-eight the fabric volume in a given time as a modern circular weft knitting machine.[25] Thus, weaving's four-fifths share of textiles is rapidly being axed by knitting.

Table 9.5
World Imports of Weaving Machinery, 1979

	Total No. of Looms	Distribution (%)		Regional Distribution of Looms (%)		
		Shuttle	Shuttle-less	Shuttle	Shuttle-less	Total
Asia and Oceania	34,183	62.0	38.0	69.6	37.6	52.6
EEC	7,648	8.5	91.5	2.1	20.2	11.8
Other Europe[1]	7,185	17.1	82.9	4.0	17.2	11.0
North America	6,376	27.6	72.4	5.8	13.3	9.8
South America	4,732	62.8	37.2	9.8	5.1	7.3
Africa	3,285	75.1	24.9	8.1	2.4	5.0
EFTA	1,625	11.4	88.6	0.6	4.2	2.5
Total	*65,034*	*46.8*	*53.2*	*100.0*	*100.0*	*100.0*

1. Includes Greece, Turkey, Spain, and the Centrally Planned Economies.

Source: Computed from data in IFCATI, *International Textile Machinery Statistics,* Vol. 1, 1979.

Knitting

Whereas the spectacular advances in weaving straddle a period of thirty to forty years, those in knitting have taken place in a shorter time, commencing in the mid-1960s with the boom in doubleknit machines.[26] Between 1972 and 1977, warp-knitting machine speeds shot up from 1,000 courses per minute to about 1,700; speeds of Raschel knitting machines doubled from 550 to 1,000 courses per minute.[27] Knitting has a higher productivity than weaving for two reasons. First, the distance yarn travels in weaving is far greater than in knitting. In the latter, the latch needle moves with a stroke of only 15–20 mm, whereas in the former warp and weft are separated spatially by about 100mm. Second, most weaving machines operate only on the basis of one cycle at a time, while in knitting many cycles occur simultaneously. Knitting has certain technical advantages as well. It employs only one set of yarns, as against two in weaving. As one textile engineer pointed out, 'yarns are not subjected to high strain during any part of the knitting cycle, making yarn breakage rare. In weaving machines, however, the yarns are subjected to continuous rubbing during shedding and high strain during weft yarn "beat-up" and the resulting fault rate has been a major constraint on weaving productivity.'[28] Knitting machines, again far better than looms, can incorporate greater design flexibility through computer control, for high fashion items. Finally, knitting machine designers and producers have made extensive use of the highly regular continuous filament chemical fibres developed since World War II. A graphic illustration of this was the technical advances in interlock knitting in the late 1940s that launched acrylic as a major clothing fibre. Fibre makers have also been active in creating fibre sub-species, specifically engineered to the fault-free demands of the knitting industry. The knitting revolution is thus a major ingredient in chemical fibres' success.

The latest innovation, the 'presser foot', opens the door for a qualitative change in the entire textile industry. Developed by Courtaulds over thirteen years of research, the machine can produce partially or completely finished garments rather than simply knitted fabric.[29] The Swiss firm Dubied was the first to produce the presser foot under a Courtaulds licence, but now the British fibre giant has sold exclusive rights for the machine (in Japan) to Mitsui. This one innovation represents a major step in blurring the division between textiles and clothing, and its impact on labour-intensive clothing shops will prove devastating.

Clothing

The colossal strides towards comprehensive automation in spinning, weaving and knitting partially explain DCEs' global market dominance in these sectors. Up to the end of the 1960s, the clothing industry failed to undergo any comparable technical change, and this in turn explains the UCEs' relatively high global market shares in this specific manufacturing sector and no other. Conversely, this technological backwater has been a deterrent — thus far — to the retention — let alone recovery — of their market shares by the DCEs.

In considering advances in the clothing industry, it should be borne in mind that its products are relatively low-value consumer products, endowed — given present technology — with an extraordinarily high labour content. Since the innovation of the sewing machine in the late 19th Century,[30] hardly any significant advances have been made in the clothing industry up to the 1970s. Marking, pattern-cutting, ironing, inspection, labelling and packing are still mainly manual processes. And innovations in sewing, the major machinery input to the industry, have traditionally been geared towards higher operating speeds.

The industry is now making far-reaching innovations, however, in both machinery and plant reorganization. In addition to the application of lasers to the laying and cutting field, developments have already been triggered in computer applications to grading, marking and cutting.[31] Water-jet cutting, a technology tested successfully for leather cutting in the footwear industry, is now being applied to cloth. Also, improved die-cutting and laser-beam cutting methods are major innovations achieving improved accuracy and other cost advantages. Mass production cutting, however, is required to offset the high capital costs of these processes and therefore diffusion is confined to large-scale plants. In sewing, the main emphasis is on workplace engineering and automatic transfer lines carrying out complex specialized operations. Research is being undertaken to replace sewing altogether with textile bonding agents and meltable interlining fabrics. A recent device pioneered by Cluett Peabody, one of the 'big clothing ten' in the United States, can pick up a piece of fabric and position it for sewing, a break-through vital to replacing the sewing machine operator. The overall perspective for the immediate decade ahead is equipment of higher capital cost and automation.[32] The cost dimensions involved are seen in the new $500,000 Gerber cutter, the latest in computerized clothes design equipment, whose major users have been the denim giants, such as Blue Bell and the Vanity Fair Corporation.[33] Through such a variety of interlinked technology, the time of shirt making dropped from twenty minutes in the 1930s to twelve minutes at present — and will fall still further in the current decade.

In the context of oligopolistic capitalism and the international division of labour, technical innovations will further trim labour inputs, thereby further blunting the major cost advantage of UCEs. Inevitably, the price of remaining in the global market hinges on their capacity to automate, or more accurately on whether, given the new technology, the transnational corporations will still perceive UCEs as desirable off-shore locations. Ironically, even if the transnational corporations were to shift clothing production back to Europe, North America and Japan, the collapse in DCE clothing industry jobs would still be hastened.

Apart from affecting the competitive capabilities of UCEs and DCEs, the new breed of technology will mostly be confined to the biggest clothing corporations, thereby accentuating the concentration and centralization of capital within an industry that is still fragmented. Table 9.6 indicates some of the major innovations of the industry.

The British Experience

As one of the world's primary textile machinery producers, the UK exports nine-tenths of its output. Its grim losses on the world textile market have been almost matched on the domestic market. While its share of world exports slipped from 19 per cent in 1963 to 13 per cent in 1970, and to around 10 per cent in 1974–6, its domestic share went from 52 per cent in 1970 to 38 per cent in 1975. By mid-1977, output in real terms was one-half, and numbers employed three-fifths, of 1970 levels.[34] This debacle has led many smaller manufacturers to seek higher profits as sales representatives for established European machinery groups. A corollary of the demise of the smaller companies has been the consolidation of three larger groups: Platt-Saco-Lowell, Bentley, and James Mackie. Such ominous market losses provoke questions as to the quantitative and qualitative nature of technical innovations in the British textile machinery industry. Professor Rothwell's findings, which we summarized here, are suggestive and could well be generalized to explain the losses and — by inversion — gains in market shares.[35]

An average of 27 per cent of all British textile corporations' respondents purchased foreign-built machinery because similar British machinery was not available. This response was marked in weaving, knitting and finishing machinery. The most widespread reason (32 per cent) for purchases of foreign-built machinery was superior overall performance and design, and therefore higher levels of operational efficiency. An ancillary reason (13 per cent) was that 'foreign machinery was technically more advanced in design'. In those cases where similar British machinery was on the market, 'at least 62 per cent of the reasons for buying foreign relate to the performance or quality of the machinery; if the category "no suitable UK alternative" is included, this increases to 76 per cent'.[36] Conspicuously, price figures less prominently than quality; or, more accurately, expected differences in operating and maintenance costs, not initial capital cost variations, were perceived as dominant.

Table 9.6
Major Technology Changes in the Clothing Industry in the 1970s

Technology	Description	Diffusion
Automatic contour seamers, profile stitching machines, and numerically controlled sewing machines	Equipment which transports cloth through sewing operations automatically.	Limited to the larger plants. More widespread use is expected with the anticipated growing use of PROMS (Programmable Read Only Memory Units) — mini-memory units which greatly increase equipment flexibility.
Laser cutting	Computer guided laser cutting systems cut fabric at high speeds with high accuracy, reducing material losses and ensuring uniformity.	Used to a very limited degree in cutting men's suits. High capital costs will limit its use to the largest firms.
Numerically controlled cutting devices	Numerical control equipment directs devices through their operations with improved product quality and higher cutting speeds.	Used to a limited degree in larger apparel plants. High capital cost will limit diffusion.
Ultrasonic sewing	High frequency sound wages (ultrasonics) are used to create a frictional bond between layers of thermoplastic cloth. The bond acts as and simulates stitching, though no thread is used. Similar to fusing, except that no adhesive is required.	Use limited to materials with a high synthetic content unless a thermoplastic bonding layer is used. Limited growth is expected.
Electronic computers	Computers are being used by management for sales analysis and forecasting, process inventory, and workflow management. In the production process they are being used in conjunction with numerical control equipment and marker preparation.	More widespread use of computers expected. In 1974, 297 computer installations were reported. The use of computers in pattern grading and marker preparation is expected to continue to grow rapidly.

Source: United States Department of Labour, *Technological Change and its Labour Impact in Five Industries*, Bureau of Labour Statistics, Bulletin 1961, Washington, DC, 1977.

Indubitably, technical change and research perceived by users as reducing average unit operating costs will continue to play a vital role in the export capability of textile machinery. Yet it would be wrong to assume that technological innovations *per se* are a guarantee of cracking the global market.[37] Sales services, punctual delivery dates, meeting users' requirements, comprehensive training courses, and systematic spare parts flow, that is, a comprehensive marketing web, were also mentioned as necessary for entering the world market. No less crucial is the role of finance capital, stressed by the NEDO report: 'The world market for textile machinery is expected to continue to "move south and east" and in these less developed countries orders will not be placed unless long term credit is available. The Sector Working Party considers that it will be difficult, if not impossible, to achieve its export market share objectives unless a way can be found of financing and insuring additional exports to these developing countries.' Such prescriptions apply not merely to the world's major machinery producers, but *a fortiori* to aspiring UCE producers themselves.

The Choices for the UCEs

In view of the circumstances that bedevil the United Kingdom, it may be inferred that UCEs are faced with only two options: producing conventional machinery for domestic, and perhaps other UCE, markets, such as India; or having recourse to foreign capital via transnational machinery affiliates, as in Brazil. In either case, independent research and development capabilities are precluded, or at least peripheralized. Continuing control of textile machinery TNCs over the fledgling UCE industries (South Korea and Hong Kong are the only other UCEs in the field) is the 50/50 joint venture of Britain's Stone-Platt in South Korea.[38] Stone-Platt retains proprietary control over the technology as well as a definitive say in choice of markets.

With an annual production capacity of around Rs. 2,800 million, India's textile engineering industry, non-existent before World War II, is today one of its three largest engineering industries. Output is overwhelmingly domestic -oriented, supplying 85 per cent of the country's textile equipment for integrated cotton mills. Partly due to the industry's fragmentation (450 producers of which ten to fifteen could perhaps be considered as majors[39]) there has been an almost complete absence of coherent research efforts. In consequence, by the mid 1970s machinery still embodied designs of the 1950s and early 1960s. Further, as against the transnational giants, India's textile machinery industry is yet to develop a strong component supplier base and hence relies on in-house production for a large share of its components. This, plus the need to maintain large inventories of raw materials and components as a hedge against interruptions in supply, substantially escalates its working capital requirements,[40] contributing (amongst a wide array of other factors) to the constriction of its global competitive capabilities.

237

A Brazilian textile machinery industry has likewise sprung up to supply conventional spinning, weaving, dyeing and finishing equipment to the domestic market. Its tentative breakthrough onto the world market, however, has been accomplished through large-scale installations of corporate subsidiaries. Among these, the German giant Schubert and Salzer is now producing cards, flyers, and ring spinning machines, France's SACM, looms, SOTEXA and Barmag, texturizing machines.[41]

Foreign corporations have entered Brazil despite its higher production costs. These are 5–20 per cent higher than West Germany, owing in large part to smaller production units, costlier production runs and lower labour productivity.[42] Their overriding goal, however, is to capitalize on lower wage costs within a huge and expanding Latin American market and – at least at present – only peripherally to export. Brazil has also conferred lucrative export incentives in the form of refunds twice the amount of the domestic excise tax.[43] As with other UCEs, prospects for a sustained and independent high technology industry remain remote, and entirely dependent on the strategic policy dictates of transnationals.

For the 1980s, one aspect of the technological changes described in this chapter threatens to ignite one of the most sweeping social, political, and economic transformations since the industrial revolution of the 18th Century: the micro-electronics revolution. Based on the silicon chip used in integrated circuits in computers and other devices, labour-saving cost reductions are being realized in almost every manufacturing and service sector.[44] In the entire gamut of the textile and clothing industries, the increasing application of integrated circuits in computerized processes is well under way in DCEs. While vastly enhancing DCE labour productivity and its cost competitiveness as against lower labour cost UCE imports, its job-displacing potential (in both DCEs and UCEs) threatens to far outstrip new job-generating investment.

In sum, the constant and accentuated revolutionizing of textile technology will provide one of the major strategic elements that will shape the contours of, and sharpen the conflicts within and between, oligopolistic and non-oligopolistic capital. Here we perceive, in yet another textile branch, new directions being imparted to the ongoing economic war now raging within national and international markets.

References

1. United Kingdom Joint Textile Committee, *Trends in Textile Technology* (London, May 1976), p. 3.
2. *The New York Times*, 9 May 1977.
3. West, 'The futures of synthetic fibres . . .'.
4. R. Rothwell, 'Technological change in textile machinery: manpower implications in the user and producer industries'. unpublished paper prepared for the NSF/BMFT Seminar, Geneva, June 6–10, 1977.

5. In the first half of the 1970s, general machinery exports were around 35 per cent of total exports, of which textile machinery exports amounted to 18 per cent.
6. *Financial Times,* 16 November 1977.
7. An example of the role finance capital played is the £17 million contract for Bolivia's largest textile spinning plant. The loan of $23 million provided by Hill Samuel, Midland Bank and Midland and International Banks (at a fixed rate of 7.5 per cent) will enable the Bolivians to import nearly three-quarters of all goods and services required for the entire project − including 90 per cent of the spinning machinery − from the UK. *Financial Times,* 1 November 1977.
8. F. McNeirey, 'Switzerland: some observations on its textile machinery manufacturing industry', *Modern Textiles,* June 1976.
9. It was recently able to consolidate its world position through the annexation of a world-wide customer and marketing service for a range of ribbon weaving machines built by Texnovo of Italy, now joined to the newly set-up Filatex. Its marketing linkages have also been extended to the Federal Republic of Germany.
10. Quoted in *Textile World,* May 1977.
11. *Financial Times,* 10 October 1979.
12. Quoted in R. Rothwell, 'Innovation in textile machinery', *Textile Institute and Industry,* December 1977.
13. R. Rothwell, 'The Role of Technical Change in International Competitiveness: The Case of the Textile Machinery Industry', *Management Decision,* Vol. 5, No. 6 (1977).
14. *Textile Month,* December 1976.
15. A universal feature of these innovations has been the price increases resulting from their growing technical complexity coupled to intensified world inflation. Between 1965 and 1970, textile machinery prices sprouted at an annual compound rate of 4.7 per cent; in the subsequent five years they almost trebled to 13.7 per cent. For more sophisticated machinery lines the rise has been even steeper. A single-shuttle automatic loom, for example, almost quadrupled in price over the last fifteen years. Government regulations on noise and air pollution have imparted a further upward push to costs. See *Textile World,* January 1976; and R. Verret, 'Capital Investment May Lead to Leadership, Mere Survival or Bankruptcy', *IFCATI,* Vol. 16, 1975.
16. The 100,000-rpm machine was developed in Poland and is capable of spinning viscose and synthetics, as well as blends. See *Textile Asia,* January 1978.
17. *Textile Asia,* June 1979.
18. A shift from long staple cotton to shorter staples typifies the direction of change, since the latter are better adapted to fast spinning velocities.
19. Woven cloth is comprised of two sets of interlacing yarns running at right angles to each other. Those yarns that run lengthwise are known as the warp; those that run across are the weft. Weaving consists of three steps: shedding, which is the separation of alternate strands of the warp; weft insertion − the transmission of single weft threads (picks) through the warp; and, beating, where the weft pick is pushed by a comb into the previously made fabric. For a more elaborate commentary on

these processes, see R. Gray, 'From silks to sack-cloth on a puff of air', *New Scientist,* 16 June 1977.

20. See L.P. Miles, 'Benefits from process advances', *Ciba-Geigy Review,* Vol. 1, 1975.
21. The shift from handlooms to mechanical looms led to a five-fold jump in productivity. Cf. Paul Mantoux, *The Industrial Revolution in the Eighteenth Century* (London, 1964), originally a state doctoral dissertation for the University of Paris, 1906.
22. It involves propelling continuous waves of picks across the machine so that at any one moment there are several picks at different stages of insertion.
23. Sulzer, *Weaving Machine Bulletin,* No. 47, 1977, p. 5.
24. For example, a US mill may be running its 600 picks-per-minute (ppm) capacity looms at only 350 ppm, owing to broken filaments, fuzz balls and denier variations at the higher speeds. See *Textile World,* May 1976.
25. Gray, 'From Silks to Sackcloth. . .'.
26. By the early 1970s, doubleknit accounted for more than half the fabric in men's and women's apparel. See *Business Week,* 27 October 1973.
27. These machines make lace, foundation garment fabric, and other patterned goods. See *The New York Times,* 9 May 1977.
28. Gray, 'From Silks to Sackcloth . . .'.
29. *Financial Times,* 26 April 1979.
30. Chandler, *The Visible Hand.*
31. One manifestation of this development is the slide in the cost of the latest mini-computers, allied to a parallel boost in their power from developments that have steadily progressed over the last three decades. This has influenced the technology of using data bases for management control purposes. Cf. P.M. Steele, 'Computerized clothing', *Textile Asia,* January 1978.
32. NEDO, Joint Textile Committee, *Trends in Textile Technology* (London, 1976).
33. *Business Week,* 29 October 1979.
34. NEDO, *Report to the National Economic Development Council,* Textile Machinery MLH No. 335, February 1978.
35. R. Rothwell, 'Users' and Producers' Perceptions of the Relative Importance of Various Textile Machinery Characteristics', *Textile Institute and Industry,* July 1977. The findings were based on answers derived from 107 textile manufacturers.
36. *Ibid.*
37. *Ibid.*
38. *Financial Times,* 6 July 1979.
39. According to *The World Bank Textile Report on India,* twenty firms accounted for 90 per cent of the industry's output. Twenty-five to thirty per cent of output was internationally competitive in quality and price, all from these twenty firms.
40. *The World Bank Textile Report on India,* quoted in *Textile Asia.*
41. The first machine for processing synthetic fibres built in a developing country.
42. ICME/CONDOR Consultants, *Study on the Possibilities of Manufacturing Textile Machinery in Mexico* (UNIDO, Vienna, March

1975), p. 83.

43. *Ibid.*, p. 78.

44. According to one estimate, the impact of micro-electronics on the expanding French banking system will be that employment will plummet by almost a third in the course of the 1980s. See Ward More-house, 'Micro Electronics: Chips with Everything', *Development Forum,* United Nations, August–September 1979.

10. The 1980s: Reordering the Debate

The 1980s marks the era of permanent and irreversible social, political and economic crises ushered in by the internationalization of conglomerate capital. The unrelenting push of global recessionary forces unleashed in the 1970s epitomized by rampant inflation, mass unemployment, unprecedented levels of indebtedness, currency and trade wars will continue to exercise an unequal impact both within and between UCEs and DCEs.

The interlaced commodity sectors that we have analysed illustrate some of the complex antagonistic relationships now tearing at the vitals of international economic relations. Productivity gaps even between certain DCEs are one of the visible manifestations of the current economic war being waged at increasingly intense levels nationally and globally. Despite an overall deceleration in DCE productivity growth between the periods 1963–73 and 1973–79, differentials between countries have become larger. For the United States and Japan the differential in the first period was 1:4; in the second it widens to 1:34.

Table 10.1
Annual Growth in GNP per Employed Worker in Major Industrial Countries, 1963–79 (% change per annum)

	1963–73	1973–79
Japan	8.7	3.4
West Germany	4.6	3.2
France	4.6	2.7
Italy	5.4	1.6
Canada	2.4	0.4
UK	3.0	0.3
USA	1.9	0.1

Source: *Economic Report of the President,* transmitted to Congress, Washington, DC, 1980, p. 85.

The bulk of manufacturing exports emanating from the UCEs is produced and marketed by transnational corporations. While US manufacturing exports between 1960 and 1976 — a period that witnessed the swift ascendancy of the internationalization of conglomerate capitalism — rose from $12.3 billion to $76.6 billion, sales of US TNC foreign affiliates leaped from $23.6 to $212.8 billion; that is, the ratio of foreign sales to US exports of these firms moved from 2:1 in 1960 to 3:1 in 1976.[1] The conglomerate battles for bigger shares of the global market are also being fought, in many cases using UCEs as trojan horses. 'The Maruzen Sewing Machine Co. of Osaka', notes *The Japan Economic Journal* (13 May 1980) 'will launch a sales drive in Italy, using its subsidiary in Taiwan ... Italy now bans virtually all imports of household sewing machines from Japan — a fact which compels the Osaka company to avail itself of its Taiwanese unit for indirect sales on the Italian market.' In the 1970s these production and marketing strategies of transnationals became widespread, covering a wide spectrum of sectors and commodities. Divergences of transnational production and marketing practices stem from the respective political and economic weight assigned to regional 'profit centres' (to use the current designation of the transnational accounting establishment) in core and peripheral countries.

In such an embattled arena, where almost the entire production and marketing complex is dominated by transnational conglomerate power, misleading conceptualizations such as 'market access', 'favourable (or unfavourable) terms of trade', 'fair and remunerative prices to the producers', lose much of their coherence as rigorous categories of analysis.

Although the word 'crisis' permeates this book, a word of caution is called for, as the question arises of crisis for whom, as well as the sectoral and corporate magnitude of the crisis. It is at once apparent from the annual returns of the top 500-odd transnational corporations (those that have already annexed more than half of all international trade) that they have by no means been uniformly affected by the buffetings of the global economic crisis. Five of the top eight US corporations in 1980 were petroleum conglomerates with combined sales of $281 billion in that year.

Uneven development, which historically remains an inherent feature of capitalist development, has been quickened during the relatively short history of the transnational conglomerate. Moreover, the vast current account surpluses generated by the OPEC oligarchy ($115 billion in 1979) in conjunction with the petroleum majors are overwhelmingly being tapped by the financial markets of the developed capitalist countries. The sheer size of these transfers, which are unprecedented in the annals of economic history, illustrate the intricate meshing (involving at once an antagonistic and complementary relationship) of the OPEC oligarchy and the transnationals. These vast surpluses further widen the rift and intensify the antagonisms between the UCEs themselves, as well as between the latter and the DCEs.

This book gives no credence to the puerile belief that there will be a return to 'the normalcy of the 1950s', however such 'normalcy' may be construed. Rather its findings illuminate the sharpening of the crisis of the 1980s, which will speed up two forces inherent in the capital accumulation process: the elimination of small- and medium-scale enterprises (in which the liquidity problem will continue to play a pivotal role);[2] and a speed-up of the conglomerate thrusts of the transnationals. In this respect, the chemical, textile and apparel industries are the proverbial drops of water that provide a clue to the chemical composition of the sea. In the absence of counter-vailing measures, deployment of such massive aggregations of conglomerate power points to further intensified corporate annexationism and economic conflict which, in its own specific way, could be portrayed as a new inter-national economic order, albeit a perversely distorted one.

Global capitalism is now far removed from the 'representative firm' model of Marshallian analysis, which operates within atomistically competitive structures where market power is diffused, and where producers sell at an externally and objectively determined price with price equilibrium attained when marginal cost and marginal revenue are equal. That was an idealized competitive model purporting to explain what should have been happening theoretically but was not happening historically. On the contrary, the giant firm in concentrated industries is faced with a different set of constraints and other patterns of pricing and profit decisions. As has been demonstrated throughout this work, transnational oligopolistic and conglomerate structures target prices and profit rates on the basis of several factors: profit positions of similar corporate structures, market power, the presence or lack of a price leader, and so on.

The upsurge of the conglomerate, particularly since its internationalization, has had other impacts. In the formulation of Wachtel and Adelsheim,

> In the first place the importance of conglomerates does not show up in the statistics on economic concentration. The expansion of these con-glomerates could explain why industries classified in the low or medium concentration sectors began, in the 1960s, to take on more of the mark-up pricing posture of the sector of high concentration. Take Hostess Bakery, for example. Because it is part of ITT, it has access to the pricing ability, managerial talent, capital markets and advertising resources of a company in a very concentrated industry. However, the data make Hostess appear as a company in a sector of low or medium concentration. Despite that classification, its actual price markup behaviour will be like that of a highly concentrated industry. Thus, the data in the 1960s which reveal more perverse behaviour in the sectors of low and medium concentration can be explained in part by the behaviour of subsidiaries that took on the pricing characteristics of their conglomerate parents.
>
> A second part of this argument is the leverage that conglomerates can exercise in the market by using different price policies in different sectors according to an overall market strategy to maximize their economic power. They might, for example, price like an oligopoly in a sector of low or medium concentration where they have newly acquired economic power and use their superior marketing and distributional

systems to sidestep competition; at the same time they might set prices more like a quasi-competitive industry in a sector of higher concentration in order to undercut oligopolistic competitors. The conglomerate, in short, need not necessarily price like an oligopolist only in the sector of high concentration. It can realize its market power by pricing in that fashion in sectors that are statistically classified as of low or medium concentration. The result is manifested in the increased inflationary bias of the economy in general as indicated by the increasingly perverse pricing behaviour of the sectors of low and medium concentration in the 1960s.[3]

The impact of such pricing policies adopted by oligopolistic transnationals, and particularly their conglomerate extensions, is by no means uniform in time and space. Within this theoretical and empirical framework we have highlighted certain major facets of contemporary capitalism refracted through the prism of selected commodities. Our study, following the vertical off-shoots of the production and distribution of cotton and other fibres down through their end-uses, embraces eight sectors (cotton, the cotton trade, petrochemicals, chemical fibres, textiles, apparel, wholesaling and retailing, and textile machinery) at very different stages of concentration. The inescapable conclusion in each sector is that mergers, acquisitions and concentration are moving apace and the boundaries between sectors are rapidly blurring.

In view of these developments, we have reforged a framework for analysing the global economy and hence have reordered the debate based on the major categories of this work, beginning with cotton Asey.

Since the 1950s the debate on cotton's prospects and changing fibre proportions reflects the larger debate on all natural commodities. The relative shrinkage of some of these commodities on the global market has traditionally been explained in the context of the two battering rams of cheap synthetics and declining UCE terms of trade. In this explanation, the political economy of corporate power gives way to the spindly constructs of neoclassical general equilibrium theory. Power relations have been shrouded in the price fetishism and quantitative analysis of formal mathematical techniques in which the international social relations of capitalist power, dependence and marginalization have been deliberately obscured by the creation of models that give wrong answers to trivial questions.[4]

The evolution of power configurations in UCEs is glimpsed in the movement toward land consolidation by landed oligarchies in Guatemala and the late Somoza's Nicaragua. In the all-too-familiar case of Brazil, a land stricken by chronic malnutrition, where most export crops are the preserve of *latifundistas* and transnational corporations, *The New York Times* notes that the Brazilian government 'has favoured agribusiness with its subsidy and credit provision program, bringing rapid improvements to productivity, but leaving unattended long-range social problems posed by the continuing movement of small farmers to the overcrowded cities'.[5] Brazil's farm priorities in

descending order are export crops, crops yielding alcohol for energy and
food crops for domestic consumption. Traditional analyses suggesting that
'the government', which is the crystallization of ruling class interests, should
be 'concerned' with the existence of lower income groups are virtually plead-
ing with the tiger to become a vegetarian. In effect, 'the continuing
movement of small farmers' stems basically from the expropriation and at
times forcible eviction of small-scale producers in the interests of foreign and
domestic ruling classes, who in turn are dovetailed into the state and military
bureaucracies.

In the trade-off between food and export crops (cotton being our central
focus) the choice in most UCEs is clear. The scandalous neglect of domestic
food production in the UCEs is by no means fortuitous. On the modest
assumption (very modest in view of rising populations and cost run-ups of
farm inputs) that annual food import growth will continue at the same rate
as between 1960 and 1977, the UCE food bill can be expected to exceed
$58 billion by 1985. The sheer magnitude of this sum must be seen in relation
to the outstanding UCE debt (including short-term and IMF lending) which
soared from $80 billion in 1972 to $330 billion in 1979, and is forecast to
shoot up still further to $440 billion in 1981. In addition, their current
account deficits are forecast to almost double between 1978 and 1981,
rising from $36 billion to $70 billion.[6]

Table 10.2
Food and Cereal Imports of UCEs[1] ($ million)

	1960	*1977*	*Projected 1985*
Food	5,090	25,230	58,143
Cereals			
UCEs	1,940	9,105	19,517
OPEC	307	3,403	11,156

1. Excluding the socialist underdeveloped countries.

Source: Computed from United Nations data.

The 1980s will testify whether the UCE oligarchies are capable of sustaining, let alone increasing, the wretchedly low *per capita* food and cereal
consumption of their subjects. Present evidence points tragically to the
opposite. But of one thing we can be sure: no matter whether millions die
of famine or are afflicted by endemic malnutrition, the multi-commodity
giant trading companies will continue to expand as luxuriantly as they have
done since the Marshall Plan and the advent of the US PL 480 legislation.

While there certainly is a playoff between food and cotton, so there
is between agriculture and armaments; as far as the oligarchies are concerned,

the choice is just as clear. In 1960, UCE arms outlays stood at $14 billion; by the end of the 1970s they had soared to almost $80 billion, a sixfold increase that is bound to escalate in the 1980s in the wake of inter-UCE wars such as that between Iran and Iraq.

Although a great deal has been written in recent years to demonstrate the gains of price stabilization to the UCEs via commodity agreements, there are few signs that such measures would improve the economic well-being of the waged and unwaged labour force in UCE agriculture. In DCEs, cotton farmers are constantly being hit by rising prices due to growing oligopolization in the industries that supply their inputs: fertilizers, pesticides, fuel, etc. Concentration of land holdings in these countries has also been swift. Also obscured in the formal debate over synthetics and terms of trade is the much more germane issue of how cotton economies were imposed on colonial UCEs. Finally, if commodities are to be viewed in their totality (as we argue that they must), the debate must be widened to encompass the forces that control different shares of the cotton retail breakdown. The cotton grower, like most agricultural producers, seldom gains more than 10 per cent of an apparel item's retail price, and sometimes receives as little as 2 per cent.

Cotton Trade
International commodity trade is one of the least understood areas of economics. The traditional emphasis on the doctrine of comparative advantage of commodities has obscured the role of one of the major actors of international trade: the multi-commodity trader. Once again the absence of coherent research in this domain is not an aberration; traders continue to hand out vast sums to conceal their activities and to silence meaningful research in this field.

While a great deal of work is required to dismantle the labyrinths of concealment and chicanery, some modest beginnings have been made in this book in unravelling the extensive intelligence networks of the big traders and their links to the transnational banking structure. Unlike industrial sectors, their oligopolistic stature has granted them unquestioned licence in the realm of price manipulation (as opposed to administered prices or price leadership). Facing this oligopoly and their manipulated prices, UCE governments and peasants, with their meagre warehousing and intelligence capabilities, are in a position of almost total subordination. Future research in this area must be centred on the techniques of manipulation, as well as finding out precisely how manipulated futures operations affect prices of the traded commodity in all countries.

Oil and Chemicals
An understanding of the immense power, as well as corrupt accounting and pricing practices, of the oil oligopoly was greatly advanced in the 1960s and 1970s. Combined with the increasingly conglomerate chemical oligopoly (perhaps the most openly cartelized industry in the world), the oil companies largely control the global petrochemical market and most of their members

are already well diversified in natural resource and energy fields. Our portrayal of just one manifestation of chemical corporate power – chemical fibres – attempts to demonstrate the many and varied strategies that corporate oligopolies deploy to create and annex new markets. Through research, advertising, brand names, transfer pricing, blending and other devices of economic war, corporations have now extended their putput tentacles over Eastern Europe, China, the Middle East, and otherf UCEs. In the general conjuncture of global crisis, their over-expansion has proved lethal to many small producers and creates prospects of an indefinite glut on the petrochemical and chemical end-use markets.

Our most crucial finding in this sector was the increasingly enmeshed networks between oligopolies (in the case of chemical fibres, with textile and textile machinery corporations) buttressed by state support in the form of subsidiaries, tariffs, and cartel formations. The oil and chemical corporations have further fanned the global crisis by their inflationary oligopolistic pricing practices.

Textiles and Clothing

The textile industry is already past the first stages of oligopoly. The clothing industry, under the pressures of technical change, economic crises and UCE imports, is witnessing the winnowing out of smaller firms and the rapid growth of several large firms (many of them conglomerates) which also foreshadow the emergence of oligopoly. Outside the realm of oligopoly, our study of these two sectors exposes the shallowness of the concept of the so-called 'Third-World' and its industrial strategies. Trade statistics reveal that seven or eight UCEs exercise almost complete control over UCE exports in these sectors, with some minimal competitive pressure from a few other UCEs who process their own cotton. For the remaining one hundred-plus UCEs, there is little prospect of any significant breakthrough into world markets in these or any other industries. Indeed, stratification is more pronounced among UCEs than between DCEs and leading UCEs.

The Immediate Future

The laws of motion of contemporary capitalism can only be grasped by a study of the extending horizons of conglomeration and oligopoly within the changing constellation of the internationalization of capital. The drive to oligopoly, so conspicuously marked in Japan in the 1920s, became universal throughout DCEs and the giant dwarfs in the 1960s and 1970s. The classic utopian model of liberal capitalism made popular by Freidman, Hayek and Samuelson presents capitalism as an immutable social order embodying the highest expressions of economic 'freedom'. But now, incongruous as it may appear, these timeless pieties are even being mouthed by the custodians of transnational enterprises. For the aim of market manipulation and aggrandizement can be aided by representing capitalism as the historical adversary of legal restraint, with monopoly attributed to unwarranted state intrusion into economic life. Such exhortations deliberately abstract from the power of monopoly at successive phases of capitalist development. Between the 16th and 19th centuries, the birth of the modern bourgeoisie both stimulated capital accumulation and, at times, acted as a brake on it. As Maurice Dobb so trenchantly put it more than four decades ago, in the springtime of its growth capitalism assaulted the monopolistic privileges of craft guilds and trading corporations only to turn about subsequently and demand — successfully — mercantilist economic privileges and state regulation of trade to consolidate its class interests.

> In the nineteenth century, again, especially in England the new factory industry raised the banner of unfettered access to markets and to labour supplies, and claimed the right to compete on equal terms with older established rivals, in order to give headroom to its remarkably enhanced productive powers. But, except in the specially favourable circumstances of England as pioneer of the new technology, this enthusiasm for freedom of trade was seldom unqualified; and by the end of the century competition was once again to yield place to monopoly, and free trade to retire before the dawn of what has been termed an era of neo-mercantilism.[7]

Over recent decades the state has continued to underpin bourgeois rule. Indicators of this, such as government expenditure as a share of GNP, are inadequate; whereas the figures for Japan are relatively low, for instance, it is precisely in that country that state machinery and corporate capital reveal their most intricate and sophisticated forms of coordination.

Table 10.3
Government Expenditure as a % of GNP, 1962–78

	1962	*1978*
Sweden	35.0	61.6
Italy	32.4	47.3
West Germany	35.6	46.5
Canada	34.4	46.0
UK	40.5	43.9
France	36.3	43.0
Brazil	12.0	35.0
USA	28.4	32.2
Australia	19.3	24.5
Japan	12.3	16.5

Source: Computed from United Nations data.

Nothing is more glaring at this point than the total inability of bourgeois political and economic theory to differentiate the qualitative changes within capitalism at specific stages of development. State interventionism, to further the interests of the capitalist class as a whose, has varied from one country to another depending on the historical, cultural and geographical specificities in which capitalism evolved in each case. Japan, Switzerland and Germany are perhaps more extreme examples of these forces at work: save at the purely formal level, they have no government policies to limit un-bridled economic concentration. But they are by no means exceptional, for even in such over-ripe capitalist economies as the United States, govern-ment agencies in the last two decades have deftly moved towards consolidat-ing economic concentration. It is at this juncture that we see how huge is the divide between the claims of 'liberal' ideology and the power realities of the state apparatus shaped by corporate design.

Large-scale government interventionism in the foreign trade sector, for example, has vastly accelerated the tempo of economic concentration. Notwithstanding the clamour of liberal ideologists for the 'unfettered operation of market forces', the United States is now spending more than $12 billion yearly on three types of export promotion activities undertaken by various specialized segments of the state apparatus. For general manufactured products, assistance is provided by the Department of Commerce, the Department of State and the Export-Import Bank. Secondly, the foreign military sales programme of the Department of Defense and the Commodity Credit Corporation of the Department of Agriculture provide export promotion programmes, as well as export financing for agricultural commodities. Thirdly, aids are offered by certain government agencies such as the US International Development Office, which promotes, insures, and finances private development projects in UCEs. The Overseas Private Investment Corporation (OPIC) facilitates US private equity and loan investments in UCEs as well. The EXIM (Export-Import) Bank of the United States has underpinned the Foreign Credit Insurance Association (FCIA), a syndicate of fifty leading American insurance firms, which insure exports of manufactures made in the United States.[8] But that is only the foreign trade sector. Much the same can be said of heavy US federal expen-ditures on basic and applied scientific research, which redound overwhelmingly to the big corporations.

The encroachments of oligopolistic capitalism have narrowed the opera-tions of smaller firms to certain sectors traditionally considered labour-intensive. The point that should be emphasized here is that even in the United States, privately held, family-owned businesses still generate almost half of the nation's GNP. They account for 99 per cent of all construction firms and 88 per cent of all sales in that sector; in wholesaling, 94 per cent of all firms and 70 per cent of aggregate sales; in retail service and distribution, 96 per cent of all firms and 72 per cent of sales.[9] But it is precisely this social stratum of capitalists occupying a narrow sectoral domain which is slated for liquidation by oligopolistic capitalism.

The very specific conceptual categories of 'capital'-intensive and 'labour'-intensive, traditionally embodied in the textile and clothing industries respectively, are losing their relevance. We are faced with a world of technology related to the silicon chip and fully automated production lines, and this fact alone throws doubt on the widespread belief, nourished by corporate capital and echoed by certain of its clients within the academic community, that such a new wave of Schumpeterian innovation or 'creative destruction' offers capitalism a new respite.

The micro-electronics revolution is just part of an already diversified range of robotic equipment now being developed by Hitachi, Digital Equipment, International Business Machines (IBM), Texas Instruments, and others.[10] Rapid strides towards the fully automated factory have already been made by such corporate giants as Hitachi, Messerschmidt, Renault, Olivetti and Fiat. With sensory robots Fiat believes that it will be possible to slash its labour force to 10 per cent of its current level, leaving mainly a white-collar cadre of computer technicians. Likewise, General Electric, in perhaps the most ambitious undertaking in its history, is poised to launch a sweeping automation offensive that will eventually replace half of its assembly plant workers with robots, and is even now already in a position to wipe out 2,000 blue-collar workers.

These cataclysmic consequences for the labour force have already been spelt out by a leading organ of capitalist power, *Business Week:*

> With such a payoff in sight, the push to develop robotic sensory systems is worldwide . . . The French auto-maker [Renault] has a robot with a television camera 'eye' that can identify each of 200 parts presented to it at random on a conveyor, then reach out and grasp each part at the proper spot for whatever the next operation may be. Other vision systems that work at 'real time' speed, or almost instantaneously, are starting to make commercial debuts . . .
>
> The next increment toward 'thinking' robots will be to integrate sensory systems with more sophisticated computer software that will enable robots to make limited decisions. Instead of having to look at parts individually, such discretionary robots will pull parts from the jumble of a bin, examine each part for defects, and use or reject a part after analysing any defects observed. If analyses of long-term defect rates indicate the need for corrective action, the robot could also communicate with a counterpart machine overseeing the manufacture of the part.[11]

At the labour base of the micro-revolution, giant corporations hire small numbers of highly-paid DCE scientists to design the components while workers throughout Asian 'free trade zones' assemble them for as little as 10 cents an hour.[12] Job liquidating capacity, however, will quickly outstrip job generating capacity. Nor are these processes by any means confined to manufacturing industries. Siemens, one of the biggest German conglomerates and the second biggest European producer of microchips after Philips, contends that about two-fifths of office employment can be wiped out by automation. In sharp contrast to earlier industrial revolutions, giant corporations from other industries have rapidly oligopolized major segments of this industry. In microchips, for example, five US corporations and the Dutch conglomerate Phillips appropriated over half the world market by 1980; Texas Instruments and IBM garnered over 10 per cent each.[13] Jointly, five US corporations, four Japanese and four European producers already control about three-quarters of the microchip market. At the same time, five of these giant microchip producers are manufacturers of robotic equipment.

Aspects of the ongoing war for supremacy of the global microchip/ robotic world market are demonstrated in the current struggle between the United States and Japan. The present $10–20 billion semi-conductor market is expected to shoot past $100 billion yearly by the century's end. In the 1960s, the United States was the leading designer, innovator and producer of computer hardware and integrated circuits. That lead time — as in other manufacturing sectors — has now been clipped: Japanese transnationals have already annexed about a quarter of the global market. Even within the USA, the inroads of the Japanese transnationals appear nothing less than staggering. Not only have they annexed two-fifths of the US market for a highly specialized microchip (the 16 K RAM, or random access memory chip, capable of handling 16,000 bits of information); but the speed of their advance, and that of the industry as a whole, can be gauged by their work, expected to be completed by 1983, on a super microchip (the 256 K RAM) capable of handling 262,144 bits of information. This amounts to a sixteen-fold increase in power in three years. The implication for economic concentration is that whereas the cost of a semi-conductor plant to produce a state-of-the-art chip was $2 million in the United States at the end of the 1960s, a decade later these costs had catapulted to $50 million. Research expenditure on microelectric technology has already outpaced 15 per cent of industry revenues and is steadily rising, with expenditure-to-sales ratios more than doubling since 1976. These bare numbers in an industry whose sales are still globally small, but whose technological impact is immensely larger, highlight not merely inter-imperialist rivalries, but the growing gap between UCEs and a handful of giant corporations.

Moreover, as our study has stressed, these technical innovations — which will be increasingly enmeshed with others — must be studied in relation to the global market and to a rapidly expanding labour force. The very notion of a 'reserve army of labour' in this context will perhaps lose much of its potency. The following labour force estimates and projections to the year 2000 are ominously suggestive: in 'low-income Asia', to use the classification of the World Bank, the labour force swelled by 125 million between 1950 and 1975; between 1975 and 2000 however, despite a projected slight decline in the participation rate, it is expected to leap further by almost 250 million to around 630 million. Likewise, the projected increments for the last quarter-

century in Sub-Saharan Africa (120 million) and Latin America and the
Caribbean (100 million) must be evaluated not in terms of the blinkered
racism of 'population problems', but in the global framework of power,
proprietary and profit considerations of corporate capital and their domestic
client oligarchies.

As we have emphasized, microelectronics and robotic technologies are
neither independent nor neutral variables in the process of capitalist development. As Professor Ward Morehouse has argued:

> We may end up with a different global economy all right, but not the
> one contemplated . . . But for both groups of countries [developed and
> underdeveloped] the critical problems are economic and political —
> in a word: who controls? who benefits? who pays? It would be naive in
> the extreme to think that the task of distributing the productivity gains
> will be easily or equitably solved as long as control over development
> and use of microelectronic technology is concentrated in a handful of
> powerful corporate and other dominant political and economic
> institutions.[14]

Flexibility is one of the hallmarks of the transnational corporation, which
can easily shift labour and capital resources. A 1980 study revealed that in
the United States alone, 15 million jobs were wiped out by plant shutdowns
between 1969 and 1975.[15] Technological innovation played its role, but it
was by no means the only factor. Other workers were replaced by non-
unionized workers in the southern states, or their plants shifted to lower-
cost labour enclaves in Mexico, Puerto Rico, and throughout the UCEs.
Over 600 'in-bond' US transnational subsidiaries have been set up just over
the Mexican border, where the Mexican state relaxes the usual customs duties
on assembled parts produced by US corporations.[16] Obviously, corporate
policy at the national or global level is neither concerned with nor capable
of coping with the global employment problem — a truth descriptive of all
stages of its development; and one which has become even more wantonly
visible in an age of endemic economic crisis. Its very class position and
profit-maximizing orientation precludes it from embracing a full employment policy. To believe otherwise is to believe in a capitalism minus
capitalists. In 1979, TNC investments of around $70 billion in UCEs created
fewer than 4 million jobs for the 680 million in UCEs who need them.[17]
Increasing numbers of these jobs are located in tax-exempt UCE 'free trade
zones' which have no productive linkage effects to the local economy.
Growing global unemployment and recession are cutting demand growth
everywhere and will thus accelerate the movement toward conglomeration as
corporations attempt to spread producer risks across industries.

The era of conglomerate capitalism has not merely speeded up concentration within specific sectors, but has also meant that firms at the upper
limits of growth within one industry, measured in national and international
market shares, have turned to sustained annexationism in other sectors

as well. Whereas the large conglomerate complex is able to withstand the
batterings of inflation – generated by its own production and marketing
policies – smaller firms are becoming increasingly vulnerable to growing costs
and marketing pressures. This applies with even greater force to the 'independent' export-oriented industries of the UCEs. The transnational oligopolistic
conglomerate has thus become the representative force of contemporary
capitalism, perhaps the ultimate stage in the system's development.

The attempt to resuscitate economic liberalism merely reveals the gap
between illusion and reality. The disintegration of the framework of the
Bretton Woods Agreements was merely the opening sally in the assault on,
and decline of, the dollar. The economic disorder of this market was
recognised with admirable candour by a spokesman of corporate capitalism:
'it has been apparent for some time that our economy was out of control,
our currency in danger, and that the ability of our government to react was
inadequate. Inflation is accelerating . . . various measures have been tried –
dollar support packages, gold sales, wage price guidelines, windfall profit
taxes – but the deterioration has continued.'[18] True enough, but such bourgeois despairs voice only a part of the crisis, for bourgeois thought is incapable of going beyond appearances to the essence of phenomena.

The 'strong medicine' prescribed to halt the crisis is itself indicative of the
forces at work: mass unemployment, cuts in social and educational services
and housing, cutbacks in public services, matched by a senseless arms race,
are just some of the devices used to hold off the onslaughts. The monetarist
and fiscally minded managers of conglomerate capitalism do not need even to
justify the savage stockpiling of human misery, for it is perpetrated not so
much in the name of economic dogma but in terms of 'human rights'. In the
UCEs, the refurbished fiscal and monetarist rationalizations have at least
yielded to open military repression on a mass scale, the most appropriate
institutional technique of conglomerate capitalism in these countries.

Increasingly, the bulk of the underdeveloped capitalist economies are
unable to meet the upsurge in the price of manufactured goods, soaring
interest rates, and petroleum inputs with their traditional raw material and
manufacturing industrial exports. In an atmosphere of mounting protectionism, the crisis has been met by two expedients: cutback in imports and/
or rising levels of indebtedness. The conjunction of petroleum and
manufactured goods imports, higher interest rates and military outlays have
conspired not merely to stoke the fires of inflation higher but also to deepen
the level of unemployment.

Even for the South Koreas, Taiwans, Brazils, Mexicos, and Singapores
which have broken into world markets by purchasing transnational technology, marketing and managers, the twin battering rams of DCE protectionism
and skyrocketing oil prices spell much slower growth rates in the 1980s.

There are no easy ways out of the present dilemma for international
capitalism. Political events over the last decade eroded imperialism's power
base in several countries and now threaten the political 'stability' of almost
all UCEs (i.e. corporate capital's capacity to govern them without inhibition).

This has been matched by the high unemployment now affecting DCEs, expected to soar to 26 million by the end of 1982, and this in the face of $250–400 billion of unused industrial capacity. But the economic slide is merely one aspect of the crisis in a system racked by every kind of corporate scandal. Throughout the DCEs bribery scandals should continue to spread and provide political fuel for movements opposing corrupt oligarchies from Saudi Arabia to Chile. Cries from DCE labour unions and workers about total disregard for health and safety should grow louder as such incidents as the dumping of thousands of gallons of highly toxic chemical wastes across the United States since World War II continue to be exposed. Despite the estimated $108 billion that global corporations poured into advertising in 1980,[19] glossy commercials cannot conceal corruption, rampaging inflation or mass unemployment. In this atmosphere of demoralization it is not surprising that illegal drug imports – for the United States alone – reached $35–51 billion in 1980.[20] It is difficult to find a more tragic commentary on the symptoms of degeneration within oligopolistic capitalism.

Nonetheless, it scarcely needs saying that we cannot expect the total disintegration of imperialism by the end of this decade. That would be little more than wishful thinking; but already the convulsive and irreversible contradictions unleashed by corporate capital and analysed in this book – albeit with respect to a limited sector – will swell to even greater crescendos in the 1980s. Corporate capital on a world basis has already been wedded to increasing militarization. It is inevitable that its policies will also lead to an intensified class confrontation, within both the developed and underdeveloped segments of the global economy.

References

1. See *International Report of the President,* Washington, DC, 1977; and various numbers of United States, Dept. of Commerce, *Survey of Current Business,* from September 1962 to March 1978.
2. Attempts to impose credit controls via monetary restraints in the era of conglomerate capitalism have lost much of their potency. Transnational corporations such as Blue Bell have access to millions of dollars in foreign banks that they could use to sidestep credit controls in the United States. This is true of most transnational corporations (as against small and medium enterprises), which have the possibility not only of tapping the large Eurodollar market but all capital markets. Moreover, as *Business Week* (3 January 1980) has argued: 'If Washington then moves to control lending to domestic companies by foreign branches of US banks, the multinationals are positioned to borrow cash from German, Swiss, British and Japanese banks out of London, Frankfurt, Paris or Geneva.' And the conclusion appears inescapable: 'Of course, smaller US companies that do not have the clout or the sophistication to gain access to funds overseas would almost certainly be hit hard by credit controls.' 'Extinction' would perhaps be a more appropriate choice

smaller US companies that do not have the clout or the sophistication to gain access to funds overseas would almost certainly be hit hard by credit controls.' 'Extinction' would perhaps be a more appropriate choice of word.

3. H.M. Wachtel and P. Adelsheim, 'How Recession Feeds Inflation: Price Markups in a Concentrated Economy', *Challenge*, September/October 1977.
4. See F.F. Clairmonte, 'The Banana Empire', *Ceres* (FAO), January/February 1975.
5. *International Herald Tribune*, 24–5 May 1980.
6. UNCTAD, *Interdependence of Trade, Development Finance and the International Monetary System*, TD/B/783, Geneva, 11 March 1980.
7. M. Dobb, *Studies in the Development of Capitalism* (London, 1944), p. 25.
8. See Y. Tsurumi and R. Tsurumi, *Sogoshosha: Engines of Export-Based Growth* (Montreal, Institute for Research on Public Policy, 1980), pp. 78–9.
9. *Across the Board: The Conference Board Magazine*, Vol. VII, No. 5, May 1980.
10. These include industrial robots, pick-and-place robots, programmable robots, computerized robots, sensory robots and assembly robots.
11. *Business Week*, 19 June 1980.
12. For an excellent overview of the industry, see John Markoff and John Stewart, 'The Microprocessor Revolution: an office on the head of a pin', *In These Times*, 7–13 March 1979.
13. Figures from Philips, quoted in *The New York Times*, 29 January 1980.
14. Ward Morehouse, 'Chips With Everything', *UN Development Forum*, August–September 1979.
15. Study by Barry Bluestone of Boston University and Bennett Harrison of MIT entitled 'Capital and Communities: the causes and consequences of private disinvestment', See *The New York Times*, 13 April 1980.
16. The Fortune 500 is well represented in this zone, led by General Motors, Westinghouse, Zenith, Levi Strauss, RCA, IBM, Burroughs and Chrysler. See *The New York Times*, 3 March 1980.
17. United Nations estimates, quoted in *Wall Street Journal*, 25 September 1979.
18. See the observations of Mr Felix Rohatyn, senior partner of Lazard Freres and Company: 'Strong medicine', *Across the Board: The Conference Board Magazine*, Vol. VII, No. 5, May 1980.
19. From McCann Erickson, quoted in *The Economist*, 20 September 1980.
20. Figures from a U.S. General Accounting Office report, quoted in *The New York Times*, 11 May 1980.

Bibliography

Books, Monographs and Documents

Aaronovitch, S., and Sawyer, M., *Big Business, Theoretical and Empirical Aspects of Concentration and Mergers in the United Kingdom*, (London, 1975).

Aiyer, H.R., *Economics of Textile Trade and Industry in India* (Bombay, 1977).

American Chemical Society, *Chemistry in the Economy* (Washington, DC 1975).

Aries, R.D., *Anatomy of the World Drug Giants*, (Paris, 1977).

Baran, Paul, and Sweezy, Paul, *Monopoly Capital* (New York, 1966).

Barnet, Richard, and Muller, Ronald, *Global Reach*, (New York, 1974).

Bernal, J.D., *Science and Industry in the Nineteenth Century*, (London, 1953).

Bernal, J.D., *Science in History*, 3 vols, (London, 1969).

Blair, J.M., *Economic Concentration: Structure, Behaviour and Public Policy* (New York, 1972).

Blume, Hans, *Organizational Aspects of Agro-Industrial Development Agencies; 9 Case Studies in Africa: Tea, Cotton, Oil-Palm* (Munich, 1971).

Board of Trade, Great Britain, *Reorganization of the Cotton Industry*, (London, 1959).

Bolsa de Mercadorias de Sao Paulo, *Relatadorio da Directoria Contas, Documentas e Parecer da Commissao Fiscal*, (Sao Paulo, 1976).

Bolton, Brian, *The MNCs in the Textile, Garment and Leather Industries* (Brussels, 1976).

Bonbright, T.C. and Means, G.C., *The Holding Company: Its Public Significance and its Regulation* (New York, 1969).

Borkin, Joseph, *The Crime and Punishment of I.G. Farben* (London, 1978).

Braverman, Harry, *Labor and Monopoly Capital* (New York, 1974).

Briscoe, L., *Textile and Clothing Industries of the United Kingdom* (Manchester, 1971).

Burns, Arthur, *The Decline of Competition: A Study of the Evolution of American Industry* (London, 1936).

Business International S.A., *Ivory Coast: Strategic Base for Developing West Africa* (Geneva, 1977).

Carr, W.H., *The Du Ponts of Delaware* (New York, 1964).

Chandler, A.D., and Salisbury, S., *Pierre D. Du Pont and the Making of the Modern Corporation* (New York, 1971).

Chandler, Alfred D., *The Visible Hand: the Managerial Revolution in American*

Business (London, 1977).

Chandler, A.D., and Salisbury, S., *Pierre D. Du Pont and the Making of the Modern Corporation* (New York, 1971).

Chase Manhattan Bank, *An Analysis of Major Chemical Fibre, Textile, Apparel and Retailing Companies* (New York 1977).

Clairmonte, F.F., *Economic Liberation and Underdevelopment: Studies in the Disintegration of an Idea*, (London, 1960).

Clapham, J.H., *The Economic Development of France and Germany, 1815–1914* (Cambridge, 1963).

Clark, J.B., and Clark, J.M., *The Control of the Trusts* (New York, 1912).

Chow, Archibald and Nan, *The Chemical Revolution* (London, 1952).

Coates, Jane, *Prices of Fibres and Fibre Products* (Washington, DC, 1919).

Cochrane, W.W., *American Farm Policy, 1948–1973* (Minneapolis, Minnesota, 1976).

Cohen, J.B., *Japan's Economy in War and Reconstruction* (Minneapolis, Minnesota, 1949).

Coleman, D.C., *Courtaulds: An Economic and Social History*, 2 vols. (Oxford, 1969).

Commodity Futures Trading Commission, *Commitments of Traders* (New York, 1977).

Cotton Board, Great Britain, Labour Department, *Equipment and Labour Utilization in the Cotton Industry* (Manchester, 1948).

Counter Information Services, *Courtaulds on the Inside* (London, 1977).

Crouchley, A.E., *The Economic Development of Modern Egypt* (London, 1938).

De Jung, H.W., *Onderneningsconcentratie* (Leiden, 1971).

Der Marktfuhrer im Textileinzelhandel, *Institut des Deutschen Textileinzelhandels* (Zurich, 1977).

Direction de la Conjoncture et des Etudes Economiques, France, *Le marche mondial du coton* (Paris, 1948).

Dodd, Wilham E., *The Cotton Kingdom; A Chronicle of the Old South* (New Haven, 1919).

Dominguez, John R., *Devaluation and Futures Markets* (Lexington, Mass., 1972).

Dun and Bradstreet International, *Europe's 500 Largest Companies*, (London, 1978).

European Economic Community EEC, *Etude sur l'evolution de la concentration dans l'Industrie du textile en France: cotton, laine* (Luxembourg, 1975).

EEC, *A Study of the Evolution of Concentration in the United Kingdom Textile Industry* (Brussels, 1975).

E.I. Du Pont Co., *The Chemical Industry* (New York, 1935).

The Economist Intelligence Unit, *A Study on Retail Distribution in Britain* (London, 1976).

The Economist Intelligence Unit, *World Textile Trade and Production*, EIU Special Report No. 63 (London, 1979).

Eichner, Alfred S., *The Emergence of Oligopoly: Sugar Refining as a Case Study* (Baltimore, 1969).

Eichner, Alfred S., *The Megacorp and Oligopoly: Micro-Foundations and Macro-Dynamics* (Cambridge, 1976).

Eli, Max *et al, Sogo Shosha: Strukturen und Strategien japanischer Welthandelsunternehmungen* (Hamburg, 1977).

Empire Marketing Board, Great Britain, *Fibres: A Summary of Figures of Production and Trade Relating to Cotton, Wool, Silk, Hemp, Flax, Jute* (London, 1933).

Fair Trade Commission, *Report on the Investigation of General Trading Companies* (Tokyo, 1974).

Faulkner, H.U., *The Decline of Laissez-Faire, 1897–1917* (New York, 1951).

Federal Trade Commission, Bureau of Economics, *Concentration Levels and Trends in the Energy Sector of the U.S. Economy* (Washington, DC, 1974).

Federal Trade Commission, *Economic Report: Conglomerate Merger Performance: An Empirical Analysis of Nine Corporations* (Washington, DC, 1972).

Feldman, G.D., *Army, Industry and Labour in Germany, 1914–1918* (Princeton, 1966).

Fitzgerald, P.F., *Industrial Combination in England* (London, 1927).

Food and Agriculture Organization (FAO), *Per Caput Fibre Consumption 1968 to 1970: Cotton, Wool, Flax, Silk and Man-made Fibres* (Rome, 1972).

FAO, Terminology and Reference Section, *Fibres and Fibre Products: Terminology* (Rome, 1976).

FAO, *Per Capita Fibre Consumption Levels, 1948–1958* (Rome, 1960).

FAO, *Yearbook of Trade* (Rome, 1976).

Framji, K.J. and Mahajan, I.K. (eds.), *Irrigated Cotton: A Worldwide Survey, 1973* (Washington, DC., 1973).

Franks, Lawrence G., *The European Multinationals* (London, 1975).

Galbraith, John K., *The New Industrial State* (Toronto, 1968).

General Agreement on Trade and Tariffs (GATT), *Arrangement Regarding International Trade in Textiles* (Geneva, 1974).

GATT, *Report of the Working Party on Trade in Textiles* (Geneva, 1972).

GATT, *Production and Trade in Textiles and Clothing, 1974 to 1976,* (Geneva, 1977).

Gibb, G.S. and Knowlton, E.H., *The Resurgent Years: History of the Standard Oil Company, 1911–1927, (New York, 1956).*

Gold, Gerald, *Modern Commodity Futures Trading* (New York, 1968).

Goss, B.A. and Yamey, B.S., *The Economics of Futures Trading* (London, 1976).

Granger, Clive William John, *Trading In Commodities and Investors Chronicle Guide* (Cambridge, 1975).

Haber, L.F., *The Chemical Industry during the Nineteenth Century* (Oxford, 1969).

Hadley, E.M., *Antitrust in Japan* (Princeton, N.J., 1970).

Hamby, Dame S. (ed.), *The American Cotton Handbook (London, 1965).*

Hannah, Leslie (ed.), *Management Strategy and Business Development: An Historical and Comparative Study* (London, 1976).

Hannah, L., and Kay, J.A., *Concentration in Modern Industry* (London, 1977).

Henderson, Hubert D., *The Cotton Control Board* (London, 1922).

Hieronymus, Thomas, *Economics of Futures Trading* (New York, 1971).

Hobsbawm, E.J., *The Age of Capital, 1848–1875* (London, 1975).

Hoffmann, Alex, *Le marche mondial de coton brut sous la dependence de la politique agricole americaine* (Geneva, 1968).

Hornbeck, B.M., *Knits in Western Europe – Their Impact on Cotton* (Washington, DC, 1973).

Instituto Centroamericano de Investigacion y Tecnologia Industrial, *An Environmental and Economic Study of the Consequences of Pesticide Use in Central American Cotton Production,* 2nd edition (Guatemala City, 1977).

International Cotton Advisory Committee (ICAC), *Report on the Developing World Cotton Situation* (Washington, DC, 1950).

ICAC, *Annual Review of the World Cotton Situation, 1975/76* (Washington, DC.).

ICME/CONDOR Consultants, *Study on the Possibilities of Manufacturing Textile Machinery in Mexico* (Vienna, 1975).

International Federation of Cotton and Allied Textile Industries (IFCATI), Congress, Burton-on-Trent, England, 1954, *The Cotton Industry Today and Tomorrow* (Manchester, 1954).

IFCATI, Congress, Venice, 1957, *The Cotton Industry in a World Economy* (Manchester, 1958).

IFCATI, Congress, Deauville, 1962, *Technical Progress and Textile Marketing* (Zurich, 1963).

IFCATI, *The Structure of the Cotton and Allied Textile Industries, 1975* (Zurich, 1977).

International Institute of Agriculture, *World Cotton Production and Trade* (Rome, 1936).

International Institute for Cotton, *Cotton's Importance to the Developing World* (Brussels, 1976).

International Labour Organization (ILO), Textiles Committee, Report III: *Conditions of Work in the Textile Industry Including Problems Related to Organization of Work* (Geneva, 1978).

ILO, Textiles Committee, *The Effects of Structural and Technological Changes on Labour Problems in the Textile Industry* (Geneva, 1968).

ILO, *Yearbook of Labour Statistics.*

International Textile, Garment and Leather Workers' Federation, *The Leading Multinational Companies in the Textiles, Garment and Leather Industries* (Amsterdam, 1972).

International Trade Centre, *Marketing of Pakistan Polyester Products in International Markets* (Geneva, 1977).

Japan External Trade Organization, *The Role of the Trading Companies in International Commerce* (Tokyo, 1976).

Keynes, J.M., *A Treatise on Money* (London, 1930).

Koch, Sung Jae, *Stages in Industrial Development in Asia: A Comparative History of the Cotton Industry in Japan, India, China and Korea* (Philadelphia, 1966).

Kojima, Kiyoshi, *Japan and a New World Economic Order* (London, 1977).

Kotz, Nick, 'Agribusiness' in Richard Merril (ed.), *Radical Agriculture,* (London, 1976).

Kroese, W.T., *The Textile Industry on the Threshold of Development Decade*

II: A Quarter of a Century of Textile History, 1945–1970 (IFCATI General Assembly, Barcelona, 1971).

Labys, Walter C., *Speculation, Hedging and Commodity Price Forecasts* (Lexington, Mass., 1970).

Lappe, Frances Moore, and Collins, Joseph, *Food First* (Boston, 1977).

Lavington, F.E., *The English Capital Market* (London, 1921).

Ludwig, Mario (ed.), *The Cotton Industry in a World Economy* (IFCATI, Manchester, 1958).

Lynch, John, *Toward an Orderly Market: An Intensive Study of Japan's Voluntary Quota in Cotton Textile Exports* (Tokyo, 1968).

Maizels, Alfred, *Exports and Economic Growth of Developing Countries* (Cambridge, 1968).

Malaterre, Guy, *L'organization internationale du marche du coton* (Toulouse, 1965).

Manchester, W., *The Arms of Krupp, 1587–1968* (Boston, 1968).

Mantoux, Paul, *The Industrial Revolution in the Eighteenth Century* (London, 1925).

Manzanilla, F., *Development and Outlook of the Petrochemical Industry in Mexico* (UNIDO, Vienna, 1978).

Marson, H.M., Knowlton, E.H., and Toptle, C.S., *New Horizons: History of Standard Oil Company, 1927–1950* (New York, 1971).

May, J.M., and MacLellan, D.L., *The Ecology of Malnutrition in Mexico and Central America* (New York, 1972).

Medvin, N., and Law, I.J., *The Energy Cartel: Big Oil vs. the Public Interest* (Washington, DC, 1975).

Mercier, C., *The Petrochemical Industry and the Possibilities of its Establishment in the Developing Countries* (Paris, 1966).

Moore, Barrington, *Social Origins of Dictatorship and Democracy* (London, 1966).

Morgan, Dan, *Merchants of Grain* (New York, 1979).

Mueller, Willard F., *The Celler-Kefauver Act: The First 27 years*, study prepared for the Subcommittee on Monopolies and Commercial Law of the House Committee on the Judiciary, (Washington, DC, 1978).

Murray, R. C., 'Transfer, Pricing and the State', unpublished thesis presented to the Institute of Development Studies, University of Sussex, 1978.

National Christian Council of Kenya, *Who Controls Industry in Kenya?* (Nairobi, 1968).

National Council of Applied Economic Research, *Cotton and Tobacco in Andhra Pradesh: Production and Marketing* (New Delhi, 1971).

National Economic Development Council (NEDC)., Clothing EDC: *progress Report 1979* (London, 1979).

National Economic Development Office (NEDO), Joint Textile Committee, *Trends in Technology* (London, 1976).

NEDO, *Report to the National Economic Development Council* (London, 1978).

Newton, Arthur Percival, *The Staple Trades of the Empire* (London, 1918).

Nissan, A.H., *Textile Engineering Processes* (London, 1959).

Noble, David, *America by Design: Science, Technology and the Rise of Corporate Capitalism* (New York, 1977).

Organization for Economic Co-operation and Development, *Export Cartels:*

    Report of the Committee of Experts on Restrictive Business Practices
    (Paris, 1974). .

OECD, *Modern Cotton Industry; A Capital Intensive Industry* (Paris, 1965).

OECD, *Restrictive Business Practices of Multinational Enterprises: Report
    of the Committee of Experts on Restrictive Business Practices* (Paris,
    1977).

OECD, *Transfer Pricing and Multinational Enterprises: Report of the OECD
    Committee on Fiscal Affairs* (Paris, 1979).

Organization for European Economic Co-operation (OEEC), *The Future of
    the European Cotton Industry* (Paris, 1957).

OEEC, Overseas Territories Committee, *Le coton* (Paris, 1955).

Owen, E.R.J., *Cotton and the Egyptian Economy, 1820–1914; A Study in
    Trade and Development* (Oxford, 1969).

Political and Economic Planning, Industries Group, *Report on the British
    Industry, an Investigation of the Present Structure of the Industry and
    Proposals for Reorganisation with Special Reference to Competitive
    Efficiency in World Markets* (London, 1934).

Prais, S.J., *The Evolution of Giant Firms in Britain; A Study of the Growth
    of Concentration in Manufacturing Industry in Britain, 1909–1970*
    (Cambridge, 1976).

Programme Analysis Unit, *A Technological Forecast for the U.K. Textile
    Industry* (Chilton, 1973).

Reader, W.J., *Imperial Chemical Industry, 1900–1930* (Oxford, 1970).

Reidy, B., *Guide to World Commodity Markets* (London, 1977).

*Report of the Mission on Japanese Combines, A Report to the Department
    of State and the War Department* (Washington, DC, March 1946).

Retail Trade International 1977 (London, 1977).

Richards, Frank, *The Marketing of Cotton and the Financing of Cotton
    Merchants* (New York, 1949).

Roberts, John G., *Mitsui: Three Centuries of Japanese Business* (New York,
    1974).

Robson, R., *The Cotton Industry in Britain* (London, 1957).

Rodney, W., *How Europe Underdeveloped Africa* (London, 1972).

Rothwell, R., *Technological Change in Textile Machinery: Manpower
    Implications in the User and Producer Industries* (Geneva, unpublished,
    1977).

Ruttenberg, S., *et al.*, *The American Oil Industry: A Failure of Antitrust
    Policy* (Washington, DC., 1973).

Sampson, Anthony, *The Seven Sisters* (London, 1976).

Scalapino, R.A., *Democracy and the Party Movement in Prewar Japan*
    (Berkeley, 1953).

Shepherd, Geoffrey, *Exports of Cotton Textiles from Developing Countries
    to the European Economic Community and the United Kingdom,
    1958–1967* (Washington, DC, 1969).

Stanford University, California, *Symposium on price effects of speculation
    in organized commodity markets* (Stanford, 1968).

Stern, F., *Gold and Iron: Bismark, Bleichroder and the Building of the
    German Empire* (London, 1977).

Textile Council, Great Britain, *Cotton and Allied Textiles: A Report on
    Present Performance and Future Prospects* (Manchester, 1969).

Teweles, Richard J., *The Commodity Futures Game, Who Wins? Who Loses? Why?*, (New York, 1974).

Thigpen, E., *Draft Paper on Cotton* (draft of IBRD paper, Washington, D.C., 1977).

Todd, John, *The Marketing of Cotton from the Grower to the Spinner* (London, 1934).

Tsurumi, Yoshi, *The Japanese are Coming: A Multinational Interaction of Firms and Politics* (Cambridge, Mass., 1976).

Union Bank of Switzerland Reports, *Mexico* (Zurich, 1978).

United Kingdom, Board of Trade, *International Cartels 1944* (London, 1976).

United Kingdom Joint Textile Committee, *Trends in Textile Technology* (London, 1976).

United Nations, *Commodity Trade Statistics* (1974).

UN, Department of Economic and Social Affairs, Statistical Office, *Yearbook of Industrial Statistics,* 1974 Edition, Vols I and II (New York, 1976).

UN, Economic Commission for Europe, *Market Trends for Chemical Products 1970–1975 and Prospects for 1980* CHEM/GE. 1/R.3/Add.65, (Geneva, 16 May 1977).

UN, *Studies in Petrochemicals,* Papers presented at the UN Interregional Conference on the Development of Petrochemical Industries in Developing Countries, Tehran, November 1964; (New York. 1966).

UN, Trade and Development Board, Commission on Commodities, Permanent Group on Synthetics and Substitutes, *Research and Development Programmes for Natural Products Facing Competition from Synthetic Materials: R and D in Cotton Processing and Utilization,* New York, 1971.

UN, *World Economic Survey* (New York, 1958).

United Nations Conference on Trade and Development (UNCTAD), *Consideration of International Measures on Cotton: Contribution from Turkey,* TD/B/IPC/Cotton/L4 (17 September 1979, Geneva).

UNCTAD, *The Control of Transfer Pricing in Greece,* TD/B/C.6/32 (Geneva).

UNCTAD, *Dominant Position of Market Power of Transnational Corporations: Use of Transfer Pricing Mechanisms* (New York, 1977).

UNCTAD, *Dynamic Products in the Exports of Manufactured Goods from Developing Countries to Developed Market Economies, 1970–76* (Geneva, 1978).

UNCTAD, *Handbook of International Trade and Development Statistics* (New York, 1976).

UNCTAD, *Impact of the Fluctuations of Cotton Prices on the Profitability of the Mexican Cotton Industry,* TD/B/IPC/Cotton/L3 (Geneva, 1979).

UNCTAD, *Interdependence of Trade, Development Finance and the International Monetary System,* TD/B/783 (Geneva, 1980).

UNCTAD, *International Trade in Cotton Textiles and the Developing Countries: Problems and Prospects* (Geneva, 1973).

UNCTAD, *Major Issues arising from the Transfer of Technology: A Case Study of Spain* (Geneva).

UNCTAD, *Major Issues in Transfer of Technology to Developing Countries: A Case Study of the Pharmaceutical Industry,* TD/B/C.6/4 (Geneva, 1975).

UNCTAD, *The Maritime Export of Cotton,* TD/B/C.4/157 (Geneva, 10

February 1977).

UNCTAD, *The Marketing and Distribution of Tobacco,* TD/B/C.1/205 (Geneva, 1978).

UNCTAD, *The Marketing and Distribution System for Bananas* TD/B/C.1/ 162 (Geneva, 1974).

UNCTAD, *The Structure and Behaviour of Enterprises in the Chemical Industry and their Effects on the Trade and Development of Developing Countries,* TD/B/AC.11/17 (Geneva, 1979).

United Nations Industrial Development Organization (UNIDO), *Development and Outlook of the Chemical Industry in Mexico,* ID/WG. 268/3 (New York, 1978).

UNIDO, *The Petrochemical Industry* (New York, 1973).

UNIDO, *World-Wide Study of the Petrochemical Industry* (Vienna, 1978).

United States, Bureau of Agricultural Economics, *The World Cotton Situation: Foreign Cotton Production* (Washington, D.C., 1965).

U.S., Bureau of Economic Analysis, *Input-Output Structure of the U.S. Economy: 1967* (Washington, DC, 1974).

U.S., Bureau of Labour Statistics, *Productivity Indices for Selected Industries* (Washington, DC, 1939-76).

U.S., Department of Agriculture, *Cotton Prices and Markets* (Washington, DC, 1926).

U.S., Department of Agriculture, Economic Research Service, *Cost of Storing and Handling Cotton at Public Storage Facilities, 1970-1971, with Projections for 1972-1973* (Washington, DC, 1972).

U.S., Department of Agriculture, Economic Research Service, *Interfibre Competition with Emphasis on Cotton: Trends and Projections to 1980* (Washington, DC, 1973).

U.S., Department of Agriculture, Economic Research Service, *Supplement for 1976 to: Statistics on Cotton and Related Data, 1920–73* (Washington, DC, 1976).

U.S., Department of Agriculture, Economic Research Service (A.B. Paul), *Treatment of Hedging in Commodity Market Regulation* (Washington, DC, 1976).

U.S., Department of Agriculture, Economic Research Service, *U.S. Textile Fibre Demand: Price Elasticities in Major End-Use Markets* Washington, DC, 1974).

U.S., Department of Agriculture, Economic Research Service, *World Demand for Cotton in 1980 with Emphasis on Trade by Less Developed Countries* (Washington, DC, 1971).

U.S., Department of Agriculture, *National Cotton Marketing Study Committee Report* (Washington, DC, 1975).

U.S., Department of Agriculture, *Statistics on Cotton and Related Data* (Washington, DC, various years).

U.S., Department of Agriculture, *The Structure of American Farming,* Issue Briefing Paper 16 (Washington, DC, 6 July 1979).

U.S., Department of Agriculture, *The World's Cottons: A Summary of Cotton Fibre and Textile Results* (Washington, DC, 1973)

U.S., Department of Agriculture, *U.S. Team Reports on USSR Cotton Production and Trade* FAS-M-277 (Washington, DC, 1977).

U.S., Department of Commerce, *Annual Survey of Manufactures* (Washington, DC, 1972).

U.S., Department of Commerce, *The Cotton Textile Cycle: Its Nature and Trend* (Washington, DC, 1963).

U.S., Department of Commerce, *U.S. Industrial Outlook 1975: with Projections to 1980* (Washington, DC, 1976).

U.S., Department of Labor, *Technological Changes and Manpower Trends in Six Industries,* Bulletin 1817 (Washington, DC, 1974).

U.S., Federal Energy Administration, *Report to Congress on Petrochemicals* (Washington, DC, 1974).

U.S., Foreign Agriculture Service, Cotton Division, *How U.S. Cotton is Sold for Export* (Washington, DC, 1972).

U.S., Foreign Agriculture Service, *Cotton Use by the Textile Industry of the European Community* (Washington, DC, 1975).

U.S., Foreign Agriculture Service, *Developments in the Japanese Textile Industry* (Washington, DC, 1975).

U.S., Interstate and Foreign Commerce, *Report on Pipelines,* 72nd Congress, 2nd session (Washington, DC, 1933).

U.S., House, Committee on Agriculture, *General Farm Program Cotton Provisions: Hearings before the Subcommittee on Cotton of the Committee on Agriculture,* 93rd Congress, 1st Session (Washington, DC, 1973).

U.S., House, Committee on Agriculture, *Review of Cotton Marketing System: Hearings before the Subcommittee on Cotton,* 93rd Congress, 2nd Session (Washington, DC, 1974).

U.S., House, Committee on Foreign Affairs, *Overseas Private Investment Corporation* (Washington, DC, 1974).

U.S., House, Committee on Ways and Means, *Library of Congress Study on Imports and Consumer Prices* (Washington, DC, 1977).

U.S., House, Permanent Select Committee on Small Business, *Small Business Problems Involved in the Marketing of Grain and Other Commodities* 92nd Congress, 1st session (Washington, DC, 1973).

U.S., National Advisory Commission on Food and Fiber, *Food and Fiber for the Future* (Washington, DC, 1967).

U.S., Senate, Committee on Military Affairs, *Economic and Political Aspects of Military Cartels,* Monograph 1, (Washington, DC, 1944).

U.S., Senate, *Disclosure of Corporate Ownership,* 93rd Congress, 2nd Session (Washington, DC, 1974).

United States, Senate, *Competition and Public Policy in the Petroleum Refining Industry: Hearing before the Senate Judiciary Committee,* 95th Congress, 2nd Session (Washington, DC, 1978).

U.S., Senate, *Export Policy: Hearing Before the Subcommittee on International Finance of the Committee on Banking, Housing and Urban Affairs,* 95th Congress, 2nd Session (Washington, DC, 1978).

U.S., Senate, *The Role of the Giant Corporations in the American and World Economies, Corporate Secrecy: Overview: Hearings before the Subcommittee on Monopoly of the Select Committee on Small Business,* 92nd Congress, 1st Session (Washington, DC, 1972).

U.S., Senate, *Mergers and Industrial Concentration: Hearings before the Sub-committee on Antitrust and Monopoly of the Senate Judiciary*

Committee, 95th Congress, 2nd Session (Washington, DC, 1978).

U.S., Senate, *Oil Company Ownership of Pipelines: Staff Report of the Sub-committee on Anti-Trust and Monopoly,* 95th Congress, 2nd Session (Washington, DC, 1978).

U.S. Senate, *U.S. Export Policy: A Report to the Committee on Banking, Housing and Urban Affairs,* 96th Congress, 1st Session (Washington, DC, 1979).

Varon, Bension, *Cotton: Current Situation, Major Issues, and Recent International Discussions* (Washington, DC, 1969).

Warley, T.K. (ed.), *Agricultural Producers and Their Markets* (Oxford, 1967).

Winkler, P.K., *The Du Pont Dynasty* (New York, 1935).

World Bank, *Ivory Coast: A Basic Economic Report,* Report No. 1147b-IVC (Washington, DC, 1977).

World Bank, *World Trade and Output of Manufactures: Structural Trends and Developing Countries' Exports,* World Bank Staff Working Paper No. 316 (Washington, DC, 1979).

Yanaga, Chitoshi, *Big Business in Japanese Politics* (New Haven, 1968).

Yates, P.L., *Forty Years of Foreign Trade* (London, 1958).

Yoshino, Michael Y., *Japan's Multinational Enterprises* (London, 1976).

Zilg, G.C., *Du Pont: Behind the Nylon Curtain* (New York, 1974).

Articles

Adame, Julian R. 'Economic and social implications of cotton production and textile manufacturing in Latin America', *IFCATI* Vol. 18, 1977.

Bardan, Benjamin, 'The cotton textile agreement, 1962-1972', *Journal of World Trade Law,* January-February 1973..

Besson, V.T. "New Developments in ethylene production', *Chemical Economy and Engineering Review,* October 1971.

Blackburn, J.A., 'The new textile industry — a 25 year revolution in the U.K.', *Textile Month,* November 1976.

Bonus, J., 'Man-made fibres and natural fibres: competition in end-uses in Western Europe', paper presented at Shirley Institute, 29-30 November 1977.

Burch, C.G., 'So you want to go into business for yourself', *Fortune,* April 1972.

Collins, Joe, and Lappe, F. Moore, 'Whom does the World Bank serve?', *Economic and Political Weekly,* 12 May 1979.

Dabman, A., 'New developments in the field of polyester fibres', *Opportunities for Man-made Fibres,* 11th Shirley Institute International Seminar, 4-6 September 1979, p. 8.

Encinas, Roberto R., 'The textile industry in Mexico', *IFCATI,* Vol. 18 1977.

Evans, R., 'Man-made fibres gain more markets in '77', *Foreign Agriculture,* 30 January 1978.

Finch, L., 'Structural changes in the agricultural industry: their meaning for American business and world food production' in *Feeding the World's Hungry: The Challenge to Business,* conference sponsored by Continental Bank, 20 May 1974.

Firch, Robert S., 'Adjustments in a slowly declining U.S. cotton production industry', *American Journal of Agricultural Economics,* December 1973.

Gray, R., 'From silks to sack-cloth on a puff of air', *New Scientist,* 16 June 1977.

Hornbeck, B.M., 'Developments in the Japanese textile industry', USDA, Washington, DC, FAS M-267, May 1975.

Johnson, L.L., 'The theory of hedging and speculation in commodity futures', *Review of Economic Studies,* Vol. 27, 1960.

Juvet, J.L., 'The cotton industry and world trade', *Journal of World Trade Law,* September-October 1967.

Kofi, Tetteh A., 'MNC control of distributive channels' a study of cocoa marketing', *Stanford Journal of International Studies,* Spring 1976.

Korn, F.P., 'Trade in deals with Comecon countries', talk given to the Society of Chemical Industry, London, 6 March 1978.

Kotz, Nick, 'Agribusiness', in Merril, R. (ed.), *Radical Agriculture* (London, 1976).

Kuczynski, Michael, 'The U.S. Agricultural Act of 1965 and its Effects on Cotton Prices and Receipts from Cotton Exports', *International Monetary Fund Staff Papers,* Washington, DC, March 1966.

Lynn, F., 'Profit and lint: the dust in Willie's lungs, byssinosis or brown lung', *The Nation,* 21 February 1976.

McNeiry, F., 'Switzerland, some observations on its textile machinery manufacturing industry', *Modern Textiles,* June 1976.

Miles, L.P., 'Benefits from process advances', *Ciba-Geigy Review,* No. 1, 1975.

Morehouse, Ward, 'Micro electronics: chips with everything', *Development Forum,* United Nations, August-September, 1979.

North American Congress on Latin America, 'Agribusiness targets Latin America, *NACLA Report on the Americas,* Vol. XII, No. 1, January-February 1978.

Parikh, A., 'A comparative study of the production structure of the cotton textile industry in India and the USA', *Journal of Development Studies,* July 1975.

Parikh, J.G., 'Research and development in man-made fibres in Europe', *Indian Cotton Mills Federation Journal,* February 1977.

Pickett, James and Robson, R., 'Technology and employment in the production of cotton cloth, *World Development,* March 1977.

Quinlan, M., 'Planning for 1980s feedstocks', *Petroleum Economist,* November 1977.

Ramaswany, P., 'Export marketing of raw cotton; some problems', *Foreign Trade Review,* New Delhi, July-September 1970.

Richards, A.R., 'Primitive accumulation in Egypt, 1798–1882', *Review,* Fall 1977.

Richardson, B.L., 'Dyeing and finishing in 1990: energy bound', *Textile World,* December 1977.

Robson, R., 'Importance of natural fibres . . .', Shirley Institute, December 1977.

Rothwell, R., 'Innovation in textile machinery', *Textile Institute and Industry,* December 1977.

Rothwell, R., 'The role of technical change in international competitiveness: the case of the textile machinery industry', *Management Decision,*

Vol. 15, No. 6, 1977.

Rothwell, R., 'Users' and Producers' perceptions of the relative importance of various textile machinery characteristics', *Textile Institute and Industry*, July 1977.

Sirhan, Ghazi and Johnson, Paul R., 'A market-share approach of the foreign demand for U.S. cotton', *American Journal of Agricultural Economics*, November 1971.

Smith, B., and Dardis. R., 'Inter-fibre competition and the future of the United States cotton industry', *American Journal of Agricultural Economics*, May 1972.

Steele, P.M., 'Computerized clothing', *Textile Asia*, January 1978.

Stern, W.A., 'Turkey ups investment in textile industry', USDA, *Foreign Agriculture*, 31 October 1977.

Subrahmanian, K.K., and Pillai, Mohanan, 'Implications of technology transfers in export-led growth strategy', *Economic and Political Weekly*, 30 October 1976.

Sung, K., 'The development of mainland China's textile industry with special reference to the changing pattern of its foreign trade', *Cotton and Allied Textile Industries*, Vol. 16, 1975.

Turner, L., and Bedore, J., 'Saudi and Iranian petrochemicals and oil refining: trade warfare in the 1980s?' *International Affairs*, October 1977.

Vanderwicken, P., 'And so U.M.M. decided to trim its capital budget', *Fortune*, September 1975.

Verret, R., 'Capital investment may lead to leadership, mere survival or bankruptcy', *Cotton and Allied Textile Industries*, Vol. 16, 1975.

Wallace, D.M., 'Saudi Arabia building costs', *Hydrocarbon Processing*, November 1976.

West, K., 'The futures of synthetic fibres: opportunities and problems, *Opportunities for Man-made Fibres*, 11th Shirley Institute International Seminar, 4-6 September 1979.

Working, H., 'Speculation on hedging markets', *Food Research Institute Studies*, Vol. 1, 1960.

Zwick, H., 'Man-made fibre marketing at Hoechst', *Cotton and Allied Textile Industries*, Vol. 15, 1974.

Periodicals and Journals Consulted

Various issues of the following publications were consulted:

Annual reports of several chemical, oil, textile and trading companies
Annual Review of the World Cotton Situation
Business Eastern Europe
Business Japan
Business Latin America
Business Week
Chemical Age
Chemical Economics Newsletter
Chemical Economy and Engineering Review
Chemical Insight

Chemical Week
Chemiefasern
Chemistry and Engineering
Ciba-Geigy Review
Cotton
Cotton Growing Review
Cotton, Monthly Review of the World Situation
The Cotton Situation
Cotton, World Statistics
The Cotton Year Book
Daily News Record
European Chemical News
Far Eastern Economic Review
Financial Times
Forbes
Fortune
Hong Kong, Monthly Digest of Statistics
L'Humanite
IFCATI, *Cotton and Allied Textile Industries*
IFCATI, *International Cotton Industry Statistics*
IFCATI Newsletter
Indian Cotton Mills Federation Journal
Industrie Chimique
Industrie Textile
International Cotton Industry Statistics
International Herald Tribune
Japan Textile News
Knitting Times
Korean Herald
Livestock
Management Today
Melliand Textilberichte
Metal Monthly Bulletin
Milling and Baking News
Modern Textiles
Le Monde
Le Monde Diplomatique
Neue Zurcher Zeitung
New York Times
OECD, *Trade by Commodities*
Petroleum Economist
Retail Trade International
Shell Chemicals
Sulzer, *Weaving Machine Bulletin*
Textil-Wirtschaft
Textile Asia
Textile Council, *Quarterly Statistical Review*
Textile Month
Textile Organon
Textile World

United Nations, *Monthly Bulletin of Statistics*
United Nations (UNCTAD), *Handbook of International Trade and Development Statistics*
United States, National Science Foundation, various reports
United States, Department of Agriculture, *Foreign Agriculture*
Wool Record

Subject Index

Ministry of International Trade and
  Industry (MITI): 5-6, 20, 62,
  74, 106, 142, 150, 163, 178,
Mitsubishi: 4, 61-2, 75, 82, 106,
  109-10, 142, 178
Mitsui: 61-2, 64, 75, 106, 108,
  110, 122, 137, 142, 178, 181,
  187, 234
Mitsukoshi: 214
Mobil Corporation: 107, 132
Molsen: 72
Monsanto: 117, 127-8, 140, 153,
  209
Montedison: 127, 141, 151, 153,
  157
Multi-commodity traders: 16, 19,
  40, 43, 45, 53-78, 82, 85-6,
  92, 247
Multi-Fibre Arrangement (MFA):
  165, 187-9

Nazism: 136-9
Nestle: 58
Netherlands: 141, 151, 186, 215-6
Netherlands Antilles: 184
New York Cotton Exchange: 94
Nicaragua: 29, 37-8, 40-1
Nichimen: 61, 66, 71-2
Niger: 43
Nigeria: 109, 186-7
Nissan: 226
Nissho Iwai: 61
Norway: 105

Office du Niger: 30
Oligarchy: 15, 29-30, 40-1, 51, 55,
  68, 100, 179, 245-6, 255
OPEC: 104-5, 109, 120, 122, 128,
  155
Outward processing: 200-1, 206

Pakistan: 27, 43, 69, 71, 154,
  183-4
Pan Overseas: 67-8
Panama: 94
Payoff complex: 55
Pechiney Ugine Kuhlmann: 137,
  150
Penny, J.C.: 206
Peru: 43

Pesticides: 39-40
Petrochemicals: 14, 100-11
Petroleum companies: 17, 103,
  108, 125, 128-35, 148, 155-6,
  243
Philippines: 71, 117
Philips: 252
Picanol: 226
Plains Cotton Cooperative: 72
Plantations: 25, 30, 39, 43, 55,
  68, 82, 186
Platt Brothers: 64
Platt-Saco-Lowell: 226
Portugal: 105
Procter and Gamble (P & G): 216

Qatar: 108

Ralli Bros.: 54-5, 71, 73-4
Reed, Austin: 215
Research and development: 11, 16,
  44, 104, 125, 144-8, 210,
  223-38
Reynolds, R.J.: 30
Rhone Poulenc: 127, 137, 140-1,
  150, 176
Rieter: 226
Rio Tinto Zinc: 132
Ruti: 226-7

Samsung: 8, 67, 181, 195
Sandoz: 157
Sanwa Bank: 66
Saudi Arabia: 104, 108, 121-2
Saurer: 226-7
Schlafhorst: 226
Schubert and Salzer: 226
Sears: 198, 211-4
Securities markets: 86-7
Shell: 50, 107, 127, 132
Shopping malls: 209, 212
Siemens: 251
Singapore: 15, 117, 188, 254
Singer: 226
Snia Viscosa: 141
Societa Italiana Resine (SIR):
  153
Societe de Banque Suisse: 55
Sogo Shosha: 16, 53-6, 60-7, 71,
  74, 77, 110, 117, 127, 178, 190

Name and Author Index